The historical impact of national movements in Europe has been dramatic and continues to be an issue of major importance. This volume by leading historians discusses authoritatively the national question in Europe in its historical context.

The national question is not of course a specifically European phenomenon, but for reasons of space and intelligibility coverage has been limited geographically. The aim is that the essays should attract readers interested in a historical problem that has been difficult to encompass theoretically and to deal with practically. A glance at what is being shown or written in the media with regard to national and ethnical issues demonstrates the validity of this aim, not only with regard to the multinational former Soviet Union or former Yugoslavia in eastern Europe, but also (for example) to the four nations of the British Isles or binational Belgium in the West.

This volume forms part of a sequence of collections of essays which began with *The Enlightenment in national context* (1981) and has continued with *Revolution in history* (1986, 1987), *Romanticism in national context* (1988), *Fin de siècle and its legacy* (1990), *The Renaissance in national context* (1991), and *The Scientific Revolution in national context* (1992). The purpose of these and other envisaged collections is to bring together comparative, national and interdisciplinary approaches to the history of great movements in the development of human thought and action.

THE NATIONAL QUESTION IN
EUROPE IN HISTORICAL CONTEXT

Volumes edited by Roy Porter and Mikuláš Teich

Already published

The Enlightenment in national context
Revolution in history
Romanticism in national context
Fin de siècle and its legacy
The Renaissance in national context
The Scientific Revolution in national context
The national question in Europe in historical context

In preparation

The Reformation in national context (with R.W. Scribner)
The Industrial Revolution in national context: Europe
and the USA
Drugs and narcotics in history
**Sexual knowledge, sexual science: the history of
attitudes to sexuality**

THE NATIONAL QUESTION IN EUROPE IN HISTORICAL CONTEXT

EDITED BY

MIKULÁŠ TEICH

Emeritus Fellow, Robinson College, Cambridge

AND

ROY PORTER

Professor of the History of Medicine, The
Wellcome Institute for the History of Medicine, London

CAMBRIDGE
UNIVERSITY PRESS

Published by the Press Syndicate of the University of Cambridge
The Pitt Building, Trumpington Street, Cambridge CB2 1RP
40 West 20th Street, New York, NY 10011-4211, USA
10 Stamford Road, Oakleigh, Melbourne 3166, Australia

First published 1993
Reprinted 1994

Printed in Great Britain by Athenæum Press Ltd, Newcastle upon Tyne

A catalogue record for this book is available from the British Library

Library of Congress cataloguing in publication data
The national question in Europe in historical context / edited by
Mikuláš Teich and Roy Porter.
p.   cm.
ISBN 0 521 36441 8 – ISBN 0 521 36713 1 (pbk)
1. Nationalism – Europe. 1. Europe – politics and government.
I. Teich, Mikuláš. II. Porter, Roy, 1946–.
D217.N38 1992
940 – dc20   92-6359   CIP
ISBN 0521 36441 8 hardback
ISBN 0 521 36713 1 paperback

D217
.N38
1993

CONTENTS

List of maps   *page* ix
Notes on contributors   x
Acknowledgements   xiv
Introduction   xv

1   The British Isles: Celt and Saxon   1
    VICTOR KIERNAN

2   The making of the French nation   35
    DOUGLAS JOHNSON

3   The national question in Italy   63
    ADRIAN LYTTELTON

4   The roots of the national question in Spain   106
    SIMON BARTON

5   Shifting nationalism: Belgians, Flemings and Walloons   128
    LOUIS VOS

6   The nation in German history   148
    WALTER SCHMIDT
    (translated from German by David Thompson)

7   Nationalism and nation-state in Germany   181
    HEINRICH AUGUST WINKLER
    (translated from German by Richard Hockaday)

8   The national identity of the Austrians   196
    ERNST BRUCKMÜLLER
    (translated from German by Nicholas T. Parsons)

9   The Czechs   228
    ARNOŠT KLÍMA (translated from Czech by Milan Hauner)

vii

10 The national question in Hungary 248
EMIL NIEDERHAUSER (translated from Hungarian by Mari
Markus Gömöri)

11 The union of Dalmatia with northern Croatia: a crucial
question of the Croatian national integration in the nineteenth
century 270
MIRJANA GROSS

12 The national question in Poland in the twentieth century 293
JERZY TOMASZEWSKI
(translated from Polish by Anna Zaranko)

13 Finland: from Napoleonic legacy to Nordic co-operation 317
MATTI KLINGE

Index 332

MAPS

1   Ethnic divisions of the Habsburg Empire, *c.* 1910   *page* 250
    (based on a map in C. A. Macartney, *The Habsburg
    Empire 1790–1918*, 1968)
2   The Croatian lands in Austria-Hungary (1867–1918)   272
3   Poland, *c.* 1937   294
4   Finland's borders in the twentieth century   318

NOTES ON CONTRIBUTORS

SIMON BARTON is Research Fellow and Praelector of Robinson College, Cambridge. He graduated in history from Aberystwyth and took his D.Phil. at York. Since 1990 he has held a British Academy Postdoctoral Fellowship at Cambridge. He is currently working on a major study of the nobility of medieval Spain and is preparing a book on *Aristocratic Society in 12th Century León-Castile*.

ERNST BRUCKMÜLLER studied history and German philology at the University of Vienna. There he is Extraordinarius Professor and teaches at the Institute of Social and Economic History. His principal publications are: *Landwirtschaftliche Organisationen und gesellschaftliche Modernisierung. Vereine, Genossenschaften und politische Mobilisierung der Landwirtschaft Österreichs vom Vormärz bis 1914* (Salzburg, 1977); *Nation Österreich. Sozialhistorische Aspekte ihrer Entwicklung* (Vienna, 1984); *Sozialgeschichte Österreichs* (Vienna, 1985). He is currently researching into the history of the Austrian bourgeoisie (with Hannes Stekl and Peter Urbanitsch).

MIRJANA GROSS is Emeritus Professor in the Department of History of the Philosophy Faculty at the University of Zagreb. She was Visiting Professor and held lectures at the universities of London, Oxford and Lancaster, and at a number of universities in the United States. Her special field of interest is social development in Croatia in the second half of the nineteenth century, and she has written several books on this subject. Her book *The Beginning of Modern Croatia* (Zagreb, 1985) was awarded the Anton Gindely Prize of the Österreichische Forschungsgemeinschaft in Vienna in 1988. Her latest book is *Towards a Middle Class Croatiān Society* (Zagreb, 1991).

DOUGLAS JOHNSON was educated at Oxford and the Ecole Normale Supérieure, Paris. He was Professor of Modern History at the University of Birmingham (1963–8), and Professor of French History at University College, London (1968–90), where he is Emeritus Professor of French History. He is the author of numerous books and articles, mainly on French history.

VICTOR KIERNAN was educated at the Manchester Grammar School and at Trinity College, Cambridge, where he read history and in 1937 became a Fellow. In 1948, after some years in India, he joined the History Department of Edinburgh University, from which he retired in 1977 as Professor Emeritus.

ARNOŠT KLÍMA was Professor of History at Charles University, Prague, until his retirement in 1981. He has published eight monographs (in Czech) dealing especially with economic and social history, and contributed articles – among others – to *The Economic History Review*, *Past and Present* and *The Journal of European Economic History*. From 1962 to 1982 he was a member of the Executive Committee of the International Economic History Association, and Visiting Professor at the universities of Leipzig, Wisconsin (Madison), Bielefeld and Vienna.

MATTI KLINGE has been Professor of History at the University of Helsinki since 1975. He is Doctor *honoris causa* of the University of Uppsala. He taught at the Sorbonne and has published a great number of historical works and essays, mainly in Finnish and Swedish.

ADRIAN LYTTELTON is now Professor of Contemporary European History at the University of Pisa. From 1979 to 1990 he was Professor of History at the Johns Hopkins Center in Bologna. His publications include *The Seizure of Power: Fascism in Italy 1919–1929* (London, 1973; 2nd edn, London and Princeton, N.J., 1988); *Italian Fascisms*, ed. (London, 1983); 'Revolution and Counter-Revolution in Italy', in *Revolutionary Situations in Europe, 1917–1922*, ed. C. L. Bertrand (Montreal, 1977); 'Landlords, peasants and the limits of liberalism', in *Gramsci and Italy's Passive Revolution*, ed. J. A. Davis (London, 1979); 'The language of political conflict in pre-fascist Italy' (Bologna, 1988); 'Society and culture in the Italy of Giolitti', in *Italian Art in the 20th Century*, ed. E. Braun (London and Munich, 1989).

EMIL NIEDERHAUSER has been Professor of History at the universities of Debrecen and Budapest, and since 1987 Corresponding Member of the Hungarian Academy of Sciences. His field of interest is comparative history of eastern Europe in the eighteenth and nineteenth centuries. His books include *The Rise of Nationality in Eastern Europe* (Budapest, 1982) and (together with Imre Gonda) *Die Habsburger. Ein europäisches Phänomen* (Budapest, 1983). He is presently preparing a historical monograph on the historiography in eastern Europe up to the Second World War.

ROY PORTER is Reader in the Social History of Medicine at the Wellcome Institute for the History of Medicine. He is currently working on the history of hysteria. Recent books include *Mind Forg'd Manacles: Madness in England from the Restoration to the Regency* (London, 1987); *A Social History of Madness* (London, 1987); *In Sickness and in Health: The British Experience, 1650–1850* (London, 1988); *Patient's Progress* (Oxford, 1989) – these last two co-authored with Dorothy Porter; and *Health for Sale: Quackery in England 1660–1850* (Manchester, 1989).

WALTER SCHMIDT, Member of the Academy of Sciences of the GDR, was Director of its Central Institute of History since 1984 until its dissolution. He has published extensively on German history, including the history of the labour movement in the nineteenth century. His other works deal with the comparative history of revolutions (especially the bourgeois revolutions in Germany and the revolutions of 1848–9) and the history of historiography and historical thinking.

MIKULÁŠ TEICH is Emeritus Fellow of Robinson College, Cambridge, and Honorary Professor of the Technical University Vienna. His publications include work on the history of chemistry and biomedical sciences, social and philosophical aspects of the development of science, technology and the economy, and on the history of scientific organizations. His *A Documentary History of Biochemistry, 1770–1940* (with the late Dorothy M. Needham) was published by Leicester University Press in 1992.

JERZY TOMASZEWSKI is Professor at the Institute of Political Sciences of the University of Warsaw, and Member of the Board and Council of the Jewish Historical Institute in Poland. His publications focus on the economic history, diplomatic history and national minorities of east-central Europe (mainly Poland, Czechoslovakia and Bulgaria). They include (with Zbigniew Landau) *The Polish Economy in the Twentieth Century* (London and Sidney, 1985) and *The Socialist Regimes of Eastern Europe* (London, 1989).

LOUIS VOS studied modern history at the Katholieke Universiteit in Leuven where he received a Ph.D. in 1980. His dissertation dealt with the conflict between Catholic students and bishops about the Flemish-nationalist orientation of the general Catholic Flemish Student Association in the interwar period. He has been Scientific Assistant at the universities of Tilburg and Leuven, and became Professor of Modern History at the KU Leuven in 1984. He holds the Chair for Nationalism in European History in the European Studies Programme for Graduate Students from Abroad. He has published several books and articles on the history of nationalism, the Flemish movement, student movements and youth associations.

HEINRICH AUGUST WINKLER was Professor of Modern and Recent History at the University of Freiburg in Breisgau from 1972 to 1991. He is currently Professor of Modern History at the Humboldt University in Berlin. He has held visiting posts and Fellowships at Princeton University (1974–5), the Woodrow Wilson International Center for Scholars in Washington, D.C. (1977–8), the Wissenschaftskolleg zu Berlin (1985–6), Maison des Sciences de l'Homme in Paris (1988) and Historisches Kolleg in Munich (1990–1). His numerous works cover political and social history of the nineteenth and twentieth centuries and include the collection *Nationalismus* (Königstein, 1978), edited by him. Recently second editions appeared: *Der Schein der Normalität. Arbeiter und Arbeiterbewegung in der Weimarer Republik 1924–1930* (Berlin, 1988) and *Der Weg in die Katastrophe. Arbeiter und Arbeiterbewegung in der Weimarer Republik 1930–33* (Berlin, 1989).

ACKNOWLEDGEMENTS

IN view of the unforeseeable events in the late autumn of 1989 we may like to think of the contributions on the countries in eastern Europe as documents in their own right. Except for some revision by Walter Schmidt in mid-December 1989 and by Heinrich August Winkler in early 1991, the 'Eastern' authors left their texts unchanged. We should like to express our heartfelt appreciation to them, as well as to the other contributors, for their patient understanding of the delay in the appearance of this volume. For one thing, we had great difficulty in commissioning translators willing to undertake the challenging task of rendering texts originally written in Czech, German and Hungarian into English. For another, the prospective author on Spain withdrew, after repeated postponements over a period of at least two years. In this connection particular thanks are due to Simon Barton for accepting the invitation to contribute to the volume at very short notice indeed. Our colleagues (and contributors to previous volumes) Clarissa Campbell Orr, Alice Teichova and Joachim Whaley have helped to oversee manuscripts and translations for which we are truly grateful. Again we renew sincerest thanks to William Davies of the Cambridge University Press for consistently supporting the purpose of the sequence we are editing. Thanks are due also to Frieda Houser from the Academic Unit of the Wellcome Institute for the History of Medicine for her considerable help with correspondence, and Gillian Law for her copy-editorial suggestions.

INTRODUCTION

MIKULÁŠ TEICH AND ROY PORTER

THE purpose of the sequence of collections of essays that we are editing is to bring together comparative, national and interdisciplinary approaches to the history of great movements in the development of human thought and action. Among them, by any reckoning, the historical impact of national movements has been immense, and it is the awareness of the enduring significance of the national question that leads us to offer a volume in which it is discussed authoritatively by specialist historians. It goes without saying that the national question is not a specifically European phenomenon, but for reasons of space and intelligibility the volume deals with the national question in a limited number of European countries. Reflecting recent research and ever-changing patterns of interpretation, the volume focuses on the role, underestimated time and again, of the national question in European history.

Our aim is that this collection should be of use to students of history as well as to a wide range of readers interested in a historical problem that has been hard to encompass theoretically and to deal with practically. A glance at what is being written in the contemporary press or shown on the screen, regarding national and ethnical issues, demonstrates the validity of this aim, not only with regard to the multinational former Soviet Union or former Yugoslavia in eastern Europe but also (for example) to bi-national Belgium or to the four nations of the British Isles in the West. Their 'stormy, often bloody history', from the Celtic beginnings to the present, is discussed by Victor Kiernan. In the concluding part of his essay, after giving the histories of England, Scotland, Wales and Ireland a balanced, critical consideration, Kiernan writes warningly:

> All today face complex difficulties; in a sense the most acute national problem of all is whether England itself can be expected to survive in any recognizable shape, physical or moral; not so much on account of issues of race and creed arising with the new ethnic minorities, residues

of the days of empire, as of an unwholesome social-economic structure, and with it reckless fouling of air, water, landscape, culture. Wales and Scotland will not do England any good by continuing their actual relationship with it. That conservative blockages stood in the way of home-rule-all-round early in this century must be regretted. There are, at the same time, valid objections to a complete break-up; the world is quite sufficiently Balkanized already, and the conventional state, which evolved primarily for military purposes has become an anachronism, a cumbrous suit of armour for any nation to have to wear. Wales and Ireland, like Brittany or Catalonia, have proved that nationality, pride in ideas, feelings, memories, not shared by others, can live on unsupported by a state, and even in spite of efforts by a state power to banish it.

Questions such as what is meant by a nation have been repeatedly asked. Among the older treatments of major impact was *Qu'est-ce qu'une nation?* by the renowned French orientalist and historian of religion Ernest Renan. Though given as a lecture at the Sorbonne as far back as 11 March 1882,[1] it is still of interest to the historian, not least because of Renan's influential attempt, grounded in historical idealism, at systematic critical analysis of the phenomenon 'nation' – 'an idea, clear on the surface but lending itself to serious misunderstandings'. According to Renan, these arose from endeavours erroneously to attribute to nations, racial, linguistic, religious or physiographical connotations. Instead Renan conceived of a nation as a spiritual human community, endowed with a past and also a desire (wish) to uphold it through a day-to-day vote of confidence – *un plébiscite de tous les jours*. In Renan's terms this was a metaphor for the use of which he – curiously – apologized to the audience. While it has often been quoted, his further observation that nations are by no means eternal entities has hardly been commented on. It deserves to be cited:

> Nations are not something everlasting. They have a beginning, they will have an end. Probably a European confederation will replace it. But this is not the law of the century in which we live. At the present time, the existence of nations is a good, even necessary thing. Their existence is a guarantee of liberty which would be lost if the world had only one law and one master.

Thirty years later a professional Georgian revolutionary travelled to Vienna, the imperial capital of a monarchy in the throes of national(ist) confrontations, to look for an answer to the very question posed for Renan. Here the primary concern with *Marxism and the National Question* (1913) is not that it was authored by Joseph Stalin,[2] neither is the historical and political context that had put its stamp on this work of particular moment. Rather the interest lies in the common ground, accepted by both Renan and Stalin when identifying the issues, and in the dissimilar conclusions they came to. Thus Stalin, like Renan, stressed that 'a nation, like every historical phenomenon, is subject to the law of change, has its history, its beginning and end'. He also examined the national question in systematic terms and to some extent looked at the same categories as Renan (race, language, religion, geography). But developing a materialist analysis, Stalin had arrived at a different answer than Renan: 'A nation is a historically constituted, stable community of people, formed on the basis of common language, territory, economic life, and psychological make-up manifested in a common culture.'

From non-Marxists and, after Stalin's demise, also from Marxists this definition has come under strong criticism, the gist of which has been that there is more to a nation than the five canonical attributes he proffered. More in what way? After recently exploring the theme afresh, the Marxist Eric Hobsbawm has concluded that 'no satisfactory criterion can be discovered for deciding which of the many human collectivities should be labelled [as a (or the) nation]'.[3] The point is made, especially if the inclination is to propound a normative concept of the nation, and in absolute terms to boot. In a sense what underlies Hobsbawm's rejection of Stalin's analysis is a shift in methodology. Like other contemporary Marxist writers, Stalin believed in the applicability of procedures in investigating nature to the social domain. This found reflection in his Linnaean-type classification, as it were, for a definition of what constitutes a nation. To Hobsbawm, writing seven decades later, such an exercise in classification of a social phenomenon appears distinctly simplistic and hence inadequate.

While a few contributors to this volume refer directly or indirectly to Renan and Stalin, they pay on the whole scant attention to the numerous general publications on the national theme that have appeared during the last twenty-five years or so.[4] Overall the perspective of the authors of the essays in which assorted 'national questions' come under concrete scrutiny is different: concrete in the sense that the writers direct factual attention at the political, military, economic, social, linguistic, territorial and other aspects of the national question in the countries under review, including their relationship and historical role. Although, or perhaps because, the contributors in their effectively particular case histories vary in their approaches, emphases and chronological reach, certain pertinent points for scholarship in this area emerge.

In a recent short piece, imaginatively entitled 'Were the English English?' Rodney Hilton has raised the question whether positive feelings of 'Englishness' existed in medieval England.[5] Writing very cautiously, he believes that they surfaced by the time of the Anglo-Scottish border wars, and the Anglo-French wars; they were growing into something like national wars. Not surprisingly, Douglas Johnson in this volume also notes that the awareness of 'Frenchness' is discernible after the English invasion of 1415: 'The idea that one should be prepared to die for one's country . . . Patriotism was still linked to religion and to the idea of a virtuous death. It could be local or regional or restricted to a segment of society. But it had also become national. '

In the Middle Ages the growth of sensibility for national 'otherness' did not necessarily depend on warfare. Take the case of the Czech Lands, reviewed here by Arnošt Klíma. There it began to make itself felt in Czech noble and Church circles in the eleventh century. They did not like or approve of the disproportionate influence of German clergy in Church affairs. The happening that reinforced and in fact heightened 'Czechness' was the mass influx of German-speaking settlers during the thirteenth and fourteenth centuries. As a result of these population movements compact German-speaking areas were established in Bohemia, Moravia and Silesia. The descendants of the settlers participated in turn as players, victors and victims in events of world historical significance that paved the road to Munich in 1938 and their expulsion from the Czech Lands after 1945.

In England, France, the Czech Lands and, for that matter, also in Hungary (Emil Niederhauser) and Poland (Jerzy Tomaszewski) varieties of ethnic/national sentiment existed in the Middle Ages. What about Germany? It is the (East) German contributor Walter Schmidt, dealing with the German case, who discusses the issue from the Marxist standpoint. Accordingly, he views the Reformation and the Peasant War in Germany as early stages of the bourgeois revolution which was defeated during 1517–25 with far-reaching negative consequences for the growth of German national sentiment. The transformation of what Schmidt calls 'the medieval feudal German nationality' into a bourgeois German nation was halted, not least because of the ensuing German territorial state fragmentation, also acknowledged by the (West) German historian H. A. Winkler in his contribution as a profoundly nefarious factor in the German national development.

During the last few years before the reunification, historians in the Federal Republic of Germany (FRG) and in the German Democratic

Republic (GDR) were deeply involved in debating the problem of German national identity. It is obvious that, although the issue stemmed directly from the existence of the two states, it has to be considered in the light of German history as a whole. This appears to have influenced the well-known (West) German historian K. D. Erdmann when he produced, in 1985, the controversial thesis regarding the existence of one German people (*Volk*), two nations (German, Austrian) and three states (FRG, GDR, Austria). The Austrian case is indeed complicated but Ernst Bruckmüller's long-term analysis abundantly clarifies why 'the Austrians have come to accept a sense of their identity which is no longer dependent upon the greater geopolitical context within which their history unfolded'. Although not perceived as such, the search for German identity was at the heart of the *Historikerstreit*, as perspicaciously pointed out by George L. Mosse at the height of the dispute.[6] 'Above all the *Historikerstreit* should stimulate deeper reflection on the relationship between nationalism and national identity.'

In general, it is inadequate to make out of national identity the alpha and omega of the national question. Thus – Spain may serve as an example – it is necessary to appreciate the historical dimension of regionalist allegiances, rooted in the feudal politics and economy of the Middle Ages, that were at work against the formation of national unity and identity. Without moving our eyes backward into the medieval past, it is difficult to come to grips with national issues in post-medieval Europe.

The established opinion is that the actual impulses that gave rise to the national question in Europe in its modern sense were the French Revolution and the Napoleonic wars respectively. This is the starting-point of the essay on Italy, but the view is reflected in other contributions as well. What also emerges is that the writers on Croatia and Finland, Poland and Belgium (for instance) take 'history from below' more seriously than has been the case in theoretical publications on the national theme of late.[7] A by-product of this approach is, as it were, that they do not make light of bench-marks of nationhood such as language, peasantry and the economy but pay to them, at times complementary, scholarly attention.

We live in a world, like it or not, in which the national dimension of history haunts us in ways from which we are finding there is no easy escape. Therefore the following comment is of interest. It is by a sensitive observer of recent events not only in eastern Europe but also resurgent nationalisms and liberation movements of the Basques, the Kosovans, the Kurds and other suchlike 'peripheral' peoples:[8]

Independence movements all make economic and territorial demands, but their first claim is of a spiritual order ... All nationalisms are at heart deeply concerned with names: with the most immaterial and original human invention. Those who dismiss names as a detail have never been displaced; but the peoples on the peripheries are always being displaced. This is why they insist upon their identity being recognised, insist upon their continuity – their links with their dead and the unborn.

NOTES

1 E. Renan, *Qu'est-ce qu'une nation?*, 2nd edn (Paris, 1882). For quotations, see pp. 1, 28.
2 Actually when the piece was first published in the spring of 1913, it bore the signature K. Stalin. Cf. J. V. Stalin, *Works 1907-1913* (Moscow, 1953), vol. II, pp. 300-81. For quotations, see p. 307.
3 E. J. Hobsbawm, *Nations and Nationalism since 1780: Programme, Myth, Reality* (Cambridge, 1990), p. 5.
4 Cf. 'in the opinion of the present author the number of works genuinely illuminating the question of what nations and national movements are and what role they play is larger in the period 1968-88 than for any earlier period of twice the length'. Hobsbawm, *Nations and Nationalism*, p. 4. Hobsbawm offers a list of ten books 'which may serve as an introduction to the field'.
5 R. Hilton, 'Were the English English?', in R. Samuel (ed.), *Patriotism: The Making and Unmaking of British National Identity*, 3 vols. (London, 1989), vol. I, pp. 39-43.
6 G. L. Mosse, 'Die lückenlose Geschichte Ernst Noltes Antwort an seine Kritiker', *Frankfurter Allgemeine Zeitung*, 19 January 1988.
7 E. Hobsbawm's one major criticism of E. Gellner's stimulating *Nations and Nationalism* (Oxford, 1983) is 'that his preferred perspective of modernization from above makes it difficult to pay adequate attention to the view from below'. Hobsbawm, *Nations and Nationalism*, p. 10.
8 J. Berger, 'Keeping a rendezvous', *Review Guardian*, 22 March 1990.

ONE

THE BRITISH ISLES: CELT AND SAXON

VICTOR KIERNAN

High the vanes of Shrewsbury gleam
Islanded in Severn stream . . .
The flag of morn in conqueror's state
Enters at the English gate:
The vanquished eve, as night prevails,
Bleeds upon the road to Wales.
A. E. Housman, *The Welsh Marches*

Of the stormy, often bloody history of the British Isles, a great part has consisted of the Germanic occupation of what is now England, followed by a millennium of English penetration into Celtic regions to the west and north, and their assimilation or conquest. Pushed back into hills and backlands, and with a malign social and psychological heritage from times when they themselves were alien conquerors, the Celtic peoples were left with little chance of a healthy evolution. In turn their fate could scarcely fail to have a malign influence on the Germanic mixture which was supplanting them – itself to a great extent composed of 'Celts' forcibly or otherwise transformed. In many ways this can be called the formative experience of the English people, especially of its ruling classes, leaving it as Cobbett said, with its treatment of Ireland in mind, 'arrogant, greedy, fond of power, and of dominion all over the world'.[1] There has been more than one parallel in Europe to this situation of a stronger people learning to be a 'nation' by dominating weaker, more 'backward' ones; the closest is the rise of Austria through subjugation of Slav territories on its mountainous south and south-east, and then of the Slav kingdom of Bohemia. Nationalism in Europe owes to a background of this kind a great deal of its domineering temper; it helped to mould the modern militarist state, ambitious of triumphs such as England sought in the

I

Hundred Years' War, and in later times in imperialist expansion
outside Europe.

Celtic peoples of today descend from an amalgam formed ages ago of
ethnic groups unknown to history and aggressors speaking Celtic
languages and wielding iron swords. Today they are cooped up in the
north-west fringes of Europe, almost pushed off their narrow ledge
into the Atlantic, which millions of their children have been forced to
escape across. Yet their Celtic-speaking ancestors once spread across
much of Europe, and were warlike enough almost to nip in the bud
the Roman Empire destined to bring most of them under its sway.
George Borrow, travelling among the Cymry or Welsh of his time,
associated their name with Cape Comorin, and concluded that 'The
original home of the Cumro was southern Hindustan.'[2] This and
many other guesses about Celtic origins gave way to a supposition
that the speakers of a first Indo-European or 'Aryan' language had
their cradle in the lower reaches of the Volga; that from there some of
them migrated across Europe; and that in middle Europe a convergence of many currents of settlement and influence brought about a
complex development, and a separating out of Celtic, Slav, Germanic
and other linguistic families. A first, Goidelic or Gaelic, pattern of
Celtic speech was established in Ireland, perhaps coming partly by
way of northern Spain, by the sixth century BC; a later, Brythonic or
British, variety was in Britain by the fourth century. Each may, or
must, have been carried by advance parties considerably earlier.
Lately this picture has in turn been challenged, by the archaeologist
Colin Renfrew. He thinks of the original Indo-European tongue
spreading across Europe at a very early date, along with farming and
the increased density of population this brought with it; subsequent
changes were due not to large-scale migrations but to a very gradual
separating out of ethnic and linguistic groups from the common stock,
taking place in the same areas where they make their first appearance
in history.[3]

Pre-Aryan languages, whatever they were, disappeared, apart from
Basque and probably a substratum persisting in some of their
successors, for instance in the mysterious Pictish of Scotland about
which modern enquirers like Scott's Antiquary have argued indefatig-
ably. In historical times it would seem to have been a kind of British,
with survivals from the tongue of an older, submerged people.[4] War
and conquest were the vocation of the charioteering Celts when they
emerged into the dim light of history, with a nobility and its followers
at the top of a social structure whose patterns of behaviour they could

never shake off. Slavery was one component. 'A servile class was an integral part of the Celtic system.'[5] There was too little resistance from a sparse population below to compel petty rulers to unite. Confronted by well-drilled Romans, these crumpled quickly except where protected by nature, as in the Welsh or Scottish hills. Only in Scotland, when Gael and Briton collided, was statehood achieved.

Rome's decline released a new flood of 'folk-wandering', long dammed up by the legions. Saxons and others from beyond the North Sea were ready to pour into Britain. Their colonizing, though they came or soon fell under powerful war-leaders, had more of the character of a 'people's imperialism', with plough instead of chariot for vehicle. In the course of it many Britons perished, many others were pushed westward, to keep up for long a scattered rearguard action whose fabled hero is King Arthur. Probably most stayed where they were, gradually absorbed into the lower orders of the new nation taking shape. Formerly they had drudged for Roman-British land-owners; 'it simply meant a change from one master to another'.[6] Britons and slaves were called by the same Saxon word. It is no wonder that the British ingredient in the population left 'no significant impression on English society'.[7] Only an odd freak of history has left the English with no other collective name for themselves and their Welsh and Scottish neighbours than 'Britons'.

British speech survived in Wales, in the shelter of the hills. It lingered in Dorset and Devon until after 900, in Cornwall much longer. How savage was the Saxon onslaught, however, is shown by a mass emigration from the south-west which gave Brittany its start. Both Wales and Cornwall suffered from Irish as well as Saxon marauders and settlers. Ireland itself was soon being molested by Danes and Northmen. A war-leader from the south, Brian Boru, defeated them in 1014 at Clontarf near Dublin; but Irishmen from the south-western province of Leinster were among his opponents there, and his death on the field ended whatever unity he had forged.

As a nation in the making, Scotland was turning into one of the strangest conglomerates anywhere in Europe, only Spain perhaps displaying a more bizarre hotchpotch. In Argyll from the fifth century AD a Kingdom of Dalriada was being set up by Irish intruders from nearby Antrim in north-eastern Ireland, the Scots. Having to fight to secure a place, and then to keep it in face of enemies who had learned something from long contact with the Romans, they held together better than their Irish forebears. Long-drawn hostilities ended in defeat for the Picts in 839, and a kingdom of 'Alba', or 'Scotland', emerged, with the Pictish tongue fading before the Gaelic of the Scots.

Gaelic similarly ousted Cumbrian-British when the principality of Strathclyde, stretching down from south-western Scotland through Cumbria to the Welsh border, was taken over by the Scots. But what is now south-east Scotland, including Lothian, had been occupied by the English of Northumbria, and remained English, though with a partially Celtic countryside, even after Danish pressure on northern England at the beginning of the eleventh century enabled the Scots to move in and fix their frontier on the Tweed. They tried indeed, true to old Celtic expansionist instincts, to push it still further south.

Saxon kings aimed at a degree of suzerainty over all of what came to be called in the Middle Ages 'Great Britain', and contests with Welsh and Scots, as well as Danes, promoted 'a massive centralisation of royal power', especially in taxation.[8] The country was being overstrained, class division deepening; only this can explain how in 1066 England, apparently so vigorous, was so easily humbled by a small force of brigands from across the Channel. Its complex machinery of state was ready to be taken over and run by other hands, with a further worsening of conditions for the masses. A precocious trend towards hegemony over the British Isles was now accelerated.

There may have been some poetic justice in the fact that among William the Conqueror's followers were Breton soldiers of fortune, descendants of Cornishmen driven out by Saxons whose descendants they were helping to subdue. His son Rufus captured Carlisle, and with it Cumbria, or Strathclyde south of the Solway: a loss to Scotland of one of its mainly Celtic provinces. 'Marcher' or frontier lords were nibbling at the southern, more vulnerable valleys of Wales. Now and then northern leaders organized efforts at union for defence. Llywelyn the Great (1173–1240) profited by divisions in King John's England. Owen Glendower led the biggest of all later rebellions, which broke out in 1400. He sought support from Scotland and Ireland, with little success. Celtic countries were frequently to receive aid from Continental enemies of the English, scarcely ever from one another.

Celtic society, revolving round the warrior chief, and contemptuous of any utilitarian activity, was everywhere deficient in urban and mercantile talents. To make up for this lack, a continuing inflow of settlers from England and the Low Countries was furnishing Scotland with an 'artisan bourgeoisie' centred on towns in Lothian and northward along the eastern coast.[9] Politically too, its rulers found it easier to borrow from abroad than to build on lines of their own. Malcolm Canmore (d. 1093) had an English wife who brought potent foreign influences wih her. A Celtic or 'nativist' reaction was put down. Their son David I (1124–53) had close Norman connections. Anglo-Norman adventurers came in as feudal lords, to bolster the royal power, which in later years their heirs did far more to weaken. Other interlopers made their way into the Highlands, where feudal authority soon intertwined with clan chieftainship. But Scotland's English- and Gaelic-speaking areas were not coming together; the Lowlands were now its nucleus, a smaller equivalent of England with its Celtic penumbra.

In 1286 the old dynasty, now only dilutedly Celtic, came to an end, and Edward I of England seized the opportunity to assert a feudal paramountcy. The long Wars of Independence might be viewed as in one aspect a faction-fight between two sections of an Anglo-Norman aristocracy, some of whose members owned estates in both countries. During the time when Wallace led the resistance a different note was struck, of 'protest by the "poor commons" against their sufferings at the hands of a harsh and repressive society'.[10] This did not recommend him to the nobles, who held aloof. Robert Bruce depended for much of his support on the Gaels, a lesser bugbear in noble eyes than mutinous peasants. At Bannockburn in 1314 'The Scottish army was basically Celtic in composition and largely Gaelic speaking.' Its antagonists numbered Welsh and Irish as well as English archers.[11] But Wallace's name betokens a Welsh background, and Robert's brother Edward was in Ireland for several years before his death in 1318, trying to cement an alliance. To Lowland Scots, Wallace and Bruce were always in later days the grand heroes, round whom much of a slowly growing patriotic legend clung; and the disappearance of formal serfdom – even if it left the masses miserably off – may have owed something to the part played by the commonalty in the defence of the realm.

In Ireland the O'Neills of Ulster, close to their fellow Gaels of the Hebrides, were in the forefront of sporadic resistance to English encroachments; but they boasted 'a chess-set made of the bones of defeated Leinstermen'.[12] Ireland was without any kind of *thinking* class, to digest lessons of experience; there were only the venal bards, ready to sing the praises of anyone who would fee them, and priests ready to welcome Anglo-Norman conquest when it was launched with papal blessings by Henry II. Richard 'Strongbow', Earl of Pembroke in Wales, descended on the coast with mainly Welsh recruits: one of very many instances of England's adroitness in setting Celts, as in later days Asians and Africans, to fight one another for its benefit. In 1170 he captured Waterford and Dublin. Before very long more than half the country was under English sway, but very insecurely except in the 'Pale', with Dublin for capital and a parliament of its own. As in the Highlands, and on the Welsh Marches, Anglo-Normans could all too easily fit themselves into Celtic society and turn half-Irish, the more so because their own ethnic background was so indeterminate.

Ireland's destiny was to be totally subjugated; Wales and Scotland were drifting towards a milder, never complete, absorption into England, but the former a century-and-a-half earlier. In 1485 Welsh discontents helped to bring to the throne, as Henry VII, a man with little right to it, but with a Welsh name, whose Tudor successors sought the continuing loyalty of Welshmen by pretending to Arthurian origins. But with Henry VIII Tudor policy came out clearly as one of incorporation, or more thoroughgoing annexation. Two Acts of 1536 provided for counties run on English lines, subject to English law and with English as official language; in return Wales was to have representatives in parliament.[13] Welshmen were to be turned into Englishmen. Bigger landlords were soon anglicized, while lesser ones, poor and rustical except in Glamorgan in the fertile south, and the peasantry, remained Welsh. A partial change came with the Reformation; translations of the Bible in Elizabeth's reign, necessary for the offensive against Catholicism, helped to preserve the language, though also for long to insulate it from modern ideas. Wales was growing into a more orderly land, but it was unmistakably a colony. Mining developed, chiefly to supply English wants. Extensive enclosures of land injured poorer cultivators and forced them off the better soil.

Monarchy had no very deep roots in Wales, but there were Arthur and the Welsh dragon to bolster it; and a poor, retarded region is always apt – like Brittany in Revolutionary France – to be conservative, from an instinctive feeling that any change will be for the worse. (Poverty-stricken old folk in France today vote conservative, Simone de Beauvoir discovered.)[14] In the civil wars Wales was staunchly royalist; altogether, during the seventeenth century the centre of gravity of the waning monarchy was floating westward, into reliance on the Celtic backlands. A 'barbarous squirearchy' led the way into Charles I's camp;[15] Huw Morris, the best poet of the time, aided the royal cause with songs full of loyal zeal 'which ran like wild-fire through Wales'.[16] In all this, national feeling had only a limited place; for one reason because of the north–south divide imposed on Wales – as on Scotland – in all epochs by geography. Glamorgan had more links with Devon and Cornwall, and Irish trade, than with the rest of Wales.[17] Cornwall too stood by the king, thanks to poverty and ignorance more than to any good the monarchy had done it; though

Cornishmen's chief desire may have been to keep Englishmen out, and they were reluctant to march beyond the Tamar, their river Tweed. Many royalist atrocities after the Parliamentary defeat at Lostwithiel in 1644 were blamed on rustic Cornish auxiliaries.[18]

In later medieval Scotland there was some resurgence of Gaelic life and culture. In the fifteenth century the government managed to overthrow the Lordship of the Isles which had provided the Hebrides with a kind of focal point, but royal authority there was still weak. In the mid-sixteenth century renewed English attacks found the disgruntled Gaels of the west more inclined to make common cause with the invaders than to join in repelling them. In the early seventeenth century nearly half the population of Scotland may still have been Gaelic-speaking, and the language was entering 'its period of greatest vitality'.[19] But clan enmities and feudal ambitions prevented any Celtic political progress. Although in the turmoil of civil wars in the 1640s and 1650s the Highlands played a considerable part, an overture to the Jacobite risings of 1715 and 1745, there was no Gaelic party; rival caudillos, Argyll and Montrose, set the clansmen at one another's throats.

Reformation had carried Scotland out of the orbit of its old ally France, into that of England, and the throne vacated by the Tudors was inherited by the Stuarts. James VI and I aspired to a closer union between the two countries than a merely personal one; but neither of them was eager to fall in with his wishes. After a generation of rule from London, the National Covenant of 1638, prelude to the civil wars, had a firm ring of Scottish patriotic feeling, as well as firm adherence to Scotland's own Kirk, a church Presbyterian and Calvinistic. The outcome a dozen years later was a faction-ridden country for the first time completely occupied, by a new-model army from England, and annexed. Events of those years suggests that there was no future for Scotland as an independent nation. It was not really even struggling for independence; all of the better-off classes wanted a closer tie with England than the former one, in the interests of Scottish trade and progress, even if they could not agree about the right terms. Good English administration, a uniform 'concern for social justice',[20] failed to soften the xenophobia of the masses, or of the Kirk.

Restoration in 1660 nominally brought back Scotland's autonomy and equality with England. It made little of them, and there was not much objection from those with political weight to the Union of 1707, when the exigencies of the long wars with Louis XIV, and the approaching extinction of the reigning dynasty, led England to insist on it. Scotland lost its parliament, never a representative one, but was allowed to keep its College of Justice and legal system, its established Church, and other rights. But while at Edinburgh the parliament was voting itself out of existence, clamorous crowds were filling the streets to denounce the Union.

English settlers in Ireland long continued to 'go native' with a gusto that made them very undependable subjects. There were complaints in the sixteenth century that in Dublin itself everyone talked Irish.[21] Henry VII, for all his claim to Celtic blood, issued stern prohibitions of Irish dress or customs within the Pale, and tightened control over the Dublin parliament. Tudor policy was to make the aristocracy reliable by anglicizing it, but there were many revolts, led by over-mighty subjects whether Irish or Anglo-Norman by origin. All these were put down, it is true. Besides the Celtic inability to combine, there was deep class division, going back to the Celtic dawn. Highland chiefs could be sure of the fidelity of their underlings, by fostering a clan spirit among them; Irish lords evidently could not, and very often they preferred, in the north especially, to make use of mercenaries, always forthcoming from the Hebrides. Ireland was one of the first countries where conquest was proclaimed liberation – a formula adopted by all modern imperialism. An Irish writer of our day thinks of the pretext as not altogether unrealistic, and of the invaders as having an easy task in weaning the poorer natives away from their masters.[22]

In 1603 the biggest rising, led by the O'Neill Earl of Tyrone, ended in defeat, leaving the way open for the Ulster Plantation. Gaels of Ireland and Scotland were finally pushed apart by this immigrant settlement. Many settlers on the vast confiscated estates were Scots, whose progenitors if not themselves had been Gaels; but religion was a breach never to be closed. Religion could on the other hand do much to bring together the 'Old English' settlers, many of whom were faithful to Catholicism, and Irish malcontents. After the Earl of Strafford as Charles I's governor had estranged all sections of feeling in Ireland, these two communities joined in the rebellion that broke out in 1641–2. For the first time there was something like a national movement. But unity proved fragile; there were factional jealousies, and, as always, too wide a gap between high and low. No full mobilizing of the people could be contemplated.[23] When Cromwell appeared on the scene defeat was inevitable. With the 1688 Revolution, Catholics could take up arms again, this time in the Stuart cause like Wales in the 1640s. In 1690 their hopes were extinguished by the victory of William of Orange, invited from Holland to England to reign as William III, at the battle of the Boyne.

Ireland was reduced to a colony,[24] exploited directly through extraction of wealth, indirectly through checks on production that might compete with English interests. Nevertheless, as the eighteenth century went on there was a glow of mild prosperity for the propertied classes, among them some Catholics who changed religion in order to keep their estates or enter the professions. Anti-English feeling ran mostly underground, in varied forms of peasant agitation – by Rightboys, Whiteboys, and others – against rack-renting by alien or half-alien landlords and tithes extorted by their Church. In time the parliament at Dublin learned to strike some patriotic attitudes, though it represented scarcely anything more than the landowners, completely dependent on English backing. Kohn has emphasized the freakish jumble of ideas that went into the opening phase of modern Irish nationalism.[25] It was put to the test in the 1790s, after first the American and then the French Revolution had stirred a whirlpool of political and social feeling. What was revealed was not the strength of a nation, but deadly hatred between the classes and the masses.

In 1791 – just a century-and-a-half after the united front against Charles I – the 'United Irishmen' began their brief career. Their centre was Belfast, where a Presbyterian trading class was ready to join hands with middle-class Catholics against the Anglican ('Church of Ireland') landlords and their British affiliates. But soon a rural, Catholic, secret organization of 'Defenders' was demanding much more sweeping changes. In 1795 the Orange Order was set up, with a name borrowed from the Protestant hero William of Orange, to turn the Presbyterian rank and file in Ulster against their Catholic neighbours. In 1797 government and propertied classes joined in a 'pacification' of the north, followed next year by a still more brutal one in the south, where agrarian revolt was breaking out.

It was easy now for the prime minister Pitt and his Tory Party to lay plans for the Union effected in 1800, by methods more squalid than the Union with Scotland in 1707, but with similar motives of wartime security against France. The Irish parliament could not be a serious obstacle. Its elimination, by stripping away a political sham, at least opened the door to a broader-based national movement. Daniel O'Connell, 'the Liberator', began campaigning for repeal of the Union not long after its birth, and at the same time for removal of the legal disabilities weighing on Catholics. He inaugurated a populist strategy of mobilizing mass support, with monster meetings and fiery oratory, which was only later emulated in Britain. Catholic Emancipation was granted in 1829, to conciliate the commercial and professional groups whom alone it benefited. Repeal was obstinately refused, and in the 1840s O'Connell was being left behind by the impatient leaders of Young Ireland, who in 1848 swelled the European chorus of revolution with a very small token rising of their own.

Nationalism like theirs 'developed almost wholly as a mystique', an ideology of a small middle-class or petty bourgeois elite, much of it only a generation or two removed from the soil, but in haste to forget the real hardships of those who cultivated it.[26] Instead they appealed to the potato-eaters in a romantic emotional style, akin to that of Mazzinians or Polish insurrectionists. Some of the rack-renting landlords were Irish, many middle-class men with money aspired (with better fortune after the great famine of 1840s) to become landlords. Orators therefore had to shut their eyes to social realities; they were then disappointed when the multitudes who applauded their rhetoric declined to rally round at the signal for action. From the time of Wolfe Tone at the end of the eighteenth century, failure left them, as O'Faolain says, full of indignation at the passivity and stupidity of the people.[27]

Union had been advertised as a guarantee of prosperity for Ireland. A vivid summary of the result was compiled in 1834 by William Cobbett, the radical champion of England's rural poor, who died before completing the book he meant to write. He saw clearly the *colonial relationship* between England and Ireland, and was convinced that things had got much worse for most people since the Union, if only because this was bound to increase landlord absenteeism; also Ireland was heavily under-represented in the London parliament, he pointed out in a lecture in Fishamble Street, Dublin, in November 1834, advocating repeal.[28] Decay of handicrafts was of course taking place in England too, but Ireland had little modern industry to replace them. At Limerick he was welcomed by a crowd of thirty thousand; in one street there, he says, 'I saw more misery than any man could have believed existed in the whole world.'[29]

In the countryside, the further west the more Celtic, and more wretched. An old villager in Donegal, born in 1864, recalled that in his boyhood all the folk were on a more or less equal footing, except the landlords. 'They were on the top of the world.'[30] Even their bailiffs could play the despot; 'if you met a bailiff and didn't touch your cap, you'd find yourself out of your farm or maybe in jail'. They got the best shares when community holdings surviving from the Celtic past were cut up into individual parcels in 1841.[31] All over Ireland hunger bred agrarian unrest, showing again after the repression of 1797–8 in the 'Ribbon Societies', and running through many phases, all inevitably with an anti-English and anti-Protestant tinge. Within the peasantry in less destitute areas, mainly eastward, there were distinguishable strata; but everywhere it was a sufficiently uniform mass for fellow-feeling to lead easily to collective action.

Famine in the 1840s, and massive emigration, diminished competition for tenancies, and cultivators struggling for lower rents and longer leases began to think of themselves as the rightful owners of the soil, and of the gentry as usurpers. In 1879 the Land League was formed, and from then until 1882 a 'Land War' raged. Direct action came naturally to the ordinary Irishman, who could have no sense of belonging to the same moral or legal hemisphere as his masters. Trollope embarked on his last novel, *The Landleaguers*, in order to condemn the violence of the agitation, but his purpose was at odds with 'his genuine liking for the Irish and his awareness of the harsh conditions under which they lived'.[32] He knew Ireland, and realized that between even the more decent landlords and their tenantry no meeting of minds was conceivable. His Mr Jones, who has exerted himself for the people's betterment, finds his son murdered, and feels bitterly sure that two girls nearby on the road must know who did it – 'but no one would tell in this accursed, unhallowed, godless country'.[33] Concessions had to be made by the government; they culminated in the buying out of landlords at the end of the century, under Tory auspices, as a lesser evil than Home Rule.

In the 1860s nationalist activity was reviving with the Fenian movement, which met with wide support, but not much comprehension of Irish realities, among sons of Erin far away in America, and sometimes in Britain. With the Fenians, the old type of secret organization for defence of peasant and artisan rights was turning political: usually as narrowly political as the old type had been narrowly economic. From their distant bases all problems could be seen as the single, simple one of getting rid of the British; they relied chiefly on what Anarchists in Europe learned to call 'the propaganda of the deed', acts of violence designed (like Irish Republican Army methods today) to startle or stampede. Their most spectacular attempts were to invade Canada from the USA in 1866, and to seize Chester castle in 1867. The more staid kind of middle-class politicians had little taste either for Fenian bombs or for Land League sabotage. They had to follow the national leader Parnell – a Protestant landowner – in endorsing the Land League; but they did so reluctantly and were happy to return to their parliamentary manoeuvres at Westminster.

Their reward in 1886 was Gladstone's first, very restricted, Home Rule bill, and its failure, with the right wing of the Liberal Party seceding to join the Tories. Its opponents were learning betimes to play the Ulster card, by stirring up intransigent Orangemen. In the counties round Belfast the largely Presbyterian farmers had more security of tenure than most Irish peasants, because domestic linen-weaving helped to pay rents; and there were some landowners of an Evangelical and patriarchal turn, whom they could look up to for guidance. With the growth of mills and shipyards in Belfast, competition for jobs there was quickly infected by communalism, and employers could keep their workforce divided by giving preferential treatment to Protestants.

By the beginnings of the twentieth century the steam had gone out of the agrarian movement; Home Rule seemed assured as soon as the Liberals could get back into power; it was clearly going to be rule by men who meanwhile were doing well for themselves in business and local government. The heroic days seemed over, and writers, of whom Ireland had a galaxy, were taking the place of politicians as its best spokesmen. There was much fanciful unrealism in their Irish feelings; the 'Celtic twilight' where some of them felt most at home blended easily with Oriental mysticism, theosophy, even magic. One acolyte was George Russell, who shared with the very remarkable poet Yeats a vision of an approaching world cataclysm, ushering in a new Messiah and a new Scripture.[34] Peerings into a shadowy past went with a nostalgic concern for the ancient language. Irish Gaelic had been waning in the later seventeenth and the eighteenth century; with the growth of a Catholic middle class it was being abandoned to the villager. O'Connell's grand meetings were conducted in English. Emigration, elementary schools teaching in English, modernizing currents from England, helped to weaken the old tongue. In Donegal in the north-west until past the middle of the nineteenth century everyone still spoke it, but then 'in one generation Irish went away like the snow off the ditches'.[35] In 1893 a Gaelic revival programme was launched. It harked back to the Romantic conception of language as the soul of nationhood, and was followed in 1905 by the formation of a new nationalist movement, Sinn Fein ('We Ourselves'), a more loudly populist tendency than the now humdrum parliamentary party. It had very little social thinking to distinguish it from the bourgeois politicians, and before 1914 met with little response.

Very different was the emerging Labour movement, whose out-

standing thinker James Connolly had a mind broadened by experience
in Scotland and America, as well as by Marxism. In 1896 he helped
to found a Socialist Republican Party, arguing that 'the Irish Socialist
was really the best Irish patriot', because 'the Irish National question
was at bottom an economic question'[36] – and because, as he wrote in
1898, 'The chief enemy of a Celtic revival today is the crushing force
of capitalism', pulverizing all national characteristics and flattening
Dublin or Warsaw into poor imitations of Manchester or Glasgow.[37]
Connolly insisted on Irish socialists being separately organized from
English; any notion that peoples so far apart could be won over by a
message offered them in identical terms was to him 'a doctrine almost
screamingly funny in its absurdity'.[38] He was critical of Sinn Fein for
repeating the Fenian error of wanting to jump into revolutionary
tactics prematurely; it was necessary to 'ascertain with mathematical
accuracy the moment when the majority of the Irish people were ripe
for revolution'.[39] It was to prove far from ripe in 1916 when he joined
the Easter Rising in Dublin, and was one of those executed after its
failure.

Between 1905 and 1914 capital and labour were locked in a series
of hard-fought disputes. Not all employers were English; bourgeois
nationalism might have had to align itself at times with peasant
agitation, but it was not going to take sides with the working class or
with socialism. Here it had the fullest approval of the Church, whose
attitude to the national struggle had always been one of reserve.
Labour's gravest weakness, and the cause of its ultimate defeat, lay in
Belfast, the biggest industrial centre, just where it ought to have been
strongest. In 1910 Connolly was hailing the working class as the last
remaining 'incorruptible inheritors of the fight for freedom in Ireland'.[40] Three years later he was compelled to lament the inertia of
Belfast, which was showing itself 'the home of the least rebellious
slaves in the industrial world'.[41] Celtic twilight and scientific Marxism
were in the same boat: the working class as Liberator was turning out
to be as hollow a champion as any hero of mythology. Disappointment
with it, as well as the collapse of socialist internationalism in 1914,
must have helped to make him throw in his lot with the insurgents of
1916.

In 1914 the Liberal government got a Home Rule bill through at
last; still a very limited one, but gratefully accepted by the parliamentary party, who further agreed to its postponement to the end of the
war, and to Ulster's provisional exclusion. Not all nationalists were
satisfied with this, and they might well be outraged by Orange
agitation in Ulster and the blackmailing of the government by the

British officers who refused to take part in quelling it. Carson, the ringleader, was a southerner; he and his friends were trying to block home rule for any part of Ireland, and keep the Protestant 'ascendancy' intact.[42] Still, the 1916 rising was either a very forlorn hope, or was meant only to give the country a reminder that the national spirit was not dead, and endow it with one more company of martyrs. The government reinforced the martyrs by trying to extend conscription to Ireland; and America's entry into the war raised hopes that at its end Ireland would have a powerful ally.

Lloyd George, the Welshman brought to the top by the war, was a prisoner when peace came of the Tory majority in his coalition. Ireland was in a mood to take the home rule it had been promised without waiting, and to go beyond it. A guerrilla struggle broke out; on the British side it was waged largely by the notorious 'Black and Tans', one of the proto-fascist bodies thrown up by the war, – on the other side by an Irish Republican Army (IRA). This was estimated to be never more than 2,000 strong, but it had enough popular support to be able to wreck the whole administration. Sinn Fein could set up an Assembly and take political control, without having to do much of the fighting.

In this chaotic fashion freedom came at last. After England had shown 'almost inexhaustible patience with the treasons, insults, and outrages of the Irish' – in the words of Dean Inge,[43] redolent of John Bull's perennial self-righteousness – in 1921 a treaty bestowed autonomy on an Irish Free State; but with Ireland partitioned, and an unfairly large territory, the Six Counties of the north-east, lopped off. This truncated Ulster was given a parliament of its own, as well as representation at Westminster, so that England could seem to be no longer ruling any part of the island; this it was hoped would reconcile the south to a continuing relation, however limited, with England. Partition had the opposite effect; despite the country's exhaustion, it set off the civil war of 1921 to 1923, extraordinarily ferocious despite the small numbers actively engaged. Mystic obsessions with the 'sacred soil' of an Ireland one and indivisible, an abstract entity over and above its inhabitants and their mundane wants, had acquired a potency that in some minds they have never lost.

Civil war gave the Free State a gloomy start. It was born too much out of hatred of foreigners, and religious bigotry: the Roman Empire had never conquered Ireland, but its ghost sat heavily on the country. There was too little energy or leadership for a fresh beginning to be made. Some of the writers withdrew before long to England, like

George Russell who died there disillusioned. No economic benefits accrued for years. The small rich class consisted mostly of Protestants, still in control of banking, business, even the higher civil service, and overlapping with a very conservative group of native monopolists.[44] Instead of material betterment or social reform, politicians devoted themselves to the task of cutting all political links with England one by one. The IRA, still in existence, wanted this pushed on faster. It was banned in 1936, but in 1939–40 carried out bombings in both Ulster and Britain. In 1937 a new constitution changed the Free State into Eire; in the Second World War it proved its independence by staying neutral; in 1949 it proclaimed itself a republic, and quitted the Commonwealth – unlike the new republic of India.

By way of nation-building, for too long every official post required a knowledge, or at least a smattering, of Gaelic; an ineffectual mode, as experience showed, of artificial respiration. Economic stagnation prevailed until by the 1950s it could be feared that the country was being fatally drained by emigration to Britain, and to America where a very large number of migrants are believed to have smuggled themselves in illicitly. Growth was at last set moving, with foreign investments playing a big part. Today the tourist sees a countryside dotted with neat farmhouses and cottages, and villas for the better-off, by contrast with the mansions and hovels of former days. Yet in a country for centuries so land-hungry, today the rural population has to be subsidized to keep it from drifting away into the towns. Intellectual as well as material activity has grown, and made wider contacts. Study of Irish history has been one of its chosen fields, from which there is still a great deal to be learned.

In Britain, as soon as peace and partition were agreed on the public 'heaved a sigh of relief and forgot about Ireland, Free State and Ulster together'[45] – just as it did a generation later when India was similarly disposed of. There were smiles of agreement when the historian Namier, addressing a college society at Cambridge in the early 1930s, declared that if Ireland could be towed out into mid-Atlantic and left there, 'How happy we should all be!' No attention was paid to the condition of Ulster; all parties were content to leave it to the Unionists in the Stormont, the meeting-place of the parliament, who kept themselves and their wealthy friends in perpetual power by flattering the self-esteem of the Protestant majority, its sense of superiority over the Catholic minority. This left things to get worse and worse, with an outbreak fated to come sooner or later, and when it happened, to cost John Bull a great deal of his precious money. Already during the

Second World War Britain was forced to realize what it had lost through Partition keeping Eire neutral, and potentially pro-German. There was much anxious debate in London about what could be done to remedy this, if only by gaining permission to make use of southern Irish ports. Churchill was obliged to go so far as to say that, although Ulster could not be coerced, reunion brought about by the two Irelands sharing together in the war effort would be welcomed. De Valera, the Eire premier, believed just after Pearl Harbor that he was being offered Ulster in return for abandoning neutrality. Even so, he was not to be tempted. Like Gandhi in his parallel situation in India, he may well have thought any such offer a 'postdated cheque on a failing bank'. Ulster was, as always, obdurate.[46]

A time came some years after the war, that loudly announced freedom struggle, when it seemed that progressives from the two sides in Ulster might be coming together in a civil rights movement, akin to the one in Black America. In 1964 a Campaign for Social Justice was launched, and in 1967 a Northern Ireland Civil Rights Association. But inflammatory anti-Catholic talk was kept up by 'Loyalists' such as the Orangemen and rabble-rousers like the Rev. Ian Paisley. Marches and demonstrations in support of the demand for civil rights were too often attacked and broken up by police or Loyalists. In 1970 an old IRA leadership grown moderate and progressive was brushed aside by a 'Provisional' command pledged to answer force with force. In the same year, by way of reply, the Ulster Defence Regiment was set up; in 1971 internment of Catholic suspects, and – in Amnesty International's belief – brutal treatment of them, led to rioting. In the slide into violence and counter-violence, what has ever since appeared to have been the point of no return was reached on 'Bloody Sunday', or 30 January, 1972, when a civil rights march at Derry (or London-derry, as Britons and Unionists call it) ended in a clash, and thirteen demonstrators were shot dead by soldiers of an irresponsible Para-chute Battalion.

Since then much destruction has taken place, but power is still lodged firmly where it always was. 'Loyalism' seems to have come to mean that England is in duty bound to go on being loyal to Ulster Toryism for ever. On the other side it has been demonstrated that in modern times a well-organized terrorist group with financial backing and popular sympathy can keep going indefinitely. It may be true, as disgruntled Unionists and soldiers complain, that the IRA could have been finished off long ago if the army and police had been given a free hand. This has been ruled out by public opinion in Britain and abroad; but public opinion has been only a negative force: Unionists have been obdurate against any real concessions, any power-sharing with the minority, in spite of lavish British subsidies. With a permanent majority of votes against reform, the Stormont regime never had any meaning, and the IRA made it unworkable; in 1972 London was obliged to shut it down and undertake direct responsibility. The police continued to be nearly all Protestants (partly because of Catholic reluctance to join), so that it was hard for them to be impartial, and impossible for Catholics to believe in their ever being so; though they have in fact been forced into some sharp clashes with Loyalist mobs. Paramilitary organizations have been set up by right-wing diehards, to take the law into their own hands – the Ulster Volunteer Force, Ulster Defence Association, Ulster Freedom Fighters. There has been feuding among them at times, and both they and the IRA have been accused of Mafia-style methods of raising money. Protestant reprisals for their bombs must have been foreseen by the IRA leaders, and perhaps welcomed.

The trial of strength and endurance has gone through many stages. The early attempt to disrupt resistance by internment of suspects without trial had too much resemblance to discredited colonialist procedures outside Europe to be easily justified. IRA claims for their men when caught to be given the status of political prisoners were firmly rejected, though it may be hard to frame a definition of 'political prisoner' that would not cover them. At one time, after the death of some children in an affray, a band of women set up a peace council; it soon fizzled out. Visits by preachers of peace from outside, Mother Teresa among them, have had as little success. Pillars of religion on both sides have deplored the killings, in principle; no one listens to them, unless they listen to themselves.

From the very long record of Ireland's earlier struggles the IRA has inherited the lesson that the only argument John Bull can be made to listen to is a gun. But rebels sometimes learn, as well as forget, as little as the Bourbons or Bulls they grapple with; and the IRA, for all the skill it has displayed in its own vocation, suffers from many of the same blindnesses that Engels criticized in the Fenians. It invokes the rooted rancours and grievances of the Catholic minority, putting forward no rational proposals. For a while it seems to have hoped that if it could get rid of the British and precipitate civil war in Ulster, Eire would have no choice but to intervene, drawing America after it. Any such dream has faded; it is too obvious that Britain is of more importance to Washington than Ireland can ever be. But for any underground organization a shift of stance is very awkward; anyone suggesting it is liable to be denounced as a renegade. Fanatic gunmen like these come to resemble the earliest Assassins, the drugged killers who did the work of the Old Man of the Mountain.

Connolly realized during the pre-1914 labour conflict how hard it was to spread twentieth-century ideas 'amidst the mental atmosphere of the early seventeenth century'.[47] Ostensibly the IRA creed is that the British are the only enemy, and as soon as they have been bombed out of the country all Ulstermen will fly into one another's arms. Really what we see is more a recrudescence of the old spirit of the blood feud, still very much alive at the time of the Plantation. Most of the belligerents are workmen, or of not much higher station, while their betters are comfortably untouched. Those of the IRA have often perhaps been casual labourers, roaming from job to job, free of the sober respectability of the workman in most times and places, and in need of a cause, a fraternity, to give them anchorage and a purpose in life.

A middle-aged woman in an Edinburgh public house one evening in the early 1950s, hearing two strangers talking of Ireland, struck in abruptly with the words 'My name is Kelly, and I hate the English.' Only a community with a very long history of injustice and oppression could give its backing so unquestioningly to such a campaign for twenty years on end. What seems to move Ulstermen, in Belfast above all, is an ingrained neighbourhood feeling, a closing of ranks – and minds – in one street against a hostile street nearby. This has of course been worsened by the segregated schools and the principles of blind faith and obedience instilled into the young. Ulster Catholics may not relish the never-ending insecurity, especially when bombs or bullets happen to hit the wrong targets, but they fall back on a not unfounded conviction that 'it was the British who began it', or their Loyalist henchmen. After the explosion in a London store before Christmas 1983 Irish men and women in Britain could be heard saying the same: the British started all the trouble, and it is up to *them* to end it.[48] Sinn Fein as the political wing of the IRA has gone on winning the Catholic vote, despite its equal lack of any intelligible programme. On such a battlefield there is no middle ground to be occupied; the Social Democratic Labour Party set up in 1970 to preach sanity and mutual understanding has made small impression on either wing, and discussions between it and Sinn Fein have got nowhere.

With a preferential right of entry for Eire citizens into Britain, and settlement there, and equal membership in the European Community, there is no 'Irish problem' left, except that of Ulster. The republic's constitution claims *de jure* sovereignty over all Ireland. There have been proposals to drop this, as offensive to Ulster Protestant feeling, but attachment to it has hardened into rigidity. It is increasingly a dead letter. Most of the IRA's funds have come from Irish America. In Eire the public is more interested in its own economic and other difficulties than in happenings in Ulster, which even in nearby Donegal seem to have the sound of a faraway civil war. No Irish ministers can disclaim some concern with them; but they cannot extol terrorism, for fear of repercussions in their own house. Dublin has been cautiously willing to collaborate in the policing of the border, and in extraditions, but in return it has had to insist on a right to be at least consulted about Ulster questions. This the Tory government, after many wooden refusals, was at length constrained to agree to, if very grudgingly, in November 1985. In Ulster the Unionist parties have denounced the accord from the start; Dublin has pressed in vain for its extension to serious political discussion, an indispensable condition for any ultimate solution. In September 1988 the Labour Party gave its backing to this, and in November 1988 the third anniversary of the agreement brought at least further exchanges of views.

At bottom the whole issue is far more social than national (or theological). Protestant workers have had, and intend to keep, the upper hand in jobs and earnings, and have been bribed with them by a ruling class that wants to keep the working class divided. This may not invalidate historical materialism, but it does make nonsense of the Marxian corollary that all workmen are brothers. Catholic farmers are conscious that Protestant farmers have been in occupation of most of the best land, ever since the conquest turned so many Catholics into 'mountainy men', relegated to inferior hill soils, and not in the Six Counties only. A guidebook to Donegal refers to the Lagan district as very fertile, and Protestant. 'It is not prosperous because it's Protestant. No, it is Protestant because it was good fertile land, the best in the county and so was earmarked for Protestant Settlement.'[49] It would seem a logical conclusion that Protestants in Ulster with good farms – or good jobs – should give them up. Otherwise it is not clear how Catholics would benefit from a British withdrawal. But nothing in IRA or Sinn Fein thinking has ever been clear.

A compulsory relocation of minority groups from district to district, on the model of the Greek–Turkish population exchange after 1918, would scarcely be practicable. A redrawing of the frontier has been mooted in Britain, off and on, since as long ago as 1972, with the aim of transferring as many Catholic areas as possible to Eire. One objection is that both Eire and the IRA would jib at any new border agreement, as amounting to an admission that Ireland will always be divided. A Berlin Wall would be needed to uphold it. Another is that not all Catholics, whatever their grievances, would wish to be handed over to Eire, with its inferior social services and oppressively clerical atmosphere. The alternative is economic growth, accompanied by bold social reform, equality of opportunity. A recent American initiative, making aid or investment conditional on a fair share of jobs going to Catholics, was a useful pointer. If Stormont is ever to be viable, equality will have to be protected by an entrenched place for the minority, a share of all ministerial and civil service appointments.

No radical new departure will come from a Tory government in London, always morbidly afraid of showing 'weakness' – or common sense – in any surviving scrap of empire; or from a Labour government mortally afraid of doing anything that Tories would not like. British statesmanship in Ulster was neatly captured by a cartoon of the time of Edward Heath's premiership two decades ago when direct rule was inaugurated, with Reginald Maudling in charge. It showed Heath standing in the turret of an armoured car bogged down in mud, and shouting to the driver, 'Give her more power, Reggie, give her more power!' On 22 August 1988, after the IRA had brought off a startling coup, the responsible minister Tom King declared that the British army would continue to defend civilization and 'what is good and right'. But the social order it is defending is neither good nor right; and the shooting eight days later, by a special army unit, of three men vaguely alleged to have 'strong IRA links' looked too much like a revenge killing in response to the Tory clamour for 'firm action'. There was shock in Eire, and an official call for an explanation.

London having had no constructive ideas in twenty years, it may well seem high time for a British withdrawal. Marxists and other left-wingers have thought so all along, endorsing uncritically the IRA thesis that nothing else is needed to deliver Ulster from its plight. Everyone in England by now (except military men addicted to the study and practice of 'counter-insurgency', or repression) would rejoice, openly or privately, at a withdrawal. A pledge from the IRA, underwritten by Dublin, that hostilities would then be halted for at least a year, to give time for negotiations and a fresh start, *might* bring some reciprocal turning over of a new leaf. But it is only too easy for opponents of disengagement to maintain that the sequel would be worse bloodshed, something maybe like the savage civil war of 1921–3.

If a solution cannot be worked out within Ulster, or the British Isles, sooner or later the problem will have to be taken up by an international body. Most likely this will be the European Parliament, with the enhanced authority it can be expected to have assumed before many years go by, and a European Community with sufficient economic and financial power to put pressure on any of its members, in this case Britain and Eire. It will be easier if by then Scotland and Wales have secured home rule, with a right to a voice in Community affairs as well. England and its Unionist clientele will have to be made willing to go much further in sharing the problem with Eire than occasional 'consultations' on odds and ends of business. An England moving by then towards merger with Europe should be better able to see the case for a merger or federation of Ulster with Eire. Apart from any mysticism of Unity by divine right, the two form in many ways a natural economic unit.

Cornwall in the early eighteenth century could still be thought of as the lair of 'a fierce and ravenous people', as Defoe called the 'wreckers' along the southern coast, who preyed on shipwrecked vessels. Cornishmen, he said, played a 'brutish and furious' game called 'the Hurlers'.[50] Their language was disappearing, though a few individuals were trying to preserve old texts; but they were still, as viewed by a clergyman in a remote parish in the next century, primitive in manners and morals, thanks in part to their abysmal poverty; they subsisted chiefly on potatoes, for the good of absentee landlords.[51] Methodism was coming in; it was inimical to all old customs or ways of thinking.[52] In our day, when regional feeling has been having a reawakening in many corners of Europe, a reaction against the vast impersonal State, enthusiasts have been trying to resurrect the old language, still current in Brittany. In 1951 a society of 'Sons of Cornwall', Mebyon Kernow, was set up. As in other situations of this kind, socialists have been in two minds about it.

To Defoe the towering Welsh peaks appeared 'barbarous'.[53] Mountains or bogs gave all the Celtic lands a forbidding, mysterious aura; and they had all been on the wrong side in the civil wars, so that the victory of Parliament was in one aspect their conquest or reconquest. 'Wales is a conquered country', a clergyman argued in an eighteenth-century law-suit, '. . . and it is the duty of the Bishops to endeavour to promote Englishmen, in order to introduce the language.' His plea, it is true, was rejected.[54] Welsh cattle, like Scottish and Irish, were driven off to be eaten in England, to pay rents to often absentee landowners: an epitome of England's parasitic position, London's especially. North Wales was so poor that when De Quincey ran away from the Manchester Grammar School in 1802 and wandered among

the hills, the 'preposterously low prices' of food made it hard for him
to spend five or even three shillings in a week.[55] Touring in 1793 the
Hon. John Byng judged the Welsh in every way '60 years behind the
English', and the country a godforsaken place, 'all in dirt, and misery,
– with insolent natives, and horrid provisions'.[56] A special disappointment was the women, 'little, coarse, thick-legg'd things, and as dirty
as possible'.[57]

Nevertheless, a rebirth of interest in Welsh antiquities and literature
was under way, and Welsh Societies were being formed. This might
often be mere dilettantism, but it could have a deeper meaning. 'The
national culture of Wales was becoming a weapon to be used against
the ruling classes.'[58] Class and nation were nearer to identity than in
any more developed country; it is not surprising that the Honourable
tourist detected a note of 'insolence'. Nascent consciousness however
could be diverted by Methodism into some less fertilizing channels.
Calvinist Methodism became the favourite choice, so much so as
almost to constitute 'a distinct Welsh Church'; but in the early
nineteenth century it was a mostly right-wing one,[59] like the Anglican
'Church of Wales'.

Antipathy to the English sway was not to be exorcized. The 'Ladies
of Llangollen' found that 31 October was always celebrated with
bonfires, 'in Commemoration of a Victory gained over the English',
and in 1785 they counted from their lawn nineteen hilltop fires.[60] This
spirit was soon breaking out in louder demonstrations, under the spur
of the protracted French wars and the Industrial Revolution. Protest
both industrial and agrarian in the early nineteenth century was well
organized and more obstreperous than anywhere else in Britain, and
radicalism quickly took on a nationalist tinge, the more so because the
Welsh language was still intact. Industrialism was being thrust from
outside on a peasant society, as the whole Celtic fringe still very
largely was. As enterprises were planted in Wales, their English
owners liked to have English foremen, which added to the bitterness
of disputes;[61] and as mining expanded in south Wales there was
always dislike of the Englishmen who flocked there for work; it often
led to fighting. In Cardiganshire in the 1820s a secret-society struggle
was waged against an English enclosing landowner.[62] Agitation in the
countryside culminated in the 'Rebecca Riots' of 1839.

Chartism, the mass movement for political reform and votes for all
men, was vigorous in Wales, with a temper sharpened, as among Irish
Chartists in Britain, by national bitterness. It faded surprisingly soon
after mid-century, under the spell of relative prosperity and Liberal
ideology, just as in England. Welshmen were taking part in British

politics, and coal gave their country an importance in foreign trade. By comparison with Scots, on the other hand, they showed no love of army or empire. Nonconformity disapproved of jingoism, and Wales was itself still too much a colony to want to help in turning other nations into colonies. In a letter to the Polish novelist Sienkiewicz in 1907 Bernard Shaw commented on 'the implacable hostility of the Welsh voters to the established church and to all measures, good or bad, of an imperialist tendency'.[63] National consciousness was still stirring, with a touch of that freakishness inherent in all nationalism, but to which a small isolated people, long shut in on itself, was more prone than most. Some landowners were ready to patronize studies of the Welsh past, by scholars like the celebrated Iolo Morganwg, who brought to light many forgotten texts and made no scruple of improving or enlarging them. Druids, those shadowy priests of ancient Britain, took on a new lease of life in the *eisteddfod* festivals that were being held from 1789 on.[64] They could at times be harnessed to the car of Progress; a Dr William Price clothed Chartism in Druidic costume, and, warming to his work, went on to claim Homer as a Welshman, the builder of Caerphilly castle.[65] A more sober approach to Welsh studies emerged by degrees, and the founding of a Welsh university college at Aberystwyth in 1872 set the seal on it. Welshmen in London had done much to bring this about.[66]

Desire for independence showed itself first in the religious sphere, as a demand for disestablishment of the Anglican Church. Starting in the early 1870s, the movement did not reach its goal until 1914, forty-five years later than in more pugnacious Ireland. Anglicans endeavoured to disguise their false position by trying to look Welsh; there was a recognition that they had failed to win a hold on the people by not making use of the native language, and Welsh could be recommended by conservatives as a barrier against the modern evils of infidelity and socialism. With these motives churchmen made a contribution of their own to the cultural revival; but the motives came more into the open from the 1880s, when reactionary Catholic thinking in France exerted a strong influence.[67]

In the Welsh mind thoughts of spiritual home rule could not fail to lead on to the idea of secular autonomy, even though sectarian bias prevented Welshmen from sympathizing with the Irish struggle. By 1887 Gladstone was prepared to accept home rule – of his own watered-down brand – for Wales as well as Ireland. Home-rule-all-round soon had an eloquent exponent in the ambitious young lawyer Lloyd George. Opposition from south Wales, increasingly English in speech and connections, blocked the path, and after 1898 the idea was fading. What took its place was a bowdlerized patriotism, a trivializing cult of Welsh bric-à-brac and quaintness.[68]

Great War sufferings and lost illusions brought a less complacent mood. By 1918 a Welsh parliament was a widely raised cry, and in England there was again talk of some kind of federal arrangement. Ulster was, as always, a stumbling-block, and John Bull's interest in anything calling for serious thought has never lasted long. In 1924 Plaid Cymru, the Welsh nationalist party, was formed to campaign for self-government. Its pioneer leader J. S. Lewis, son of a Dissenting minister, wanted no mere devolution, but full Dominion status; his dream was of the English language expelled, and the south de-industrialized to make room for a return to agricultural and pastoral life. Few votes were forthcoming for any such utopian programme, except from small farmers of the northern valleys. Subsequently the party has been more realistic, but its advance has been fitful, and dependent on the state of the economy. With a general improvement of conditions since 1945 television and the rest of the media have been able to restore some of the pre-1914 illusions, and conjure up 'a new, false image, cosy and heart-warming, sentimental and nostalgic about the past'.[69]

In sharp contrast is the recent steep decline of the southern coal and steel industries. But the resulting unemployment has befallen English and Scottish workers as well; self-government holds out no ready cure, as it may for a grievance like the buying up by English families, as holiday homes, of cottages needed by local people to live in. Some nationalists have resorted to direct action, by burning them down. Cultural development has continued, with four university colleges now to promote it; but the mass media, those insidious invaders, have pushed their way in far more quickly. Whether an authentic Welsh culture can survive has become for its well-wishers an anxious question. By comparison with Ireland or Scotland, an uncomfortably unstable turning-point has been reached. Enough Welsh-speakers are left to feel able to give first place to the language, as the bedrock of national existence, but in another generation there may be far too few. In 1979 when a referendum was held to test feeling in Wales and Scotland about devolution, only 11.8 per cent of the Welsh electorate voted for it. Wales will not disappear, it can be hoped, but patriots will have to come to terms with the fact that it is turning into a new as well as old nation; they will have to learn to wear their old emblem the leek, so dear to Shakespeare's Captain Fluellen, with a difference.

*

After the Union of 1707, which Scots soon felt was regarded by Englishmen as a Scottish surrender, popular disgust with it went on smouldering. It found vent in 1736 in the 'Porteous riots' at Edinburgh, when there was nationwide applause for the lynching of an officer who had fired on a crowd. The Jacobite risings of 1715 and 1745 in favour of the dynasty overthrown in 1688 were divisive, in spite of their appeal for national support against the Union; the Stuarts were Catholics, and most of their forces Highlanders; Lowlanders looked on instead of joining in.

More and more educated Scots were moving into England, where their presence and their clannishness made them the butt of much satire, though they were not modern England's first prominent ethnic minority. Scots were also, however, making rapid progress before long at home; this was stimulated by the English connection, partly through a new awareness of being looked down on by the southerners as a backward people, and a desire to prove their capacity. Agriculture was going through a capitalist revolution, modern industry was finding footholds, and four universities were helping to nurture the 'Scottish Enlightenment' that gave their country a place in the intellectual life of Europe. To be catching up with more advanced neighbours, and on some lines surpassing them, must be an exhilarating experience for any nation.

Radicalism ignited by the French Revolution had a distinctive colouring in Scotland. In the 1790s clubs of United Scotsmen were springing up, partly on the model of the United Irishmen. Besides wanting reforms, as English progressives did, they shared Robert Burns's regret at the obliteration of Scottish nationhood by the Union. They were soon snuffed out by Tory reaction and the clamour of the wars with France. Lower down in society legends of Wallace and Bruce could still work like yeast, as they did in Scott's boyish mind. Social discontents found an outlet in talk of a recovery of Scotland's lost 'rights'. It might be more than usually seductive to a decaying class like the hand-weavers, squeezed out of the market by new machines and at a loss for any practical cure for their ills. It is clear that the west country radicals, mostly Ayrshire weavers, in their pathetically small insurrection in 1820 were thinking of Scottish independence as a prime aim.[70] Years later the same aspiration showed itself in the Chartist excitements of 1848.

But modern life was in many ways deepening Scotland's diversity of regions, classes, modes of thinking, instead of harmonizing them. Landowners and iron-workers had not much more in common than Zulus and Eskimos. Compared with the old craftsmen, the new industrial working class was uprooted from the past and its memories; and it was conscious of exploitation by employers mostly Scots. Rational class feeling took precedence over patriotic sentiment; Scottish workers saw their natural allies in English workers, and joined in trade unions covering all Britain. 'National' feeling meant with them chiefly dislike of the Irish labour pouring in and undercutting their wages. Highland and Island crofters, struggling tenants on small farms, in their sometimes un-pacific agitation in the early 1880s had no natural allies in England, but they had natural enemies in their own Scottish landlords.

For the rest of the public a harmless, sterilized patriotism was purveyed by hack novelists and shopkeepers, a sentimental cult of the past much like the one worked up in Wales. There was much 'deplorably unhistorical' fuss over kilts and clans,[71] with tales of Bonny Prince Charlie and Flora Macdonald of 1745 as seasoning. A more honourably cherished tradition was that of the Covenanters, diehard defenders of Kirk independence in the late seventeenth century, though it too came further and further adrift from its seventeenth-century setting. Doggerel verses carved on a stone beside the Covenanters' Monument at Dreghorn on the outskirts of Edinburgh contain the mildly reproachful lines –

> If Brother Bull complacently maintain
> Union secured us clear and wholesale gain,
> Softly demurring we yet grudge him not
> Haply more gain by equal link with Scot,
> In warmth and mutual love old feuds forgot.

It may be arguable whether on the whole Scottish nationality was overlaid and smothered by the Union, or in the long run could develop best within its framework. Tories waved the Union Jack all the more industriously to make up for their lack of popularity in Scotland, where their most prominent figures were the landlords; at the end of the century the Boer War hysteria marked a climax. Yet Scots had so great a share in both the acquisition and the management of the Empire[72] that their self-esteem and sense of identity may have been fortified rather than weakened by the imperial adventure, even though the bulk of its profits ended in London.

Proposals for devolution made only a very hesitant start. Parliament's neglect of Scottish business was the main ground for complaint. One who took up early the call for political and administrative change was the reforming landowner Kinloch;[73] but Tory demagogy had more to do with its first stages. In 1853 the writer W. E. Aytoun was in the forefront of a brief spell of protest. In the 1880s a good deal of impatient talk of home rule was heard; in 1895 a concession was made by the setting up of a Secretary of State for Scotland, to be responsible for seeing that Scottish wants were not overlooked. Gladstone's Home Rule for Ireland bill in 1886 had split the Liberal Party, normally in command of Scotland. In 1907 the Liberals, back in office, started a Grand Committee, made up of all MPs from Scotland, to scrutinize Scottish business. A series of private home rule bills failed; but when home rule was granted to Ireland in 1914 it was with the intention of a similar gift to Scotland and Wales.

Socialism made headway in Scotland sooner than in England, and helped to give the Labour movement there a more Scottish orientation. In 1888 Keir Hardie and others formed a Scottish Parliamentary Labour Party (later the Independent Labour Party), separate from the Liberal Party. In 1916 the Scottish Trade Union Congress came out in favour of a Scottish parliament; in 1918, partly at least as a response, the Labour Party now getting on its feet put home-rule-all-round in its election programme. In Scotland this was overshadowed by heated industrial disputes, arising from wartime discontents in the Glasgow area along the 'Red Clyde'. These were more quickly forgotten than they might have been if industrial and national questions had been fused. An exceptional figure was John Maclean, a Marxist of true originality like Connolly in Ireland, and with much pride in his Highland roots and sympathy for the Irish struggle. He advocated a 'Scottish Communist Republic', freed from England but not submitting to the yoke of 'traitor kings or chiefs'. He saw in Bolshevism the spirit of the old Russian *mir* or village commune in new guise, and held that in like fashion 'The communism of the clans must be re-established on a modern basis.'[74]

Further Home Rule bills were introduced in 1922, 1926, 1929; but by 1929 Ramsay Macdonald, Scotsman and Labour premier, was turning away from the idea. One may wonder whether he feared it might give fresh ammunition to the Congress movement in India that plagued him so much. A National Party had lately been formed; another was started in 1932, by no less than a duke. In 1934 – the year when a Scottish Office was set up at Edinburgh, to bring government business nearer home – the two joined in the Scottish National Party (SNP), which has never altogether shaken off weaknesses traceable to its dubious parentage. For long it was 'a resilient little sect rather than a political movement',[75] preoccupied with cultural matters and with academic queries about violations of the Treaty of Union, not all of whose provisions, it has been pointed out in reply, can have been expected to last for ever.[76] Lack of realistic planning for Scotland's future spelled electoral failure, when the Slump was casting its shadow, population was annually dwindling, and tales of Bannockburn could offer small comfort. Not until 1945 was a parliamentary seat won.

Soon after the Second World War a new body, the Scottish Convention, was able to claim 2 million signatures for a 'National Covenant' – its title an echo of 1638 – demanding home rule and a parliament. Much was being heard of a Scottish literary renascence. An audacious group of students carried off from Westminster Abbey the 'stone of destiny' or coronation seat carried off from Scone Palace by Edward I. Some zealots went further, by attacking pillar boxes with the obnoxious inscription 'ER II', implying that the reigning monarch was the second Queen Elizabeth of Scotland as well as of England. Later on a 'Scottish Republican Army' was heard of, but whether it existed seems doubtful. Armed action is only feasible where there is intense popular feeling to endorse it, and where there has been a recent past of violence as in Ireland or the Basque provinces.

A decline of cordiality towards the English connection must be attributed in part to the loss of the empire. Every now and then there has been grumbling about too many posts in Scotland, in the universities for example, being held by Englishmen. A weightier contention is that Scotland has been starved of industrial development, with the result of workers being less well paid than in England. In recent years the gap in wages has been narrowed; and if much of Scottish industry is under foreign control, the same is true of England. 'Why the Scots themselves have not revitalised their industries remains a mystery.'[77] For years nationalist excitement spurted up by fits and starts; in individuals it often seemed no more than a mode of working off passing annoyances. A sudden change came over it when North Sea oil was discovered in 1971, and came into production in 1975. It belonged to Scotland, patriots urged, and would make everyone in a free Scotland rich.

In 1973 the Kilbrandon Report recommended a Scottish parliament, chosen by proportional representation, and a cabinet responsible to it. In the elections of February 1974 the SNP was suddenly winning votes and seats at a rate that threatened to push Labour out of the lead. Next year two Labour MPs broke away to found a Scottish Labour Party; but socialism and nationalism were not easily harmonized, and the new body soon vanished. In July 1978, however, the Labour government felt obliged to placate Scottish feeling, and passed a bill providing for devolution for both Scotland and Wales, but the parliamentary opposition was strong enough to insist on a referendum.

In Scotland only 32.9 per cent voted in favour. Nationalists complained that the question had been confusingly phrased; none the less, the old High School on Calton Hill at Edinburgh, which had been got ready for sittings, stayed empty.

Oil fever was not long in abating. For one thing, an even better claim to the wealth might be by the Shetland islanders, and they might be as ready to separate from Scotland as Scotland from England. In a more general way the current has gone on flowing in a nationalist direction. A long spell of right-wing rule has brought Toryism into deeper disrepute. Scotland has been picked as first victim of a highly inequitable system of local taxation. Elections in 1987 left the Tories with only one-seventh of Scottish seats, a grotesquely narrow base for a Secretary of State who has to make a travesty of his office by imposing unwelcome measures on a country which has utterly repudiated his party.

Most of the gains of 1987 went to Labour rather than to the SNP, but a good many of them because defeat of Thatcherism was the overriding need; and Labour itself has been feeling more Scottish. A 'Campaign for a Scottish Assembly' organized after the referendum can point to opinion polls showing as many as 80 per cent of voters to be in agreement with its aim; also to a range of affiliated bodies from Liberals to Communists. In November 1988 the SNP's by-election victory at Govan, in one of Labour's safest seats, dramatically advertised the trend of opinion. It was primarily a protest vote against Thatcherism, and in the longer run most Scots may be expected to hesitate at complete severance, for fear of economic dislocation. Still, a break-away now looks possible, and if it does come it may well spread further, with Scotland again, as in 1638, inaugurating a revolution in British affairs. Scotland and northern England, various of whose regions have changed hands between them in times gone by, might well make a better combination than either of them with the south. A gloomy vision seen by Walter Scott in 1826 has come to look prophetic. Britain he feared was coming to resemble the image in Belshazzar's dream. 'London, its head, might be of fine gold – the fertile provinces of England, like its breast and arms, might be of silver – the southern half of Scotland might acquire some brass and copper – but the northern provinces would be without worth or value.'[78]

People are still abandoning the Highlands and Islands, Gaelic speech is dwindling in spite of devoted efforts to preserve it. Patriots have looked to Lowland English, or Lallans, as a second line of linguistic defence. It stems from the Northumbrian dialect which in medieval Scotland, though not in England, served as a true written language. With all its rich flavour, in modern Scotland it has sunk to not much more than a patois, as it did long ago in northern England. Even Burns could only make use of it for poetry, Scott for dialogue in novels; it is hard to see how any writer today could expand it beyond these limits. As for the need of a substitute for Gaelic, in the Scotland where nearly all Scots live the loss of a Celtic language is something that happened centuries ago; not a loss of fairly recent times as in Ireland, or of an all too probable tomorrow as in Wales.

What then have the Celts bequeathed to a progeny here, or far away, who no longer know their ancient tongues? All dwellers in the British Isles are in some measure Celtic (and pre-Celtic). Here we venture on deceptive ground, illuminated by *ignes fatui*. A historian of the Scots takes for granted 'the inheritance of qualities from racial stock', and is convinced that 'the Gaelic qualities in the Scot' have always been evident.[79] A Welshman dwells on 'the impulsiveness and susceptibility that belong to the Celtic family'.[80] These are nebulous assertions. All the same, outsiders may be struck by unaccustomed traits of character or temperament; by volcanic stirrings under the surface in Scotsmen ordinarily reserved and self-enclosed. Despite the talent displayed by the latter-day clansmen for running banks or newspapers, there was much in their earlier story better fitted to foster the poetic than the practical faculties. Conan Doyle, himself of Irish descent, ascribed to Celtic blood the 'intense glowing imagination' of the Brontës.[81] An enthusiast might even let his mind stray so far as to recall that Shakespeare was born not very many miles from the Welsh border.

One index of the gap between England and the rest of the British Isles is that Wales, Scotland, Ireland, which in early times had a Christianity not dictated by Rome, all rejected the official Church that English kings sought to impose on them. All today face complex difficulties; in a sense the most acute national problem of all is whether England itself can be expected to survive in any recognizable shape, physical or moral; not so much on account of issues of race and creed arising with the new ethnic minorities, residues of the days of empire, as of an unwholesome social-economic structure, and with it reckless fouling of air, water, landscape, culture. Wales and Scotland will not do England any good by continuing their actual relationship with it. That conservative blockages stood in the way of home-rule-all-round early in this century must be regretted. There are, at the same time, valid objections to a complete break-up; the world is quite sufficiently Balkanized already, and the conventional state, which evolved primarily for military purposes, has become an anachronism, a cumbrous suit of armour for any nation to have to wear. Wales and Ireland, like Brittany or Catalonia, have proved that nationality, pride in ideas, feelings, memories, not shared by others, can live on unsupported by a state, and even in spite of efforts by a state power to banish it.

The Celtic lands were never able to co-operate, because too uneven in development; Scotland had the great advantage of political unity, if of a rough and ready sort. In our day, in the wake of Pan-Slav, Pan-Turanian, Pan-African movements, some Pan-Celtic thinking might have been looked for, beyond a few linguistic conferences where a De Valera could try to understand Manx. Wales and Scotland within a federated Great Britain, and a federal Ireland, all within a Europe moving towards federal union, may be able to meet and reinforce one another for the first time.

It is fair to say that England had not a few things of value to contribute to them, even if these were too often cancelled out by its greeds, or those of the rich men who have always ruled it. There may be some further palliation of its bullying in the fact that the decisive steps towards English hegemony were taken by a foreign race of kings and lords. Before the battle of Poitiers the Black Prince is said to have gingered up his troops by reminding them of how their Plantagenet kings were wont to conquer at home and abroad, as far afield as the Holy Land, by the 'lively courageousness' that had 'brought under the stiff-necked Scots and unruly Irishmen, yea, and the Welchmen also which could well endure all labour'.[82]

NOTES

I have benefited from discussions, leading to agreement or disagreement, with many friends; I owe thanks in particular to Neil Belton, Owen Edwards, Rhodri Jeffreys-Jones, Alfred Jenkin, Roisin Mulholland, Robert Young; and to the late James Maclean and Esmond Robertson.

1 Cobbett in Ireland, ed. D. Knight (London, 1984), p. 190. On England and its 'Celtic fringe', cf. N. Evans, in a debate on current British historiography, in Past and Present, 119 (1988), 194ff.

2 G. Borrow, Wild Wales (1862), ch. 109.

3 See C. Renfrew, Archaeology and Language: The Puzzle of Indo-European Origins (London, 1987), especially ch. 9: 'Ethnogenesis: who were the Celts?' For earlier views cf. G. Herm, The Celts (1975; London edn, 1976); A. A. M. Duncan, Scotland: The Making of the Kingdom (Edinburgh, 1975), ch. 1.

4 D. S. Thomson (ed.), The Companion to Gaelic Studies (Oxford, 1983), p. 224; Duncan, Scotland, p. 51; Renfrew, Archaeology and Language, pp. 226–70.

5 W. C. Mackenzie, The Highlands and Islands of Scotland (revised edn, Edinburgh, 1949), p. 81.

6 M. Wood, Domesday: A Search for the Roots of England (London, 1987), pp. 76–7.

7 Sir F. Stenton, *Anglo-Saxon England*, 3rd edn (Oxford, 1971), pp. 314–15; cf. D. Whitelock, *The Beginnings of English Society* (Harmondsworth, 1952), pp. 17–18.

8 Wood, *Domesday*, pp. 102–4.

9 A. A. M. Duncan, *The Nation of Scots and the Declaration of Arbroath (1320)* (Historical Association, London, 1970), p. 7; cf. T. C. Smout, *A History of the Scottish People 1560–1830* (1969; London edn, 1972), pp. 23, 28–9.

10 Duncan, *The Nation of Scots*, p. 16; cf. T. Johnston, *History of the Scottish Working Class* (Glasgow, [1925]), pp. 22–3.

11 Gen. Sir P. Christison, *Bannockburn* (National Trust: revised edn, Edinburgh, 1970), pp. 8, 10.

12 J. Carney (ed.), *Early Irish Poetry* (Cork, 1975), p. 15.

13 See P. R. Roberts, 'The union with England and the identity of "Anglican" Wales', *Transactions of the Royal Historical Society*, 1972. Cf. G. Jones, *The Gentry and the Elizabethan State* (Llandybie, 1977).

14 S. de Beauvoir, *Old Age* (1970; Harmondsworth edn, 1977), p. 310.

15 P. Jenkins, *The Making of a Ruling Class: The Glamorgan Gentry 1640–1790* (Cambridge, 1983), p. 70; G. Williams, *The Land Remembers: A View of Wales* (1977; London edn, 1978), pp. 149ff.

16 Borrow, *Wild Wales*, ch. 20.

17 Jenkins, *The Making of a Ruling Class*, p. 210.

18 B. Donagan, 'Codes and conduct in the English Civil War', *Past and Present*, 118 (1988), 89–90.

19 W. Ferguson, *Scotland's Relations with England: A Survey to 1707* (Edinburgh, 1977), pp. 8–9.

20 *Ibid.*, p. 138.

21 Mackenzie, *The Highlands and Islands of Scotland*, p. 171.

22 S. O'Faolain, *The Irish* (1947; revised edn, Harmondsworth, 1969), p. 76.

23 N. Canny, 'The formation of the Irish mind . . . 1580–1750', *Past and Present*, 95 (1982), 113.

24 See generally R. F. Foster, *Modern Ireland 1600–1972* (London, 1988); *Ireland and Scotland 1600–1850: Parallels and Contrasts*, ed. T. M. Devine and D. Dickson (Edinburgh, 1983), and *Nationalism and Popular Protest in Ireland*, ed. C. H. E. Philpin (Cambridge, 1987).

25 H. Kohn, *The Idea of Nationalism* (New York, 1945), pp. 466ff.

26 O'Faolain, *The Irish*, p. 148. Cf. T. Dunne, 'Haunted by history: Irish Romantic writing 1800–50', in R. Porter and M. Teich (eds.), *Romanticism in National Context* (Cambridge, 1988), pp. 68–91.

27 O'Faolain, *The Irish*, pp. 101–2.

28 *Cobbett in Ireland*, ed. Knight, pp. 86, 186ff.

29 *Ibid.*, pp. 142, 149.

30 C. McGlinchey, *The Last of the Name*, ed. B. Friel (Belfast, 1986), p. 24.

31 *Ibid.*, p. 45.

32 R. Tracey, Introduction to A. Trollope, *The Landleaguers* (1883; New York edn, 1981).

33 *Ibid.*, ch. 30.

34 S. Bolt, *A Preface to James Joyce* (New York, 1981), pp. 189–90.

35 McGlinchey, *The Last of the Name*, p. 7.
36 J. Connolly, *Selected Political Writings*, ed. O. D. Edwards and B. Ransom (London, 1973), p. 166.
37 J. Connolly, *Socialism and Nationalism* (anthology, ed. D. Ryan; Dublin, 1948), p. 58.
38 *Ibid.*, p. 105.
39 *Political Writings*, pp. 69–70.
40 *Socialism and Nationalism*, p. 3.
41 *Ibid.*, p. 101.
42 N. Mansergh, *The Irish Question 1840–1921* (1965; 3rd edn, London, 1975), pp. 219ff.
43 W. R. Inge, *England* (New York, 1926), p. 66; cf. 148–9.
44 D. Gwynn, *De Valera* (London, 1933), p. 220; J. Hawkins, *The Irish Question Today* (Fabian Society, London, 1943), p. 17.
45 R. Coupland, *Welsh and Scottish Nationalism* (London, 1954), p. 333.
46 A detailed study of Anglo-Irish relations during the war will be found in chapter 6 of J. Bowman, *De Valera and the Ulster Question 1917–1973* (Oxford, 1982); see especially pp. 246–7.
47 Connolly, *Socialism and Nationalism*, p. 107.
48 Information from an Irish Catholic socialist resident in Britain. On how the troubles actually started, and events leading up to them, a useful chronology will be found in J. Darby, *Conflict in Northern Ireland* (New York, 1976), pp. xiff.
49 J. J. Tohill, *Donegal*, 3rd edn (Ballyshannon, 1985), p. 70.
50 D. Defoe, *A Tour through the Whole Island of Great Britain* (1724–6; abridged edn, Harmondsworth, 1971), pp. 236, 243.
51 P. Brendon, *Hawker of Morwenstow* (London, 1975), pp. 69–70, 73.
52 R. Green, *The National Question in Cornwall* (London, 1981), p. 26.
53 Defoe, *A Tour through Great Britain*, pp. 382–3; cf. 376–7.
54 A. H. Johnes, *Dissent from the Established Church in the Principality of Wales* (reprint, London, 1970), p. 67.
55 T. De Quincey, *The Confessions of an English Opium-Eater* (1821).
56 J. Byng, 'A Tour of North Wales, 1793', in C. B. Andrews (ed.), *The Torrington Diaries*, vol. III (London, 1936), pp. 251, 301.
57 *Ibid.*, p. 277.
58 Jenkins, *The Making of a Ruling Class*, p. 215.
59 Coupland, *Welsh and Scottish Nationalism*, pp. 119, 218. Cf. D. W. Smith, 'Berriew in the eighteenth century', in *The Montgomeryshire Collections*, vol. 70 (1982), pp. 123ff.
60 E. Mavor, *A Year with the Ladies of Llangollen* (1984; Harmondsworth edn, 1986), p. 185.
61 A. H. Dodd, *The Industrial Revolution in North Wales* (Cardiff, 1933), p. 399.
62 G. A. Williams, 'Locating a Welsh working class', in D. Smith (ed.), *A People and a Proletariat: Essays in the History of Wales 1780–1980* (London, 1980), p. 16.
63 B. Shaw, *Collected Letters 1898–1910*, ed. D. H. Lawrence (New York, 1972), p. 743.
64 Cf. G. A. Williams, 'Romanticism in Wales', in Porter and Teich (eds.), *Romanticism*, pp. 9–36.

65 B. Davies, 'Empire and identity: the "case" of Dr William Price', in Smith (ed.), *A People*, pp. 73–6, 81–2. Cf. S. Piggott, *The Druids* (1968; Harmondsworth edn, 1974), pp. 142ff.

66 See B. B. Thomas, *'Aber' 1872–1972* (Cardiff, 1972).

67 See E. Sherrington, 'Welsh nationalism, the French Revolution, and the influence of the French Right 1880–1930', in Smith (ed.), *A People*.

68 Smith (ed.), *A People*, Introduction, p. 8.

69 D. Smith, 'Wales through the looking-glass', *ibid*., p. 237. Cf. an account of the revival in this century of the medieval ceremonial of investiture of the Prince of Wales, as an antidote to Welsh nationalism, in T. Nairn, *The Enchanted Glass: Britain and Its Monarchy* (London, 1988), pp. 120–32.

70 See P. B. Ellis and S. Mac A'Ghobhainn, *The Scottish Insurrection of 1820* (London, 1970).

71 R. L. Mackie, *A Short History of Scotland*, ed. G. Donaldson (Edinburgh, 1962), p. 301.

72 For a graphic narrative and pictorial record see H. Smailes, *Scottish Empire* (Edinburgh, 1981).

73 C. Tennant, *The Radical Laird: A Biography of George Kinloch 1775–1833* (Kineton, 1970), p. 234.

74 J. Maclean, *In the Rapids of Revolution* (essays, etc., ed. N. Milton, London, 1978), p. 218. See also N. Milton (his daughter), *John Maclean* (London, 1973).

75 C. Harvie, *Scotland and Nationalism: Scottish Society and Politics 1707–1977* (London, 1977), p. 236. See generally part 2 of this work, on the period since 1945; and T. Nairn, *The Break-up of Britain: Crisis and Neo-Nationalism* (London, 1977), and *The Enchanted Glass*. A more general study is J. Osmond, *The Divided Kingdom* (London, 1988).

76 J. G. Kellas, *Modern Scotland*, 2nd edn, revised (London, 1980), p. 76.

77 *Ibid*., p. 162. See generally G. Brown (ed.), *The Red Paper on Scotland* (Edinburgh, 1975), and R. Saville (ed.), *The Economic Development of Modern Scotland 1950–1980* (Edinburgh, 1986).

78 W. Scott, *The Letters of Malachi Malagrowther* (1826; fascimile reprint, Edinburgh, 1981), p. 112.

79 W. Notestein, *The Scot in History* (London, 1946), p. xi.

80 Johnes, *Dissent from the Established Church*, pp. vii–viii.

81 A. Conan Doyle, *Through the Magic Door* (London, 1912), p. 92.

82 Geoffrey le Baker, cited by D. L. Simms, 'Archimedes' weapons of war and Leonardo', *British Journal for the History of Science*, June 1988, 204.

TWO

THE MAKING OF THE FRENCH NATION

DOUGLAS JOHNSON

INTRODUCTION

When was the French nation born? This has for long been a subject of discussion and controversy. Auguste Longnon, who taught at the Collège de France at the end of the nineteenth century, and who specifically wrote on the formation of French unity, claimed that it was 'une merveilleuse histoire'. He saw what is now the familiar visage of France, of which the contours seem to have been sketched out in advance of the achievement of unity, as the result of a long series of obstinate and determined struggles.[1] Longnon was lecturing well after the war of 1870, when France had been defeated by Germany, when Alsace and Lorraine had been annexed and when many writers, including historians, had written about France's past in order to encourage 'a holy passion' for *la patrie* and to discover a long-standing tradition of patriotic poetry and writing.[2] Such historians invariably looked to a political date as one that could be seen to mark the beginning of the French nation. Clovis was the king of a Frankish tribe who defeated a Roman general in 486 and established his royal residence in Paris, thereby representing the transition from a minor barbarian king to the claimant of an imperial ruler, whose authority was accepted by what remained of the Roman Empire. General de Gaulle always considered that Clovis was the first French sovereign. Another possible political figure who could claim that title was Charles the Bald, Charlemagne's grandson, who swore an oath with his brother at Strasbourg in 842, which became the first document known to be written in the Romanic and Germanic languages (which eventually became modern French and German) and who, by the Treaty of Verdun in 843, became the ruler of the territories situated to the west of the rivers Meuse, Saône and Rhône, that is to say, the essence of modern France.

This was followed by a confused history, consisting of skirmishes and wars, mainly between uncles and nephews, and surrounding kinglets who were manipulated by nobles. This period is usually described as ending with the accession of Hugh Capet in 987. When he was elected king he thereby founded the Capetian dynasty, and this has frequently been accepted as the starting-point of France. Although Hugh Capet was in no way the ruler of the territory that is now accepted as France, and was master of little more than an assortment of lands, towns and châteaux, which was smaller than several of the other principalities in the kingdom, this was the dynasty which, from its origins until 1792 (or 1848), established an important continuity in French history. It profited from four main advantages. The royal domain included fertile lands; they contained Paris and Orleans, two towns of considerable strategic and commercial importance; there was no serious conflict over the question of succession; the fact that the king was the anointed king made him the bearer of a priestly power and the elect of God, so that the Church considered him as a protector and the nobility saw in him a natural arbitrator.

Historians have stressed that these advantages varied in importance, as circumstances changed. But more importantly they have posed the problem of whether one has the right to talk about the History of France before one can speak about the emergence of a French national sentiment. It was Guizot, the nineteenth-century historian and politician, who denied this. There was, he claimed, no national sentiment in a country which was feudal. The French nation, the sentiment of being French, French patriotism, did not exist. It was not until the accession of the Valois dynasty that a true and real France came into existence. It was in 1328, after a number of kings had died without leaving male heirs, that Philip of Valois, the eldest cousin of three preceding kings, was recognized as king by an assembly of prelates and nobles. It was contested by the king of England, Edward III, who was the son and the grandson of the eldest daughters of two kings of France, but there was hostility to an English king. Frankish customs were recalled (or possibly invented) to impede any female succeeding to the throne or transmitting a right of succession. The result was, after an interval of time, that the king of England claimed the throne of France, and the wars that began in 1337 did not properly end until 1453. It was through these wars, according to Guizot, and through the many upturns of fortune that accompanied them, that for the first time the nobility, the burghers and the peasantry became united morally, united by a name, by a sense of honour, and by the same desire to defeat the foreigner.[3]

Guizot's rebellious and hostile associate, Michelet, expressed a similar point of view, although he was, somewhat untypically, more circumspect. Speaking about the many tragedies that France experienced at the time of the accession of Philip of Valois, he explained that France was beginning to know itself, to become conscious of itself. The wars brought together the populations from many provinces. But the nation could not become united, even if the fundamental division was that of the Midi and the Nord.[4] Later he was more direct. France, he wrote, owes a great debt towards England. It is England who caused France to become aware of itself. It was England which was the pitiless guide of this painful initiation. After the long enchantment of the Middle Ages France was immersed in a deep sleep. At first the English attacked the nobility, but after Crécy (1346), they took refuge in their castles and refused to accept battle. Therefore the English attacked the ordinary people, the peasant. They cut down his trees, destroyed his vines and burnt down his dwelling-place; they starved him, they beat him, they killed his pigs, took his wife, fed their horses on his harvest before it was ready. And at last the peasant, whom Michelet calls 'le bonhomme Jacques', awoke. He attacked his lord who had failed to protect him and such a revolt was called 'la Jacquerie'. And when the English returned he realized that God was on the side of the French. Women joined him and led their men to battle, and Jacques was also called 'Jeanne la Pucelle'.[5]

Modern historians believe that their nineteenth-century predecessors exaggerated this awakening of the population in a national sense. For them the so-called Hundred Years' War (supposedly 1328–1453) is a period of crises and depressions, and they talk about the three horsemen of the Apocalypse, war, plague and famine, as dominating French history. If, for example, one examines the long career of the constable of France, Bertrand du Guesclin (c. 1320–80), one has to ask whether he was in any way a patriot, and if so, what he might have understood by patriotism. Born into a minor family of the nobility in French-speaking Brittany, du Guesclin took part in the war of succession to the duchy of Brittany that was fought in the 1340s and 1350s between the partisans of Charles of Blois, who was accepted by the French, and those of John de Montfort, who was supported by the English. Then, the future Charles V (who as Dauphin had assumed the government of the realm during the captivity of his father John II, who had been taken prisoner in battle) took him into his service to fight against the Anglo-Navarrese armies. Supported by loyal Bretons, du Guesclin had mixed fortunes in his wars, but what was remarkable was that the king sent him beyond the

Pyrenees to conquer Castile and also to invade Provence (which was
not part of the kingdom of France). What one must also note was the
way in which at times he opposed his king and supported the
anglophile Duke of Brittany, John IV, and planned to invade Sardinia
without the support or permission of the king of France. He struck the
imagination of his contemporaries and when he died his remains were
treated as if they were religious relics. He undoubtedly performed
many services for the king of France and a marble tomb bearing his
effigy was constructed in the royal mausoleum in Saint-Denis. But he
was a soldier at a time when bands of mercenaries were roaming the
countryside holding towns and individuals to ransom. He was similar
to their commanders and he established comradely relations with
them, including some who were English. He amassed much wealth
and sought to gain more. If he were a patriot at all he was a Breton
rather than a Frenchman. Yet it remains true that patriotism, like
nationalism, cannot exist in a vacuum. Such sentiments and aspirations generally occur as a by-product of some political unit's relationship with the world that lies outside and beyond it.[6]

THE MEDIEVAL MONARCHY

The question has been asked, was it the kings of France who created
the French nation or was it the contrary, a geographical reality which
created the kings of France? In pre-Roman Gaul, and ever afterwards, there was a geographical unity which corresponds, after
certain adjustments to the frontiers, such as Alsace-Lorraine and
Dunkirk, with a modern conception of France. In this sense it is
suggested that there was, geographically speaking, a Gallo-Roman
predestination of the country, however vague it might have been.
France could not be created just anywhere.[7] But geographers these
days are anxious to deny this form of determinism. Faced with a
map, from which all political frontiers had been removed, no one, it
is argued, could identify France.[8] The so-called natural frontiers of
France are not barriers at all, and never were barriers. The Rhine
meant trade, the Channel was a means of transit, the Pyrenees, the
Alps and the Jura never prevented the movement of peoples, and the
river Loire helped to link the north and the south together. Whilst
rejecting the theory of France's natural frontiers as pure imagination,
some historians have claimed that the France that did eventually
emerge was an accidental creation and they have amused themselves
by imagining the different types of France that might well have
evolved had circumstances been different. Thus there could have

been a southern Mediterranean France, a Franco-English empire, or a Burgundian France.[9]

If one is to believe that the creation of the French state contains, to say the least, an element of the accidental or the haphazard, then this has implications for the study of the French nation. The historian is obliged to concentrate on those signs that indicate the emergence of the political power of the French king. Thus we find that in the mid-fourteenth century the role of the monarchy was the subject of considerable debate, and not simply a struggle between conflicting personal ambitions. Nor was it simply a struggle between a feudal nobility and a rising bourgeoisie (the latter being represented by Etienne Marcel, a rich cloth manufacturer who was the provost of the merchants of Paris and who was murdered in 1358) in which one side could call on help from outsiders, such as the English. The debate was on the extent of the power of the king and the manner in which it could be controlled.[10] For some time it had been accepted that the king had to possess not only all the powers but also all the virtues of wisdom and knowledge.[11] In a France which, possibly because it had played such a prominent part in the Crusades, considered that it was the favoured offspring of the Church, it is noticeable that the kings were tightening their grip on ecclesiastical appointments. Canonries were increasingly reserved for services in the court bureaucracy, a procedure which led to unexpected results, such as the conservatism of the music performed at Notre-Dame de Paris at a time when polyphony was flourishing in other parts of Europe. For the first time in the history of France, in 1328, a fiscal document appeared which surveyed the population of the royal domain. This is an indication of the growing efficiency of the administration, but also a sign of a preoccupation with finance which can only be explained by the necessities brought on by the wars. Not only were there armies to be raised but, most expensive of all, boats had to be built, equipped and manned as the war against the English became a naval war as well as a conflict on land. In 1338 a French force invaded Southampton and proceeded some miles inland; in the 1370s there were several attacks against the English coast and in 1386 plans were made for an invasion of England, although they never came to anything. On a number of occasions the French allied with the rulers of Castile in order to attack the English fleet. It is not surprising that the French word for frontier (*frontière*) should have appeared at the beginning of the fourteenth century.[12]

But the position of this monarch had seemed to be in serious danger. In 1360 the Treaty of Brétigny ceded Calais and an enormous ransom to the king of England, as well as greatly enlarging the English hold on south-west France from the Pyrenees practically to the Loire (the region of Gascony had been English ever since Eleanor of Aquitaine had married Henry II in 1154). After 1380 a dynastic dispute opposed the Duke of Burgundy, who held the east and the north of the kingdom, to the Duke of Orleans, who held the west and the south. In 1415 Henry V of England overwhelmed the French nobility at Agincourt, conquered Normandy and marched on Paris. The kingdom of France was divided into three parts, the one being English, the other being Burgundian, and the third was organized around Poitiers and Bourges. It was then that the extraordinary adventure of Joan of Arc took place. The English suffered a reverse at Orleans; Charles VII was crowned and anointed at Rheims in 1429; and four years after Joan was burned at the stake in Rouen, he became reconciled with the Duke of Burgundy in 1435. Paris was recaptured, the English were driven out of Normandy, and with the French victory at Castillon in 1453, Gascony ceased to be English. Only Calais remained in English hands. Whether by purchase, reversion, inheritance or negotiation, other regions became part of France: Dauphiné in 1456, Burgundy in 1477 and Provence in 1481.

The process was continued into the sixteenth century with the reigns of Louis XII (1498–1515), Francis I (1515–47) and Henry II (1547–59). Control over the church was regularized by the Concordat of Bologna in 1516. Brittany was absorbed in 1532. Royal power was limited in the sense that the king had to be a good Christian, he had to respect existing agreements and customs, he had to be accepted as the source of justice. In practice the court (and royal government) was itinerant and therefore the royal bureaucracy was far from effective. But the monarchy was accepted as legitimate and sacred. In its journeys it impressed the realm with its presence. It had acquired the right to levy direct taxation. And amongst the reasons why it was venerated was that patriotism required it.

Of course it was true that in France, the most heavily populated of European countries, the mass of the population lived in villages and their culture was a local culture with a limited mental horizon which could hardly take in such concepts as the state or the nation. But there was fear of invasion, and the fear of outsiders became associated with the consciousness of foreigners. This certainly existed in towns. When the news of the French defeat at Pavia in 1525 reached Paris there was something approaching panic, special guards were set up and some of the gates were closed. In contrast to this apprehension there was a growing consciousness of the existence of the king and a belief that everyone's salvation, whether in this world or in the next, was somehow associated with him. The churches cultivated and supported these sentiments. The monarchy put out propaganda and made itself more widely known emblematically. Thus the victory of Francis I at Marignan, in Italy, in 1515 presented the young king to those who were educated as a new Hercules, a new Hannibal, a new Caesar. But the legend of a messianic personality, leading his army towards a great destiny in distant lands, was more widespread.[13]

France could not be called a unified state and the French could not be described as a united nation. Although there is a long-standing historical tradition that views French history as the gradual formation of a centralized state and can ascribe it to 'the forty kings who made France', it is usually now accepted that this view is too much influenced by the conditions that prevailed in nineteenth- and twentieth-century France.[14] In institutional terms, when new territories were absorbed they kept their old institutions, such as the provincial estates which represented the different orders (clergy, nobility and third estate) of the province. They carried out certain administrative tasks on behalf of the crown, but they also sought to safeguard provincial liberties against the crown. So great could be resistance to the crown on financial matters, and so widespread and persistent were the privileges enjoyed by individuals, classes, corporative bodies and municipalities, that the history of the crown from the fifteenth century onwards is often one of great precariousness.[15] Furthermore, in a region such as Gascony, the population inevitably bore the mark of three hundred years of English rule, especially when they had received commercial benefits and favoured treatment in their municipal institutions. At the beginning of the fourteenth century the burghers of Bordeaux expelled French soldiers from their city, and in 1451 they called on the English to liberate them from the French. When Dax, further to the south, was occupied by the French in 1442, its inhabitants were only too eager to welcome the English back some weeks later.

There were five main languages spoken in medieval France. There was Basque, Breton and Flemish; and there was the *langue d'oeil* in the north, and the *langue d'oc* in the south, both of which were subject to a number of regional variations and to a multitude of local dialects. It was undoubtedly difficult for an ordinary person in one part of France to be understood in another part of France; Latin was only the language of the church, the university and the royal administration. French (in the sense of *langue d'oeil*) was slow in imposing itself, even after the decree of Villers-Cotteret, issued in 1539. This made it obligatory for French, which was referred to as the maternal language, to be used in place of Latin, in all public declarations, as well as in marriages, baptisms and burial monuments. It took some time for royal officials to adapt themselves (it was not until 1600 that the effect of the decree was to be discerned in the Pyrenees, for example) and the ordinary people were largely unaffected by it. But although the principle had been put forward many times, even as early as the twelfth century, that men speaking the same language would the more easily live harmoniously together, and although at the beginning of the sixteenth century it was claimed that the story of the heroes of France should be told in French because they were held in affection by 'la nation de France', there seems to have been little hostility to Breton or Occitan or other languages. English was rejected because it was the language of the would-be conquerors of France (in 1420 it was claimed that the French could not obey the English because they could not understand them). Flemish was despised, possibly because it represented a region which was very different from France and which was closely linked to England through the wool trade.[16]

The idea that one should be prepared to die for one's country appeared most clearly in the fifteenth century, after the English invasion of 1415. Until then it had been rather generally (and vaguely) assumed that a readiness to die in battle was reserved for knights and crusaders. But in 1422, after the English had been forced to lay a protracted siege to Meaux, they took vengeance on the defender of the town (known as the bastard of Vaurus) by killing him and several of his companions. It would have been more normal to have held him to ransom or to have persuaded him to change sides. This act aroused widespread comment, but one reaction was to say that the death of the bastard of Vaurus was an example to all Frenchmen and to future generations. Patriotism was still linked to religion and to the idea of a virtuous death. It could be local or regional or restricted to a segment of society. But it had also become national.[17]

Yet it is always possible to write about the history of France in terms of civil war. This is not merely the conflict between king and feudal lords, between town and country, between north and south, that existed in many continental states and embryo states. Nor is it simply a question of faction, whereby individuals with ambition advance their cause by joining with others who have similar or complementary goals. This is a commonplace in most modern societies. Some historians prefer to avoid the term 'civil war' and to say, more simply, that the political history of France can be interpreted in terms of antagonisms.[18] But some have not hesitated to speak of the recurrent conflict between the crown and the duchies of Brittany, Normandy and Burgundy, as a case of civil war.[19]

There can be no doubt that between 1559 and some time around 1600, the wars of religion in France constitute such a conflict, that one can not only speak of civil war, one should also speak of a kingdom that is broken.[20] The development of Calvinism, since it constituted a section of the population which practised a religion different from that of the sovereign, threatened the unity of the kingdom. Furthermore, it coincided with the death of Henry II in 1559, and an ensuing dynastic crisis, since his three sons were either young, sickly or degenerate. (Francis II, who died in 1560 and Charles IX, who died in 1574, were both minors when they became king, and Henry III, who was assassinated by a Dominican monk in 1589, had no heir.) These wars were marked by endless cabals and intrigues, individual and family ambitions, national negotiations and foreign interventions, all of which affected both personal and collective religious convictions. They are remembered today for their assassinations and their massacres (that of Saint Bartholomew, 24 August 1572, when some 3,000 Protestants were killed in Paris, is still remembered by the French as an atrocity in their history). More significant perhaps, although less sinister, was the fact that these wars implied a reawakening of those desires for political autonomy that had been challenged and repressed by previous monarchs, and sometimes in these years, the governors of the provinces found themselves acting independently of royal control. This could be the case in Languedoc, Dauphiné and Brittany.

Another consequence was that the central government found itself in acute financial difficulties and, given the principle that it is easier to raise money with the consent of the taxed rather than without it, even if the consent is somewhat unrepresentative and superficial, it called frequently upon the Estates General. This was a body which was first called in 1484, after the death of Louis XI in the previous year, when his successor Charles VIII was aged only thirteen. This assembly was made up of representatives of those who prayed, those who fought and those whose duty it was to work so as to support the other two. It was thus a replica of a divinely created hierarchy and, since those who worked never included peasants, manual workers or traders, it could claim to be representative of the elites in society. It might have become a body which could permanently have provided a check on royal power, but it never won the initiative and never became the equivalent of the English Parliament. Historians these days do not find this in any way surprising since they regard the success of the English Parliament as being exceptional rather than the

failure of the French Estates to develop.[21] Nevertheless, the dangers
for the unity of the kingdom and the prestige of the monarchy were
real, and it was not possible to foresee that after the death of Henry
III, his successor would be the Protestant Henry of Navarre (Henry
IV), and that by a neatly judged conversion to Catholicism and by a
series of military victories, the power and the prestige of the monarchy
would be re-established, the extent of the kingdom increased and its
unity reaffirmed.

Two developments must be stressed. The one is that whilst, at the
beginning of the sixteenth century, and possibly still by the 1550s, the
idea of France is linked to the theocratic concept of divine inspiration
and intervention, the religious wars and the accession of Henry IV
(the first of the Bourbons) created a more lay interpretation of the
country's history and development. Once the three lilies symbolizing
the French monarchy had been represented simply as a miraculous
gift from the angels. But they became symbols representing 'justice,
finance, government' or similar concepts. The mythical origins of
France were largely forgotten, and although even those who put
forward the notion that it was the institutions which were important
might still claim that Joan of Arc had been sent by God in order to
assist France, nevertheless a more rational and objective view of
French history began to prevail. Protestants could not believe in the
divinity or the virtue of a king who persecuted them.

The other is that when Henry III died and when it seemed possible
that his successor would be a heretic, the suggestion was made that a
Spanish princess or a Savoyard duke, both of whom had certain
claims to be monarch, might be offered the throne. But the Estates
General, meeting in 1593, rejected the possibility of a foreigner. As
has been said, 'la synthèse national était en marche'. It was not only
the Protestants who rejected the Spanish nation. There were Catholics
also who resented foreign intrusion, whether it came from the Papacy,
or from a neighbouring state. The cry of 'Vive la France', or at least
'Vive Roi, Vive France', is said to have been heard for the first time
in Marseilles, in 1585. The king, the law and the country were part of
the common interest of the nation.[22]

Henry IV, who was assassinated by a Catholic fanatic in 1610, had
been a popular king. He had succeeded in creating, at least in legend,
a rapport between himself and the people. It was said by some of
those who visited him, that they had found the king, but that they had
not found the majesty. This was remedied in the seventeenth century.
A strong sense of royal greatness and an insistent use of royal
propaganda, the concept of a unified and powerful state, an insistence

upon order, an ambitious and warlike foreign policy which led to constant demands for money, these were the characteristics of the seventeenth century. Richelieu, the chief minister of Louis XIII, and Mazarin, the chief minister of Anne of Austria during her regency, were significant preludes to the personal reign of Louis XIV which has usually been seen as the apogée of the *ancien régime*. His presence in the château of Versailles, the ritual of his court, his role as an absolute monarch, his determination to play the supreme role in French politics, all meant that his glory was felt throughout France and through most of Europe. French culture was dominant on the Continent, and the Absolutism of this monarchy was the model for all other sovereigns.

Yet although the rule of Louis XIV impressed both contemporaries and subsequent historians, it is clear that his absolutism was never total. His reign, like that of his predecessor, had its share of revolt and dissent. Indeed the whole of the seventeenth century sees instances in the history of the French nation which could fairly be called civil wars, whether we are speaking about peasant revolts, the obstinacy of provincial administrations, the armed resistance of a variety of magnates, or the protests of Protestants whose very existence was linked to the idea of provincial autonomy.

The most obvious example is that of the Frondes. These revolts were organized by those who believed that the royal authority should be limited, and who profited from the the fact that at the death of Louis XIII in 1643 (Richelieu having died seven months earlier), his son was aged only four years. They were also, especially in Paris, incensed that the financial crisis of the government, brought on essentially by the expense of war, had caused the Italian, Cardinal Mazarin, to introduce (via other Italian officials) new taxes, new methods of pressurizing taxpayers, and new procedures for delaying the payment of government debts and of withholding official salaries. The Parlement of Paris, which was a group of judges directing a court of law, and whose powers were delegated by the throne, claimed in 1648 that they would play the same role as the English Parliament had against Charles I. At first they were successful and they manufactured a type of Magna Carta. But the regent, Anne of Austria, having pretended to accept it, suddenly arrested the ringleaders. A hundred barricades appeared in Paris. This was the first of the Frondes. There were three others, and the last did not end until October 1652. They all failed, because they were organized by privileged classes and they created disorder and suffering amongst those who were not privileged. They failed too because they were unable to define a system whereby the power of the monarchy would be legally restrained and would be shared by some other institution.[23]

These episodes can be said to inaugurate the real crisis of the *ancien régime*. Did France have a constitution? Were the French people united? Was not the role of Paris in French life becoming preponderant? The evolution of the nation within France and the role played by the French state both in Europe and in the world had clearly changed dramatically since late medieval times.

It has been said that when Louis XIV died in 1715, France was impoverished, vanquished, riddled with internal dissent and buzzing with criticism of the government.[24] This was more than the general crisis of the seventeenth century, which affected many countries. The government's debts were colossal. Protestants were persecuted once again and some 300,000 went into exile, including much of the elite of the business and scientific world. Within the Catholic Church many had been attracted towards the heresy of Jansenism, and in the provinces, especially in Brittany, the population both resisted and resented the missionary activities of the Catholic Church and clung obstinately to their superstitions. Although some of the powerful aristocrats were tamed by Louis XIV, the majority of the nobility remained influential, especially at a local level. Although many of the judicial, fiscal and courtly offices could be purchased and, on payment of further money, were bequeathed to a chosen successor, the role of the rich man in the state could still be restricted by considerations of birth and status. Conventional wisdom of the time said that if a financier failed, then genteel folk would mock and despise him. But if he succeeded they would hope that they could marry his daughter. If there was, to some extent, a shift in the social basis of the state, it did not necessarily mean that the government guided by men from the new bourgeoisie was more efficient or dynamic. There was a continuous war between the crown and the localities, in which the power of the king was accepted as unlimited and in which the privileges of various institutions and social groups were accepted as firmly entrenched in tradition. The politics of the kingdom consisted of compromise and bargaining, interspersed with moments of royal ferocity and provincial revolt.

Perhaps this could have continued indefinitely. But there were two factors which meant crisis was always present. The one was that the population of France continued to grow, from some 18 million in the mid-sixteenth century, to some 22 million in 1710 and possibly to some 28 million by 1790. Life was precarious when there were so many mouths to feed. The system whereby money or produce had to be paid to seigneurs, to landowners, to the church and to the state, and whereby the towns profited from the peasants' need to sell their produce in the autumn when prices were low, created constant tension. The other is that France continued to grow. With a population which, at the beginning of the eighteenth century, represented a quarter of the continent's population, France absorbed Alsace, Artois, Roussillon, Flanders and Franche Comté. France expanded into Canada and the West Indies, and began to establish itself in India and in Madagascar. French trade spread to the furthermost parts of the world and ports such as Brest, Sète, Rochefort, Dunkirk and Marseilles grew rapidly. And France, whether through the ambition of its rulers or because of the natural consequences of its geographical position in Europe, seemed determined to play a predominant role in the Europe of national states that was developing. For most of the last thirty years of Louis XIV's reign France was at war. Its army grew from some 70,000 men in the 1670s to some 400,000 in 1703; its navy from some 20 ships in 1660 to more than 270 in the 1680s.

THE FRENCH REVOLUTION AND THE EMERGENCE OF THE FRENCH NATION: MYTH AND REALITY

All these features of French life were to persist throughout the eighteenth century, and they explain the Revolution of 1789. Wars, debts, the pressure of population on food resources, disagreement about the role of an absolute monarchy, the failure of crown and provinces to agree, social tensions, the difficulties of a rapidly growing economy, a refusal to accept Catholic orthodoxy, these were always present. There were many reformers, but they never succeeded in getting their way.

There should be no problem in understanding the Revolution. Towards the end of the eighteenth century the government of France ceased to function. There was no revolutionary party; there was no revolutionary opposition; there was no revolutionary situation; there was no accumulation of crises which exploded. There were many features that made government more difficult. Some of these were in the realm of ideas, which undermined the traditional authority of an anointed king. Some were in the nature of hard facts, such as inflation and rising expenditure. Some were in the nature of accident, such as bad harvests. Some were in the nature of circumstances, such as the presence of a young and well-intentioned king who drew attention to problems and ills which he was unable to solve. And some were to be found in the fact of innovation, when Frenchmen found themselves, for the first time, englobed in a parliamentary assembly and involved in a situation that created confrontation, dispute, attitudinization and division. And out of all these features, the French nation emerged.

France of the *ancien régime* had been governed by a king, by an aristocracy and by a church. The king disappeared with the Revolution, Louis XVI being a prisoner from 1792 and being executed in January 1793. To a limited extent the royal authority was resuscitated by the three monarchs who ruled between 1815 and 1848 (Louis XVIII, Charles X and Louis-Philippe) and in a different manner by the two Bonapartes (Napoleon I from 1799 to 1815, and his nephew, Napoleon III, from 1849 to 1870). The nobility lost its privileges and its power, although it did not disappear altogether as a social force. The role of the Church was diminished and although Catholicism was to remain the dominant religion in France, its influence has, since 1789, constantly been contested. For these three powers the Revolution substituted the nation. The Declaration of the Rights of Man and of the Citizen stated explicitly that the principle of all sovereignty was vested in the nation. No institution and no individual could exercise any authority that had not been conferred by the nation.

Although the word 'nationalism' was not at all in common use during the revolutionary period, the word 'nation' and 'national', accompanied by references to 'le patriot' and 'la patrie', became increasingly widespread. Many of the matters relating to the state which had earlier been described as 'royal' began to be described as 'national'. *La national* replaced *le roi* in the hierarchy of the state.[25] Furthermore, it was accepted that a nation was not a chance collection of humanity, brought together by the rule of a royal family and growing and shrinking according to the hazards of inheritance, matrimonial alliances and wars. Each nation had its characteristics, as the *Encylopédie* had pointed out,[26] but the nation existed as the result of the general will of the people. The Fête de la Fédération in 1790 (which commemorated the first anniversary of the fall of the Bastille) claimed that it was for the people to decide whether or not they would adhere to the the national community, even if, according to old feudal laws, they had been seen to be the property of some foreign lord when they lived in Alsace, or of the Pope when they lived in certain enclaves in Avignon or the Venaissin. The Revolution, by proclaiming the right of peoples to dispose of themselves, was challenging the existing political map of Europe.[27]

From its very origins the Revolution offered to the many who had, as the result of tumultuous events, achieved a certain political awareness, the possibility of being proud of being French. It was in

France that the old order had been overthrown, that Absolutism and privilege had been ended, and that the rights of man had been proclaimed. The principle of government was that what was right for one part of France was right for all parts of France. This principle could apply to all parts of Europe. France was the model for the rest of the world.

To begin with, the Revolution was pacific. Wars were rejected, policies of aggrandizement were seen as characteristics of selfish dynasties. The other peoples of Europe would see the French as their brothers. But soon the Revolution became aware of the hostility of the European powers. The most constant theme of the Revolution began to emerge, that it was in danger, in danger from enemies who were in alliance with foreigners. And as fear and belief in conspiracy began to grow, the rival groupings in the Assembly began to become aware of the advantages that they could derive from an aggressive and nationalist rhetoric. The Revolution created a new community, with a belief in a mythical past which linked it to Greece and Rome, and with its own symbols and rituals. Before 1789, there had been no national flag. Each regiment of the army had its flag. Only the emblem of the lilies represented French royalty and the French state. But from 1789 the red, white and blue *cocarde* made its appearance and was worn by Lafayette's National Guard. Probably deriving from the red and blue colours of Paris and the white of the royal army, a red, white and blue flag emerged, and from June 1790 it became the national flag (although it was not until 1794 that its design was officially fixed by decree).[28] Oaths of loyalty were taken around trees of liberty, which were connected with ancient rural ceremonies that were meant to commemorate change and to mark the need to consolidate the new order.[29]

The nation and the Revolution were synonymous, the one to the other. The one had to be prepared to die for the other. Deputies rivalled each other in their nationalist fervour. It was said that every citizen was a soldier and that no power on earth could overcome 6 million free soldiers. In January 1792 the whole Assembly, including those who were present as ushers or spectators (both male and female), swore on oath that they would die rather than renounce the constitution that the Revolution had created. The following year a deputy admitted that he loved all men, especially free men, but that above all men in the universe he loved the Frenchmen and above all else in nature he preferred his motherland.[30]

To the sound of ferocious war-songs there developed the idea that territories adjoining France should be annexed. The whole of the

French nation, old and young, male and female, was supposedly mobilized in order to defend France against enemies and in order to demonstrate the superiority of France. Belgium was annexed in 1795; sister republics were created on France's borders; the term *la Grande nation* entered common use; young generals began to revise the frontiers of Europe and one of them, who named himself the Emperor Napoleon in 1804, solved his domestic political difficulties by fighting battles in distant lands and returning to Paris enveloped in an atmosphere of victory and glory.

Historians who have difficulty in explaining how different social classes endured many hardships and made many sacrifices in order to defend the Revolution, have claimed that they were united by the idea of *la patrie*. Labourers and shopkeepers, men and women, people who were politically so far distant from each other as the moderate Girondins and the extremist *enragés*, were all zealous partisans of their country, and were hostile to foreigners whom they tended to treat as suspects if not as enemies.[31] 'The French Revolution', as one historian has put it, 'completed the nation which became one and indivisible.'[32]

This interpretation of the Revolution has been completed by the legends concerning this period of French history. These legends were almost contemporary to events as certain propagandists, such as the artist Jean-Louis David, created a series of national revolutionary heroes, who could be venerated with a fervour that was akin to religious fervour. France was represented on offical seals and coinage (from September 1792 onwards) by the figure of a woman, dressed in classical costume and holding in her right hand a spear (or pike), her head covered by a Phrygian bonnet. Thus France, Republic and Liberty were linked to the past. Napoleon too cultivated his own legend, with his official communiqués and with popular engravings suggesting that he personally possessed powers that were almost supernatural. The legend of patriotism was fostered all the time. 'Are you ashamed to wear the same uniform that your Emperor wears?' was the sort of remark attributed to Napoleon when he encountered a reluctant recruit.

These legends were perpetuated in the course of the nineteenth century both by events and by writers. The fact that Napoleon was defeated and that by the 1815 Treaty of Vienna the frontiers of France were reduced to those that had existed in 1792, was made into an issue by those who were thought of as being on the Left in politics. Since the political and ideological differences within French society were considerable, politicians gave great importance to foreign affairs, and France was represented as the natural champion of nations which were struggling to be free, such as the Greeks, the Poles or the Italians. Weak governments sought to strengthen themselves by organizing successful forays abroad. Under Louis XVIII there was an expedition into Spain; under Charles X Algiers was invaded and the conquest of Algeria was begun; even the bourgeois Louis-Philippe was urged to consolidate his throne by waging a foreign war, and much of his unpopularity came from his alleged subservience to England and his failure to extend French influence into neighbouring countries, such as Belgium or Spain, or into more distant parts of the world, such as the Pacific. Napoleon III, whilst professing that his Empire meant peace, was conscious of the need to demonstrate that France was actively present on the world scene, whether in the Crimea or in Mexico. Writers such as Victor Hugo, popular poets such as Béranger, or a historian like Michelet kept the legends of patriotism alive. The last expressed it dramatically. France, he wrote, is a religion.[33]

The humiliating defeat of France in 1870, the creation of the German Empire and the annexation, by Germany, of Alsace and Lorraine, created a new nationalism, linked to the idea of a war of revenge. The rising in Paris in 1871, known as the Commune, was an experiment in socialism and the last of the classic French revolutions, but it was also a movement of hostility against those who had acquiesced in the German victory. Fundamental to the ideas of those who founded the Third Republic in September 1870 was that France must be regenerated and that the French nation should reassert itself and rediscover its greatness.

Yet there are reasons to doubt that this version of national history is altogether correct. It has been claimed that after the crisis years 1792 to 1794, the mass of the people did not identify itself with France and with the nation. The bourgeoisie supposedly rejected the lower orders and their aspirations. Patriotism no longer united the social classes.[34] The resistance to the Revolution was, in Brittany and in the Vendée particularly, a resistance to conscription as well as a rejection of any orders which came from Paris. Whilst it was often claimed that this resistance was inspired by aristocrats, bigoted priests and English gold, it is understood now that it was a movement that was deeply rooted in the ordinary people. Nor were these the only regions which objected to the actions of the republican government.[35] There is a great deal of evidence to show that soldiers were preoccupied by material considerations more than by patriotism. Desertion was frequent, and under Napoleon was extremely important.[36]

Furthermore, it was during the Revolution that the regional diversity of France was fully apprehended. The linguistic survey carried out by the abbé Grégoire in 1790 showed that three-quarters of the population knew some French but that only a little more than one-tenth could speak it properly. Important revolutionary documents had to be translated so that they could be understood in the provinces. It appears that the march of the men from Marseilles on Paris in 1792, when the Marseillaise was supposedly sung, was, in fact, a march made by men who spoke Provençal rather than French.[37] Even in 1863, according to official figures, about a quarter of the country's population spoke no French, and there is every reason to believe that this is an underestimate. The persistence of languages other than French, and of the many patois and dialects of the French provinces, lasted well into the twentieth century. There is ample evidence to suggest that substantial parts of the population did not feel that they belonged to a French nation, just as they were ignorant of the vital facts of French history, such as the significance of 1789 or of 1870 and just as there were many communes which did not possess a tricolour flag.[38]

The unity of France was supposedly assured by the system of administrative centralization, as it was by the creation of a statistical survey for the whole of France (from 1840 onwards) and by such devices as the careful visits to the whole of France by the head of state, which were initiated by Napoleon III. But how powerful were the instruments of government, such as the prefect? In his novel *Lucien Leuven*, Stendhal's hero, living in Nancy in 1832, states that in the provinces everyone makes fun of the prefect and that it is the local aristocracy (present-day historians would prefer to use the word notabilities) who take all the decisions. At the same time, this local nobility is both unknown in Paris and has no knowledge of Paris. Was the French population moved by the desire to live together? The answer must be in the negative, and some would suggest that it is not only south of the national line drawn from Saint-Malo to Grenoble that this reluctance existed.[39]

THE THIRD REPUBLIC AND THE TWO WORLD WARS

The accomplishment of the Third Republic was the homogenization of the nation. The laws of the 1880s (associated with the name of Jules Ferry) instituted free, compulsory and lay primary education. Trained teachers applied an established school practice and produced a nationalist pedagogy in history, geography and civics. The French language spread to the detriment of other tongues and patois, even although bilingualism flourished. The growth of railways, which was accompanied by a considerable improvement in roads, facilitated the spread of newspapers, and by 1913 the sort of individual who fifty years earlier had been lamenting the fact that people did not read at all was regretting the fact that certain popular newspapers were to be found everywhere. The greater ease of communications within a framework of prosperity also encouraged the growth of fairs, markets and shopping centres. Areas became less isolated, sociability was extended, and it was often said that peasants learned to speak and understand French more readily at the market than they did at school. From 1889 all young Frenchmen who were passed as being physically fit were obliged to do military service, and thereby received a further education, however imperfect, that was patriotic and that sought to show the connection that existed between local and national interest. In 1881 it was decided that 14 July should be celebrated as a national holiday.

Thus the administrative structure of France became associated with a cultural infrastructure. This coincided with the development of a threat to France which was first revealed by a speech made by the German Emperor, William II, when he visited Tangiers in 1905 and violently attacked French and British policy in Morocco. Rightly or wrongly this was seen by a wide section of French opinion as a revelation that France was in mortal danger. The newspapers were filled with such fears. Typical was the attitude of Clemenceau who declared that for the first time since the Hundred Years' War, France was faced by a power which was implacable in its determination to be superior. It was the combination of a cultural preparation and an awareness of an international crisis which created French unity in August 1914 and the four years of catastrophic fighting that followed. The popular sense of the nation had been formed by certain symbols, such as the tricolour flag, the Marseillaise, the festival of 14 July, as well as by street names, museums, school textbooks, illustrations and Larousse's dictionary. Politics are a matter of memory and the threat from Germany recalled the volunteers of 1792, the greatness of Napoleon and the defeat of 1870.

This is all the more remarkable because the theory that there were two Frances, invariably at conflict with each other, whilst it has been applied to wide periods of French history, has seemed particularly relevant to the Third Republic, when parliamentary democracy and universal manhood suffrage were in force. It has been claimed that politics has its own laws, and that the social relationships, the economic life, religious beliefs and ethnic characteristics of a region determined the way in which it would vote. This being so, France, especially at moments of tension, was irresistibly divided into two antagonistic *blocs*, the Right and the Left. People are supposedly different from each other, according to whether they belong to one or the other of these *blocs*, and they differ in their attitude towards the family, the local authorities, the state, the church or the army. Since these blocs are irreconcilable, the unity of the nation is always in doubt.[41]

During the last decades of the nineteenth century these differences became more acute. Catholics objected to the policy of state schools as they objected to what they believed was the anti-clericalism of successive republic governments, and they were sustained by the history (and the myth) of the Vendée and its resistance to the Revolution. Nationalists, concerned with the recovery of France and its greatness, were shocked by the instability of governments and the opportunism of politicians, and they were disgusted by the scandals of the Panama Canal Company (which was financial) and of Dreyfus (which concerned spying). They wanted an end to parliamentary government. They denounced as enemies of France all those who were Protestants, Freemasons, Jews and foreigners. The socialists opposed the supremacy of the bourgeoisie, the aristocratic elements that dominated the army, the reactionary influence of the Church, the scandal of colonial adventures and exploitation. They turned to international socialism and pacifism and rejected war as a device used by capitalists and militarists. In all these ways sections of French society were inexorably, and apparently permanently, hostile to each other.

But the Catholics were anxious to demonstrate that they were no less patriotic than the others. Given the fact of war, nationalists had to support the army that they had always defended. Socialists remained Jacobins, determined to defend the country that had given birth to the principles of the Revolution, of progress and civilization. August 1914 was therefore in France (as in other European nations) the triumph of the idea of the nation. It is true that Frenchmen accepted being turned into soldiers with resignation rather than with enthusiasm. Officers distrusted each other for reasons of politics and religion. Munition workers were not prepared to abandon their rights. Peasants saw opportunities for amassing wealth. Government agents reported on groups or individuals who were hostile to the war. Nevertheless, in 1919, on the first July 14 of peace, it was a victorious and united France that celebrated itself as the greatest power in Europe.

Attempts were made to maintain that spirit. November 11, Armistice Day, became a day of national remembrance. Many towns and villages used to have a special annual ceremony commemorating the terrible battle of Verdun. The war memorial became a melancholy but meaningful presence in every commune. But as economic and political difficulties grew increasingly important, so discord rather than unity became the characteristic of the nation. Lacking the mass political parties that are associated with modern democracies, with a large peasant population, a small and largely isolated working class and with commercial and industrial enterprises based upon the family firm, the political leadership tended to be stuck in a cul-de-sac of cliques, moderates and opportunists. Therefore extremes developed, whether on the Left or the Right, denouncing the essential bases of French society, whether it was the predominance of the bourgeoisie and the role of the banks and the monied classes, or whether it was the parliamentary system, with its weaknesses and its incompetence. The Communist Party (founded in 1920) proclaimed itself the party of revolution and looked to Moscow for leadership. Fascist and crypto-fascist groups looked to Mussolini or the French concept of authoritarianism. Catholic leagues called for a return to the traditional values, but they were divided amongst themselves, since there were those who were ultramontane and intolerant, those who were liberal and those who believed that their religion could be reconciled with socialism. Anti-clericalism was sometimes an ideological rejection of superstition and priest power, but it could also be a tactic to bring together left-wing groups which were otherwise divided over class and economic issues. Pacifist ideas spread, not only because the elementary school-teachers' union and many former combatants' associations claimed that this was the only doctrine that could decently be taught to the children of France after the massacres of the war, but because the Communist Party attacked the socialists who had betrayed the cause of peace in 1914.

All these differences evolved in what has been described as an atmosphere of civil war.[42] The victory of the Popular Front in 1936 was associated with the greatest movement of strikes that France had ever seen; factories and departmental stores were occupied by workers in what appeared to be an assault on private property; there were those who were indignant that the Prime Minister of Gallo-Roman France was a Jew, Léon Blum; when workers were granted holidays with pay (*congés payés*) there were seaside hotels and restaurants which put up notices saying that 'congés payés' were not admitted. Again France was divided against itself. But the real civil confrontation came with the war of 1939 and the military defeat of 1940. There were those who had never wanted a war. Many wanted an armistice and accepted it. But they did not necessarily accept the regime which organized and signed the armistice and which sought to govern France in a new way. There were those who believed in this regime and welcomed its policies, including its persecution of Jews, Freemasons, Communists and foreigners. Others turned to resistance movements, although they themselves were divided between Communists, socialists, Catholics and followers of the unknown General de Gaulle who had established Free France in London. During the war, and at the time of the Liberation of France, Frenchman killed Frenchman, both at home and abroad.

THE FIFTH REPUBLIC

Nor did these 'franco-français' wars cease in 1945. Fear of a communist revolution, fear of an allegedly fascist rising led by de Gaulle; opposition to and support for the colonial wars that France fought in Indo-China and in Algeria; apprehension that France would no longer be able to organize its own defence if its army was to be merged into some western European force; dismay that French politics were locked into sterile and archaic debates about relations between church and state in education matters or about the protest movements of particular economic groups which were suffering decline; regret that France was economically backward: these divisions appeared to come to another climax when, in 1958, a revolt organized by a number of army officers and settlers in Algiers, inspired by the fear that a weak government in Paris would abandon the French possession of Algeria, brought about another threat of civil war. Parachutists were dropped into Corsica and disarmed the local police and gendarmerie. Threats of further parachutists landing in Paris brought about the prospect of barricades over which army unity would confront socialists and communists.

The result was the coming to power of de Gaulle and the foundation of the Fifth Republic. A new constitution which gave considerable powers to the President who was a prestigious figure on the world scene, enabled him to proceed to complete decolonization. By 1962 France was at peace for the first time since 1939. In the favourable economic climate of the 1960s France modernized its economy and, equipped with nuclear weapons, became the champion of national independence and the opponent of the domination of the world by two superpowers. France, claimed de Gaulle, cannot be France without greatness. It was through this concept of greatness, he believed, that the French nation could escape the internal demons which would otherwise destroy it. His preoccupation was with unity. Gaullism supposedly belonged neither to the Left nor to the Right in politics. Everyone, said de Gaulle, is, or has been, or will be, Gaullist.

Naturally, de Gaulle had his opponents. There were those who refused to accept the manner in which he came to power. Some rejected the constitution. Others protested against a prosperity which left many still in poverty. Students revolted in 1968 and were joined by many workers in a series of events that demonstrated the fragility of power. But after de Gaulle three further Presidents demonstrated the continuity of the Republic. By the 1980s the word 'consensus' achieved a certain popularity. The ideological struggles of yesterday seemed to have passed away. The institutions of the state, the principles of national independence and defence, the need for continued modernization, the desirability of a consumer society and the extension of a sophisticated communications system, all seem to have been accepted by the French nation. The celebrations of the bicentenary of the French Revolution in 1989 did not lead to the controversy that had been anticipated. As one historian had put it, the Revolution was over. France had come into harbour.[43]

Conflicts still exist; the largest demonstrations ever held in France were organized in 1984 by those who thought that the administrative reforms proposed by the socialist government threatened the nature of private schools, essentially Catholic schools; the railway strike of December 1986 and January 1987 was unusually protracted and received unexpected public support. But these, and other conflicts, affect specific sectors, are usually unpredictable and sometimes reflect isolated resentments and emotions. They do not reflect popular ideology, what the French people think of themselves. And this is particularly interesting at a time when the French seem to be indulging in so obsessive a search for their identity that such recurrent questions as 'who are we?' and 'what are our collective values?' have been assessed as forming a national identity crisis.[44]

There are many reasons for this. Undoubtedly, like all consumer societies the French are conscious of the fact that they are subject to the same influences, pressures and aspirations as others, and that they have necessarily lost much of their distinctiveness as they have been submerged by the same technology. Traditional sources, such as identification with patriotism, have not been available over a long period of peace and are not appropriate to modern conditions (one cannot fly the tricolour flag on an Exocet missile). But in the case of France there are three particular considerations that are relevant.

The first is regionalism. It was for a long time an accepted axiom that France would be nothing without the existence of the French state. This was the fundamental principle of Gaullism, and was restated by his successors in the Presidency of the Fifth Republic, Pompidou and Giscard d'Estaing. Centralization was part of the Jacobin tradition to which both socialists and Communists adhered. But after 1945, and particularly after the Algerian war and the student–worker revolts of 1968, the number of associations and movements which sought or demanded regional autonomy increased steadily.[45] It was partly to combat these demands (Corsican, Breton, Occitan, Basque, Alsatian) that the socialist government followed up the more timid reforms of its predecessors by a law on decentralization that came fully into effect in 1983. The powers of the prefects were reduced. The powers of regional and local administrations have been increased, as was the role of the regional and local electorates. This reform has been accompanied by a certain cultivation of regional cultures and languages and by a new assessment of the importance of pluralism in French history. The effects of these reforms are still debatable, but whilst they have calmed down some of the more aggressive of the autonomous movements, the importance given to local notabilities and the high economic stakes for which certain regions are playing, have created a situation whereby many French people identify themselves increasingly with their regions rather than with the centralized, hierarchical French state.[46]

Secondly, there is Europe. French statesmen were prominent in the post-1945 moves to create a united Europe, as a means of avoiding future conflicts and as a means of controlling West German power. Although opinion was divided, France became one of the six founder members of the European Community and soon found that it was an excellent instrument for furthering French interests. This was particularly the case after General de Gaulle had established a special relationship with West Germany. The European Community appeared all the more likely to continue to be used by the French for their advantage because demographic projections suggested that relatively early in the twenty-first century France would replace West Germany as the most populous country in the European Community (with a population of 58 million in the year 2025). But by the late 1970s and 1980s it became clear that the situation had changed. French governments were obliged to accept that they were forced to adopt policies as the result of pressures originating beyond the boundaries of France and which they had not voluntarily chosen. Europe ceased to be an instrument. The Community appeared instead to be the essential means whereby the French could ensure their prosperity, their defence and their importance in the world. If France could dominate the Community in alliance with West Germany then all would be well, but from November 1989 the prospect of the reunification of Germany became more immediate and the centres of the Community seemed likely to shift to Bonn and Berlin. One French response was to insist upon a greater political and economic integration of the Community. 'France is my country but Europe is my future' became a rallying cry. It was possible that France could dominate the European Community. Many Frenchmen began to protest that they thought of themselves as Europeans, or that they thought of themselves as Breton and European, rather than simply as French. But resentments against a European bureaucracy, or against Spanish competition in agricultural produce or against Belgian acquisition of desirable French property, are obvious examples of traditional French assertiveness.

Third, there is the pattern of immigration. France has always been a country which has received many foreign immigrants. But whereas, after the last war, nearly 90 per cent of this foreign population was of European origin (Italian and Spanish, for example), by the 1970s some 40 per cent of this population came from North Africa. More than 4 million immigrants are present in France; the Muslim religion has become the second religion, after Roman Catholicism and easily outstripping Jews and Protestants. The panic idea was put forward in a widely spread publication that soon nothing would remain of French culture.[47] A political party, the Front National, was partly successful in the municipal elections of 1983, the European elections of 1985, the parliamentary elections of 1986 and the Presidential election of 1988, largely because it claimed to represent purely French interests as opposed to the interests of immigrants and other outsiders. This contemporary version of nationalism is associated with a certain Catholic fundamentalism (which was violently opposed to the showing of the Scorsese film, *The Last Temptation of Christ*) and even with a certain Republican fundamentalism, which was, for example, opposed to Muslim girls wearing headscarves when they attended a state school. However, the fierceness of these responses is much palliated by the repeated desire of immigrants to become, and to be accepted as French.[49]

Naturally, a preoccupation with regionalism, with the organization of Europe and with immigrants is not confined to the French. But in certain respects the problem is worse for them, since they have invariably seen themselves as intrinsically special, frequently occupying a position of leadership, whether political or cultural. Within a comparatively short space of time they have had to adapt to defeat and occupation, to the traumas of having assisted in the persecution of the Jews and of having fought obstinate colonial wars, and they have had to accept the brooding burden of guilt which these successive events have generated. The French have had to accept loss of power and prestige; they can no longer rely upon unlimited patriotism (a recent film, *La Vie et rien d'autre*, views the 1914 war without any mention of national sentiment); they have had to reconcile the traditional apparatus of their state with the network of regional and European institutions; they have to put up with a complex spectrum of political loyalties (bearing in mind, as one French President recently put it, political parties bring discord just as clouds bring rain).

But the French have certain advantages. They have excellent administrators; they have modernized with remarkable success; their contacts with eastern Europe are good. No one can ignore the nation that is both a maritime and a continental stronghold. The French have their rhetoric and they have their myths. *La France éternelle* is a myth shared both by them and by the rest of the world.

NOTES

1 A. Longnon, *La Formation de l'unité française* (Paris, 1922).
2 C. Beaune, *Naissance de la nation France* (Paris, 1985), p. 7 mentions writers such as Georges Guibal and Charles Lenient.
3 Guizot, *Histoire de la civilisation en Europe*, 1st edn (Paris, 1826).
4 Michelet, 'Précis de l'histoire de France', *Œuvres complètes*, vol. III (Paris, 1973), p. 107.
5 Michelet, 'Discours d'ouverture à la faculté des lettres', *ibid.*, p. 222.
6 K. Fowler, *Medieval Mercenaries* (Oxford, 1989).
7 The question is put by Emmanuel Le Roy Ladurie in *L'Express*, 21 August 1987, pp. 33–5.
8 See the argument put forward by E. Julliard in *Une Leçon d'histoire de Fernand Braudel (18, 19, 20 October 1985)* (Paris, 1986), pp. 175–82. Braudel's discussion of the subject is to be found in the chapter, 'La Géographie a-t-elle inventé la France?', *L'Identité de la France: espace et histoire* (Paris, 1986), pp. 237–336.
9 See R. Pernoud, *La Formation de la France* (Paris, 1966).
10 R. Cazelles, *La Société politique et la crise de la royauté sous Philippe de Valois* (Paris, 1958), and by the same author, *Etienne Marcel: champion de l'unité française* (Paris, 1984).
11 Jacques Le Goff, 'Portrait du roi idéal', *L'Histoire*, 81 (September 1988), 70–6.
12 Braudel, *L'Identité de la France*, p. 280.
13 Janine Garrisson, '1515: Marignan', *L'Histoire*, 114 (September 1988), 26–32.

14 For an interesting discussion of the strengths and weaknesses of this orthodox view see P. R. Campbell, *The Ancien Régime in France* (Oxford, 1988).

15 This is shown for the late sixteenth century and for the seventeenth century by R. J. Bonney, *The King's Debts: Finance and Politics in France, 1589–1661* (Oxford, 1981).

16 Beaune, *Naissance de la nation France*, pp. 291ff; A. Brun, *Recherches historiques sur l'introduction du français dans les provinces du Midi* (Paris, 1923).

17 Beaune, *Naissance de la nation France*, pp. 332–5.

18 A. Duhamel, O. Duhamel and J. Jaffré, 'Consensus et dissensus français. Table ronde', *Le Débat*, May 1984. The preoccupations of these historians and political scientists were with the last two hundred years of French history, but their arguments are applicable to a wider period.

19 See for example, Emmanuel Le Roy Ladurie, *L'Etat royal 1480–1610* (Paris, 1987), p. 348, with regard to 'la reprise de la guerre civile' in 1467.

20 This phrase is used by J. Garrisson, 'Deux vieilles France en Echaugette: les guerres de religion', *Vingtième Siècle*, 5 (January–March 1985), 91.

21 Emmanuel Le Roy Ladurie, *L'Etat royal*, p. 95.

22 *Ibid.*, pp. 346–7.

23 R. J. Bonney, *Political Change in France under Richelieu and Mazarin, 1624–1661* (Oxford, 1978); E. H. Kossman, *La Fronde* (Leiden, 1954); C. Jouhaud, *Les Mazarinades: la Fronde des mots* (Paris, 1985).

24 R. Mettam, *Power and Faction in Louis XIV's France* (Oxford, 1988), p. 319.

25 J. Godechot, 'Nation, patrie, nationalisme et patriotisme en France au XVIIIᵉ siècle', *Actes du colloque Patriotisme et nationalisme en Europe à l'époque de la Révolution française et de Napoléon* (Paris, 1973), pp. 20–6; A. Dupront, 'Du sentiment national', in M. François (ed.) *La France et les Français* (Paris, 1972), pp. 1423–72.

26 Dupront, *ibid.*, p. 1435.

27 J. Godechot, *La Pensée révolutionnaire* (Paris, 1964), p. 122.

28 R. Girardet, 'Les Trois Couleurs', in P. Nora (ed.), *Les Lieux de mémoire* (Paris, 1984), vol. I, pp. 5–35.

29 M. Ozouf, *La Fête révolutionnaire 1789–1799* (Paris, 1976).

30 These speeches are quoted in C. Emsley, 'Nationalist rhetoric and nationalist sentiment in revolutionary France', in O. Dann and J. Dinwiddy (eds.), *Nationalism in the Age of the French Revolution* (Oxford, 1988), pp. 42–3.

31 M. Slavin, *The French Revolution in Miniatures* (Princeton, N. J., 1984), p. 344.

32 Albert Soboul quoted in E. Weber, *Peasants into Frenchmen: The Modernisation of Rural France*, 1979 edition, p. 95.

33 Jules Michelet, *Le Peuple* (Paris, 1876), pp. 276–8.

34 A. Soboul, 'La Révolution française: problème national et réalités sociales', *Actes du colloque Patriotisme et nationalisme*, pp. 29–58.

35 F. Lebrun and R. Dupuy, *Les Résistances et la révolution* (Paris, 1987).

36 C. Emsley, 'Nationalist rhetoric and nationalist sentiment', pp. 45, 86.

37 M. de Certeau, D. Julia and J. Revel, *Une Politique de la langue: la Révolution française et le patois* (Paris, 1975); E. Weber, 'Who sang the Marseillaise?', in J. Beauroy, M. Bertrand and E. T. Gargan (eds.), *The Wolf and the Lamb: Popular Culture in France from the Old Régime to the Twentieth Century* (Saratoga, 1976).

38 Weber, *Peasants into Frenchmen*, pp. 67, 86.

39 *Une Leçon d'histoire de Fernand Braudel*, p. 180.

40 Quoted in R. Girardet, *Le Nationalisme français* (Paris, 1983).

41 D. Johnson, 'The two Frances: the historical debate', *West European Politics*, 1, no. 3 (1978), 3–10.

42 S. Berstein, 'L'Affrontement simulé des années 1930', *Vingtième Siècle*, 5 (January–March 1985), 48.

43 See R. Rémond, 'Les Progrès du consensus', *ibid.*, pp. 123ff.

44 D. Pinto, 'The Atlantic influence and the mellowing of French identity', in J. Howorth and G. Ross (eds.), *Contemporary France*, vol. II (London, 1988), pp. 117–33; Espace 89, *L'Identité française* (Paris, 1985); J. Schmitt, *Fin de la France? Histoire d'une perte d'identité* (Paris, 1986); D. Schnapper, *La France de l'intégration* (Paris, 1991).

45 W. Beer, *The Unexpected Rebellion: Ethnic Activism in Contemporary France* (New York, 1980); C. Gras and G. Livet (eds.), *Régions et régionalisme en France du XVIIIᵉ siècle à nos jours* (Paris, 1977); M. Philipponeay, *La Grande Affaire: décentralisation et régionalisation* (Paris, 1981).

46 J. Rondin, *Le Sacre des Notables* (Paris, 1985).

47 'Serons-nous encore Français dans 30 ans?', *Le Figaro Magazine*, 26 October 1985.

48 P. A. Taguieff, 'Nationalisme et réactions fondamentalistes en France', *Vingtième Siècle*, 25 (January–March 1990), 49–74.

49 A. G. Hargreaves, 'The Beur generation: integration or exclusion?', *Contemporary France*, 3 (1989), 147–59.

THREE

THE NATIONAL QUESTION IN ITALY

ADRIAN LYTTELTON

IN THE SHADOW OF FRANCE, 1796–1814

The Italian question did not exist as a political reality before 1796.[1] The Italian Jacobins[2] were the first to pose the creation of a united Italy as a concrete political project, and their concept of the nation was derived from the French Revolution. For the French revolutionaries, the nation was not a given; it had to be created. The historical heritage was irrelevant, even dangerous. Just this abstract quality of French nationalism favoured its transplantation into Italy, where the historical basis for a political concept of nationality was lacking.[3] The adoption of this concept was also prepared by a shift in the meaning of the word *patria* and its derivatives. Originally used in a neutral sense to refer to a person's place of birth, or, at most, the state of which he was a subject, it became charged with a new political significance. The *patria* could only be an association of free citizens, and a patriot was someone who worked for the cause of freedom against despotism. Paradoxically, it was the universality of the new idea of patriotism which prepared the ground for a new idea of the nation, because it implied a refusal of the legitimacy of the existing absolutist states. The gesture which typified this new attitude was the tragedian Vittorio Alfieri's solemn renunciation of his status as a subject of Piedmont, which implied the loss of his privileges as a noble. Alfieri called on his fellow writers to become expatriates and to 'seek liberty wherever it is to be found'.[4]

The propaganda for the new ideas of the French Revolution was effective because the victories of Bonaparte's armies demonstrated the weakness and vulnerability of the old states and created a political vacuum. Austria was expelled from Lombardy, and it soon became clear that the the other states of northern and central Italy only retained their independence on French sufferance. One response to the crisis of the old states was the resurgence of old municipal aspirations to 'liberty'. But this, curiously, gave a base to unitarianism: the call for a united Italy found its greatest response in provincial cities like Brescia and Reggio Emilia, where it was seen as a way of challenging the hegemony of the old capitals (Venice and Modena). The most important discussion of the national question took place in the context of a literary competition organized under the supervision of the French as the occupying power in Lombardy. At a time when the French military position was precarious, it suited Bonaparte to create a party which would agitate for the liberation of the other Italian states from their 'tyrants'.[5] The famous *concorso* announced in September 1796 offered a price for the best essay on the theme *Quale dei governi liberi meglio convenga alla felicità d'Italia* ('Which form of free government is best adapted to the happiness of Italy'). The terms of the competition assumed the existence of an Italian 'nation'. Writers were actively to serve the cause of revolution by exposing their rulers: 'show them naked to the people and they will become hateful to the nation'. They were also to promote national sentiment by 'recalling the ancient glories of Italy'.[6] Within these parameters, the problem was that of adapting the ideas of the French Revolution to Italian realities. The experience and the language of the Revolution exerted a powerful fascination. The formula of 'the Republic, single and indivisible' was frequently repeated with almost religious reverence. 'Federalism' had become a dirty word in French political discourse, and this helps to explain the reluctance of many participants in the competition to advocate federal solutions. However, one of the leading Italian patriots, Giovanni Ranza, argued that federalism, though mistaken in France, was necessary in Italy because of the great differences between regional 'customs' and 'dialects'. He warned his compatriots against copying French political 'fashions', which might be unsuitable for Italy.[7] For Matteo Galdi, perhaps the most widely read of any of the publicists who discussed the national question, however, all compromises were unnecessary and unwise. A single Italian republic should be established by a process of continuous revolutionary struggle. The creation of a free and united Italy was a necessary step in the process of universal 'regeneration' set in motion by the Revolution.[8] This programme had the advantage of simplicity. Unitarian propaganda attempted to win popular support and to diffuse a new idea of nationality through education. A kind of republican catechism was drawn up for children: they were to be taught that they were Italians, that Italy's boundaries had been set by nature, and that the division of Italy constituted 'violence against natural rights'.[9]

At the time when the competition was set, ideas like Galdi's might have been acceptable to the French; but already nine months later, when the results were announced, the political balance had shifted in favour of a more moderate approach. The winner of the competition, Melchiorre Gioia, rejected federalism and took the French constitution of 1795 as his model. However, he rejected violent revolution as a method. Unity should only be achieved gradually, through the spontaneous imitation of the positive example set by the republic in the liberated territories. This programme did not preclude the possibility of compromise with the existing Italian states, and it did not arouse the fears of the Directory that the adoption of a radical programme in Italy might favour the revival of Jacobin extremism in France itself. Gioia, who became one of Italy's leading economists, can be seen as a link between the native Enlightenment tradition of practical, modernizing reform and the new Jacobin patriotism. The leading Lombard reformer, Pietro Verri, was the president of the commission which judged the competition. Gioia preserved a typically eighteenth-century faith in legislation. He rejected federalism, because it would merely perpetuate those local differences which would weaken the Republic. It was the task of the legislator to destroy harmful and obsolete local prejudices by a uniform system of laws, and thereby to create the new 'customs' which would give a moral basis to the new state. Gioia also produced a more cogent economic argument against any form of federalism based on the old state units; with few exceptions, they had favoured the maintenance of anachronistic urban privileges, particularly in favour of their capital cities. The only remedy for the decadence of Italy's city-centred economies was, instead, to encourage the reorientation towards the country which was already taking place. Federalism would also provide insufficient guarantees for national security. The example of Switzerland, invoked by federalists, was misleading, because Italy lacked the protection given by the former's mountainous terrain. Exposed to the constant threat of invasion by more powerful neighbours, Italy needed a political system capable of reacting with more rapidity and decision.

The Italian patriots had been roused not only by the example of the French Revolution but by the propaganda of the Convention, which had promised 'fraternity and assistance to all the peoples who wish to reconquer their liberty'.[10] But the political climate after Thermidor was suspicious of libertarian and egalitarian ideas which might favour the revival of Jacobin extremism in France itself. By an unhappy coincidence, the beginning of Bonaparte's conquests coincided with the discovery of the conspiracy of Babeuf. The most important Italian revolutionary, Filippo Michele Buonarroti, was one of its leaders. During the Jacobin ascendancy Buonarroti had been officially employed as the political agent of the army of Italy, and then as *commissaire* for Oneglia, occupied during the campaign of 1794. His ties with Saliceti, the Corsican *commissaire* of the army of Italy in 1796, made him dangerous. The example of Buonarroti helped to create the stereotype of the Italian patriot as 'anarchist'. In any case, the Directorate saw the uses of Italian 'patriotism' as purely instrumental. Prior to 1796, they did not recognize an Italian question, only an Austrian question; and even after Bonaparte's conquests they valued the acquisition of Italian territory above all as a means of bringing pressure on Austria to make peace and concede the Rhine frontier. Ideas of Italian unity would be an inconvenient obstacle to this policy. Realists argued that it was in any case in France's long-term interest to keep Italy weak, divided and dependent. It was easier to justify this policy, since there were in fact good reasons for scepticism about the feasibility of the patriots' programme and the extent of their support. At first, it suited Bonaparte to give a greater degree of encouragement to the cause of Italian liberty and independence, as part of a personal policy designed to free himself from the restrictions which the Directorate would have liked to impose on his sphere of action. But for him too the Italian patriots were a tool which should not be allowed to interfere with the requirements of *realpolitik*, or his own personal ambition. This became brutally obvious with the Treaty of Campoformio (18 October 1797), which surrendered Venice to Austria.

The discordance between French propaganda and French policy created a paradoxical situation. The first had encouraged the ideal of a free and united nation; the second was an obstacle to its realization. Italian patriots were forced either to redefine their aims or to contest their patrons. French help appeared vital if any kind of national independence was to be realized, and yet it might be regarded as an insidious threat. Patriots were torn between admiration for French models and the need to assert Italian autonomy. For a long time, the terms of the national question in Italy were to be essentially defined by this dilemma. The easiest way out was through a reaffirmation of Jacobin ideals. The abandonment of the cause of national liberation could then be perceived as merely an aspect of the general betrayal of the ideals of the revolution after Thermidor. This solution appealed most to those, like Buonarroti, for whom national independence was a means towards egalitarian social revolution, rather than the other way around; however, the logic of the situation in any case produced a natural alliance between Italian patriots and those who criticized the Directory from the Left. By 1798 the *Società dei Raggi* had organized an active conspiratorial network designed to work for Italian independence, in conjunction with the overthrow of the Directory by the Jacobins in France. Naturally, this made the patriots even more suspect in the eyes of the French government and its local representatives. Free speech was severely restricted. Many of the more outspoken patriots, including even a relatively moderate figure such as Gioia, paid for their independence with prison or exile; the journals which called for the union of Italy were suppressed. Yet French policy was sufficiently ambiguous and the Directory sufficiently unstable to keep alive the hopes of Italian revolutionaries. The overcoming of local differences was favoured by the presence in Milan of political exiles from Rome, Naples, Venice and other areas of Italy awaiting liberation. In alliance with elements in the French army and administration who saw the creation of new republics as an opportunity for plunder and profit, they formed an effective pressure group. If unitarian ideas were discouraged, the number of independent republics none the less multiplied, and this could be seen as a stage on the road towards national liberation. In particular, the foundation of the Roman Republic (February 1798) revived revolutionary hopes for national unity.[11] The cause of Italy was associated with the victory over papal 'fanaticism'. The liberation of Rome and the destruction of the Papacy as the dawn of a new era for humanity: this was to be the link between the French Revolution and the messianic nationalism of Mazzini. In 1798 Matteo Galdi published a treatise on 'The political and economic relations between free nations', which shows the survival of a somewhat utopian form of patriotism, pervaded by the optimistic ideals of the Revolution.[12]

It was an article of faith for Galdi that monarchs were responsible for all wars and conflicts between peoples. There was no reason therefore to fear French supremacy. Italy must fight alongside France not only for her political independence from Austria, but against the more subtle threat of the economic domination of the 'new Carthage', England. England had introduced a new system of commercial exploitation and subjugation through the power of wealth: 'the poor nation becomes the slave of the rich', and Naples, like Portugal, had in this way become an English dependency. Having destroyed English supremacy in the Mediterranean, France and Italy could share a common civilizing mission in Egypt and the Near East. Galdi's analysis strikingly anticipates that of twentieth-century movements in the Third World which have seen national independence and the struggle against economic imperialism as inseparable.[13] However, Galdi differs from them in his faith in free trade. For all its ingenuousness, Galdi's was one of the first attempts to define the strategic and economic functions of a future united Italy.

Even in 1796 we have seen that among the patriots there were gradualists who believed that unity would have to come by stages. As French reservations became apparent, the argument for this approach grew stronger. Rather than pursuing chimeras of unity it could be held that the most important task was to build up the Cisalpine Republic as a model of a self-governing Italian state. Just as unitarian nationalism tended to appeal to radicals, this policy tended to appeal to moderates. A pragmatic approach seemed to make possible collaboration with the French on at least limited objectives. The reward for faithful collaboration would be administrative autonomy and the stabilization of a viable state. Unfortunately, during the brief and tormented history of the first Cisalpine Republic even these objectives proved impossible to achieve. The autonomy of the Republic was reduced almost to zero by a series of coups organized in Paris. After the initial union with the Cispadane Republic, hopes for further territorial expansion and consolidation were frustrated. In an uncertain international situation, the mere existence of the Cisalpine Republic remained evidently provisional.

The brief and tragic history of the Republic of Naples touched on the national question only indirectly. Naples was easily the largest Italian state, and for geographical reasons it had the best chance of maintaining its independence, even if economically and militarily it was weaker than Piedmont. For this reason, although exiled Neapolitan patriots like Galdi had played a very important role in the development of an Italian nationalism, the national question was not of primary importance during the revolution of 1799. To some extent, indeed, one can say that the national question was never the decisive issue during the dramatic moments of the struggle between revolution and reaction in Naples (1820, 1848). In 1799 the 'nation' which served as the point of reference for most patriots was Naples, not Italy.

One important legacy of the Naples revolution – or rather its failure – to the national question was in the field of theory. Vincenzo Cuoco's famous concept of the 'passive revolution' for the first time succeeded in comprehending within a coherent intellectual framework the contradictions of revolutions which come about through foreign intervention and not through an autonomous internal process.[14] His criticism of dependence on abstract French models as a prime cause of the Republic's failure gave moderate politics a new national justification. It could be argued that a conservative policy which aimed to secure the active co-operation of the clergy and the nobility was not merely a falling-away from the democratic national ideal, but that on the contrary its divergence from French revolutionary models was a proof of its national authenticity. Cuoco should not be read as an Italian Burke, and his insistence on the importance of adapting institutions to local conditions was not intended as a counter-revolutionary argument against change. After 1799, he worked with the republican and Napoleonic regimes in northern Italy. He should rather be seen as the first (and certainly the most original) of the theorists of a 'middle way' which would try to reconcile revolution with tradition within a national framework.

1799 was a year of disasters. The Republic of Naples was swept away by the vast popular insurrection of the *Santa Fede*. Even in enlightened Tuscany, Catholic and royalist reaction triumphed with the armed bands of the *Viva Maria*. In Lombardy, the return of the Austrians was greeted with popular enthusiasm. Everywhere, the 'Jacobins' were the target of mass hostility. For the first time, the problem of the isolation of the intellectuals and the absence of popular support for Italian nationalism appeared in its full gravity. However, in one sense 1799, like 1797 (Campoformio), contributed to the growth of nationalism by bringing home the disastrous consequences of dependence on foreign support. The whole situation radically changed again with the coup of Brumaire and Marengo. The repression carried out by the Austrians in Milan and the Bourbons in Naples had convinced the intellectuals that French rule was the lesser evil. The situation in both France and Italy had stabilized, and there was no practicable alternative to the moderates' policy of collaboration with the First Consul. From now on, the national question became, at least in political terms, almost exclusively that of the forms and limits of Italian autonomy which Napoleon could be persuaded to concede. Napoleon was conscious of the advantages to be gained by creating a façade of independence. In 1802 he summoned an assembly of Cisalpine representatives (*Consulta*) to Lyons to approve the new constitution which he had had drafted by Roederer, the president of the French Council of State. This was the act of foundation of the first state to call itself Italian. Although Bonaparte had himself elected President, he nominated the widely respected Francesco Melzi d'Eril as Vice-president.

Melzi had cultivated the illusion that an independent north Italian state could play a neutral role as a buffer between France and Austria. The stabilization of the new state could only be achieved in the context of a restoration of the European balance of power, and of a period of peace. Instead he found himself responsible for the government of a satellite republic whose policy was subordinated to the needs of a militarist state. However, he could at least attempt to build up an efficient administration staffed exclusively by Italians. 'No, we are not yet a people and we must become one, and we must constitute ourselves a Nation, strong through unity . . . independent through true national sentiment. We do not have an ordered government; and we must create it. We do not have an organized administration and we must organize it.'[15]

Essentially, the Republic faced the same difficulties that the government of united Italy had to contend with sixty years later, when it annexed the south. Gradually, the resistance to conscription was overcome and an efficient army was created. The army became in some respects a genuine national institution, in spite of its total subordination to Napoleon's imperial aims. However, a state of almost constant war greatly intensified the human costs of conscription and ensured the permanence of peasant hostility to the Napoleonic regime. Popular identification with the *patria* was still a mirage.

Under the Empire, even the very limited autonomy which Melzi had been able to achieve was further reduced. In 1805 Marshal Duroc wrote to Napoleon's stepson and viceroy, Eugene de Beauharnais, 'if Milan is on fire . . . you must let Milan burn and wait for your orders'.[16] The Kingdom of Italy was to be governed on French principles and in French interests. Nowhere was this more apparent than in the economic field. Military costs and contributions to France continued to absorb more than half of a greatly expanded budget. The Republic had been partly successful in evading the commercial restrictions imposed by the renewed war with Britain, but after 1806 the creation of the Continental System and the British blockade put a stranglehold on Italian trade. By 1810–11, Italy had been deliberately reduced to the status of a 'continental colony' of France. The Italian market served as a unique outlet for the exports of French manufacturers, deprived of overseas markets.[17]

There was no place for national self-determination in Napoleon's imperial vision. The Kingdom of Italy was allowed to annex new territory, in the Veneto, the Tyrol and the Marche; but the smaller independent states were absorbed piecemeal into the French Empire.[18] They were governed directly from Paris by French prefects, and only Napoleon's family policy preserved a vestige of independent existence in the little courts of Turin and Florence, headed by his sisters Paolina and Elisa, and their husbands. Naples was different; even Napoleon had to realize that it could not be governed from Paris, and Murat, who succeeded Joseph on the throne in 1808, was more successful than most of Napoleon's vassals in cultivating his independence. There was not much logic or feeling of permanence about Napoleon's territorial arrangements. On the other hand, his powerful belief in rational, centralized administration left a lasting mark. Napoleon was a unifier by temperament and conviction. This was apparent in the programme he had sketched out for the Republic of Italy when he became president: 'You have only particular laws and you need general laws. Your people has only local customs and it is necessary that you acquire national habits.'[19] In fact, not just the Kingdom of Italy, but all the territories directly or indirectly controlled by Napoleon came to share a broadly similar system of administration. The Napoleonic legal codes were extended to Italy and Naples with little modification, and the same was true of the prefectoral system. Taxation and the public debt were reformed and simplified. The Napoleonic reforms consolidated the new elite of bureaucrats, magistrates, legal and financial experts and statisticians which had already begun to form during the Enlightenment. The gains in efficiency and state power which they made possible were so great that both the reforms and their executors in large part survived the Restoration. In the end, the Napoleonic system emerged as the dominant model for the construction of the modern, unified national state. Undoubtedly, the Napoleonic legacy in this way furthered the solution of the national question in political and administrative terms; but were the results at the social and cultural level equally positive? Certainly, the Napoleonic period posed the foundations for that 'unconditional unitarianism' and uniformity of response to diverse local conditions which has often been seen as the besetting sin of the new Italian state. 'General laws' did not necessarily produce 'national habits', and in their absence the former's significance might be distorted.

Napoleon was remarkably successful in controlling and manipulating Italian national sentiment. The unitarians posed no serious threat until the Empire started to dissolve, and even then their influence on events proved only marginal. As in France, Napoleon recognized 'the men of learning' as one of the three social groups whose support was essential for the stability of his regime, and through an adept policy of co-optation and symbolic concessions he was able to win over many former patriots. Dissent was controlled by a rigorous system of censorship and police repression. The official press, often managed directly by the prefects, achieved a degree of stultifying uniformity and adulation of the ruler not to be matched until fascism. Nevertheless, the Napoleonic regime may have actually encouraged the growth of a feeling of Italian national identity. Both the positive attempts to win consensus by appealing to 'national' symbols, and the realities of French supremacy combined to work in this direction. 'Aesopism', or the masking of political opposition by cultural debate, contributed to the formation of another dimension of the national question. The defence of the Italian language was no longer an academic question now that strenuous attempts were being made to impose the use of French as the only official language in the departments annexed to France.

In a sense, the reaction against French cultural imperialism[20] was nothing new. Literary nationalism in Italy was far older than political nationalism, and, as elsewhere in Europe, it had originated in a defence of native originality against the universalizing claims of French Classicism.[21] In the later eighteenth century this literary response had fused with a more diffuse reaction against the *mœurs* of fashionable French society, and had often been reinforced by conservative doubts about the radical, egalitarian and anti-religious ideas of the *philosophes*. However, now that the dominance of France was political, military and economic as well as cultural, the two strands of nationalism could become intertwined. Napoleon's frustration of the national aspirations which the French Revolution had aroused lent a new edge to cultural polemic and the search for national identity. Yet, it is important to realize, the peculiarity of Italy's situation and history would make any assimilation of this process to the paradigm case of German Romantic nationalism decisively misleading. The Italians could reject academic Classicism, but they could not reject the classical tradition. Furthermore, Romanticism in Italy did not, for its chief representatives, imply a repudiation of the heritage of the Enlightenment.

In the age of nationalism, poets enjoyed a peculiarly privileged role as the guardians and even creators of national identity. Nowhere was this more true than in Italy. After all, Dante was the founding father of the Italian language. The diffusion of the Italian language had been the work of a literary and humanistic elite, unassisted by a powerful central state, as in France, or by a vernacular reformation, as in Germany. Dante and the other great poets of the past were elevated to the status of patron saints in the national revolutionary cult.[22] Even before that, cultural nationalism had already become a political question with Alfieri. Alfieri's revival of tragedy was at one and the same time a vehicle for the protest against tyranny and the achievement of a new, 'virile' form of expression in conscious reaction to cosmopolitan *politesse*. This went with an idealization of the reserves of primitive, even barbaric, energy and courage to be found in the Italian race. This is summed up in his famous expression of faith in the soundness of the 'pianta-uomo' (man-plant) in Italy, and his appeal to the proof of 'the sublime crimes which every day are being committed'.[23] As a Piedmontese, Alfieri was particularly conscious of the cultural hegemony of France; high culture in Piedmont was bilingual, and Alfieri chose Italian. Like Manzoni later, he made a pilgrimage to Florence in search of linguistic purification. His idea of the nation recognized language as the decisive criterion; it is significant that even when most hostile to the French he recognized that Savoy should belong to them. 'As they both say *oui*, they are and deserve to be the same nation.'[24]

Alfieri's republicanism did not survive contact with the reality of revolutionary Paris. Forced to flee in great danger with his mistress, the Countess of Albany, he became a decided counter-revolutionary and towards the end of his life even identified with the Piedmontese legitimism he had earlier so decisively rejected. He published a violent anti-French tract, the *Misogallo*. For these reasons he could be claimed as a precursor by twentieth-century nationalists and fascists. But, aside from anachronism, this ignores the real influence of Alfieri. It was not the second, reactionary, Alfieri who inspired the next generation. In spite of his current views, Alfieri's tragedies were the focus of patriotic enthusiasm during the *triennio giacobino*; they were the model of a new national, civic drama. It was the patriotic rebel and not the reactionary who became the object of a cult. However, at a later date his warnings against the French and his claims for the vitality of the Italian character were congenial to those who saw in national independence a third way which could avoid both revolution and reaction. He was particularly influential among the young Piedmontese nobles of the *Accademia della Concordia* like Cesare Balbo and Santorre di Santarosa. Defenders of the Piedmontese monarchy and military tradition, they none the less saw the need to abandon the heritage of Absolutism; inspired by the Prussia of 1813, they aimed to base state and army on a genuine national spirit. Sooner or later, this implied the choice of going beyond liberalism and domestic reform and persuading the monarchy to assume the leadership of the fight for Italian independence and even unity.[25]

In the years of Bonaparte's first conquests, no one experienced and expressed the alternation between hope and disillusionment with more

drama than the young Greco-Venetian poet Ugo Foscolo. In exile
from Venice in the spring of 1797, he wrote an ode 'To Bonaparte the
Liberator'. During the brief existence of the 'democratized' Venetian
municipality he became a prominent member of the patriotic *Società di
Pubblica Istruzione*. The news of Campoformio shocked him into a
display of histrionic violence: 'armed with a dagger and making
horrible exclamations and contortions, he swore to strike to the heart
of the perfidious Bonaparte'.[26] It is unlikely that he seriously contemplated tyrannicide; but he did become a conspicuous member of the
group of advanced unitarian critics of French rule in the Cisalpine
Republic. His 1799 *Discorso su l'Italia* shows his strict faithfulness to
the Jacobin model, complete with National Convention, Committee of
Public Safety and *levée en masse*.[27] But by 1802 no such illusions were
possible, and he could only turn again to Bonaparte as 'the father of
the peoples'. Liberty was redefined more modestly as 'not having
(except Bonaparte) any magistrate who is not Italian, any captain
who is not Italian'.[28] Disappointed of his hopes of political advancement, Foscolo became a symbol of the writer who refuses to compromise his independence for the sake of official favour, in contrast to
men like Vincenzo Monti, the poet laureate of Napoleonic Italy.
Monti gave Foscolo the friendly advice that he should observe the
'custom' of adding 'a couple of words' of praise of Napoleon or Eugene
to his writings.[29] In this climate, Foscolo's stated preference for the
freedom of Homer over the servility of Virgil and Horace had a clear
contemporary significance. In reaction to Napoleon's identification
with Imperial Rome, Italian writers could only express their opposition by repudiating the Roman heritage. Cuoco developed a full-
blown myth of an autochthonous Italian civilization, identified with
the Etruscans, which had preceded and influenced both Greece and
Rome.[30] The later revival of the 'idea of Rome' obscures the fact that
in its origins the Risorgimento was predominantly anti-Roman. After
1815, the interest in primitive Italic antiquity was largely superseded
by the new attention paid to the free communes of the Middle Ages as
the true nursery of Italian nationality.[31] The Genevan historian
Sismondi wrote his great history of the Italian Republics with the aim
of combating the Napoleonic system, even though he recognized the
positive aspects of Napoleon's regime in Italy.[32] Pre-Roman or post-
Roman: in both cases the origin of the Italian nation was divorced
from Rome as a reaction against French imperialism.

Already in Foscolo nationalism expresses itself in the new language
of Romantic sensibility. Passion and patriotism are associated in
opposition to 'cold and calculating' reason. In Italy, Foscolo did more

than anyone else to create the new figure of the Romantic exile, imbued with melancholy.[33] Foscolo spent the last twelve years of his life in England, where he succumbed tragically to debt and disappointment, and in retrospect[34] this gave his patriotism an added poignancy. But Foscolo also invented the category of internal exile: 'all Italians are exiles in Italy'. Above all, in his poetic masterpiece, the *Sepolcri*, Foscolo instituted a new cult of the nation. The occasion which gave rise to the poem was highly significant. The French government had proposed, for utilitarian reasons of public health, that burials should no longer be allowed in churches. This, for Foscolo, was to deprive the Italians of the continuity of their collective memory.[35] The tombs of the great Italians of the past in Santa Croce in Florence were to inspire a religious sense of reverence for the national past. They were to be, literally, a shrine for the celebration of the religion of the nation. Italians should make pilgrimages to Santa Croce and kneel before the tombs. History, conceived in monumental terms, was to furnish the scriptural texts for the national cult through the commemoration of great men. The Romantic pathos of tombs fused with patriotism and the memory of the classical heritage in a peculiarly Italian blend. Alfieri was sanctified as the latest of the great and the first prophet of the new Italy. Similarly, Mazzini was later to give a definitive sanction to Foscolo's status in the apostolic succession of patriotic bards, among other things devoting himself to the collection of his literary 'relics'.

LIBERALISM, REPUBLICANISM AND THE RESTORATION, 1814–1831

The activity of the unitarian secret societies continued under the Napoleonic regimes. As hopes in Napoleon faded, patriots started to look for foreign assistance, particularly from England. With the arrival of Lord William Bentinck in Sicily as commander of the British occupation forces and minister to the Bourbon court of Palermo, the idea of British support for a national rebellion against Napoleonic rule in Italy started to appear as a concrete possibility. Bentinck saw his pressure on the Bourbons to grant a constitution to Sicily as a means towards this end. Spain had risen against Napoleon: so why should Italy not do so? 'The Italians are an intelligent people. They have long desired a constitution which should give them national liberty. They will never submit to be transferred from one despotism to another.'[36] Unfortunately, Bentinck found that Italian discontent stopped some way short of rebellion.[37] It was only when the Napoleonic Empire was in evident dissolution that Bentinck was able to act. In March 1814 a small force of English and Italians landed in Tuscany; the Italians carried a flag with the motto 'Italian union – national independence'. But the ingenuous Bentinck, a genuine and idealistic supporter of Italian independence, had failed to realize that his government's interest in the question was purely instrumental. He was sharply called to order by Castlereagh: 'It is not insurrection we now want in Italy or elsewhere – we want disciplined force under sovereigns we can trust.'[38] Italy was a vital element in the European balance of power, and it suited Britain that it should be under Austrian control. The admirers of English freedom, particularly in Milan, who had been encouraged to believe that it might be possible to achieve independence under English protection were rapidly disillusioned. None the less, the idea of a liberal nationalism which would take England and not France as a political model had taken root among the younger generation of the nobility in northern Italy during the last years of the Napoleonic Empire.

No loyal Austrian could fail to desire the recovery of Lombardy. Nevertheless, the Austrian commander, Field Marshal Bellegarde, warned Vienna that only the concession of a large measure of home rule could appease the strong national sentiment of the Italians. 'Italy must be treated always as a body completely different from the other lands of the Monarchy.'[39] Metternich at first inclined towards Bellegarde's view. He thought that the efficiency of Austrian government was appreciated, but none the less admitted that discontent was widespread. 'National consciousness must be met half-way.'[40] He argued for the appointment of a viceroy with real powers, whose court could serve as a magnet for the nobility, and the institution of a special department of Italian affairs (*Hofkanzlei*) at Vienna. But Metternich was defeated by the Emperor Francis I's obstinacy and by the renewal of the drive towards bureaucratic centralization which had started in the time of Joseph II. Although Francis did agree to appoint his brother as viceroy, he insisted that his powers should be merely symbolic. 'It is not my will that the viceroy of the Lombardo-Veneto kingdom should delve into administrative affairs and thus infringe on the governor's efficient conduct of affairs.' Worse still, the Italian monopoly on posts in the local administration was infringed, and functionaries of German origin colonized the higher ranks of the administration and the judiciary. Universities and schools had to conform to a centrally imposed curriculum.[41] In the eighteenth century, Habsburg rule had been associated with a policy of Enlightened reform. Under the Restoration, although the Austrian administration of the Lombardo-Veneto was still more efficient than that of the rest of Italy, its obtuse bureaucratic uniformity lacked any similar justification. Metternich recognized that 'the moral influence' of literature had become a 'mighty lever for governments', but the days of fruitful co-operation between Habsburg officials and the *lumi* of Milan were over. Censorship, police control and the restriction of employment opportunities all combined to coagulate the spirit of opposition among the new intellectual and professional classes, whose growth, ironically enough, had originated with the Josephine reforms.

Elsewhere in the peninsula, the Austrian spy system, although probably more feared than really effective, contributed to the feeling of oppression. Italy was the object of a 'Metternich doctrine' which claimed the right of Austria to intervene to restore monarchic order wherever it was threatened. In order to put Austrian hegemony on a sound footing and at the same time concede something to Italian desires for recognition, Metternich had tried at first to organize a Confederation similar to the German.[42] But Piedmont saw this as a menace to her recently regained independence, and the papal Secretary of State, Cardinal Consalvi, also raised objections. The idea of an Italian Confederation in fact revived the medieval problem of the conflicting rights of Emperor and Pope. Here were to be found the seeds of the 'neo-Guelph' programme of a Confederation under papal leadership and excluding Austria.

For the moment, however, insurrection seemed to be the only practicable way of loosening the Austrian grip on the peninsula. The continuity of the Franco-Italian Jacobin conspiratorial tradition was remarkable; the post-1815 secret societies most probably derive from the French republican sects whose networks were extended to Italy by dissident officers and bureaucrats of the Napoleonic regimes. They absorbed the faithful remnants of the Italian Jacobin unitarians. The relationship of the *Carbonari* and other secret societies of the epoch to Italian nationalism is problematic. In a sense, they had both wider and narrower aims than a solution of the national question. On the one hand, the arch-conspirator Buonarroti and other Jacobin diehards still saw Italian unity as merely a stage on the road to the universal social revolution. Buonarroti was inspired by the Masonic model whereby members were progressively initiated into the secrets of the organization as they attained higher grades in the hierarchy. At the centre of the conspiratorial network, Buonarroti and a few intimates alone knew that communism was the real aim. The lower grades of his Society of Sublime Perfect Masters only had to accept deism, popular sovereignty and democracy; the Perfect Masters were in turn supposed to act as an elite or advance-guard, who should lead, manipulate and co-ordinate the activities of other organizations, whose members would be instructed only in the aims of independence and constitutional reform. On the other hand, the *Carbonari* of southern Italy, who were more successful in winning mass support than any other Italian revolutionary organization of the nineteenth century, were in the main more interested in achieving a democratic constitution in Naples than in the national question.[43]

It is nevertheless in the Restoration period that the Italian national movement came to see itself as one among a number of similar movements, all working together for the cause of national liberation and democracy. The example of Spain was important here; Spain had not only given the example of national resistance to Napoleon, but had given itself a democratic constitution, based on that of the French Republic of 1791, before the deviation of the Terror. The Spanish revolution of 1820 directly inspired the Neapolitan revolution, and the *Carbonari*'s key demand was for the Spanish constitution. The technique of the Spanish revolution also seemed suitable for Italy. The quickest way to achieve a revolution is by subverting the army, and in Italy it was easier to subvert the post-Napoleonic armies than to organize civil society against the state. The example of Spain was succeeded by that of Greece; here, Christian solidarity and classical reminiscences lent a particular pathos to the struggle for national freedom against Asiatic despotism.[44] The Italian solidarity with Greece and Spain was active; Italians were among the earliest and most numerous of the Philhellenes, and many Italian exiles fought at one time or another for the liberal cause in Spain, and also in Portugal. It was in the later phases of the struggles of the Spanish- and Portuguese-speaking world on both sides of the Atlantic that the most important military cadres of the Risorgimento were formed. Garibaldi acquired his unique military skills in the obscure and bitter wars of Rio Grande and Uruguay. In both cases, Garibaldi was fighting for the independence of a small republic against a large monarchist or dictatorial state. In fighting for the freedom of others, the exiles were convinced that they were fighting also for their own.

In Italy itself, however, military conspiracy brought disappointing results. The Austrians proved better at co-ordinating reaction than the revolutionaries were at co-ordinating resistance. Unlike the *Carbonari* of Naples, those of Piedmont, with a much weaker popular and military base, could not hope to win any lasting success unless the revolution spread to other regions of Italy, especially Lombardy. Another secret society, the *Federazione Italiana*, in fact succeeded in linking the young liberal aristocrats of Lombardy, led by Confalonieri, with the young nobles and officers of Piedmont, led by Santarosa. The Piedmontese conspirators hoped to win over the royal prince Charles Albert (second in line in the succession to the crown) and through him to persuade the king, Victor Emmanuel I, not only to grant a constitution but to lead a war of liberation against Austria. In March 1821 the moment looked favourable because a large part of the Austrian army was engaged in the expedition to suppress the revolution in Naples. But Victor Emmanuel abdicated rather than yield to the conspirators' demands, Charles Albert played them false, and the sentiment of the rank and file of the army turned out to be more monarchist than national. Neapolitan resistance proved unexpectedly weak, and the Austrians had no difficulty in sending reinforcements to support the loyalist troops in Piedmont. Over the next three years, the Austrians broke up the conspiratorial networks in Lombardy and arrested their leaders, except for those who had escaped abroad. The failure of the revolutions of 1820–1 shifted the centre of gravity of the movement for national independence, with the formation of important communities of political exiles. The largest number settled in London, thanks to the tolerance of the British government. England became an important point of reference, and this favoured the growth of a liberal tendency, opposed to Buonarroti's egalitarian extremism. In 1823 the London group of exiles were able to unite behind a programme of 'Liberty, Unity and Independence', leaving the difficult question of the form of government to be settled by a future constituent assembly.

For most of Italian opinion, however, France was still the decisive country. The July Revolution, therefore, could not fail to have enormous effect, especially since it was followed by the outbreak of national revolutions against foreign rule in Belgium and Poland. It was widely believed that if revolution broke out in Italy, France would not allow it to be suppressed again by Austria. Italian conspirators were already in contact with Lafayette and the French liberal opposition before 1830. But after some initial doubt the new regime of Louis-Philippe decided that war with Austria would be too risky from both an internal and an international point of view, and this, more than anything else, doomed to failure the revolutions which broke out in Modena and Bologna in spring 1831. This failure had two effects on the conception of the national question. The first was to revive in an acute form the problem of the ideological and political subordination of Italian patriotism to French republicanism. In the short term, the result of the 1830 revolution had been to revive the Jacobin tendency represented by Buonarroti at the expense of the more moderate tendency of the London exiles. Even in Paris, the majority of the exiles at first favoured the idea of a constitutional monarchy, in the hopes of winning the support of the Orleanist regime. This was also the line taken by Ciro Menotti, the organizer of the Modena revolution. However, by January 1831 Buonarroti's conspiratorial skill had enabled him to set up a secret triumvirate to direct the most important exile organization.[45] The failure of the revolutions in central Italy discredited the policy of moderation and collaboration with the French government. But this did not yet mean an end of faith in France. Rather, it was followed by a transition period similar to that of 1796–9, in which there was an alliance between Italian patriots and the revolutionary opposition in France. On this occasion the alliance was facilitated by a more understanding attitude on the part of the French opposition towards Italian nationalism. Both republicans and Bonapartists saw the agitation for a war on behalf of Italian independence as a way of destabilizing the Orleanist regime and relaunching the revolutionary process in Europe.[46] But, as hopes for a further revolution in France faded, the argument that Italians should rely on their own efforts instead of looking to France for leadership became more persuasive.

The other, long-term, effect of the failure of the revolutions of 1831 was to drive a wedge between liberals and democrats. The former abandoned secrecy for 'conspiracy in the light of day', through journalism and the organization of civil society. This meant playing down the objectives of unity and independence and working within the framework of the existing states, including the Austrian Empire. For this reason, the democrats accused the liberals of having virtually abandoned the national cause. The controversy became particularly acute in Piedmont, where both sides charged the other with a lack of realism. The liberals could argue that the outcome of 1821 had shown that the active and voluntary support of the House of Savoy was necessary if the movement for independence were to succeed; the democrats could argue that it was quite unrealistic to continue to put any hope in the monarchy, and in particular in the treacherous Charles Albert, who succeeded to the throne in April 1831. At the most, he might offer reforms, but collaboration signified, in Mazzini's words, remaining 'Piedmontese always, Italians never'.[47] Mazzini's famous open letter in June 1831 appealing to Charles Albert to take up the struggle for independence was designed to clarify the situation; if he refused, as Mazzini had every reason to believe he would, then it would be seen that nationalists had no alternative but to be republicans.[48]

THE EMERGENCE OF YOUNG ITALY

The emergence of Mazzini and of Young Italy must be placed in the context described in the last section. Mazzini's participation in the intellectual debate between liberals, republicans and socialists in France was intense. The break between Mazzini and the Jacobin tradition was neither as early nor as complete as he later claimed. In the first period of his exile, he sympathized with Blanqui and admired Buonarroti. He accepted the need for a transitional dictatorship to be exercised by a 'committee of public safety' during the revolutionary war. Nor did the original creation of Young Italy represent a clean break with the model of organization and the practices of the secret societies. Most important, Mazzini still accepted the idea of a move-ment involving different grades of membership and levels of knowl-edge. He conceived of Young Italy as a higher-level, co-ordinating association, which would work to achieve the union of other secret societies under its own direction. This was not so very different from the idea behind Buonarroti's latest creation, the *Veri Italiani*. In fact, the short-lived union of the two associations did not prevent a struggle for hegemony between the two leaders and their followers. It was only in the course of this contest that Mazzini's repudiation of the sectarian model took shape, and that romantic patriotism and Jacobin socialism finally diverged. In breaking with Buonarroti, Mazzini dissociated nationalism from all ideas of communism or class struggle; the people was 'the aggregate of all classes'. He rejected the right of a revolution-ary dictatorship to speak for, and indeed 'form', the people. Universal suffrage was a necessary condition of national sovereignty.[49] Finally, he proclaimed that France had lost its role of revolutionary leadership for good; the 'initiative' had passed to Italy, and only a new, truly Italian association could promote it.[50] At first thrown on the defensive by Buonarroti's customary tactics of penetration and control by a determined minority, Mazzini eventually emerged the victor through his eloquence and skill in winning converts by open propaganda. The repudiation of the sectarian model undoubtedly entailed a loss of conspiratorial efficiency, as the uniformly dismal results of Mazzini's attempts at revolution were to testify. But Mazzini's methods brought a new simplicity and clarity to the hitherto tangled undergrowth of nationalist politics. They established Young Italy on the foundation of clear, unambiguous, easily understood and publicly proclaimed principles, and they demanded a new intensity of moral commitment. Mazzini's own example of complete personal disinterestedness and his extraordinary tenacity in the face of defeat did more than anything else to maintain a tenuous but unbreakable thread of continuity between the various phases of the nationalist movement over the next thirty years.

Mazzini's intransigent unitarianism owed much to the Jacobin tradition. His first formulations were directly influenced by Buonarroti's polemic against federalism. He retained the insistence that the popular sovereignty of the nation must be indivisible, and the rejection of all forms of federalism as devices for prolonging the hegemony of local ruling classes. Mazzini's mystic belief in the unity and sanctity of the popular will was not, however, just rewarmed Rousseau, but drew on new sources. On one decisive issue Mazzini distanced himself with great effect from the Jacobin tradition: his repudiation of terror. In his one brief experience of actual revolutionary government, the Roman Republic of 1849, Mazzini was to prove that this was a sincere and deeply felt moral conviction. But Mazzini was no liberal, prepared to admit that the truth might emerge from the clash of opposing ideologies or interests. The people still had to be 'formed'; and faced with the reality of a divided Italy what radical unitarian could think otherwise? Mazzini found the solution to the problem in the doctrines of Saint-Simon and his followers, in their ideal of a civic faith which would overcome in a new synthesis the sterile eighteenth-century antithesis between reason and orthodox belief.[51] The new religion of Humanity was to rest on the foundation of the historically revealed law of progress. It was in Saint-Simonianism, also, that he found the specific idea of the end of the era of individualism and the beginning of a new era of collective behaviour. Before 1830, Mazzini had been much influenced by Guizot and by the eclecticism of Victor Cousin, who argued that European civilization was in an epoch of transition; but his disgust at their political cowardice and conservatism in the post-revolutionary period led him to reject their ideas and to proclaim the new era of the collective.

If Mazzini outdid all previous propagandists for Italian nationality and succeeded in combining a universalist perspective with a full recognition of Italy's cultural and intellectual independence, this too was made possible by his absorption of the heritage of Romanticism. He learned from Mme de Staël that each nation must find its own original form of expression. But literature was not the expression of an immutable national character; it reflected the evolution of a nation's history and the nature of its institutions. By taking this position Mazzini was able to avoid the alternative between the sterile defence of a static Classicism and the admission of an intrinsic Italian inferiority.[52] Without liberty or independence, Italian literature could only be an erudite, academic and courtly pastime: 'useful and national, never'. However, in modern times the power of public opinion gave literature a new role: it could precede and help to shape political development. Contemporary writers must 'explore the needs of the peoples', and study 'social man in action'. Intellect must be united with enthusiasm, philosophy with poetry.[53] Then Italian literature (and music) could inspire and direct the revival of the nation. Also important was Mazzini's concrete experience as an exile of the brotherhood of oppressed peoples; the idea of Young Europe was born out of his contacts with Polish exiles in particular. There was nothing exclusive about Mazzini's nationalism: for him, the different national questions were essentially interdependent. Each nation had to discover its own special interests, aptitudes and functions in order to perform its particular 'mission' in the general cause of humanity. When all nations had been freed, a 'United States of Europe' would become possible and desirable. Mazzini was accepted as the prophet of nationalism not only in Italy but throughout Europe, and as far away as India.[54]

However, it is true that Mazzini did not resist the temptation to assign Italy a higher and more universal role than that of other nations; if Germany represented thought, and France action, it was Italy's mission to unite the two, and thereby to restore 'moral unity to Europe, and through Europe to humanity'. There was a Messianic streak in Mazzini's thought, which responded both to something in his temperament and to a deeply felt need of the epoch. The centrality of Italy's 'mission' was justified by an argument which certainly, again, originates in the period of the French Revolution: it was the struggle against the Papacy which gave the cause of Italian liberation its universal significance. Only Rome could give the word for 'modern unity', because only Rome could end the 'old unity'.[55] The completion of Italian unity entailed the destruction not only of the Papacy's temporal authority, but of its spiritual authority as well. It would bring about a secular millennium in which superstition would be finally banished from the earth and the 'regenerated' nations would rise again from the dead, united in harmony by the common cult of Humanity. If many even of Mazzini's followers were not impressed by the complex architecture of his secular religion, one should nevertheless note the deep resonance for Italian nationalism of the myth of rebirth, expressed in the very name of the Risorgimento.

Mazzini's nationalism was essentially democratic. He rejected both the elitism of the moderates and the belief in revolutionary dictatorship of the Jacobin tradition. He added universal suffrage as a fourth prerequisite to the triad of Union, Independence and Liberty. The nation must be co-terminous with the people, and without democracy national unity would be an empty formula. It followed also that true independence could only come about as a result of a people's own efforts. Reliance on foreign intervention was to be avoided not just because it had proved ineffective. National consciousness could only be formed through active popular participation in the struggle for independence. How was this to be achieved? Military conspiracy was not enough; it could start a national revolution, but not bring it to fruition. The role of the secret societies must be to prepare the conditions for the outbreak of a people's war of national liberation. Mazzini's conception of 'the war of insurrection' was decisively influenced by his encounter with the Piedmontese exile Carlo Bianco di St Jorioz, one of the military conspirators of 1821. Bianco had written a manual on guerrilla warfare. He drew his examples from a number of struggles for national independence, including those of the United States, Greece and Poland. But the principal source of his theories was undoubtedly the great Spanish war of 1808–13.[56]

The efficiency of guerrilla warfare, not only in military but in political terms, as an instrument for making a nation, has been proved repeatedly. Unfortunately, there were severe problems about putting Mazzini's conception of a 'people's war' into effect in nineteenth-century Italy. A guerilla war could not succeed without the support of the peasants. Mazzini saw this more clearly than Bianco; but he had no convincing practical programme for bringing it about. The propaganda of Young Italy was almost exclusively confined to the towns, and most of its members were recruited from among students, the professional middle classes, and even the aristocracy. Strangely enough, both Bianco and Mazzini underrated one decisive lesson of the Spanish experience: that the backing of the clergy had been indispensable for winning the peasants to the national cause. The Italian republicans were never successful in overcoming the cultural gap between town and country. The populist urge to rediscover rural life and folk culture, which was so strong a component of many nineteenth-century nationalisms, was largely lacking in Italy.[57]

CATHOLICISM, THE NEO-GUELPHS AND THE MONARCHY, 1830–1848

One of the general tendencies of Romantic thought had been to revalue the importance of faith as opposed to reason. For Mazzini, it had been axiomatic that Italy could only be united by a new faith in

Humanity and progress. But was there not another way? The return to religion, in reaction to the excesses of revolutionary rationalism, did not necessarily imply the acceptance of the Restoration settlement and its underlying principles. The revived interest in Catholicism could meld with the effort to establish a national identity founded on a historical continuity of tradition. It was Manzoni who first argued, in his *Discorso sopra alcuni punti della storia longobardica* (1822), that this continuity could only be realized if attention was focused on the conquered Roman population instead of the conquering barbarians.[58] It was not, however, the classical tradition of Imperial Rome which had survived and which had civilized the barbarians, but that of Christian Rome. The hero and heroine of Manzoni's great novel, the *Promessi Sposi*, are symbols of the Christian people's capacity to survive oppression through faith in God's providence. Cesare Balbo took up the theme in his very influential historical writings of the 1840s: Christian nations can sicken but not perish, because Christianity provides the moral resources needed to overcome defeat. He added that Italy had lost its independence when Renaissance decadence had taken the place of the Christian spirit of the Middle Ages. It was possible, so to speak, to appeal from the present Papacy, the heir of the Counter-Reformation, to the great Popes of the Middle Ages, who had combined the defence of religion with that of Italian liberty, allying with the free communes to resist the German emperors. This was the basic idea of the 'neo-Guelph' school of historians, in opposition to the 'neo-Ghilbellines', who argued that the emperors had represented the cause of Italian unity, against its perennial enemies, 'municipalism' and the Church. The great advantage of neo-Guelphism (which attracted much superior literary and historical talents) was that it seemed to provide historical legitimation for a reconciliation between the Church and the nation. The practical issue was put bluntly by Niccolò Tommaseo in his *Dell'Italia* (1835): only the priests knew how to speak to the masses. Neo-Guelphism became a political programme in the writings of the Piedmontese priest Vincenzo Gioberti. Gioberti took up an idea which had surfaced on various occasions without much practical effect, that of an Italian Confederation under the presidency of the Pope. He rejected Mazzini's ideas of popular initiative as wholly impracticable; 'the Italian people is a desire and not a fact, a germ not a plant; but the Italian princes are something real, and their interests, wealth and armies . . . are forces which do not exist only in the mind'.[59] The Confederation should be formed by the union of the existing states. Gioberti combined an extremely cautious and conservative political programme with a highly successful appeal to Italian national pride, flattered by the claim to moral and civil 'primacy'.[60] In fact, he turned Mazzini's idea of Italy's mission on its head: Italy's primacy in European civilization was to be restored not by the destruction of the Papacy, but by its reconciliation with the forces of nationality and progress. Gioberti's ideas appeared to have been triumphantly vindicated when Pius IX was elected Pope in 1846. The election of an anti-Austrian and presumedly liberal Pope gave an immense stimulus to the national movement. Between 1846 and the outbreak of the 1848 revolution in Paris, Italy seemed to be in the forefront of the movement for change in Europe. It seemed as if a strange synthesis had been achieved betwen Gioberti's idea of a nation led by the Pope and Mazzini's idea of a people's war. But, of course, it was a brief moment. Even if Pius IX had really been a liberal, which, of course, he was not, it would have been unrealistic to suppose that as the head of a universal Church he could commit himself to a national war against a Catholic state. The neo-Guelph dream vanished when Pius IX withdrew his support from the war against Austria in the papal allocution of 29 April 1848. However, the liberal-Catholic movement left a lasting impact. It had made the movement for national independence (though not unity) respectable and divorced it from the image of republican, anti-clerical revolution. A significant section of the upper classes of Italian society had been won over to the conviction that it was possible to be a good Catholic and a good Italian at the same time, whatever the Pope might say.

The 1840s saw the emergence into the light of day of a third programme alongside Mazzini's revolutionary unitarianism and Gioberti's Catholic confederation: that of an alliance between the national movement and the Piedmontese monarchy. As this was the winning solution, it has acquired an air of predestination. It is worth emphasizing, therefore, that for a long time it appeared implausible. After 1821 Piedmont, under the reign of Carlo Felice, and even in the first years of Charles Albert, acquired the reputation of being one of the most reactionary and bigoted states in Italy. It appeared neither likely nor desirable that such a state should assume the leadership of the movement for national independence. However, by 1840 internal economic and administrative reforms had improved the image of the monarchy, and there were signs that a return to the traditional Piedmontese policy aim of expansion in northern Italy was being actively considered. The appearance of Gioberti's *Primato* inspired Cesare Balbo to reply. Although he was on good terms with Gioberti and regarded his book as a fundamental contribution to the national cause, he was critical of his lack of realism. 'Before aiming at primacies we should aim at parity.'[61] Independence was the only feasible and legitimate objective; 'we have no hegemonies to conquer'.[62] The cause of independence had been compromised in the past by being associated with liberty and the 'puerile' idea of unity. Instead, Balbo reinterpreted the territorial growth of Piedmont in the eighteenth century as the first sign of a genuine Italian political revival. As a strong military monarchy on the periphery of the peninsula, Piedmont had the manifest destiny to be Italy's 'Macedonia or Prussia'. He was proud of the Piedmontese army, and insisted on the need to restore the honour of the Italians through war. Yet, strangely, he did not envisage Piedmont taking the lead in a war to expel Austria from Italy. Rather, Piedmont was to take political advantage of the expected European crisis over the partition of the Ottoman Empire to bring pressure on Austria to relinquish her Italian possessions in return for territory in the Balkans. For all its air of diplomatic realism, Balbo's *Speranze d'Italia* was not a great improvement on Gioberti in its solution of the Austrian problem. It offered no programme of action, and had the great defect of pinning the hopes of the national movement on a rather unlikely set of external circumstances. However, the book was of great importance none the less in selling the idea of Piedmont's leadership of the movement for national independence both to the monarchy and its advisers, and to moderate liberal circles elsewhere in Italy. In 1845 Massimo d'Azeglio succeeded in creating a liaison between Charles Albert and the secret societies of the Romagna, and in extracting from him a promise to intervene on behalf of the Italian cause when the time was ripe. Charles Albert had no sympathy for liberalism, and he only reluctantly granted a constitution in February 1848 after revolution had already broken out in Palermo and Naples. However, this last-minute and involuntary concession resolved the internal crisis of the state and gave Piedmont a new status in the eyes of liberal opinion. The way was open for Charles Albert to assume the leadership of the independence movement, and when Milan rebelled the union of Lombardy and Piedmont seemed at first almost a foregone conclusion. But the *rapprochement* of the monarchy and the national movement was too sudden and left too many problems unsolved to serve as the basis for an effective and sincere co-operation.[63]

ECONOMIC CHANGE AND 'NATIONAL OPINION', 1830–1848

It was in the period between 1830 and 1848 that economic growth first decisively started to affect the perspective and prospects of unification. Piedmont – hitherto one of the more backward Italian states from the point of view of legislation and social attitudes – began to participate in the general transformation of the European economy. This helped to make its claims to leadership more plausible. Piedmontese commercial rivalry with Austria became an important motive for hostility, and for union with Lombardy. With the building of railways, the key issue came to be that of whether the trade of Lombardy would flow eastwards to Trieste or southwards to Genoa. Austria tried to settle the issue in favour of Trieste by refusing to link the Piedmontese and Lombard railway systems. The railway question was seen to be of immense political and social as well as economic significance. Cavour inaugurated his career in liberal politics with an article on the issue. He hoped that a new system of communications would destroy the 'petty municipal passions, the children of ignorance and prejudice' which had hitherto divided the peoples of Italy.[64] The railways were regarded as a practical means of unifying and 'regenerating' the nation. Therefore, the opposition of Austria to the integration of the railway systems helped to fuse economic and nationalist grievances. However, it would be wrong to imagine that there existed a single, advanced Italian bourgeoisie with an agreed agenda for railway building and the creation of a national market. The Milanese industrialists saw the Piedmontese as rivals and had good reason to favour integration with the larger German market.[65]

In spite of these conflicts of interest, during the 1840s intellectuals and journalists created and popularized what amounted to a programme for economic unification. The success of the German *Zollverein* made it an obvious example to follow; and the protectionist policies of Austria were, by contrast, seen as reactionary and harmful to Italian interests. The coming of the railways highlighted the irrationality of the multiple frontiers and customs barriers which divided the territory of Italy. What use would it be to build an integrated railway system for Italy if tariffs and border formalities doubled the cost and time of transport? The idea of a customs union came to be the central issue in the national programme of the new liberalism. In turn, the diversity of weights and measures, currencies, and legislative systems could be seen as just so many obstacles to the necessary expansion of the market. Once all this was conceded, political federation would be the logical last step. The bolder liberals even argued that a single national flag and a national navy were essential for the protection of Italian commerce. In the new climate of European economic expansion, with railway-building and the extension of free trade, the achievement of these aims took on an added urgency. Only the creation of an economic and political federation could prevent Italy from being left at the starting-gate in the race for commercial and industrial progress. It was this perception of the European 'peaceful revolution' and Italy's possible place in it, rather than the pressure of already formed economic interests, which accounts for the popularity of the national economic programme of liberalism. The triumphant success of Cobden's visit to Italy in the spring of 1847 marked the culmination of the enthusiasm for an English model of liberalism.

It is difficult to disentangle economic and political motives in the 'programme for a national opinion'. Liberals like Massimo d'Azeglio and Cavour saw in economic unification a way of achieving their political objectives and of advancing the national cause in a way that would make the democratic tactic of conspiracy seem irrelevant and counter-productive. On the other hand, industrial interests were frequently protectionist and tied to the policies of the existing states; they were too weak to benefit from wider markets, and in most cases had good reasons to fear the extension of competition. Even commercial interests were not always united behind the national programme. In Piedmont they feared to endanger traditional ties with France. However, in port cities such as Genoa and Leghorn the national programme was popular because it called for both internal and external free trade. The most consistent support for economic unification probably came from landlords and farmers with an interest in commercial agriculture. It is no accident that several of the most important leaders of Italian moderate liberalism were improving landlords: Cavour himself, Minghetti in Bologna and Ricasoli in Tuscany.[66]

If one wants to look for the material conditions of existence which helped to shape a national consciousness, one should perhaps look at the conditions of life and production of the intellectuals themselves. No single question served better to unite the intellectuals of Italy than the demand for a national law of copyright. The reasons for this were eloquently explained by the Florentine reformer Giovanni Fabbroni as early as 1801; he passes directly from the specific problem of the lack of copyright, which prevented Italian intellectuals from receiving a decent price for their work, to the necessity of national unity for Italian cultural development. 'The time has come to make a nation out of Italy under no matter what form of government. Otherwise we shall have to be content with the role of "simple spectators", or else console ourselves with the general progress of humanity.' Language constitutes a kind of natural system of protection for literary production, and the intellectuals could hope to be among the first to benefit from the creation of a national market. It was communication rather than the production and exchange of material goods which was most severely hindered by the existing system of states. The 1820s and 1830s saw the emergence in Lombardy and Tuscany of a new class of professional literary men, producing for the market. But the dignity which writers attributed to their role in society conflicted sharply with its meagre material rewards. The intellectuals' quest for income and status was intimately linked with their assumption of a role as the advance-guard in the creation of a national consciousness.

For literary intellectuals (and even opera librettists) censorship was a major source of dismay and discomfort.[67] Intellectuals of a more practical bent were more fortunate. From 1839 on, scientists, doctors, jurists, administrators and economists came together in the yearly national Scientific Congresses. Permission was originally granted by Grand Duke Leopold II of Tuscany, much to Metternich's anger. However, the success of the meetings was so great that the Austrian authorities gave way to the extent of allowing three congresses to be held in the Lombardo-Veneto. To have done otherwise would have simply focused discontent with Austrian rule; this would have been especially dangerous since Charles Albert had followed Leopold's example in extending his patronage to the Congresses.[68] But the Congresses were a kind of live propaganda for a federal Italy; intellectuals met to discuss questions of national interest in a national framework, and the result was the formation of a large area of consensus on what needed to be done.

The liberals had created a 'national opinion', or, in other words, a public of Italian dimensions. But how was this new public sphere to be safeguarded, and what would be the consequences of its creation? As even Mazzini recognized, Massimo d'Azeglio's reform programme was in the service of the 'great national idea'.[69] D'Azeglio seems to have envisaged a two-stage programme: Italians had first to demonstrate their 'civil courage' in the fight for reforms, and overcome the 'fraternal enmities' which divided city from city, citizens from nobles, and the laity from the priesthood, in order to prove themselves ready and fit for independence. 'Loss of independence is not only the misfortune but the fault of a people': unless the Italians showed themselves capable of effective political action it was useless to expect sympathy or assistance from abroad. However, the hopes for national independence were none the less connected with the expectation of a general crisis of the European system set up by the Congress of Vienna. 'The edifice has already in part collapsed.' In 1846–7 d'Azeglio advocated limiting action to non-violent protest against foreign occupation, and to concrete measures to secure the closer union and effective independence of the Italian states, excluding the Lombardo-Veneto. But the interests of Austria and the Italian states were 'diametrically opposed', and he did not deny that in a second stage military as well as civil courage might be necessary.[70]

THE REVOLUTIONS OF 1848

In 1847 a peaceful liberal solution to the Italian question did not appear outside the bounds of possibility. The most influential Milanese publicist, Carlo Cattaneo, believed that the Lombardo-Veneto could achieve national autonomy within a restructured Austrian Empire. The centralized structure of the Empire was collapsing under its own weight, and the crisis of its finances was a strong argument against a policy of force. In these circumstances, legal agitation could have a good chance of success, whereas 'violence and war' would play into the hands of the military party in Vienna.[71] In the Lombardo-Veneto, agitation for reform and Austrian repression produced an escalating crisis. After Field Marshal Radetzky's soldiers had killed civilians in the streets of Milan the likelihood of a violent confrontation increased dramatically. 'Opinion', as the democrat Giuseppe Ferrari noted in an acute article, had outrun the pace of reform and become revolutionary. D'Azeglio wrote triumphantly: 'Austria is an assassin! Your cause [Italy's] is won.' Italy was a nation, and the Austrian Empire was nothing more than a bureaucracy.[72] In fact, the outbreak of revolution in Vienna itself was soon to confirm the truth of the idea that the superstructure of Austrian government had been undermined by the changes in civil society and the growth of national feeling. The immediate consequence was the outbreak of revolution in Milan and Venice. By then, however, the whole international outlook had changed. Up till February 1848 the Italians had anticipated rather than followed the general European movement for change. Mazzini's claim that they were destined to be the 'initiating people' no longer looked absurd. However, the February days in Paris revived the old problem of the relationship between the movement for Italian independence and French revolutionary leadership. Democrats hoped for a new revolutionary crusade; liberals were terrified by the spectre of communism. Cavour, for example, never doubted that the fate of the European social order would be decided in France.[73] Between a revolutionary France on one side and a reactionary Austria on the other, what could become of the liberal middle way, whose chances in Piedmont had seemed so promising after Charles Albert had conceded a constitution? If, initially, these fears seemed to indicate the need for a more cautious policy towards Italy, the outbreak of insurrection in Milan pointed to a different conclusion. Only by heading the war for national independence could Charles Albert save his dynasty and bring the revolution under control. There was no disagreement between the liberals and the monarchy on this point; but whereas the liberals saw national independence as a logical consequence of the growth of civil society, expressed in free institutions, the princes of the House of Savoy saw the national movement in purely instrumental terms. It could be used to further traditional dynastic aims, and even perhaps turned against its original promoters; as the future King Victor Emmanuel II wrote, 'the spirit of Italian independence is a great spirit, a spirit of immense force . . . we must take care not to suffocate such a spirit, but instead to use it to destroy liberalism'.[74] The war of 1848 was conducted in a royal rather than in a liberal spirit. With an army and a bureaucracy still imbued with the tradition of Absolutism, it could hardly be otherwise. Until the middle of May, in fact, the war was 'federal'; all the Italian states sent contingents of regular and volunteer troops. But the democrats were either unable or unwilling to oppose any effective resistance to the conservative programme of immediate fusion with Piedmont, albeit with the promise that a future Constituent Assembly would be held to determine the form of what would in any case be a constitutional monarchy.

The democrats had led genuine popular revolutions; but they were municipal and not national revolutions, and they did not have either an organization or a programme capable of contesting the alliance between local aristocracies and the Piedmontese monarchy. The Venetian leader Manin's failure to secure the support of the mainland cities of the Veneto was emblematic.[75] Even Cattaneo and the Milanese Council of War, which had led the insurrection, had no alternative to suggest except the neo-Guelph programme of calling for a congress in Rome under Pius IX's presidency.[76] It has been suggested that the fundamental error of Mazzini and his supporters was in their enthusiastic and ingenuous acceptance of Charles Albert's famous slogan that *l'Italia farà da se*. Mazzini has been charged with blindness for his hostility to the idea of French intervention. Although the French government was reluctant to act, they were under strong pressure from public opinion, in the streets, in the National Assembly and in the army.[77] But by the time the failure of the 'royal war' had become clear, the June days in Paris had blunted the edge of revolutionary radicalism. French intervention might still have been a possibility, but only if it had been requested by Charles Albert.

The distastrous conclusion of the 'royal war' gave the initiative back to the democrats, in spite of their deficiencies in leadership. They called for the resumption of war against Austria, backed by a *levée en masse* and popular mobilization throughout Italy. At the same time, the federal idea revived, and for a time Gioberti became the leading personality in Piedmontese politics. He always liked to reconcile opposites, and his programme for a Confederation was meant to provide a middle way between municipalism and unity, between the rights of princes and peoples. He tried to persuade Pius IX to accept the idea of an Italian Confederation in return for a guarantee of the Temporal Power. But the Pope was not enthusiastic, and the divergent interests of Rome and Piedmont prevented an agreement. On the other hand, democrats in Tuscany and Rome rejected Gioberti's cautious agenda. In October 1848 Giuseppe Montanelli – a former neo-Guelph – trumped Gioberti's idea of a Confederation by calling for a Constituent Assembly. This was a radical, Mazzinian idea, but Montanelli tried to differentiate his position from Mazzini's by insisting that his proposal left the choice between republic and monarchy open, and that the creation of a new federal 'Diet' would not imply the destruction of the existing states. But it was unlikely that the rulers of the Italian states would willingly accept the revolutionary principle that popular sovereignty should be the foundation of legitimacy. And even if the democrats were to win power and force the adoption of their programme, would Austria stand by and watch the 'recomposition of the nation' by the decree of an assembly, without taking action? Montanelli's programme gave the democratic movement a new impetus, but it did not, as he hoped, provide a rallying-point around which Italians could regroup in order to continue the struggle for independence.

By the summer of 1848 Mazzini recognized that his policy of collaborating with the monarchy in the interests of national unity had failed. The monarchists had not respected the political truce and had imposed fusion. Worse, their conduct of the war had discouraged popular participation and had proved ineffective. The only solution could be a return to a 'people's war', fought according to the guerrilla tactics which Mazzini had advocated since the 1830s. However, though Mazzinian propaganda had been successful in winning converts among the artisans of the cities, he had neither the programme nor the cadres needed to inspire and guide a movement of resistance in the countryside.[78] The other side of the problem was that the landowners were unwilling to make the concessions which would have been necessary if patriotic unity were to be preserved. There was no

Kossuth among the gentry of northern Italy. Neither radicals nor moderates succeeded in bridging the age-old gap between town and country.

The last act of the Italian revolutionary movement was over-shadowed by the general triumph of reaction in Europe.[79] When the war between Piedmont and Austria broke out again in March 1849, it took Field Marshal Radetzky only four days to win a decisive victory. Once again, the action of the Piedmontese army was poorly co-ordinated with that of the Lombard democrats and volunteers. The patriots had organized an efficient network of secret committees, and Como, Bergamo and Brescia all rose in revolt. But without Pied-montese support the insurrection was doomed, although the desperate ten-day resistance of Brescia showed what might have been achieved if more confidence had been placed in popular participation in the independence struggle.[80]

If the 'people's war' never became a serious alternative to the 'royal war', Mazzini and the republicans could at least claim a symbolic victory. The ideal of the people's war inspired a last-ditch resistance whose determination formed a striking contrast to the performance of the regular Italian armies. The heroic defence of the Roman and Venetian Republics, led by Mazzini and Manin respectively, redeemed many failures. In the eyes of the European Left, the Italian cause took on an epic grandeur; in the whole of Europe, Italians had been the first to rebel and the last to submit. The defence of Rome founded the legend of Garibaldi, the greatest popular hero of the nineteenth century. In spite of the personal friction between Mazzini and Garibaldi during the Roman Republic, Garibaldi's fame gave a new lustre to the Italian Left as a whole. In so far as Garibaldi had clear political ideas at this stage, they were those of Mazzini; his first military enterprise in Italy was carried out in the name of 'God and the People'.[81] The defence of the Roman Republic had another consequence. It re-established the status of Rome as the ideal capital of Italy. For those who believed in Italian unity no other capital would be ultimately acceptable. For Mazzini Rome was 'the natural centre' of Italian unity:

> But the Italians had almost lost the religion of Rome; they began to call it a tomb, and so it appeared . . . Rome was regarded with aversion by some, with scornful indifference by others . . . nothing revealed in her that ferment of liberty which every so often agitated Romagna and the Marches. It was necessary to redeem her and place her again on high so that the Italians could reaccustom themselves to regard her as the temple of the common fatherland.[82]

The 'religion of Rome' and the 'religion of the nation' were henceforward to be inseparable, and this was to be a fateful legacy for the future of Italy.[83]

In 1848 and 1849 all the programmes for resolving the Italian question had been tried and found wanting. The solution was to come not from a radically new departure, but rather from a combination of elements previously separated or opposed: Piedmontese expansion and French intervention, Right and Left, regular armies and volunteers, royal conquest and revolution. This did not mean, of course, that all these elements worked together harmoniously, or that no one was excluded. Unity was to lack the popular and democratic foundation which Mazzini and other democrats had regarded as indispensable. Federalists, whether of the Right or the Left, lost out to centralizers; Piedmontese statism was reinforced by the 'unconditional unitarianism' of former democrats, who clung all the more fiercely to unity as their belief in democracy waned. Liberalism and Catholicism were not reconciled. The reality of Italian unification was to be somewhat different from what the bright hopes of 1848 had suggested.

> The Italian 1848 died, and there died with it the hopes for a country united by nationality and yet allowing for urban, local and regional differences. Certainly it died through its own intrinsic weakness, Guelf and municipal as were its deepest roots. But it was buried by 'Europe', in other words by the great modern states, France with the cynicism of Louis Napoleon, Germany with its disdain for whoever was not German, the Austria of Schwarzenberg with its renewed imperial expansionism, and even England with its desire for peace at any price.[84]

THE ROAD TO UNIFICATION, 1849–1860

1849 raised Mazzini's prestige among European democrats to a new height. No one, except perhaps Kossuth, could match his eminence. Mazzini made use of this position to try to revive, on a sounder footing, his old project for an union of European democrats. In his analysis of 1848, the battle for democracy and national freedom had failed because the democrats had fought divided and had been unable therefore to translate their local superiority into general victory. The Poles, the Hungarians and the Italians had allowed themselves to be crushed separately, and French and German democrats had been unable to translate their sympathy for the oppressed peoples into effective action. This was a convincing enough diagnosis, but the cure proved illusory. Ironically, Mazzini was forced to pin his hopes on a revival of the radical Left in France, in spite of their earlier failure to save the Roman Republic from Louis Napoleon's intervention. The coup of Brumaire put paid to these hopes. In the meantime, Mazzini's attempt to find a minimum common denominator on which the various groups of European democracy could agree had run into predictable difficulties. Even among the Italian exiles Mazzini's insistence that the social question must take second place to the national question was increasingly challenged. Carlo Pisacane, the young Neapolitan officer who had played a vital role in organizing the defence of the Roman Republic, made an interesting and new attempt to reconcile the idea of social revolution with that of the Italian initiative. In his first major work, an analysis of the wars of 1848–9, he argued that leadership had consistently lagged behind popular initiative. It was significant that the revolution had started in Sicily, the region furthest removed from the moderate influence of the 'Albertists', and also the region where the people were 'most oppressed'. The war for national independence could only succeed if it were also a social war; he argued that the backwardness of Italy was actually an advantage, as it meant that the bourgeoisie could put up less resistance. Pisacane's new 'socialism' in many respects harked back to the old Jacobin tradition, for example in its distrust of popular sovereignty and insistence on the need for a single 'legislator'. He failed to appreciate the positive value of Garibaldi's leadership, and criticized him for having failed to form a true revolutionary army.[85] Pisacane's own attempts at starting a revolution in the Kingdom of Naples foundered tragically at Sapri in 1857, when his tiny expeditionary force was massacred by the local peasants.

However, the idea of a 'southern initiative' took hold among the Mazzinian democrats, with in the end fruitful results. Mazzini's old lieutenant, Nicola Fabrizi, argued that only a 'southern initiative' could start a new war of independence. The 'Galvanic current' would rapidly transmit itself from south to north, and the House of Savoy would be forced by public opinion to back the popular movement.[86] Fabrizi did not, of course, foresee that Piedmont would take the initiative; but the second half of his prediction proved accurate.

Public opinion compelled Cavour first to allow and then to support Garibaldi's expedition to Sicily. Garibaldi succeeded where Pisacane had failed for two reasons, other than his own genius. First, he did not attempt to create an artificial revolution from outside; he found a peasant insurrection already raging, and local leaders who would cooperate with him. Secondly, he could turn to advantage the considerable force of *Sicilian* nationalism. This had inspired two revolutions, and had briefly succeeded in establishing an independent state in

1848–9. But the suppression of the Sicilian state by the Neapolitan army had shown the impossibility of independence. Liberal and democratic opinion became convinced that the only way to achieve autonomy from Naples was through union with the rest of Italy. With Sicily as a base, Garibaldi could go on to conquer Naples; but he could not free himself from dependence on the monarchy. In fact, this was never his aim; Garibaldi fought in the name of 'Italy and Victor Emmanuel'. Cavour was afraid that once Garibaldi had reached Naples he would become 'the absolute master of the situation',[87] but this proved too pessimistic a forecast.

Garibaldi's conversion to the necessity of working with the monarchy preceded the new war of independence by several years. In fact, after the Crimean War a whole section of the democratic leadership came to accept collaboration with the monarchy as the only realistic alternative. The argument was put most bluntly by the Lombard exile Pallavicino; Austria cannot be defeated without soldiers and cannon, and only Piedmont has soldiers and cannon.[88] The old distrust of Piedmontese Absolutism was gradually removed by Cavour's liberal policy. It remained true that Cavour was not committed to Italian unity, nor the unitarians to him. In 1856, Cavour could still comment that the most illustrious of the democratic converts, Manin, unfortunately believed in 'Italian unity and other such nonsense'.[89] However, Cavour and the unitarians were at one in the aim of independence from Austria, and each could be useful to the other's purposes. The foundation of a National Society by Pallavicino, Manin, La Farina and other former democrats, with the all-important support of Garibaldi, gave Cavour the instrument he needed for exerting control over the independence movement. He placed himself in a strategic position where he could impress the great powers as the only person who could channel the national movement into orderly, non-revolutionary channels, and at the same time impress Italians as the only person who could create the diplomatic conditions needed for success. It was a difficult game; for opposite reasons, both sides frequently suspected his intentions. But in the end it paid off.

In 1848 Cattaneo and other democrats had criticized the royal war effort for failing to make effective use of the volunteers, and for omitting to seek the solidarity of other national movements, particularly the Hungarian. In both these respects, in 1859 Cavour incorporated elements of the 'revolutionary' strategy in a war in which none the less the initiative remained firmly in the hands of the governments and their armies.

Garibaldi was given an important if auxiliary role in the campaign, and Cavour laid serious plans to provoke an insurrection in Hungary. Cavour even called for a 'general insurrection' in Lombardy, but here the limits of Cavour's willingness to use popular forces made themselves felt. The National Society proved ineffective as a promoter of revolution. One could not really say that this denoted its failure. In large part, its shortcomings derived from the inherent limitations in the idea of a controlled and orderly revolution. The leaders of the Society pursued unification with a single-minded and reductive logic. Instead of a problem, Italian nationhood became an assumption. There was little disposition to discuss its moral and political implications, or the form of the future Italian state. Even independence and liberty became secondary goals; the most important thing was that a unified Italian state should exist.[90] Out of the reflection on the failures brought about by 'municipalism' there emerged the paradoxical conclusion that division was a worse evil than oppression. It followed, evidently, that national unification was the only legitimate aim for revolution; to raise any 'question of liberty or social structure' would be divisive. In this way, the idea of national unity was purged of the democratic content which it had previously possessed. The religious pathos of Mazzini's republicanism had no place in a 'prosaic century'; what was needed was realism, force and an iron hand.[91] It is understandable, therefore, that Cavour's 'party' lacked the boldness and the contacts with popular forces needed for insurrection, and he frequently failed to give it clear directives. Even when he did, its action usually fell short of what he required.[92]

The mechanism of unification followed the precedent set in 1848. The Kingdom of Italy was formed through a process of successive 'fusions' or annexations, ratified by plebiscites. The character of these plebiscites as expressions of popular sovereignty was highly dubious; even the plebiscites of 1848 in Lombardy and the Veneto were fair by comparison. In Tuscany, Parma, Modena and the Papal Legations the mechanism worked smoothly because the hegemony of the moderates was unchallenged; the only significant opposition came from the Tuscan autonomists. It was in this phase that the National Society proved most useful, as a source of cadres for the provisional governments which paved the way for annexation. When Cavour returned to power in 1860, however, he had to deal with a much more delicate situation. The two main dangers which Cavour had to face were that the revolutionary forces might escape from his control, and that the Italian war might broaden into a general European war, in which the balance of forces would be unfavourable to Italy. The two dangers were connected; if Cavour showed himself unable to control the revolution, he risked alienating the great powers. The gravest danger was that the Party of Action (which could once again count on the support of Garibaldi) might succeed in launching a volunteer invasion of the Papal States. This was still the project most favoured by Mazzini; he did not agree with those of his followers who assigned a primary role to the 'southern initiative'.[93] It was the necessity to forestall a possible action by Garibaldi against Rome which offered Cavour the argument he needed to persuade Napoleon III of the necessity to launch an invasion of the Papal States himself. The 'national question' continued to divide the moderate Right from the Party of Action during the decade after the formation of the kingdom of Italy in 1861, with the centre-Left of Rattazzi playing a murky double game in the middle. Only with the annexation of the Veneto in 1866 and Rome in 1870 did it cease to be the major issue in Italian politics. Rather than analysing these conflicts, however, it will be more profitable to end by asking two questions: what was the relationship between the new Italian state and the 'nation', and what residual forms did the 'national question' take in the later history of united Italy?'

EPILOGUE: UNRESOLVED PROBLEMS

The rapid completion of the process of unification signified that the process of 'nation-building' would have to be completed by the action of the state. The major problem lay in the narrow social boundaries within which the national idea had really taken hold. Italian nationality was based on a sense of common culture and language; but this was the culture and language of an educated minority. The number of those who were both literate and for whom Italian was their first language did not exceed 2.5 per cent of the total population.[94]

Even among the educated it cannot be taken for granted that all identified with the new Kingdom of Italy. In both Naples and Sicily a strong sense of collective identity survived. The centralized form assumed by the new state ensured that there could be no easy reconciliation between the desire for autonomy, widely diffused in the 'two Sicilies', and identification with united Italy. Liberal opinion had always been favourable to decentralization, in reaction to the Jacobin and Napoleonic cults of unity and the strong state. But in the emergency of 1860–1 Cavour and his successors abandoned their previous support for regionalism and local self-government.[95] The result was widespread disaffection and apathy in Naples, and open protest in Sicily, where most supporters of unification had imagined that it would mean an increase rather than a reduction in the island's political autonomy. The bitter war with the brigands in the Neapolitan provinces between 1861 and 1865 employed over 100,000 regular troops, and led Massimo d'Azeglio to wonder if, faced with such strong popular opposition, the only way for the government to maintain its liberal principles might not be to allow Naples to secede. In fact, brigandage further strengthened those who argued that only a policy of centralization and the readiness to use force could keep the new state together. In the face of crisis, the ruling class tended to take refuge in an 'unconditional unitarianism'.[96] Any fundamental criticism of the institutions of the new state was dismissed as anti-national.

In the north and centre of Italy the sense of national identity was much stronger. At least in urban Italy, the national propaganda of the democrats had won converts outside the upper and middle classes, among the artisans. But the nation of popular feeling was far better represented by Garibaldi than by Victor Emmanuel. Garibaldi, in fact, was a living symbol of all those popular forces which had contributed to the Risorgimento but which had been relegated to the margins of the new state. As Ferrari and Cattaneo had pointed out, republicanism had deeper roots in Italian history than monarchy.

On the other side of the political spectrum, the denial of the new state's legitimacy by the Church was a grave handicap. It combined with material grievances (high taxation, conscription, the appropriation of Church and communal lands by the new bourgeoisie) to ensure the continued alienation of the rural masses.

Under the shadow of the Vatican, the 'new Rome', far from assuming a role of universal significance, failed even to perform the functions of a true political and cultural capital.[97] Certainly the moral unity of which Mazzini had dreamed was far away. The 'national question' survived in united Italy first and foremost under the form of a persistent unease about the incompleteness of the transformation accomplished, and about the failure to bring about the 'nationalization of the masses',[98] or to create a strong national identity. The cult of the 'great memories' of the Risorgimento was employed as a surrogate for a deeper sense of historical unity.[99] Secondly, the national question survived in the more obvious form of irredentism, with the claim on Trento and Trieste. Until the twentieth century, irredentism remained a left-wing cause, linked to the heritage of Risorgimento republicanism. Thirdly, the great emigration from Italy starting in the later nineteenth century gave nationalists a new pretext for expansion. Only the acquisition of an empire, it could be argued, would stop the haemorrhage and allow the reintegration of the Italian people in the

Italian state. All these motifs were appropriated by fascism, which claimed to embody the heritage of the Risorgimento, while denying the democratic, liberal and progressive impulses which had brought it into being.

NOTES

1 See F. Chabod, *L'idea di nazione*, 2nd edn (Bari, 1962), pp. 46–7.

2 The term 'Jacobins' is in common usage to refer to Italians who supported the French occupation, and who were, in the words of Napoleon Bonaparte, 'partisans of the French constitution or of pure democracy'. But Carlo Capra points out that 'democrats' or 'patriots' would be a more appropriate description, since they were only called 'Jacobins' by their opponents. The patriots were, in fact, divided in their attitude towards the French Jacobins. See C. Capra, 'Il giornalismo nell'età rivoluzionaria e napoleonica', in V. Castronovo and N. Tranfaglia (eds.), *Storia della stampa italiana*, vol. I: *La stampa italiana dal cinquecento all'ottocento* (Rome and Bari, 1976), p. 425.

3 See F. Venturi, 'L'Italia fuori d'Italia', in R. Romano and C. Vivanti (eds.), *Storia d'Italia*, vol. III: *Dal primo settecento all'Unità* (Turin, 1973), p. 1130.

4 M. Fubini, *Ritratto dell'Alfieri e altri studi alfieriani*, 2nd edn (Florence, 1963), p. 34. In the Italian world of the eighteenth century there was one concrete example of a people fighting for freedom and independence which had enormous importance for the formation of the new patriotic ideal: the Corsica of Pasquale Paoli. Paoli was compared to an ancient hero, and Alfieri dedicated his tragedy *Timoleon* to him. See F. Venturi, *Settecento Riformatore*, vol. V: *L'Italia dei lumi*, pt 1 (Turin, 1987), pp. 6, 86.

5 See A. Saitta, *Alle origini del Risorgimento: I Testi di un 'Celebre' Concorso (1796)* (Rome, 1964), vol. I, pp. vii–viii.

6 *Ibid.*, p. x.

7 S. J. Woolf, 'La storia politica e sociale', in Romano and Vivanti (eds.), *Storia d'Italia*, vol. III, p. 168.

8 M. Galdi, 'Necessità di stabilire una repubblica in Italia', in Saitta, *Alle origini del Risorgimento*, pp. 276–329. It might be profitable to investigate the connections between the revolutionary idea of 'regeneration' and the concept of the Risorgimento. See S. Mastellone, *Giuseppe Mazzini e la 'Giovane Italia', 1831–1834* (Pisa, 1960), vol. I, p. 337, for Mazzini's argument that the 'regeneration' of a nation requires a new religion.

9 See U. Marcelli, 'Bonaparte fra il nazionalismo ed il babouvismo italiano (1796–1797)', *Bollettino storico livornese*, January–December 1954 (*Atti del 7° Convegno Storico Toscano*), 247.

10 A. Forrest, 'Rivoluzione ed Europa', in F. Furet and M. Ozouf (eds.), *Dizionario critico della rivoluzione francese* (Milan, 1988), p. 103.

11 Venturi, 'L'Italia fuori d'Italia', pp. 1154–8.

12 M. Galdi, 'Dei rapporti politico-economici fra le nazioni libere', in D. Cantimori and R. de Felice (eds.), *Giacobini Italiani*, vol. II (Bari, 1956), pp. 209–364.

13 Galdi's faithfulness to patriotism in its original eighteenth-century sense can be seen in his argument that the destruction of England's maritime and commercial hegemony was really in her own best interests, because it would reverse the growth of 'corruption' and the national debt. For the linkage between the two in English eighteenth-century thought, see J. G. A. Pocock, *Virtue, Commerce and History* (Cambridge, 1985), pp. 69, 112, 140.

14 For antecedents, see A. Saitta, 'La questione del "giacobinismo italiano"', *Critica Storica*, 1965, 226–42.

15 G. Bollati, *L'Italiano* (Turin, 1983), p. 16.

16 C. Zaghi, 'Napoleone e l'Italia', *Bollettino storico livornese*, 1954, 57–8.

17 *Ibid.*, pp. 55, 60.

18 Piedmont was definitely annexed to France in September 1802, and Parma passed under French government in the same year, although its annexation only became official in 1808. The Ligurian Republic was annexed in 1805, Tuscany in 1807 and the Papal States in May 1809.

19 C. Zaghi, *L'Italia di Napoleone dalla Cisalpina al Regno* (Turin, 1986), p. 283.

20 For the concept of 'civilizing mission' as an administrative ideology, see S. J. Woolf, 'French civilization and ethnicity', *Past and Present*, 124 (1989), 110. One can see Mazzini's concept of national 'mission' as a reaction to this universalist concept, conveyed through the work of Guizot (see A. Omodeo, *Difesa del Risorgimento*, Turin, 1951, pp. 20–5, 34–6).

21 I. Berlin, *Vico and Herder* (London, 1976), pp. 147–8.

22 See C. Dionisotti, *Geografia e storia della letteratura italiana* (Turin, 1967), pp. 258–68.

23 The concept of 'aristocratic Romanticism' developed by Norbert Elias seems useful as an interpretation of Alfieri's moral and political revolt. According to Elias, this outlook originated among members of the feudal nobility who chafed against the constraints of state control and court ceremonial imposed by absolutist monarchy, and who constructed an idealized image of rustic simplicity and military courage in contrast. See N. Elias, *The Court Society* (New York, 1983), pp. 216–41. See also R. Romeo, *Cavour e il suo tempo* (Bari, 1969), vol. I, pp. 7–17. It should be noted that Alfieri's 'Romanticism' differed substantially from the later Romantic movement; his ideal of civic virtue was neo-classical in character.

24 Fubini, *Alfieri*, p. 158.

25 R. Romeo, *Dal Piemonte sabaudo all'Italia liberale* (Turin, 1963), pp. 17–23.

26 U. Foscolo, *Scritti letterari e politici dal 1796 al 1808*, *Opere*, vol. VI, ed. G. Gambarini (Florence, 1972), pp. xx, xxv.

27 *Ibid.*, pp. 159–62.

28 *Ibid.*, pp. 231–2.

29 P. Hazard, *La Révolution française et les lettres italiennes* (Paris, 1910), p. 290; B. Frabotta, 'Ugo Foscolo e la crisi del jacobinismo: le due inconciliabili libertà', *Rassegna Letteraria Italiana*, 1977, p. 330.

30 See Hazard, *La Révolution française*, p. 245. For Foscolo's anti-Romanism, see U. Foscolo, *Ultime lettere di Jacopo Ortis*, ed. G. Bezzola, 8th edn (Milan, 1987), p. 52.

31 See B. Croce, *Storia della storiografia italiana nel secolo decimonono* (Bari, 1964), vol. I, pp. 109–11.

32 S. Stelling-Michaud, 'Sismondi face aux réalités politiques de son temps', in *Sismondi Européen* (*Actes du colloque internationale*, Geneva, 1973) (Paris, 1976), p. 157.

33 See G. Cambon, *Ugo Foscolo: Poet of Exile* (Princeton, N. J., 1980), pp. 18, 150 and *passim*; also Fubini, *Alfieri*, p. 188.

34 Foscolo's Italian contemporaries were actually often highly critical of his pessimism, and his extravagance. See E. R. Vincent, *Ugo Foscolo: An Italian in Regency England* (Cambridge, 1953), pp. 160–70.

35 See Cambon, *Ugo Foscolo*, pp. 12, 157–63. There is a striking parallel with the practice of some contemporary dictatorships: see the brilliant story by Milan Kundera, 'Let the old dead make way for the new dead', in *Laughable Loves* (London, 1978).

36 J. Rosselli, *Lord William Bentinck and the British Occupation of Sicily* (Cambridge, 1956), pp. 30–1.

37 *Ibid.*, pp. 54, 198–9.

38 *Ibid.*, p. 142.

39 A. G. Haas, *Metternich, Reorganization and Nationality, 1813–1818* (Wiesbaden, 1963), p. 92.

40 *Ibid.*, pp. 117–18.

41 *Ibid.*, pp. 93–5.

42 See A. Wandruszka, 'La politica italiana dell'Austria nel periodo della Restaurazione', in *La restaurazione in Italia: strutture e ideologie* (Atti del XLVII Congresseo di Storia del Risorgimento italiano (Rome, 1976)), pp. 105–12.

43 However, see G. Candeloro, *Storia dell'Italia moderna*, vol. II: *Dalla restaurazione alla rivoluzione nazionale* (Milan, 1988), p. 92 for the attempts of the more radical leaders of the Neapolitan *Carbonari* to export the revolution to the Papal States and Lombardy.

44 For the effect of the Greek war of independence on Mazzini's imagination, see S. Mastellone, *Mazzini e la 'Giovine Italia' (1831–1834)* (Pisa, 1960), vol. I, p. 330.

45 A. Saitta, *Filippo Buonarroti: contributi alla storia della sua vita e del suo pensiero* (Rome, 1950), vol. I, pp. 178–9; Mastellone, *Mazzini*, vol. I, pp. 73–5.

46 *Ibid.*, vol. I, pp. 33–5.

47 *Ibid.*, vol. I, p. 57.

48 The 'Albertists' had circulated a copy of a petition to Charles Albert asking him to assume the constitutional monarchy of Italy, but the petition was never sent.

49 See Saitta, *Filippo Buonarroti*, vol. I, p. 190.

50 *Ibid.*, vol. I, pp. 215–16.

51 Mastellone, *Mazzini*, vol. I, p. 334.

52 See R. Bizzocchi, *La 'Biblioteca Italiana' e la cultura della restaurazione, 1816–1825* (Milan, 1979), pp. 37–8, 78–96.

53 G. Mazzini, 'D'una letteratura europea', in F. Della Peruta (ed.), *Scrittori politici dell'ottocento*, vol. I (Naples, 1969), pp. 271–305. For Mme de Staël and

Italy, see Hazard, *La Révolution française*, pp. 467–75. Mazzini's insistence on the union of thought and action originated as a response to Guizot, who had identified the separation of intellect and practice as the fatal weakness of Italian civilization (Woolf, 'French civilization and ethnicity').

54 See G. Borsa, 'L'influenza del modello risorgimentale nelle varie fasi di sviluppo del nazionalismo indiano', in G. Borsa and P. B. Brocchieri (eds.), *Garibaldi, Mazzini, e il Risorgimento nel risveglio dell'Asia e dell'Africa* (Milan, 1984), pp. 170–6. Mazzini's conception of the relationship between faith, morality and politics exerted a particular influence on the thought of Gandhi.

55 Mastellone, *Mazzini*, vol. I, p. 236.

56 P. Pieri, *Storia militare del Risorgimento* (Turin, 1962), pp. 107–8. Mazzini pointed out that Calabria had preceded Spain in popular resistance to Napoleon ('Della guerra d'insurrezione', in *Scrittori politici*, pp. 417–42).

57 For an explanation of the weak association between nationalism and popular culture in Italy, see P. Burke, *Popular Culture in Early Modern Europe* (London, 1978), p. 14: 'Italy, France and England had invested more in the Renaissance, in classicism, and in the Enlightenment than other countries had and so they were slower to abandon the values of these movements. Since a standard literary language already existed, the discovery of dialect was divisive.' The one leading figure of the Risorgimento who was also an important student of popular culture, Niccolo Tommaseo, came from the 'cultural periphery' of Dalmatia.

58 Croce, *Storia*, vol. I, pp. 122–4.

59 Candeloro, *Storia*, vol. II, p. 368.

60 *Primato morale e civile degli italiani*, first published in Brussels in 1843.

61 Romeo, *Dal Piemonte sabaudo all'Italia liberale*, p. 64.

62 W. Maturi, *Interpretazioni del Risorgimento* (Turin, 1962), p. 127.

63 See C. Cattaneo, 'Dell'insurrezione di Milano nel 1848 e della successiva guerra', in D. Castelnuovo Frigessi (ed.), *Opere Scelte*, vol. III: *Scritti 1848–1851* (Turin, 1972), p. 28.

64 Cavour, *Scritti* (Bologna, 1912), vol. II, pp. 3–50; Romeo, *Cavour e il suo tempo*, vol. II (1842–54), pp. 218–19.

65 See A. Caracciolo, 'L'Italia economica', in Romano and Vivanti (eds.), *Storia d'Italia*, vol. III, p. 616.

66 See K. R. Greenfield, *Economics and Liberalism in the Risorgimento* (Baltimore, Md, 1934), p. 299.

67 For opera censorship, see J. Budden, *The Operas of Verdi* (London, 1973), vol. I, pp. 23–4.

68 See Candeloro, *Storia*, vol. II, p. 347.

69 R. Marshall, *Massimo D'Azeglio: An Artist in Politics, 1798–1866* (London, New York and Toronto, 1966), pp. 86ff.

70 M. d'Azeglio, *Scritti politici e letterari* (Florence, 1872), vol. I, pp. 116–17, 276–77, 285, 306–7.

71 C. Cattaneo, *L'insurrezione di Milano nel 1948* (Milan, 1951), p. 25.

72 D'Azeglio, *Scritti*, p. 416.

73 Romeo, *Cavour e il suo tempo*, vol. II, pp. 300, 307.

74 D. Cantimori, *Studi di storia* (Turin, 1949), p. 673.

75 See P. Ginsborg, *Daniele Manin and the Venetian Revolution of 1848–49* (Cambridge, 1979), pp. 162–84, 189–202.

76 Cattaneo, 'Dell'insurrezione di Milano nel 1848 e della successiva guerra', p. 97.

77 A. J. P. Taylor, *The Italian Problem in European Diplomacy, 1847–1849* (Manchester, 1934), pp. 95–6.

78 See Ginsborg, *Daniele Manin*, pp. 258–9.

79 Taylor, *The Italian Problem*, pp. 213–14.

80 See A. Gramsci, *Il Risorgimento*, 9th edn (Turin, 1960), pp. 90–3.

81 *Ibid.*, pp. 259–60.

82 G. Mazzini, *Note autobiografiche* (Milan, 1986), p. 386.

83 See F. Chabod, *Storia della politica estera italiana dal 1870 al 1896* (Bari, 1965), vol. I, pp. 215–373 *passim*, especially pp. 224–9, for the influence of Mazzini and Gioberti.

84 Venturi, 'L'Italia fuori d'Italia', p. 1361.

85 G. Berti, *I democratici e l'iniziativa meridionale nel Risorgimento* (Milan, 1962), pp. 419–20, 424, 426, 435–7, 446–7.

86 *Ibid.*, p. 700.

87 Candeloro, *Storia*, vol. IV: *Dalla rivoluzione nazionale all'unità, 1849–1860* (Milan, 1990), pp. 475–6.

88 R. Grew, *A Sterner Plan for Italian Unity: The Italian National Society in the Risorgimento* (Princeton, N. J., 1963), p. 10.

89 D. Mack Smith, *Victor Emanuel, Cavour and the Risorgimento* (London, New York and Toronto, 1971), p. 27.

90 Grew, *A Sterner Plan*, p. 141.

91 *Ibid.*, pp. 143, 151, 157–9.

92 *Ibid.*, pp. 197, 209.

93 Berti, *I democratici*, pp. 735–40.

94 T. de Mauro, *Storia linguistica dell'Italia unita* (Bari, 1970), p. 43.

95 See Mack Smith, *Victor Emanuel*, pp. 254–74.

96 See R. Grew, 'How success spoiled the Risorgimento', in A. W. Salomone (ed.), *Italy from the Risorgimento to Fascism* (New York, 1970), pp. 51–2.

97 S. Lanaro, *L'Italia nuova: identità e sviluppo 1861–1988* (Turin, 1988), pp. 75–7.

98 See E. Gentile, *Il mito dello stato nuovo dall'antigiolittismo al fascismo* (Rome and Bari, 1982), p. 251.

99 Lanaro, *L'Italia nuova*, pp. 152–60.

FOUR

THE ROOTS OF THE NATIONAL QUESTION IN SPAIN

SIMON BARTON

WRITING in the fifth century the Spanish priest Orosius commented that 'by the disposition of the land, Spain as a whole is a triangle and, surrounded as it is by the Ocean and the Tyrrhenian Sea, is almost an island'.[1] That Nature should have endowed the Iberian Peninsula with such clearly marked boundaries has been taken by many to imply likewise that the political unity of the region was itself a natural and logical creation. But if, as Orosius noted, the boundaries of the peninsula are clear-cut, the physical landscape of the interior is far from being so. At the centre lies the vast arid tableland called the Meseta. Ringed by formidable mountain barriers, communications between this high plateau and the coastal regions of the peninsula are difficult, while the Meseta itself is bisected by a series of mountain ranges: the Sierra da Estrela, the Sierra de Gredos and the Sierra de Guadarrama. These physical divisions have endowed the peninsula with an astonishing regional diversity with the result that even if political unity has been frequently held up by some as a natural goal, Spain's 'geographical handicap', as Sánchez-Albornoz once referred to it, has in fact tended to encourage the development of regionalist and separatist movements.[2]

Accordingly, it has become customary to portray Spanish history in terms of a permanent struggle between two opposing forces: the desire of central government to overcome regional sentiment and thereby bring about a truly united nation; and the no less strenuous efforts of the peripheral regions to maintain their identity and to keep central government at arm's length.[3] Even today, when the regime of *autonomías* introduced by the democratic constitution of 1978 has, with the notable exception of the Basque provinces, largely helped to dampen regional secessionist aspirations, it is striking that the overriding allegiance of many a Spaniard remains towards his *patria chica*, to his region, and not to the nation as a whole. Even that arch-unitarian

Ramón Menéndez Pidal was forced to concede that 'the Spaniard allows his local patriotism to prevail excessively'.[4] Yet geographical features alone cannot account for the difficulty governments have encountered for centuries in forging a strong unitary state and in nurturing a widespread sense of Spanish national consciousness.[5] The roots of the Spanish national question, rather, lie deep in the past and in a complex combination of political, economic and cultural factors.

HISTORIANS AND 'THE SPANISH PREDICAMENT'

Just precisely when Spain as a nation was born is very much a moot point.[6] If the union of Castile and Aragón under Isabel and Fernando in 1479 has traditionally been presented by historians as the key moment, a series of other candidates present themselves.[7] Some would trace the origins of the Spanish nation right back to the unitary kingdom forged by the Visigothic kings in the late sixth and early seventh centuries.[8] Support can also be found for the view that Spain as a political entity is the product of relatively modern times: it has been argued, for example, that it was only after Felipe V introduced the so-called *Nueva Planta* of 1716, which did away with the traditional privileges and institutions of the Catalans, that Spain became truly united for the first time.[9] But political unity is one thing; national consciousness quite another. It could even be argued, given the persistence of strong regionalist feelings in the peninsula to this day, that Spain as a nation is still to be born.

What is not in dispute, however, is that during the brief space of fifty years, between 1492 and 1542, Spain experienced an extraordinary change in her fortunes. During this time she acquired by conquest and settlement a vast American empire and had a substantial European one thrust upon her after the accession of the Emperor Carlos V to the Spanish throne in 1516.[10] Spain was rapidly catapulted to the status of major world power. But she was not to enjoy her preeminent position for long. Already, before the end of the reign of Felipe II in 1598, the revolt of the Netherlands and the fiasco of the naval expedition against England had revealed the first embarrassing cracks in the imperial façade. The next three centuries were to be years of slow, painful decline: Portugal, annexed in 1580, broke away again in 1640, this time for good; Spanish hegemony in Europe was effectively broken after the Peace of the Pyrenees of 1659; and Spain itself was to suffer invasion by foreign armies in 1704 and again in 1808. If some historians are quick to warn us today that the decline in Spain's fortunes after around 1660 was not quite as relentless and precipitous as we are often led to believe, a decline it undoubtedly was all the same.[11] By the end of the nineteenth century the Spanish colonial empire was no more, while Spain itself, racked by invasion and civil war, had been reduced to a nonentity on the European political stage.[12]

Among the nations of western Europe none, surely, has devoted quite so much of its intellectual energies towards the analysis of its historical development as have the Spaniards. Russell has aptly spoken of the 'narcissistic tendency' which has dominated Spanish thought in modern times.[13] As early as the seventeenth century when, notwithstanding numerous reverses, Spain still ruled over a vast empire, writers dubbed *arbitristas* were declaring that the country was in decline and setting out their own remedies to the nation's political and economic ills.[14] As Spain's world role steadily diminished, so this mood of self-examination and pessimism increased. Spain's imperial experience was widely viewed as a tragic error and people looked back to the reign of the Catholic Kings as a golden age.[15] By the time of the nineteenth century, the loss of most of the Spanish overseas empire, coupled with domestic political turmoil and the ever-present fear that Spain itself might disintegrate, merely added to this sense of hopelessness and failure; men felt that Spain had lost its way in the world.[16] The year 1898 was a watershed: the humiliating defeat in Cuba by the United States saw the last vestiges of the Spanish Empire (Cuba, Puerto Rico and the Philippines) stripped away. For many Spaniards the Cuban débâcle was the final straw. In an atmosphere of anguish and self-criticism, a group of intellectuals, the so-called 'Generation of '98', just like the *arbitristas* long before them, set about examining the causes for Spain's plight and putting forward solutions for her salvation.[17] It was not just the historical development of Spain that was being probed here, however, but the very essence of the Spanish soul. To borrow Brenan's memorable metaphor, it was as if Spain itself had become a patient on the psychoanalyst's couch.[18]

For the most part, however, this debate was not carried out in a mood of detached critical enquiry. For much of the time, notwithstanding their radical statements of intent, the writings of the 'Generation of '98' and their successors merely tended to echo the rhetoric voiced by the *arbitristas* long before.[19] Spain's political decline was mostly examined on a very superficial level with any number of facile explanations being offered to account for 'the Spanish predicament'.[20] According to the essayist and novelist Angel Ganivet, for example, whose *Idearium español* was a formative influence on the work of the 'Generation of '98', the Spanish decline was due fundamentally to a lack of *aboulia*, or will-power, among its inhabitants.[21] The philosopher Ortega y Gasset, for his part, in his celebrated essay *La España invertebrada* published in 1921, attributed Spain's problems to the lack of an able 'selective minority', such as a strong aristocracy, which might have been able to dominate the innate *particularismo*, or individualism, of the masses.[22] It was this *particularismo*, Ortega claimed, exacerbated by the geographical, linguistic and ethnological divisions of the peninsula, which had throughout the ages fatally undermined the ability of governments to foster a sense of Spanish community and nationhood. For Ortega, the fact that feudalism had failed to take root in the peninsula 'fue nuestra primera gran desgracia y la causa de todas las demás'.[23] Other writers struck a similarly critical note. The proponents of the doctrine of *regeneracionismo*, notably Joaquín Costa, deplored Spain's historical isolation from the mainstream of European political and cultural thought and called for the urgent Europeanization of Spain.[24] According to Macías Picavea, meanwhile, the blame for Spain's dilemma lay squarely with the overweening pride of Castile which, by its dominance of the peripheral regions, had fatally weakened the always fissile unity of the peninsula.[25] The general tone of most of these works was one of soul-searching and disillusion. Profoundly influenced by the humiliating events of recent times, there was a marked tendency among intellectuals to reject the Spanish past. Not only was Spain's imperial adventure widely condemned as a tragic error, but the very 'historical unity' of Spain began to be called into question.

To many historians, however, for whom the unitary principle was all, such views amounted to nothing short of heresy. With memories of the disastrous federal experiment of 1873, when a group of Andalusian 'cantons' had declared their independence from Madrid, still fresh in men's minds, and with regional nationalism on the rise in Catalonia and the Basque country, the very existence of Spain appeared to be in jeopardy. It was to discredit the views of those intellectuals who, like Unamuno, had dismissed the unity of Spain as an absurd nationalist myth, that a group of scholars set themselves the task of demonstrating to their fellow countrymen that Spain, far from being a mere historical accident, had been the triumphal product of the continuous unifying impulse that had driven their ancestors.[26] For the nationalist historians, the weakness of the ties which bound Spaniards together was to be attributed above all to their uniformity of character. It was the innate individualism of the *Spaniard*, they argued, not any fundamental ethnological or linguistic differences between, say, Catalans and Castilians, that explained the strong

regional feeling that existed in Spain.[27] The mood of the unitarians
was summed up by Menéndez Pidal:

> Let us be clear on this point: the form of life of the Spaniards throughout
> these 2,000 years has not been a perpetual mistake, nor was the
> superstructure artificial; it was in fact the normal structure, the most
> natural one that the Spanish people could select in the particular
> historical circumstances in which it was involved.[28]

This interpretation of the Spanish past was to acquire particular
resonance in the years following the Nationalist rising against the
Republican government of Azaña in July 1936. Drawing ideological
inspiration from Menéndez y Pelayo's *Historia de los heterodoxos españoles*
– a rhetorical and chauvinistic account of Spanish history published
in 1882 – the supporters of Franco's *Movimiento Nacional* proclaimed
the indissoluble unity of Spain.[29] General Franco himself portrayed
the rising as a Crusade which would prevent Spain from being
deflected from her historical destiny and would crown 'la obra
unificadora' which God had entrusted to him. Spain would be reborn,
Franco promised, and a renewed feeling of patriotism and national
solidarity would prevail.[30]

The debate took on renewed vigour in 1948 with the publication of
Américo Castro's *España en su historia: cristianos, moros y judíos*.[31] Offering
a strikingly original interpretation of the Spanish past, Castro's thesis,
stylishly delivered, albeit with somewhat cavalier treatment of his
sources, was essentially as follows: Spain and the Spanish psyche were
above all the product of the eight long centuries of *convivencia*, or
coexistence, of the three religions of the medieval peninsula: Christian,
Muslim and Jewish. Accordingly, Castro believed, it was nonsensical
to seek, as other historians had done, to distinguish the essential
'Spanishness' of the inhabitants of the peninsula in Roman or Visigothic times, let alone before then.

A furious counter-blast to Castro's thesis was delivered only eight
years later by the distinguished medievalist Claudio Sánchez-Albornoz. *España: un enigma histórico*, published in two massive volumes, was
conceived above all as a fundamental refutation of Castro's work,
which Sánchez-Albornoz regarded with evident distaste as being little
more than a heretical *deformación* of Spain's true history.[32] If the
hallmark of Sánchez-Albornoz's writings hitherto had been a rigorous
and painstaking scholarship, his *España*, although underpinned by his
customary erudition, is a patriotic, passionate and at times rancorous
piece of rhetoric. Sánchez-Albornoz himself, never one to hide his own

light under a bushel, regarded his work as the 'clave de la historia española'.[33]

Unlike Castro, Sánchez-Albornoz fervently believed in the *homo hispanus*: that a basic Spanish temperament, shaped by the climate and terrain of the peninsula, had evolved even before the arrival of the Romans, although he conceded that this temperament was not immutable and had evolved over the course of the centuries.[34] Moreover, he rejected out of hand that any such fusion of the Christian, Muslim or Jewish cultures had taken place or indeed that the Muslims had had any significant influence upon Christian Spain.[35] Instead, he averred, Spain was the product of the long centuries of war and struggle between Christian and Moor.[36] To borrow the metaphor of which Spanish historians were so fond, the medieval Reconquest was the forge in which Spain had been wrought. A *cristiano viejo* of the old school, Sánchez-Albornoz passionately held that the 'black pages' that Castro had written were poisoning the national consciousness and that it was his duty to correct the grave wrong that had been served upon his country.[37] Fearful that the centrifugal forces of regionalism were in danger of destroying the 'historical unity' of Spain, Sánchez-Albornoz sought to persuade those who wished to break away that their ancestors were truly Spaniards.[38]

For all their manifest differences, however, both Castro and Sánchez-Albornoz were of agreement that the Middle Ages was the most crucial period in the historical development of Spain and provided the key to understanding not only the temperament of the Spaniard himself, but also the trials and tribulations that beset Spain from the sixteenth century onwards. As will become clear in the coming pages, this view has been widely shared and the medieval period has traditionally been the chosen 'battleground' for those historians anxious to explain the evolution of the Spanish nation and psyche.[39]

Yet for all the variety of approaches adopted in the numerous works dedicated to the nature of Spain and the Spanish temperament, written by men of widely differing political and intellectual backgrounds, we are returned time and time again to the perennial question of the unity of Spain. To attribute the nation's problems simply to a fundamental flaw in the Spanish character, to a loss of 'spirit and ancient virtue', or indeed to Spain's supposed incapacity in some way to live up to her 'historical destiny' was to avoid the real issue.[40] Behind all the cryptopsychologizing that characterized many of the socio-historical meditations on the nature of Spain there lay a crucial awareness of an imperfect sense of nationality. This, in essence,

is the Spanish 'national question' and it is to the origins of this crisis
of identity that we must now turn our attention.

THE ROOTS OF THE SPANISH NATIONAL QUESTION

To say that the Iberian Peninsula stands at the crossroads between
two continents is a commonplace, but none the less accurate for all
that. From the earliest times, waves of settlers were attracted to the
peninsula. During the first millennium before Christ, for example,
came the Celts from the north; while from the south and east Iberians,
Phoenecians, Greeks and Carthaginians were among those who were
attracted to Spain's shores. They were followed in the third century
BC by the Romans who, over the course of a long and arduous series
of campaigns, were able to destroy the Carthaginian Empire in
southern Spain and subsequently to extend their authority over the
numerous tribes who inhabited the rest of the peninsula by the end of
the first century BC.

By all accounts, Roman *Hispania* appears to have been a relatively
peaceful and prosperous region.[41] The imprint of Roman civilization
gradually made itself felt, in the form of language, religion, urbanization, engineering works, and so on. But if, as some historians have
asserted, the administrative and cultural unity imposed by Rome over
the peninsula seems in some way to presage the subsequent political
unification of Spain, recent studies have sought to emphasize the
limitations of this control.[42] 'While the impression of Roman Spain is
one of unity, and indeed in terms of architecture, engineering, art and
religion, almost of uniformity with the rest of the Empire', Collins
observes, 'it is essential to appreciate how fragile this was. It was an
artificial imposition that negated much of the geography and past
history of the peninsula.'[43] For one thing, we are told, the patina of
Roman culture was not spread evenly across the peninsula and in
some areas, notably in the mountainous districts of Galicia, Asturias,
Cantabria and the Basque country, tribal organization seems largely
to have remained in place.[44] Furthermore, it is thoroughly misleading
to attribute to the inhabitants of the peninsula any precocious self-
conscious regional identity. Though the Christian chroniclers of the
thirteenth century might later regard the indigenous inhabitants of
the peninsula as *españoles*, a tendency that has been followed by more
than one modern historian, for contemporaries *Hispania* was strictly a
geographical expression and its inhabitants citizens of the Empire.[45]
As one historian has put it, 'Hispania only existed with and because
of Rome.'[46]

By the time of the fifth century Roman political and military authority had begun to decay and the peninsula was once more subjected to invasion by waves of migrants. The first incursion came in 409 when a confederacy of tribes – the Vandals, Sueves and Alans – crossed the Pyrenees and settled in the peninsula. In the ensuing power struggle they were joined by the Visigoths who, having already established a power-base in southern Gaul, first crossed into Spain in 415. Notwithstanding their military successes over the other tribes, however, permanent Visigothic settlement in the peninsula did not begin until towards the end of the fifth century, and even then occurred on a very limited scale. A century later, however, having successfully prosecuted a series of campaigns against the Sueves, Franks, Basques and Byzantines, the Visigoths were masters of almost the whole of the peninsula.[47]

Great play has been made by Spanish historians of the energetic efforts of the Visigothic monarchs to impose a single centralized authority over the peninsula. King Leovigild (569–86), who established Toledo as the political and ceremonial centre of the realm, is usually singled out as the chief architect of this achievement, although even he was unable to bring the Basques to heel and a Byzantine enclave remained in southern Spain until it was extinguished by King Suintila (621–31) in 624. Military operations apart, however, two celebrated events provide the clearest evidence of the desire of the Visigoths to cement the fragile unity of the peninsula. The first of these occurred in 587 when Leovigild's son and successor, Recared (586–601), renounced the Arian heresy and embraced Catholicism. This act was officially confirmed two years later, at the Third Council of Toledo, thereby removing one of the principal barriers that had hitherto divided the Hispano-Roman population and the Visigothic ruling caste. In 654, meanwhile, the legislative unification of the Visigothic realm was achieved by the promulgation of the *Lex Visigothorum* or *Liber Iudicorum*, by King Reccesvinth (649–72).

Notwithstanding their ignominious overthrow by the Arabs in the early eighth century, the Visigothic kings largely enjoyed a good press among later historians. For this they had much to thank their most influential propagandist, Bishop Isidore of Seville (556–636), whose *Historia Gothorum*, compiled in 625–6, was later to enjoy enormous popularity.[48] In the first half of the thirteenth century, for example, it was incorporated by Bishop Lucas of Tuy into his *Chronicon Mundi* and shortly afterwards Rodrigo Jiménez de Rada, archbishop of Toledo, who completed his own *Historia Gothica* in 1243, used Isidore's work as the core of his chronicle and composed a glowing eulogy to the

Visigothic dynasty.[49] Modern historians, too, have tended to share Isidore's high opinion of the Visigoths. For many, the Visigothic achievement in forging an independent and united Iberian kingdom marked the birth of the Spanish nation.[50] Moreover, Isidore's chronicle, with its opening paean of praise to Spain and its inhabitants, the *Laus Spaniae*, has been widely portrayed as the voice of an incipient Spanish nationalism.[51]

All the same, such an interpretation has not been without its detractors. Ortega y Gasset, for one, memorably dismissed the Visigoths as mere 'germanos alcoholizados de romanismo', while Castro also hotly rejected the notion that the Visigoths could in any way be regarded as Spanish.[52] Likewise, doubts have been expressed about Isidore's supposed role as a nationalist spokesman.[53] More recently, moreover, we have been reminded that for all the centralizing efforts of its rulers, the Visigothic realm, like Roman *Hispania* before it, was a fragile creation.[54]

The Arab invasion of 711 brought Visigothic rule to an untimely end. The decisive defeat near Medina Sidonia in the lower Guadalquivir valley of the army led by King Rodrigo (710–11) to intercept the invaders, allowed the Arabs to proceed to capture the Visigothic capital, Toledo. By 718, the whole of the peninsula was in Arab hands.[55] Visigothic power was irrevocably shattered; with their king dead and with no clear successor to hand, several members of the aristocracy fled across the Pyrenees.[56] Most probably chose to come to terms with their conquerors.[57] Whether any nobles actually made their way north to the Asturias is not known, but that was certainly what Christian writers wanted people to believe nearly two centuries later. Which brings us to the elaboration of the neo-Gothic myth.

The earliest surviving Christian source to record the Arab invasion of 711, the so-called *Chronicle of 754*, was probably compiled in Toledo and sketches the history of the peninsula across the period 611–754.[58] Yet, while its anonymous author laments the fate of 'unhappy Spain', he none the less devotes much space to the deeds of its Muslim conquerors and has nothing to tell us of the resistance that was being met far to the north in the mountains of the Asturias.[59] Our knowledge of the emergence and expansion of the tiny Asturian kingdom is almost entirely dependent upon the testimony of a clutch of chronicles, probably produced in the capital Oviedo, in the late ninth and early tenth centuries.[60] According to their account, which admittedly varies substantially depending on which text we use, the Muslim invasion of 711 led many members of the Visigothic aristocracy to take refuge in the Asturias.[61] Some years later, we are told, an uprising against

Muslim rule was launched under the leadership of Pelayo, the former swordbearer of King Witiza according to one account, but of royal descent according to another.[62] The Asturians elected Pelayo their king and at Covadonga in 722 defeated a Muslim army sent to deal with the uprising. Shortly afterwards, the rebels killed Munnuza, the Arab governor of Gijón, and drove the Muslims out of the region.[63] 'From then on', the *Chronicle of Albelda* asserts, 'freedom was restored to the Christian people . . . and by divine providence the kingdom of Asturias was born.'[64]

Notwithstanding their differences of detail and emphasis, the message of the Asturian chronicles was clear: the sins of the Visigoths may have allowed the Muslims to invade and triumph, but Pelayo and his successors were the legitimate political heirs to the Visigothic legacy. This belief acquired particular currency during the reign of Alfonso II (791–842) who, according to a celebrated passage in the *Chronicle of Albelda*, established in Oviedo 'the Gothic order, both in the church and the palace, as it had been at Toledo'.[65] The Asturian chronicles reflect the optimistic and self-confident spirit that prevailed among the Christians towards the end of the ninth century. The Muslims had been expelled from the region and the important military successes achieved by Ordoño I (850–66) and by his son Alfonso III 'the Great' (866–910) had extended Christian authority as far south as the river Duero. Nevertheless, far greater rewards were in sight, the chronicles promised, and the expulsion of the infidel from the peninsula was imminent.[66]

In point of fact, the neo-Gothic myth does not stand up to scrutiny. Contrary to the claims of the Christian chroniclers, there is no independent evidence that large numbers of Visigothic nobles took refuge in the Asturias after 711, let alone that Pelayo, their leader, was 'ex semine regio'.[67] Instead, the campaign which culminated in the action at Covadonga in 722 was in all probability a purely Asturian affair. It seems highly unlikely, moreover, that from the outset the overriding aim of Pelayo and his followers was the restoration of national unity. As Lomax has remarked, the Asturians 'possibly had no clearer policy than a general interest in booty and expansion and a general religious hostility to the Muslims'.[68] Indeed, there is a certain irony in the insistence of the chroniclers that the nascent Asturian kingdom was the legitimate successor to the Visigothic state when, in fact, it had been one of the very regions which had most resisted the centralizing efforts of the Visigothic kings.[69] The cultural traditions of the Visigoths do not seem to have reached the Asturias until they were carried there by the Mozarabic immigrants who made their way north during the course of the eighth and ninth centuries.

Nevertheless, the myth endured. It can be found in many of the major works of Christian historiography produced in the peninsula during the Middle Ages. It was recorded and amplified, for example, by the anonymous *Historia Silense* in the early twelfth century and formed the ideological core of Rodrigo Jiménez's *Historia Gothica* in the thirteenth.[70] So potent indeed was the neo-Gothic idea that it passed into the historical consciousness of modern times. For those historians who believed in the 'historical unity' of the peninsula, the idea was followed with almost religious zeal. Had it not been for the indomitable warriors of the Asturias, they declared, Spain and possibly the rest of Christendom would have been engulfed under the tide of Islam. Despite the demise of the unitary Visigothic state after 711, the victory at Covadonga, which already in the early tenth century had assumed legendary proportions, meant that the flame of resistance was kept burning and enabled subsequent generations to undertake the Reconquest and to contemplate the restoration of the whole of the peninsula into Christian hands. Not for nothing was the Asturias regarded as 'the cradle of Spain'. In the words of Menéndez Pidal, Asturias 'served as initiator and teacher in this ideal of resistance and total restoration'.[71]

Yet if, by proclaiming the political continuity between the Toledo of the Visigothic kings and the Oviedo of the reign of Alfonso III, the court chroniclers of the late ninth century were seeking to establish the legitimate rights of the Asturian kings to rule over the whole peninsula, political realities were rather more complex. At roughly the same time as the inhabitants of the Asturias were throwing off the yoke of Muslim domination, other centres of Christian resistance were emerging too. In the Basque country to the east, for example, despite the efforts of both the Arabs and the Franks to impose their authority over the area, a small independent principality evolved in the eighth and ninth centuries, which was later to become the Kingdom of Navarre. At the eastern end of the Pyrenees, meanwhile, a series of campaigns carried out by the Franks between 785 and 801 led to the founding of the military frontier region called the Spanish March. Later, as Frankish power declined during the course of the ninth century, so the various counties into which this region had been divided became independent entities.

Two centuries later, Christian Spain had evolved into five major geopolitical areas: the Kingdom of León, which also embraced the Asturias and Galicia; Castile, which had emerged from the shadow of

León as an independent county towards the end of the tenth century and had become a kingdom on the accession of Fernando I in 1035; the Basque kingdom of Navarre; the Kingdom of Aragón; and the Catalan counties, the most powerful of which was the county of Barcelona. In the words of Vilar, the Christian principalities 'coalesced or dispersed according to the rhythm of marriage and family succession. Each accumulated and preserved the fame of its titles and its battle honours, a mistrust of its neighbours, an individualism exacerbated by free municipalities and noble adventurers'.[72]

By the middle of the thirteenth century the pattern had simplified somewhat. Aragón and Catalonia had joined together in 1137 and the definitive union of León and Castile had taken place in 1230. All the same, it is hard to agree with García Villada that these developments marked 'la tendencia a la unificación de España'.[73] After all, Portugal had declared its independence from León-Castile in 1143; Navarre, its fortunes tied to the dynasty of the counts of Champagne from 1234, remained aloof; and the reconquest of the Muslim Kingdom of Granada still lay far in the future. True, from the time of Alfonso III, the kings of Asturias-León, by styling themselves *imperator* in the charters they issued, seem to have been laying claim to political supremacy over the other Christian regions. During the reign of Alfonso VII (1126–57), these imperial pretensions were voiced with renewed insistency.[74] Yet, notwithstanding Alfonso VII's imperial coronation at León in 1135, and the fact that he might grandiloquently style himself 'ego Adefonsus, pius, felix, inclitus, triunfator, ac semper invictus, totius Hispaniae divina clementia famosissimus imperator' in the charters he had drawn up, his claims to imperial supremacy were never translated into a *de facto* domination of the other Christian kingdoms.[75] On his death in 1157, the imperial claim was quietly forgotten, never to be resuscitated. The Christian realms remained divided and fiercely independent.

For those writers who so wholeheartedly espoused the neo-Gothic idea and longed for the day when *Hispania* might once more be united, the fragmentation of Christian Spain into competing principalities was a source of profound embarrassment. As Linehan has put it, 'squaring the unitary neogothic myth with political reality called for some virtuoso conceptual gymnastics'.[76] The *Primera Crónica General*, for example, composed under the patronage of Alfonso X of Castile (1252–84) towards the end of the thirteenth century, deplored the divisions among the Christians which, it declared, had slowed down the progress of the Reconquest.[77]

Later historians sought to provide a more positive interpretation of the disintegration of Christian Spain. Though the Christian realms may have been *momentarily* separated by political circumstances, they argued, they were none the less united by a common religious cause against the Muslim invaders.[78] The *Reconquista* was above all a war of religion, a crusade, whose aim was to restore the whole of the peninsula to Christian hands. Accordingly, it was held that those who combated the Moors, whether Castilians or Catalans, were not merely acting out of local patriotism, but were all serving the cause of national reintegration. The idea of Hispanic unity, therefore, not only lived on, but was actively pursued.[79]

Nowhere was this spirit of common enterprise more clearly witnessed, they agreed, than on those occasions where Christian princes had actually joined forces to campaign against the Moors. In 1147, for example, Catalan and Navarrese knights had joined Alfonso VII and his allies from Genoa and Pisa to launch a successful attack on the port of Almería.[80] And in 1212, a new alliance between Castile, Navarre and Aragón had brought about a crushing Christian victory over the Almohads at Las Navas de Tolosa.[81] The leading role in all these actions, it was emphasized, however, was played by Castile. Indeed, the belief that Castile, 'la madre de España', had inherited the unifying mission of the Visigothic and Asturian kings and was the driving force behind the Reconquest, was to become one of the most cherished myths of Spanish historiography. It was Castile who bore the brunt of the Arab attacks during the height of the Reconquest; Castile who, by dint of supreme sacrifice, neutralized the Muslim threat and, by the conquest of Granada in 1492, removed that threat for good; Castile who by her efforts reunited Spain after centuries of division; and it was Castile who undertook, almost single-handedly, the conquest and settlement of the Spanish overseas empire.[82]

All the same, such an interpretation chose to ignore certain uncomfortable facts. For one thing, far from consistently pursuing the goal of peninsula reunification, the Christian realms were frequently at loggerheads with one another. Alfonso VII, for one, had to fight long and hard with his Christian neighbours in Portugal, Navarre and Aragón before he was allowed a free hand to campaign in al-Andalus.[83] The buoyant optimism displayed by the Asturian chronicles of the late ninth century soon gave way to a more circumspect attitude. Kings sought the aggrandizement of their kingdoms, certainly, but not exclusively at the expense of Muslim al-Andalus. During much of the eleventh century, the picture we get is not of implacable hostility between Christian and Moor, but of close political contacts and a certain religious tolerance. Treaties of friendship were made between

Christian and Muslim rulers, while Alfonso VI of León-Castile (1065–1109), the conqueror of Toledo in 1085, would style himself the 'Emperor of the Two Faiths'.[84] The principality Rodrigo Díaz de Vivar, 'el Cid', carved out for himself in Valencia in 1094 was the work of a military adventurer, not a religious crusader.[85] To claim, as did Menéndez Pidal, that the Cid's successes in the Levant 'gave new strength to the neo-Gothic idea of unity' is far-fetched to say the very least.[86]

This mood of tolerance and *convivencia* would change in the course of the twelfth century as the arrival of crusading ideas in the peninsula led to a hardening of attitudes towards Islam. There developed a 'spirit of reconquest' the like of which had not been seen since the Asturian chronicles, way back in the late ninth century, had confidently promised the imminent expulsion of the Moors from the peninsula.[87] All the same, as the kings of Castile and Aragón looked forward to the day when all Spain would be in Christian hands, they seem to have been thinking more along the lines of partition than of reunification. The treaties drawn up at Tudillén in 1151 and Cazola in 1179, which provided for the subsequent carve up of the Muslim-held lands between the crowns of Castile and Aragón, reflected the hard-nosed diplomacy of independent political powers; they were hardly the sign of monarchs bent on forging peninsula unity anew.[88]

THE LEGACY OF THE MIDDLE AGES

The political map of Spain was to remain largely unchanged until the late fifteenth century. The death of Enrique IV of Castile in 1474, however, brought to an end the uneasy equilibrium between the 'peninsula triptych' of Portugal, Castile and Aragón.[89] Civil war broke out between the supporters of Enrique's half-sister, Isabel, who in 1469 had married Fernando, the heir to the throne of Aragón, and those of his allegedly illegitimate daughter, Juana 'la Beltraneja', betrothed to Alfonso V of Portugal. The future of Castile hung in the balance.[90] Only five years later, in 1479, was Isabel able to make good her claim to the throne of Castile; the same year her husband Fernando succeeded to that of Aragón.

The union of Castile and Aragón in 1479, we are frequently told, marked the birth of modern Spain.[91] The Kingdoms of Granada and Navarre were annexed in 1492 and 1515 respectively. Only Portugal maintained her independence, although between 1580 and 1640 she did briefly come under Spanish control once more.[92] For nationalist historians, the union of Castile and Aragón was the glorious conclusion to the long process of reconquest and reunification which had been set in motion by Pelayo and his followers in the mountains of the Asturias nearly eight centuries before. Like a phoenix rising out of the ashes, a new united Spain, the rightful successor to the Visigothic kingdom, had finally been born. We would do well to take these rhetorical claims with a pinch of salt. After all, if the supporters of Juana 'la Beltraneja' had prevailed, the political map of the new *Hispania* would have been very different; the fortunes of Castile would have been inextricably tied to those of Portugal. As Hooper has rightly observed:

> That the six states which emerged in the north of the peninsula should have evolved into two nations – one of them made up of five of those states and the other consisting of the remaining one – was a matter of purest chance. Had a battle here or there gone the other way, had this or that son not died in infancy, had this or that mother not perished in childbirth, the division might have been altogether different. Contrary to what the more rabid of Spain's centralists claim, there is absolutely nothing 'sacred' about the unity of Spain, because there was nothing pre-ordained about its shape.[93]

For all its symbolic value, however, the union of Castile and Aragón changed little. As Kamen has said, 'the marriage did not, and could not, create a new united Spain'.[94] Though Fernando and Isabel might pursue a common foreign policy, no real effort was made to integrate the two kingdoms. The customs barriers between Castile and Aragón remained in place, their administrative structures unchanged. The crown of Aragón, for example, continued to be divided into five realms – Catalonia, Aragón, Valencia, Majorca and Sardinia – each possessing its own government and laws. In other words, the fundamental divisions of medieval Spain had not disappeared.

From the very beginning, moreover, the union of Castile and Aragón was not a partnership of equals.[95] Castile, the military and economic heavyweight of the two, was able to call the tune. The conquest and settlement of the empire in the New World was almost exclusively a Castilian venture and Castilians dominated the imperial institutional apparatus. Moreover, from the sixteenth century onwards there was a move to concentrate the machinery of government in the centre of the peninsula. The Catholic Kings, in common with most medieval monarchs, had been largely itinerant rulers, dealing with matters of government during the course of their travels across the length and breadth of Spain. But even before the death of Fernando of Aragón in 1516, Valladolid had emerged as the administrative centre of the realm. When, in 1561, Felipe II established his capital in

Madrid, at the very centre of the peninsula, it graphically demonstrated the governmental philosophy of the Habsburgs.

Almost inevitably, the centralization of political power led to resentment. For Aragón, in particular, which had remained independent for nigh on 700 years, its subordination to the interests of Castile proved a bitter pill to swallow. Nevertheless, as Sánchez-Albornoz observed, such ill-feeling might well have been overcome in time had a serious attempt been made to foster a sense of Spanish identity among the inhabitants of the peninsula.[96] As it was, by perpetuating the divisions of the medieval period and by leaving untouched the political and economic privileges enjoyed by the peripheral regions, the seeds were sown for future discord.

Regional discontent was later compounded by the economic decline of the centre. 'From the fifteenth to the seventeenth centuries', Vilar has written, 'the central provinces had not only played a leading role, they had also a greater population and greater production, as well as economic and demographic superiority. Such a balance between the political force of the centre and its true vitality was an exceptional moment.'[97] This equilibrium was lost from the moment Castile began to experience a downturn in her economic fortunes.[98] Thereafter, as the economic initiative passed to the regions, but political power remained firmly rooted in Madrid, there developed a widespread conviction that the centre was running Spain at the expense of the periphery, a feeling which has persisted to this day. When Olivares, the chief minister of Felipe IV, made the first serious attempt to bring about the administrative unification of the peninsula in 1640, the plan seriously backfired and he only succeeded in provoking the rebellion of the Catalans and the Portuguese.[99] Instead, it was not until Felipe V introduced the *Nueva Planta* constitution of 1716, which swept away the existing institutions and privileges of the crown of Aragón, that Spain was truly united for the first time.[100] Or was it? By riding roughshod over regional sensibilities, the Spanish rulers had merely stirred up resentments that would return to undermine the unity of the nation in the coming years. The spectre that Spain might disintegrate never quite disappeared. Even today, Spaniards are still trying to come to terms with that legacy; the struggle between centre and periphery goes on.

NOTES

This work was carried out with the support of a British Academy Postdoctoral Fellowship.

1 'Hispania uniuersa terrarum situ trigona est et circumfusione oceani Tyrrhe-nique pelagi paene insula efficitur': Orosius, *Historiarum adversum paganos libri VII*, ed. K. Zangemeister (Leipzig, 1889), p. 11.

2 C. Sánchez-Albornoz, *El drama de la formación de España y los españoles: otra nueva aventura polémica* (Barcelona, 1973), p. 22.

3 See P. Vilar, *Spain: A Brief History*, 2nd edn (Oxford, 1977), p. 3.

4 R. Menéndez Pidal, *The Spaniards in Their History* (London, 1950), p. 178.

5 'Spain's geography may not have exactly favoured unity, but it did not make it unthinkable. France is almost as varied and marginally bigger, yet the French today are a remarkably homogeneous people. What ensured that Spain would remain so divided was the course of its history': J. Hooper, *The Spaniards: A Portrait of the New Spain* (Harmondsworth, 1987), p. 205.

6 Much depends, of course, on how we choose to define 'nation'. In this essay, it will be employed in its loosest sense as 'a community of people whose sense of belonging together derives from their belief that they have a common homeland and from experience of common traditions and historical develop-ment', as opposed to its stricter modern sense, born of the French Revolution, which reflects the wish of such a community 'to assert its unity and independence vis-à-vis other communities or groups': D. Thomson, *Europe since Napoleon* (Harmondsworth, 1966), p. 119.

7 'Se cerraba una puerta en la historia de España y empezaba en verdad España a existir; afirmar que España había existido antes, a partir de este o del otro siglo ... es pura fantasía': C. Sánchez-Albornoz, *Mi testamento histórico-político* (Barcelona, 1975), p. 90.

8 'La nación española nació y se afirmó, *políticamente*, el año 573, bajo el cetro de Leovigildo, y *espiritualmente* el 8 de mayo de 589, bajo Recaredo': Z. García Villada, *El destino de España en la historia universal*, 2nd edn (Madrid, 1940), pp. 105–6.

9 H. Kamen, *Spain 1469–1714: A Society of Conflict* (London, 1983), p. 269.

10 Excellent surveys of the period are to be found in Kamen, *Spain 1469–1714* and J. H. Elliott, *Imperial Spain 1469–1716* (London, 1963).

11 Kamen, *Spain 1469–1714*, pp. 266–71.

12 On the nineteenth century, see especially R. Carr, *Spain 1808–1975*, 2nd edn (Oxford, 1982).

13 P. Russell, 'The Nessus-shirt of Spanish history', *Bulletin of Hispanic Studies*, 36 (1959), 220.

14 See Kamen, *Spain 1469–1714*, pp. 230–5.

15 *Ibid.*, p. 272.

16 Carr makes the point that radical protest at the plight of Spain was being actively voiced long before the end of the century: *Spain 1808–1975*, p. 524.

17 See, for example, D. L. Shaw, *The Generation of 1898 in Spain* (London, 1975).

18 G. Brenan, *The Literature of the Spanish People: From Roman Times to the Present Day*, 2nd edn (Cambridge, 1953), p. 419.

19 A point made by Russell, 'The Nessus-shirt', p. 219.

20 A phrase coined by Brenan, *The Literature of the Spanish People*, p. 417.

21 A. Ganivet, *Idearium español* (Granada, 1897); translated by J. R. Carey as

Spain: An Interpretation (London, 1946). On Ganivet's work, see H. Ramsden, *Angel Ganivet's Idearium Español: A Critical Study* (Manchester, 1967).

22 J. Ortega y Gasset, *España invertebrada: bosquejo de algunos pensamientos históricos* (Madrid, 1921).

23 *Ibid.*, p. 129.

24 J. Costa, *Reconstitución y europeización de España* (Madrid, 1900). On the work of Joaquín Costa, see R. Pérez de la Dehesa, *El pensamiento de Costa y su influencia en la Generación del 98* (Madrid, 1960) and G. J. G. Cheyne, *Joaquín Costa, el gran desconocido* (Barcelona, 1972) and *A Bibliographical Study of the Writings of Joaquín Costa* (London, 1972).

25 R. Macías Picavea, *El problema nacional: hechos, causas y remedios* (Madrid, 1899).

26 Unamuno's comment is cited by R. M. Nadal in the introduction to Ganivet, *Spain: An Interpretation*, p. 24.

27 See, for example, Menéndez Pidal, *The Spaniards in Their History*, p. 179.

28 *Ibid.*, p. 202.

29 M. Menéndez y Pelayo, *Historia de los heterodoxos españoles*, 2 vols. (Madrid, 1880–2). See in this context D. W. Foard, 'The Spanish Fichte: Menéndez y Pelayo', *Journal of Contemporary History*, 14 (1979), 83–97.

30 M. E. Lacarra, 'La utilización del Cid de Menéndez Pidal en la ideología militar franquista', *Ideologies and Literature*, 3 (1980), 108–9.

31 A. Castro, *España en su historia: cristianos, moros y judíos* (Buenos Aires, 1948). Translated as *The Structure of Spanish History* (Princeton, N.J., 1954) and *The Spaniards: An Introduction to Their History* (Berkeley, Calif., 1971). References in this essay are made to the 1954 translation.

32 C. Sánchez-Albornoz, *España: un enigma histórico*, 2 vols. (Buenos Aires, 1956). A very poor English translation exists, published as *Spain, a Historical Enigma*, 2nd edn, 2 vols. (Madrid, 1975). Sánchez-Albornoz later referred to 'la deformación de la historia de mi patria por Américo Castro' in *El drama*, p. 11.

33 Sánchez-Albornoz, *Mi testamento*, p. 78.

34 Sánchez-Albornoz, *Spain*, vol. I, pp. 20–2.

35 *Ibid.*, vol. I, pp. 207–45.

36 He was later to comment: 'Contra la tesis de hibridismo basada en la cópula e interpenetración de cristianos, moros y judíos, la realidad histórica atestigua la forja del pueblo español en la batalla abierta entre moros y cristianos y en la pugna, muchas veces sangrienta, de los cristianos contra los judíos y contra los nietos de los conversos': Sánchez-Albornoz, *Mi testamento*, p. 91.

37 Sánchez-Albornoz, *El drama*, p. 15. Sánchez-Albornoz referred to 'la angustia irritada ante el envenenamiento de la concienca nacional por una sombría teoría nacida de una concepción peyorativa de España de no sé qué resentimiento familiar y racial': *Mi testamento*, pp. 76–8.

38 Sánchez-Albornoz, *Spain*, vol. II, pp. 921–1045. 'Los gallegos son tan españoles como los andaluces, los catalanes no lo son menos que los extremeños, y los vascos lo son aún más que las gentes de Toledo y de la Mancha porque hablaron el castellano antes que ellos; y constituyeron la raíz cúbica de lo hispano': *Mi testamento*, p. 82.

39 A point made by Russell, 'The Nessus-shirt', p. 219.

40 Menéndez Pidal, *The Spaniards in Their History*, p. 191.

41 See F. J. Wiseman, *Roman Spain* (London, 1956).

42 Menéndez Pidal, for example, refers to the 'spiritual unity' of Spain during the Roman period 'governed by certain organic principles, by certain vital energies which endured in action and in strength': *The Spaniards in Their History*, p. 181.

43 R. Collins, *Early Medieval Spain: Unity in Diversity, 400–1000* (London, 1983), p. 6.

44 *Ibid.*, pp. 8–9.

45 The *Primera Crónica General*, for example, in its account of Hannibal's campaigns in the peninsula, relates that 'tomo aquella gente que troxiera d'Affrica e de los espannoles quantos quiso, e fuesse contra los romanos': *Primera Crónica General de España que mandó componer Alfonso el Sabio y se continuaba bajo Sancho IV en 1289*, ed. R. Menéndez Pidal, 2 vols. (Madrid, 1955), vol. I, p. 17.

46 R. B. Tate, 'The medieval kingdoms of the Iberian Peninsula (to 1474)', in P. E. Russell (ed.), *Spain: A Companion to Spanish Studies* (London, 1973), p. 66.

47 On Visigothic Spain see, for example, E. A. Thompson, *The Goths in Spain* (Oxford, 1969); J. Orlandis, *Historia de España: la España visigótica* (Madrid, 1977); Collins, *Early Medieval Spain*, pp. 11–145.

48 The latest edition of Isidore's chronicle, together with facing Spanish translation, is that of C. Rodríguez Alonso, *Las historias de los godos, vándalos y suevos de Isidoro de Sevilla* (León, 1975). For an English translation, see that of G. Donini and G. B. Ford, *History of the Goths, Vandals and Suevi* (Leiden, 1970). Isidore's history of the Goths, but not those of the Vandals and Suevi, has also been translated by K. Baxter Wolf, *Conquerors and Chroniclers of Early Medieval Spain* (Liverpool, 1990), pp. 81–110.

49 Lucas of Tuy, *Chronicon Mundi ab Origine Mundi usque ad Eram MCCLXXIV*, ed. A. Schottus, *Hispaniae Illustratae*, vol. IV (Frankfurt, 1608), pp. 1–116. For the *Historia Gothica*, see *Roderici Ximenii de Rada, Historia de rebus hispanie sive Historia Gothica*, ed. J. Fernández Valverde, Corpus Christianorum Continuatio Mediaeualis, 72 (Turnhout, 1987).

50 Above, n. 8.

51 'El sentimiento de la *Laus*, como el del resto del tratado, comporta un claro orgullo nacional y patriótico. Isidoro ve como suyo al pueblo godo y se siente parte de él, la historia de España es, para él, la historia de los visigodos': Rodríguez Alonso, *Las historias de los godos*, p. 63.

52 Ortega y Gasset, *La España invertebrada*, p. 133; Castro, *The Structure of Spanish History*, pp. 63ff.

53 'No ha hecho, creo yo, historia nacional, sino dar una historia de pueblos no romanos, con independencia, y considerar en la *laus Hispaniae* a España unida al pueblo godo. Pero no hay propiamente concepto de nacionalidad': L. Vázquez de Parga, 'Notas sobre la obra histórica de S. Isidoro', in M. C. Díaz y Díaz (ed.), *Isidoriana* (León, 1961), p. 106.

54 Collins, *Early Medieval Spain*, pp. 110ff.

55 See R. Collins, *The Arab Conquest of Spain, 710–797* (Oxford, 1989).

56 *Crónicas Asturianas. Crónica de Alfonso III (Rotense y 'A Sebastián'). Crónica Albeldense (y 'Profética'),* ed. J. Gil Fernández, J. L. Moralejo and J. I. Ruiz de la Peña (Oviedo, 1985), pp. 67–8.

57 *Ibid.,* pp. 68–9.

58 In this study I have made use of the edition in the *Corpus Scriptorum Muzarabicorum,* ed. J. Gil, 2 vols. (Madrid, 1973), vol. i, pp. 15–54. A more recent edition is that of J. E. López Pereira, *Crónica mozárabe de 754: edición crítica y traducción* (Zaragoza, 1980). An English translation of the chronicle is provided by Baxter Wolf, *Conquerors and Chroniclers,* pp. 111–58.

59 'Infelicem Spaniam . . . condam deliciosa et nunc misera effecta': *Corpus Scriptorum Muzarabicorum,* vol. i, p. 33.

60 See the excellent edition in Gil Fernández *et al., Crónicas Asturianas.*

61 The Oviedo version of the so-called *Chronicle of Alfonso III* records: 'Sed qui ex semine regio remanserunt, quidam ex illis Franciam petierunt, maxima uero pars in patria Asturiensium intrauerunt . . .': *Crónicas Asturianas,* p. 123.

62 *Ibid.,* pp. 122–3.

63 *Ibid.,* pp. 122–31.

64 'Sicque ex tunc reddita est libertas populo Christiano . . . et Astororum regnum diuina prouidentia exoritur': *ibid.,* p. 173.

65 'Omnemque Gotorum ordinem, sicuti Toleto fuerat, tam in eclesia quam palatio in Ouetao cuncta statuit': *ibid.,* p. 174.

66 The buoyant mood found its most remarkable expression in the *Prophetic Chronicle,* redacted in Oviedo in April 883, in which its author, drawing on a spurious biblical prophecy attributed to Ezekiel, predicted the imminent expulsion of the Muslims from the peninsula on 11 November 884: *ibid.,* p. 188.

67 *Ibid.,* pp. 65–71; Collins, *Early Medieval Spain,* pp. 228–9.

68 D. W. Lomax, *The Reconquest of Spain* (London, 1978), p. 26.

69 A point made by, among others, J. Vicens Vives, *Approaches to the History of Spain* (Berkeley, Calif., 1967), p. 32.

70 *Historia Silense,* ed. J. Pérez de Urbel and A. G. Ruiz-Zorrilla (Madrid, 1959). For the *Historia Gothica* of Rodrigo Jiménez, above, n. 49.

71 Menéndez Pidal, *The Spaniards in Their History,* p. 186. 'The pure unfettered religious spirit which had been preserved in the north gave impetus and national aims to the Reconquest. Without its strength of purpose Spain would have given up in despair all resistance and would have become denationalized . . . What gave Spain her exceptional strength of collective resistance and enabled her to last through three long centuries of great peril was her policy of fusing into one single ideal the recovery of the Gothic states for the fatherland and the redemption of the enslaved churches for the glory of Christianity': *ibid.,* pp. 143–4.

72 Vilar, *Spain: A Brief History,* p. 15. For a general treatment of the Reconquest, see Lomax, *The Reconquest of Spain;* among the most stimulating accounts in Spanish are J. A. García de Cortázar, *La época medieval* (Madrid, 1973) and J. M. Mínguez, *La Reconquista* (Madrid, 1989).

73 García Villada, *El destino de España,* p. 114.

74 On the imperial pretensions of the kings of Asturias-León, see, for example, R. Menéndez Pidal, *El imperio hispánico y los cinco reinos* (Madrid, 1950); J. A. Maravall, *El concepto de España en la Edad Media*, 2nd edn (Madrid, 1964), pp. 412–15.

75 A contemporary account of the imperial coronation of Alfonso VII is to be found in the *Chronica Adefonsi Imperatoris*, ed. A. Maya: *Chronica Hispana saeculi XII, Pars I*, Corpus Christianorum Continuatio Mediaeualis, 71 (Turnhout, 1990), pp. 109–248, at pp. 181–4. The charter cited here was drawn up at Peñafiel on 9 November 1156: J. A. Llorente, *Noticias históricas de las tres provincias vascongadas, Alava, Guipúzcoa y Vizcaya*, vol. IV (Madrid, 1808), pp. 164–7.

76 P. A. Linehan, 'Religion, nationalism and national identity in medieval Spain and Portugal', in S. Mews (ed.), *Religion and National Identity*, Studies in Church History, 18 (Oxford, 1982), p. 176.

77 *Primera Crónica General*, vol. I, p. 4.

78 'A pesar de que los Reinos y Condados pirenaicos estuvieron separados *políticamente* del sucessor legítimo del antiguo Reino visigodo, *espiritualmente* conservaron todos la *unidad*. Esta unidad estaba constituída por el anhelo común de extrañar a los mahomentanos del suelo patrio para reanudar el lazo que a todos, libres e invadidos, les ligaba, es decir la Catolicidad': García Villada, *El destino de España*, p. 106.

79 'But the destruction of the Gothic kingdom, followed by the long-drawn-out period of disintegration, did not blot out of men's minds the idea of unity, but only obscured it. It banished the idea from political life, but not from men's aspirations. For the mediaeval kingdoms never broke Gothic unity in an arbitrary manner but tried to patch it up and save it from destruction': Menéndez Pidal, *The Spaniards in Their History*, p. 185.

80 For a contemporary poetic celebration of the Almería campaign, see *Prefatio de Almaria*, ed. J. Gil: *Chronica Hispana saeculi XII*, pp. 249–67.

81 On the campaign of 1212 see, for example, Rodrigo Jiménez, *Historia de rebus hispanie*, pp. 259–79.

82 See García Villada, *El destino de España*, pp. 117–28.

83 *Chronica Adefonsi Imperatoris*, pp. 152–62, 184–91.

84 In this context, see the comments of A. Mackay, *Spain in the Middle Ages: From Frontier to Empire, 1000–1500* (London, 1977), pp. 15–22.

85 See the excellent study of R. Fletcher, *The Quest for El Cid* (London, 1989).

86 Menéndez Pidal, *The Spaniards in Their History*, p. 187.

87 On the introduction of crusading ideals into the peninsula, see R. A. Fletcher, 'Reconquest and crusade in Spain c. 1050–1150', *Transactions of the Royal Historical Society*, 5th ser., 37 (1987), 31–47.

88 For the treaty of Tudillén, see *Liber Feudorum Maior*, ed. F. Miquel Rosell, 2 vols. (Barcelona, 1945), vol. I, pp. 39–42. The text of the treaty of Cazola can be found in J. González, *El reino de Castilla en la época de Alfonso VIII*, 3 vols. (Madrid, 1960), vol. II, pp. 528–9.

89 Vilar, *Spain: A Brief History*, p. 16.

90 'Castile, with no male heir, was poised between the choice of an Atlantic or Mediterranean future': Tate, 'The medieval kingdoms', p. 102.

91 Above, n. 7.
92 The long independence of Portugal has not stopped some Spanish writers advocating the total unification of the peninsula: 'Respeto el orgullo nacionalista de los portugueses y vuelvo a hacer notorio mi enamoramiento de su patria, pero mentiría si ocultase mi esperanza en un futuro regreso de Portugal a la matriz de Hispania de donde había salido': Sánchez-Albornoz, *Mi testamento*, p. 194.
93 Hooper, *The Spaniards*, p. 211.
94 Kamen, *Spain 1469–1714*, p. 10.
95 *Ibid.*, pp. 12–15; Elliott, *Imperial Spain*, pp. 41–4.
96 Sánchez-Albornoz, *Mi testamento*, p. 82.
97 Vilar, *Spain: A Brief History*, p. 47.
98 Kamen, *Spain 1469–1714*, pp. 222–30.
99 *Ibid.*, pp. 235–40.
100 *Ibid.*, pp. 269–70.

FIVE

SHIFTING NATIONALISM:
BELGIANS, FLEMINGS AND WALLOONS

LOUIS VOS

THE nationality problem in Belgium, that is, the problem of two language groups living within one state, has dominated political life in recent decades. It has led to a restructuring of the state in a series of revisions of the constitution in 1970, 1980 and 1988. Through these revisions a process of federalization has been put in motion. With the latest revision of the constitution the central unitary state is to give way to a body of federal states, although at the time of writing the process has not been yet completed. The language groups – the Dutch-speaking community in the north and the French-speaking community in the south – are moving more and more towards the development of complete national entities with their own symbols, public holidays and institutions. The question now is whether the old Belgian national identity which in 1830 was so strong that it led to a successful national revolution and to independence, can withstand the centrifugal power of the new nationalist forces. It is possible of course that the appeal of complete separatism has diminished precisely because of the structural reforms recently undertaken and that a new co-ordinating role will be found for the Belgian state.[1]

The question that concerns us in this contribution is how and why the waning of a Belgian sense of identity has come about to the advantage of both a Flemish and Walloon identity. The new process of nation-formation has, it is true, witnessed its definitive break-through in the past two decades, but its roots go back to the period of early Belgian independence in the first half of the nineteenth century. At that time, in marked contrast with today, there was no question of a Flemish and Walloon nation respectively. Consideration was given only to the establishment of a Belgian nation and this nation could trace its roots back to the previous centuries.

A SOUTHERN NETHERLANDISH IDENTITY

To understand the background to this process it is necessary to go back to the growth of a Southern Netherlandish 'national' identity which formed the basis of Belgian nationhood in 1830.

In the Middle Ages there were a number of sovereign principalities in the Low Countries. From the end of the fourteenth century, when they gradually came under the control of the Dukes of Burgundy, these principalities developed a certain sense of unity.[2] This unity was confirmed in the sixteenth century with the political union of the seventeen provinces at the time of Emperor Charles V. The Low Countries – or Netherlands – thus formed an area in which the people, and in particular the ruling elite, did not consider themselves either German or French. In the first place they felt themselves bound to their own principalities and were therefore first of all loyal to Flanders, Brabant or Hainault. But alongside this they also developed a general Dutch identity. It must be said that an important part of present-day Belgium, the former princely diocese of Liège, was not included in this process. It remained completely autonomous until its annexation by revolutionary France at the end of the eighteenth century.

In the second part of the sixteenth century, there was dissatisfaction with the policies of the monarchs, at that time the Habsburgs, concerning religion (the fight against Protestantism), administration (centralization and taxation policy which chipped away at old privileges) and law and order (military actions against commercial interests). This dissatisfaction resulted in an uprising and civil war.[3] The Eighty Years' War (1568–1648) led to the independence of the seven northern provinces which, with Holland as the new centre, together formed the Republic of the United Provinces. The Southern Netherlands on the other hand remained – or again came – under the authority of the Spanish Habsburgs. The latter allowed the local nobility, the clergy and the large cities a certain measure of autonomy in the day-to-day administration of the region.

The north, where the Reformation triumphed, had its golden age in the seventeenth century. With Amsterdam as the nerve centre of expanding overseas trade, the Republic became a great political power (with Stadholder William III (1672–1702) becoming in 1688 also King of England) and a cultural leader. In stark contrast to this golden age, the eighteenth century was to experience economic and political stagnation and neglect. The Southern Netherlands in the seventeenth and eighteenth centuries (under Spain until 1700, and then by dynastic succession under the Austrian-Habsburg dynasty) became the plaything of the great powers and was also a highly desirable buffer zone. Public life, repeatedly devastated by war, was dominated by the Counter-Reformation in the seventeenth century and by administrative centralization and economic expansion in the eighteenth century.[4]

During the course of these two centuries, then, both countries, the Protestant Republic of the United Provinces and the Catholic Southern Netherlands, grew further and further apart politically, economically and culturally. The fact that both peoples largely shared a common language could not prevent this trend. Indeed the upper classes in the Austrian Netherlands underwent a great Frenchification towards the end of the eighteenth century. These two centuries of separate history led to the development of both a Dutch and a 'Belgian' mentality which could no longer be unified. The identity of the Southern Netherlands was strongly influenced by its Catholic Counter-Reformation. In this the Jesuit colleges, the University of Leuven and baroque art in newly built churches played a significant part. So too did Jansenism which had more followers and opponents here than elsewhere in Europe. But identity was also influenced by French intellectual life and by its special geopolitical function as a buffer zone between imperialist France and other European powers. Finally provincialism also played a part in this growing 'Belgian' identity. In fact for the majority of the people it continued to be of more importance than the loyalty towards the 'generality' of the southern provinces.

Throughout all this, from the sixteenth to the eighteenth century, there developed in the Southern Netherlands an ethnic community as defined by the sociologist Anthony D. Smith. He emphasizes six dimensions in the notion of ethnic community (or *ethnie* as he calls it): a collective name, a common myth of descent, a shared history, a dictinctive shared culture, an association with a specific territory and a sense of solidarity.[5] We still do not have an accurate description of the process of development of this configuration in the Southern Netherlands. That these dimensions were at last present at the end of the eighteenth century was evidenced by the conflict between that country and its legal ruler, the Emperor Joseph II of Austria.

In 1789 there was a revolution in the Austrian Netherlands. It was in fact a reaction to the politics of centralization of Joseph II. This revolution was legitimized in two diverging ways. On the one hand, it was mainly encouraged by the traditional resistance to the centralization policies of the Emperor which encroached upon the privileges of the favoured classes, that is, the nobility and clergy. On the other hand, a minority of rebels sought justification for their revolt in the ideas of the Enlightenment which had already served as an inspiration for the American revolution. Within a few months, however, this latter group were neutralized by the traditional strata. Nevertheless, through their actions, new elements came to the fore in a second movement. The resistance movement against the autocratic government of the Emperor gradually developed into a struggle for independence of national calibre.[6]

In December 1789 this so-called 'Brabant Revolution' – in reality supported not only by the Duchy of Brabant but by the other principalities of the Austrian Netherlands as well – forced the Austrian troops to withdraw, so that in January 1790 the revolutionaries could proclaim officially their independence. The then emerging 'Belgian' state (formally Les Etats Belgiques Unies/United Netherlandic States) had a federal structure with only a weak central government, so that the provincial identities (an inheritance from the former principalities) were able to coexist, while at the same time a new sense of national identity vigorously manifested itself. The growth of that nationalism took place within the existing institutional framework and followed the same path – that of the 'state-to-nation' evolution – as in the American and French Revolutions. In all these cases there emerged a new ethnic community within an existing state framework, and a new nationalism was developed with both cultural and political dimensions.

As regards content, the new Belgian national identity was characterized by three elements. First of all, 'restoration', the wish to restore the old political, institutional and religious order of the past. Secondly, the creation of national symbols: the introduction of the heraldic Brabant colours as a black–yellow–red tricolour flag, of the lion as a symbol of strength, bravery and independence, the development of a new interpretation of 'Belgian history', and the rise of a personality cult of the leaders of the revolution. Thirdly, it was very significant that the whole discourse of the revolution was imbued with religious feelings. Catholicism became the most outspoken marker of the new nation, partly as a consequence of the major role played in the revolution by the Catholic clergy, but also as a mobilizing principle for the nation's cause. Collective prayers and continuous processions were held as an expression of national solidarity with the fellow compatriots who volunteered for the defence of the fatherland. However, they did not prevail and a military defeat ensued at the end of 1790.

Although as a result the Austrian imperial authority was restored, this was not to be for long. A few years later, in 1795, the Austrian Netherlands and the princely diocese of Liège were captured by the French revolutionaries and annexed by France. The annexation, which lasted for twenty years until the capitulation of Napoleon in 1815, was to have three main consequences. First of all, it brought about the integration of Liège into the rest of the Southern Netherlands and the inclusion of the hitherto vehemently independent provinces in one centralized national structure. Secondly, it led to the complete Frenchification of public life in the Southern Netherlands and the birth of a Frenchified bourgeoisie alongside the existing Frenchified privileged classes of the *ancien régime*. Thirdly, it set in motion a process of denationalization among the enlightened progressive powers. As they were incorporated in the revolutionary state itself, these could only pursue the principles of the French Revolution, by behaving as perfect French citizens, unlike the progressives in satellite countries who could link the principles of the French Revolution to nationalism, as they were allowed to retain a certain degree of autonomy.[7]

The Congress of Vienna in 1815, which redrew the map of Europe, decided to bring both the Northern and Southern Netherlands together in the United Kingdom of the Netherlands under the leadership of King William I, son of the last 'stadholder' of the former Dutch Republic.[8] However, William's attempt to achieve a perfect amalgamation between the two parts of the new state failed. The state was to survive only fifteen years. Dissatisfied with royal policies in relation to church, politics and culture, and driven by the flame of Romanticism, both liberals and traditionalists united around the slogan 'freedom'. This culminated in 1830 in a southern revolt from which Belgium arose as an independent and national state. Apparently, the separate national identity of the 'Belgians' on the one hand and the 'Dutch' on the other hand became far too strong. The separation of the Netherlands which had taken place in the sixteenth century could not be reversed.

FROM A BELGIAN TO A FLEMISH MOVEMENT

Although the Belgian revolution was in many aspects similar to the earlier revolution in Brabant, it was nevertheless fundamentally different in origin. As in 1790, the immediate causes for the dissatisfaction lay in a number of measures taken by the authoritarian head of state. Also similar was the fact that originally the protest movement only wanted to effect some changes and adaptations in the administration, but that – through a process of escalating protest and counter-protest – the movement developed into a struggle for complete independence. In contrast to 1790, however, the movement of 1830 could not support itself on the back of an existing political framework in which nationalism had started to develop. Instead of the 'state-to-nation' evolution from three decades earlier, now a 'nation-to-state' route was followed. The national conviction was now first and foremost, and proved strong enough to create an autonomous state, adapted to the Belgian ethnic identity.[9]

Once the revolution had succeeded and independence had been established, many patriots committed themselves to the building up of their ethnic-cultural identity. Political autonomy acquired cultural expression. To understand this it is useful to keep in mind the distinction between cultural and political nationalism as recently defined by John Hutchinson:

> Political nationalists have as their objective the achievement of a representative national state that will guarantee to its members uniform citizenship rights. They tend to organize on legal rational lines, forming centralized apparatuses in order to mobilize different groups against existing polity and to direct them to this unitary end. For a cultural nationalist however ... the glory of a country comes not from its political power but from the culture of its people and the contribution of its thinkers and educators to humanity. The aim of cultural nationalists is rather the moral regeneration of the historic community, or, in other words, the re-creation of their distinctive national civilization.[10]

After independence in Belgium, the political nationalists were by and large overtaken by cultural nationalists. The latter started studying and reinterpreting the nation's history and aspired to the creation of an art and culture for the fatherland. They also wanted to replace the vernacular by the official French language, as an expression of the national character. So in the newly independent Belgium, Frenchification of public life spread rapidly. Political power was *de facto* in the hands of the dignitaries and the upper classes who chose French as the official language. Their choice was based on three considerations: the belief that a one-language policy was necessary for the building up of a stable state, the conviction that French as a cultural language was intrinsically superior to the Flemish or Walloon dialects spoken by the people, and the feeling that, for love of the fatherland, the language of the old United Kingdom of the Netherlands must be surrendered.

But a part of the new tendency towards Belgian cultural nationalism chose as its goal to make Belgium more Belgian, thus in fact fostering a bicultural state.[11] It turned its attentions to the process of Frenchification which it saw as a threat to national identity. It therefore opposed the law of 1831 which declared French to be the only official language in Belgium. From this movement's point of view, the Flemish cultural inheritance and the Dutch language were important constituent components of Belgian identity and, precisely to emphasize this identity as against that of neighbouring France, they were not to be lost in a complete Frenchification. In its origins and throughout the nineteenth century this Flemish movement was a Flemish-Belgian movement.

Originally it was also an autonomous political cultural programme, separate from the political parties which in any case were not set up until the 1840s. The Flemish movement entered the political arena in 1840 when it organized a petition calling for measures favourable to the Dutch language in Belgium. At the same time it sought contact with cultural circles in the Netherlands in order to bring Flemish cultural life to a higher level. It also wanted the linguistic unity between the Netherlands and Flemish Belgium to be put beyond doubt through the realization of uniform Dutch spelling in both countries. In 1856, as a recognition of the fact that there were causes for linguistic complaints, the government on its own initiative set up an official Commission of Grievances. In its report, published in 1859, it demanded a general bilingualism in the Flemish areas, supporting French unilingualism in the French-speaking areas. These demands marked the beginning of a new phase in the Flemish movement.

While in the early decades the movement emphasized above all a linguistic and literary renewal, in the second half of the nineteenth century it demanded equality for French and Dutch and strove for the introduction of bilingualism in the northern part of Belgium. That was to remain the programme of the Flemish movement until the end of the nineteenth century. It was under no illusions that Dutch-speakers in Belgium would have to be bilingual if they were to play a role in public life. Yet it wanted French-speaking officials in Flanders to bear at least some of the cost of bilingualism.

In the sixties and seventies the Flemish movement was increasingly absorbed by the two parties which had opposed each other since the forties: the traditionalist Catholics and the enlightened (and thus anti-clerical) liberals. The large majority of Flemish-minded public opinion was to be found in the Catholic camp. There it received support from a section of the clergy that considered the Catholic and Flemish elements to be two inseparable aspects of the national character. An appeal to the Christian Flemish Middle Ages was an integral part of this. On the liberal side, as opposed to this, freedom – thus also freedom of thought – sanctified by an appeal to the revolt against Spain in the sixteenth century, became an integral characteristic of the Flemish people.[12] Liberal Flemish militancy had much less support and had to contend with bitter opposition within its own liberal circles. Between these two poles, some Flemish radicals sought to bring about co-operation among all those who stood outside these two ideologically opposed blocks. They experienced success above all in Antwerp, where they managed to set up a pro-Flemish and democratic Meeting Party. This party was to be the first to return pro-Flemish deputies to Parliament and to couple Flemish demands with the struggle of the middle and lower middle class for a voice.[13]

In the seventies pro-Flemish parliamentarians, supported by the agitation concerning a number of controversial trials, were able to get the first language laws into the statute-books. These concerned the use of French or Dutch in the courts (1873), in the administration (1878) and in the official secondary education (1883). Those laws provided facilities only for people who knew no French. There was no question of a general bilingualism or of a geographical unilingualism. A move in this direction came only in the decades around the turn of the century.

In the eighties and nineties there was a breakthrough in the use of symbols of official bilingualism such as the introduction of coinage struck in both languages (1886), banknotes (1888), postage stamps (1891) and the official newspaper (*Le Moniteur Belge*) (1895). The jewel in the crown was the recognition, in principle, of the equality of Dutch and French as official languages in 1898. With that recognition the curtain fell on the struggle for bilingualism in Flanders. A new phase began. Voices were now to be raised in support of Dutch unilingualism in the northern regions.

FROM LANGUAGE TO ETHNICITY

The broadening of the Flemish programme around the turn of the century must be seen against the changing social, political and cultural background of that period. It was the time of the breakthrough of industrialization, the beginnings of democratization and the cultural influence of the *belle époque* which sought synthesis.

In the wake of the Industrial Revolution the tertiary sector in Belgium underwent a strong expansion.[14] In most clerical jobs knowledge of languages was very important. Large numbers of middle-class

people who were native Dutch-speakers felt themselves to be discriminated against when they found that they were being pushed to the
back when applying for jobs, compared to the French-speaking
applicants. This strengthened the pro-Flemish feelings which wanted
more room for the Dutch language within the administration and
services. The Flemish movement now claimed broader public support
with the setting up of Christian Democratic groups for workers and
the peasants around 1890. These groups threw their weight behind
Flemish demands as did a newly formed group of Catholic Flemish
intellectuals. In contrast to this, socialism in Flanders was not very
Flemish-minded but followed more in the steps of the overwhelmingly
French-speaking and anti-clerical liberalism.[15]

The large-scale popular democratic organizations were able to play
a major role in public life from 1893 onwards, when census franchise
was replaced by universal suffrage, admittedly in a way which allowed
for a second and even third vote in elections for people with a higher
income or education. This strengthened the position of the Christian
Democrats in Parliament and gave this predominantly pro-Flemish
movement greater influence in the formation of government policy.

Finally, this larger popular support and this increasing political
influence led to a stronger sense of Flemish consciousness. Around
1900 the Flemish movement stopped concentrating its energies solely
on language laws and widened its programme to that of cultural
nationalism. It became a broad movement for the realization of an
independent cultural, scientific and economic life in Flanders and thus
for the formation of a Flemish elite in these areas. This explains why
the legislative struggle now focused on making Flanders completely
unilingual. The prime objective now was the conversion of the French-
speaking state University of Ghent (in the north of the country) into a
Flemish-speaking one. Indeed a broadly based popular movement
sprang up around this objective. It was stimulated by the untiring
agitation of the students and intellectuals who employed a wide
variety of social initiatives including public meetings, the establishment of people's libraries, and organizing university extension and
people's colleges. This all fitted in with the general development of
European culture towards synthesis and 'organic work' in this period,
resulting in a spiritual renewal in different fields of culture.

So between 1890 and 1910 there was a shift from language to
ethnicity. One can perceive the emergence of a new Flemish ethnic
identity, which for the first time could be separated from the Belgian
identity, although to a certain extent still forming a part of it.
Significant in this respect was the emphasis on culture as a whole, on

group solidarity and emancipation, on economic, social and educational development of the Flemish nation and on the creation of new 'Flemish' institutions. On the eve of the First World War, a new Flemish cultural nationalism was flourishing, aiming at a Flemish national 'revival', using politics as a means to re-establish (or, more precisely, to establish) a Flemish community. This cultural nationalism was not incompatible with loyalty towards the Belgian fatherland, but on the other hand it would pave the way for a distinct Flemish political nationalism.

Naturally, opposition to these developments was to grow within the French-speaking community. The principal opponent was the Walloon movement. It sprang up in the last decades of the previous century as a reaction to the possible extension of bilingualism into Wallonia, and against the introduction of complete unilingualism into Flanders, where many French speakers had been able to get hold of the more lucrative jobs thanks to the previous policies of Frenchification. The liberals, who had been in opposition since 1884, were the first to support the Walloon movement just before the First World War. They received support from the socialists who were very strong in Wallonia. In reciprocal fashion this strengthened once again the Catholic character of the Flemish movement.

In the midst of these two movements, around 1900 a new Belgian nationalism was born in Brussels. It was a left-liberal movement, clearly and openly French-speaking, which dreamed of a greater and stronger Belgian state. This new nationalism received, as did Belgian patriotism in general, an enormous stimulus from the First World War, during which the greater part of Belgium was occupied by the Germans but which also saw the Belgian army holding out in a small remote corner of the country for four years.

FLANDERS OR BELGIUM?

In the occupied territories the German authorities developed a *Flamenpolitik* (a pro-Flemish policy), trying to gain the sympathy of the Flemish people by yielding to Flemish grievances.[16] They succeeded in gaining the support of a minority of Flemish nationalists, namely the Activists, by, among other things, setting up a Dutch-speaking university in Ghent (which reverted immediately in 1918 to a French-speaking university). The Activists formed a puppet government which had as its aim the administrative separation of Flanders and Wallonia but which lacked the support of the majority of the people.

Meanwhile, at the front, dissatisfaction within the army over discrimination against Flemish-minded soldiers had developed into a Front movement. It issued Flemish propaganda clandestinely from 1917 on and hoped to bring about a form of federal self-government for Flanders and Wallonia after the war. The majority of the Flamingants both in Belgium and abroad (many had fled the land) remained loyal to the Belgian state, and hoped that after the war the government would make concessions over some of the strongest of the Flemish grievances.

All these hopes of the Flemish cause came to nothing. The German defeat in 1918 brought with it an end to Activism which had discredited the Flemish movement in the eyes of the public. It brought with it also a strengthening of Belgian nationalism, so much so that in the twenties the Walloon movement became only a shadow of its former self, and the majority of French-speakers and those who were against the Flemish aspirations regarded themselves as Belgian nationalists.

Even the Flemish movement itself became disunited and split into two groups, each of which followed its own strategy. There was a minority radical wing, supported on one side by veterans of the Front movement and on the other by the younger generation of students and intellectuals who regarded themselves as the heirs to the Activists.[17] They developed a Flemish-nationalist politic that fought for self-government for Flanders, via a federalization of Belgium or via separatism causing the disappearance of Belgium. Some even considered the union of Flanders with the Netherlands. So an anti-Belgian attitude became the major touchstone and the first principle of this new Flemish movement. In their eyes Belgium was nothing less than the oppressor of the Flemish people.

The majority of the Flemish movement, however, remained loyal to the Belgian state and reverted to the pre-war path of focusing on the language laws and cultural nationalism. They hoped to achieve unilingualism in Flanders and a form of cultural autonomy via a legally guaranteed replacement of French by Dutch in public life without calling into question the unitary structure of the Belgian fatherland. It was primarily the Christian Democrats who advocated this course.

Despite these two different strategies, the borderline between the new and the old Flemish movement, which was very sharp in the twenties, became somewhat blurred in the thirties. On the one hand, the programme of Dutchification by means of the language laws was now settled, at least in principle. On the other hand, a cultural

nationalism had grown up which influenced both the political nationalists and supporters of the language laws. Indeed, a completely
independent Flemish culture had now grown to maturity without any
reference to Belgium, as still often was the case prior to the First
World War.

This fully developed cultural nationalism created an environment
and a mental framework within which the commitment to Belgium
gradually gave way to a solely Flemish-nationalist sentiment. This
sentiment was to attract not only the radical political nationalists, but
also the strategically moderate supporters of the language laws. There
was now a Flemish culture alongside the official and still much
stronger officially bilingual Belgian culture, which in turn had
assumed a slightly more Frenchified character. For many people in
the interwar years a Flemish national consciousness was to replace a
dying Belgian consciousness.

The situation became more complicated when in the thirties some
Flemish militants were taken by the ideal of a fascist New Order, so
that the Flemish movement was caught up in the growing polarization
between the Left and the Right. Both socialists and liberals increasingly disapproved of political Flemish nationalism which was now
identified with the New Order. This disapproval was sharpened by
the Spanish Civil War which drew sympathy for Franco from the
Catholics (and thus the Flemish-minded), and, for the Republic, from
left-wing public opinion.

During the Second World War, the most important political
Flemish-national groups opted for collaboration with the occupying
German forces.[18] In doing so they hoped to be given the opportunity
to build up a Flemish New Order. They were to be denied this once
again. To an even greater extent than during the First World War,
collaboration severely damaged the Flemish movement. The repression after the war of the supporters of the New Order and the
punishment of the collaborators wiped Flemish nationalism off the
political stage. At the same time, however, the punishment caused
dissatisfaction among large sections of the Flemish people who felt
that many idealists were punished simply because of their Flemish
sympathies.

SPLITTING BELGIUM?

In the early years after the Second World War the spontaneous wave
of Belgian-national enthusiasm following liberation gave way to a
sharp division between Flanders and Wallonia. The origin of this was

the disunity among the Belgians in assessing their king's attitude during the war.[19] King Leopold III had not followed his government to London during the war (from where he might have continued the struggle against Germany). He stayed in Belgium and had negotiated with Hitler about the situation of Belgian prisoners of war. On the eve of the liberation of Belgium, he was taken by the Germans to Austria where later he was liberated by the Americans. Leopold, however, could not return to Belgium because of the controversy surrounding his role during the occupation. The opposing attitudes in this matter led to a political showdown which divided the population into two camps, Catholics (overwhelmingly Flemings) supporting the king, versus non-Catholics (with a majority in Wallonia) who were against him. In 1950 a referendum was held on the question of whether or not the king could return to exercise his office. In the country some 58 per cent of the electorate supported the king. However, the pattern of voting was very unevenly divided: in Flanders there was a majority of 72 per cent for the king, while in Wallonia and Brussels only a minority of 42 and 48 per cent respectively supported him. What the referendum showed was that entirely different attitudes had developed in Flanders and Wallonia. It resulted, not in a coming together, but in a heightening of the tension between the northern and southern parts of the country.

Despite the backing of the majority of the Belgian population the government bowed to street violence and in the summer of 1950 forced King Leopold III to abdicate in favour of his son Boudewijn (Baudouin). Catholic public opinion in Flanders experienced this capitulation as a humiliation at the hands of Walloons and this served to strengthen their sense of Flemish identity. At the same time the sympathy of the majority in Flanders for King Leopold made the reintegration of the former Flemish-nationalist collaborators into the Flemish movement easier. Paradoxically this reintegration was also facilitated by the anti-Flemish climate in Belgium after the war which in time led to a revival of the Flemish movement. From the end of the war everything that was Flemish was regarded as unpatriotic by French-speakers, Belgian patriots and left-wing opinion. A wave of Frenchification engulfed the country. The language laws of the thirties were continually broken to the detriment of Dutch. At the same time the southern provinces saw a revival of Walloon-Belgian sentiment which was considered perfectly compatible with respectable Belgian patriotism.

This situation provoked reaction from loyal Belgian Flemish-minded people which first expressed itself via the cultural societies and then in parliamentary initiatives from some Christian Democrat representatives, for the autonomous Flemish culture had survived the war and its aftermath. Especially in the Catholic secondary schools and the Catholic youth movements, which had a huge impact on Flemish youth, in the late forties and the fifties Flemish cultural nationalism revived and was soon flourishing again, using the symbols, songs and themes of the pre-war period. It formed a fertile soil for the rebirth of Flemish militancy aiming at cultural renewal first, and then later attracted to political nationalism imbued with a certain anti-Belgian sentiment. Nevertheless, in the two decades after the war the language question remained a secondary problem in Belgian politics. It was overshadowed first by the royal question, and later by conflict over the subsidies for Catholic secondary education which was fought out between Catholics and non-Catholics from 1954 to 1958. Underneath there was a strengthening of Flemish sentiment, especially among the young.

The still relatively hidden tensions between Flemings and Walloons were brought to the forefront of political life after the pacification of the conflict between Catholics and non-Catholics in 1958. In addition to the language problems there was a strong economic component playing a role. The fifties in Belgium were marked by slow economic growth which resulted in structural reconversion. The agricultural sector declined rapidly. There was a corresponding expansion in industry which was much stronger in Flanders than in Wallonia. While in the middle of the nineteenth century Wallonia was in the forefront of the Industrial Revolution on the continent and throughout the whole century Flanders remained overwhelmingly a rural and backward area, from about 1900 Flanders set out to bridge the gap with Wallonia. The harbour in Antwerp became the focal point of an economic growth which manifested itself particularly in the expansion of the tertiary sector. After the crisis of the thirties and the interruption of the Second World War, this economic growth continued strongly through the fifties. Around Antwerp and Ghent, but also elsewhere in many new industrial estates, foreign companies, often multinationals, established themselves. They were attracted by the Flemish labour reserve with its low wages, by the favourable location of the Flemish harbours and by a new transport infrastructure.

As opposed to this the old Walloon industry experienced a rapid loss of markets and jobs. By the end of the fifties the limits of economic growth were already becoming visible in Wallonia. Dissatisfaction with this state of affairs led to a strike movement in 1960. This movement also sought federal reform and reawoke the slumbering

Walloon national movement. From then on the movement campaigned for a left-orientated self-government in Wallonia. In the meantime it appeared that there was also dissatisfaction on the Flemish side. This was for cultural rather than for economic reasons. The main grievance was that unilingualism in Flanders, which already had been declared in principle in the thirties, had not yet been realized. That was the background and the explanation for the re-emergence of a Flemish nationalist party in the sixties.

At the beginning of the sixties governmental policy brought about unilingualism in Flanders, cultural autonomy for the French- and Dutch-speaking communities, and bilingualism in Brussels and some other bilingual areas near the linguistic border. But instead of solving the problem, these measures rather heightened the tensions. They reached a peak when the position of the bilingual Catholic University of Leuven was called into question with the suggestion that its French section should be transferred to Wallonia. The removal of that section in 1968 did not, however, bring a final solution. It increased the anti-Flemish sentiment in Wallonia and Brussels, and brought more support to nationalist parties from both sides. Towards the end of the sixties and during the seventies they continued to gain important electoral support, reaching a peak of 45 seats (out of 212) in 1974, representing 22 per cent of the electorate. In the same period all 'national' parties (Christian Democrats, liberals and socialists) were split along linguistic lines, thus forming separate French-speaking and Dutch-speaking parties. The forming of governmental coalition became more and more difficult.[20]

Against this background the government tried to find structural solutions. In 1970 the constitution was reformed. Responsibility for cultural affairs was transferred from the national government to newly formed cultural councils while control over regional economic development was handed over to newly created regional authorities. That was the first step towards a federal Belgian state. Another step was taken in 1980 with a second constitutional reform. It created, alongside the National Belgian Government, two regional governments, a Flemish and a Walloon, each with their own administrations. It also introduced a greater degree of autonomy for Flanders and Wallonia in cultural matters.

The most recent revision of the constitution took place in 1988. It allowed for a very large extension of the powers – including finance – to the regions and to the linguistic communities. It also clarified the situation with regard to the Brussels region and the German-speaking community in the east of Belgium. Although no date has been set there are further plans afoot to transfer some remaining responsibilities from the central authorities to the regions and the communities, to stabilize the remaining national government, and finally to revise the function of the Upper House in the bicameral parliamentary system.

CONCLUSION

The rapid acceleration in the pace of political reforms in the last two decades reflects the fact that the Flemish and Walloon identities are increasingly growing apart. The economic crisis since the seventies has served to reinforce this trend. This new nation-building, which has taken place within an existing unitary state, demonstrates the pattern of 'nation-to-state' evolution, just as did the emerging Belgian nationality in 1830. With all this, the Flemish movement has undergone a slow evolution from a Belgian patriotism, to a Flemish-Belgian cultural consciousness, to a Flemish-Belgian cultural nationalism and a Flemish cultural nationalism *tout court*, and finally to a political Flemish nationalism which, despite its setback after the war, could revive, grounded as it was in a vigorous cultural nationalism and since the sixties opposed by a new political Walloon nationalism.

Looking at developments from a long perspective of time, it can be said that the Belgian nation had to make room gradually for the birth of a Walloon and Flemish ethnic identity which in recent years have grown into almost fully fledged nationalities. Today the waning of the Belgian national identity is almost complete. The distinct Flemish and Walloon national identities have by and large superseded it. The process however is not yet finished. Only the future can show if there will still be a function for a Belgian nationality. There are some signs that this will be the case, if only because it can serve as a common denominator for those inhabitants of the Low Countries who already for centuries have been considering themselves as being neither Dutchmen, Frenchmen nor Germans, and who – despite their linguistic differences – are sharing some sort of 'Belgitude'.[21]

NOTES

To aid understanding of this article, it may be useful to clarify some terms and concepts.

Belgium is a state that came into existence only in 1830, and since then its inhabitants have been called Belgians. Its territory covers almost exactly the same area as that covered in the eighteenth century by on the one hand the Austrian

Netherlands – a confederation of distinct principalities bound together in a dynastic, personal union – and on the other, the ecclesiastical principality of Liège.

One of the principalities belonging to the Austrian Netherlands was the county of Flanders, with its major cities, Bruges and Ghent. Its origins date back to the ninth century, and its name, whose etymology is uncertain, first appeared in the *Vita Eligii* (eighth century) as *Pagus Flandrensis*. Since Belgian independence in 1830, the term Flanders no longer refers to the old county, whose territory covered only a part of what now comprises Flanders. The term now refers to the Dutch-speaking language area north of the linguistic frontier which runs along an east–west line; while the term Wallonia, also dating from the same period, refers to the French-speaking southern part, with its inhabitants known as Walloons, a name referring to the Germanic word *Wal(l)h* = foreigner, and the Latin word *Gallia*.

Consequently, the Flemings today are the 5.5 million inhabitants of the unilingual Dutch-speaking part of Belgium, while the Walloons are the 3.1 million inhabitants living in the southern, French-speaking part. Only the capital-region of Brussels (population 1 million), situated north of the language frontier, is bilingual, with a preponderance of French-speakers. There is no such thing as the Flemish language; as an adjective, Flemish refers merely to the region. The language used in 'Flanders' is Dutch, as in the Netherlands. In the southern part of Belgium the language is French, as spoken in France.

One more remark is necessary to complete the picture. Since 1970 the 64,000 German-speakers living in two small eastern districts near the German border have been officially recognized as a separate cultural community. Its origins date back to the end of the First World War, when Belgium, in compensation for its sufferings during the war, obtained a small piece of former German territory. The population, however, is too small to influence in any significant way the process of shifting nationalism in Belgium.

1 A general introduction in English on the modern history of the Low Countries is E. H. Kossman, *The Low Countries, 1780–1940* (Oxford, 1978). The general standard work on the history of the Low Countries is *Algemene Geschiedenis der Nederlanden*, 15 vols. (Haarlem, 1977–83). Useful handbooks on political history are: T. Luykx and M. Platel, *Politieke geschiedenis van België van 1789 tot 1985*, 5th edn (Antwerp, 1985) and E. Witte and J. Craeybeckx, *Politieke geschiedenis van België sinds 1830* (Antwerp, 1982). A critical survey of Belgian historiography is in: H. Hasquin (ed.), *Histoire et historiens depuis 1830 en Belgique* (Brussels, 1981).

General introductory books in English on the history of the Flemish movement are: M. de Vroede, *The Flemish Movement in Belgium* (Antwerp, 1975); Manu Ruys, *The Flemings: A People on the Move, a Nation in Being* (Tielt, 1973). A broad range of interesting articles is offered in A. Lijphart (ed.), *Conflict and Coexistence in Belgium: The Dynamics of a Culturally Divided Society* (Berkeley, Calif., 1981). This book also contains a very useful bibliography of publications in English on language and community conflicts in Belgium. The only book – recently published – about the nature and history of the Flemish movement providing original historical documants in English translation is: *The Flemish Movement: A Documentary History, 1780–1990*, edited by Theo Hermins and co-edited by Louis Vos and Lode Wils (London, 1992).

An early scholarly work on the subject is S. B. Clough, *A History of the Flemish Movement in Belgium: A Study in Nationalism* (New York, 1930; 2nd edn, 1968), but apart from this forerunner, the scientific historiography of the Flemish movement in Belgium started in the fifties, with the publications of Lode Wils, Maurits de Vroede – both dealing with the origins and evolution of the Flemish movement in the nineteenth century – and Arie W. Willemsen on the history of political Flemish nationalism in the interwar period.

Since the end of the sixties the history of the Flemish movement has become a topic for research at the Flemish universities of Ghent, Brussels and above all Leuven. In the same period the historian and former Flemish-nationalist politician Hendrik J. Elias published his standard work in four volumes on the evolution of the Flemish ideas and ideals: *Geschiedenis van de Vlaamse Gedachte. 1780–1914* (Antwerp, 1963–5). In the seventies several important books were published on the subject. Most valuable are the broad syntheses of the movement by L. Wils, *Honderd jaar Vlaamse beweging*, vol. I to 1914, vol. II 1914–1936 (Leuven, 1977–85) and vol. III 1936–1950 (Leuven, 1989). A. W. Willemsen has dealt with the interwar period. His Ph.D. thesis (1958) was enlarged in *Het Vlaams-nationalisme. De Geschiedenis van de jaren 1914–1940* (Utrecht, 1969). This work formed the basis for *De Vlaamse beweging van 1914 tot 1940* (5th vol. in the series 'Twintig eeuwen Vlaanderen') (Hasselt, 1975).

On the post-war evolution of the movement see the currently updated chronological story (to date six volumes) written by H. Todts, *Hoop en wanhoop der vlaamsgezinden* (Leuven, 1961–88). An interesting work of reference is an alphabetic encyclopaedia on the Flemish movement, *Encyclopedie van de Vlaamse beweging* (Tielt, 1973–5). The results of new current research on the history of the Flemish movement are published in a quarterly review that since 1981 has been specially reserved for this issue: *Wetenschappelijke Tijdingen* (Ghent, 1990: vol. 50). An overview of the foreign contribution to the historiography of the Flemish movement is: L. Vos, 'Die onbekende Vlaamse kwestie. Het aandeel van de buitenlandse historici in de geschiedschrijving van de Vlaamse beweging', in *Bijdragen en Mededelingen betreffende de Geschiedenis der Nederlanden*, 100 (1985), 700–21.

For the evolution of the Walloon movement see the contributions to the general work *La Wallonie. Le pays et les hommes. Histoire-Economies-Sociétés*, 6 vols. (Brussels, 1981), and G. Fonteyn, *De nieuwe Walen. Met een inleiding over het Belgisch model* (Tielt, 1988). An evaluation of the rather limited historical research of this topic is in H. Hasquin, 'Le mouvement wallon: une histoire qui reste à écrire', in H. Hasquin (ed.), *Histoire et historiens depuis 1830 en Belgique* (Brussels, 1981), pp. 147–55.

2 W. Prevenier and W. Blockmans, *De Bourgondische Nederlanden/Les Pays-Bas bourguignons* (Antwerp and Paris, 1983); R. Vaughan, *Valois Burgundy* (London, 1975).

3 For a critical review of the historiography of the Netherlands see the contributions in W. W. Mijnhardt (ed.), *Kantelend geschiedbeeld. Nederlandse*

historiografie sinds 1945 (Utrecht and Antwerp, 1983). Some English publications are: G. N. Clark, *The Birth of the Dutch Republic* (Oxford, 1975); G. Parker, *The Dutch Revolt* (Harmondsworth, 1977).

4 See for example C. Wilson, *The Dutch Republic* (London, 1968); J. L. Price, *Culture and Society in the Dutch Republic during the Seventeenth Century* (London, 1974); R. Mortier and H. Hasquin (eds.), *Unité et diversité de l'Empire des Habsbourg à la fin du XVIIIᵉ siècle* (Brussels, 1988).

5 A. D. Smith, *The Ethnic Origins of Nations* (Oxford, 1986), pp. 22–31.

6 J. Stengers, 'Belgian national sentiments', in Lijphart (ed.), *Conflict and Coexistence*, pp. 46–60. P. Delsaerdt and J. Roegiers, *Brabant in revolutie. 1787–1801* (Leuven, 1988); J. Roegiers, 'Nederlandse vrijheden en trouw aan het huis van Oostenrijk', in R. Mortier and H. Hasquin (eds.), *Unité et diversité . . .* (Brussels, 1988), pp. 149–64.

7 Wils, *Honderd jaar Vlaamire beweging*, vol. I, pp. 16–19.

8 See E. H. Kossmann's chapter on the United Kingdom of the Netherlands in *The Low Countries*.

9 See the three important articles covering not only the period of the Belgian revolution but also its aftermath in the nineteenth and twentieth centuries, published in A. Lijphart, *Conflict and Coexistence in Belgium*: R. De Schryver, 'The Belgian revolution and the emergence of Belgium's biculturalism', pp. 13–33; J. Polasky, 'Liberalism and biculturalism', pp. 34–45; and J. Stengers, 'Belgian national sentiments', pp. 46–60.

10 J. Hutchinson, *The Dynamics of Cultural Nationalism: The Gaelic Revival and the Creation of the Irish Nation State* (London, 1987), pp. 15–16.

11 L. Wils, *De ontwikkeling van de gedachteninhoud der Vlaamse beweging tot 1914* (Antwerp, 1955), pp. 38–79.

12 For the amalgamation of the Catholic and Flemish element see for example the evolution in the world of the young Catholic Flemish intelligentsia as described by L. Gevers, *Bewogen jeugd. Ontstaan en ontwikkeling van de katholieke Vlaamse studentenbeweging. 1830–1894* (Leuven, 1987); for the liberal Flemish side see: J. Verschaeren, *Julius Vuylsteke (1836–1903). Klauwaard & Geus* (Kortrijk, 1984): a biography of one of the liberal leaders.

13 L. Wils, *Het ontstaan van de Meetingpartij te Antwerpen en haar invloed op de Belgische politiek* (Antwerp, 1963).

14 A. Zolberg, 'The making of the Flemings and Walloons: Belgium 1830–1914', *Journal of Interdisciplinary History*, 5 (1974), 179–235.

15 L. Wils, 'De historische verstrengeling tussen de christelijke arbeidersbeweging en de Vlaamse beweging', in E. Gerard and J. Mampuys (eds.), *Voor kerk en werk. Opstellen over de geschiedenis van de christelijke arbeidersbeweging 1886–1986* (Leuven, 1986), pp. 15–40. About socialism and the Flemish movement see H. van Velthoven, *De Vlaamse kwestie 1830–1914. Macht en onmacht van de vlaamsgezinden* (Kortrijk-Heule, 1982).

16 L. Wils, *Flamenpolitik en aktivisme* (Leuven, 1974).

17 On the growth of anti-Belgian radicalism in the ranks of the young Catholic intelligentsia see L. Vos, *Bloei en ondergang van het AKVS. Geschiedenis van de katholieke Vlaamse studentenbeweging 1914–1935*, 2 vols. (Leuven, 1982). See also

the chapter 'The two Flemish movements' in Wils, *Honderd jaar Vlaamse beweging*, vol. II, pp. 170–218.

18 On the wartime period in Belgium, see the regular publications of the Centre for the Study of the History of the Second World War (Navorsings-en Studiecentrum voor de Geschiedenis van de Tweede Wereldoorlog, Leuven-seplein 4, 1000 Brussels).

19 J. Stengers, *Leopold III et le gouvernement: les deux politiques belges de 1940* (Paris and Gembloux, 1980); P. Theunissen, *1950: ontknoping van de koningskwestie* (Kapellen, 1984).

20 For the facts see Todts, *Hoop en wanhoop der vlaamsgezinden*. A recent book in English on the post-war evolution of the linguistic communities in Belgium: K. D. McRae, *Conflict and Compromise in Multilingual Societies*, vol. II: *Belgium* (Waterloo, Ontario, 1986).

21 On 'Belgitude' see H. Dumont, 'Belgitude et crise de l'état belge. Repères et questions pour introduire un débat', *La Revue Nouvelle*, 44 (November 1988), 11, 21–44 and H. Dumont et al. (eds.), *Belgitude et crise de l'état belge. Actes du colloque organisé par la faculté de droit des Facultés Universitaires Saint-Louis le 24 novembre 1988* (Brussels, 1989).

SIX

THE NATION IN GERMAN HISTORY

WALTER SCHMIDT

UNDERSTOOD as the genesis, consolidation and process of change which takes place in the formation of a nation – as the structural developments with their economic, social and political components, with their ethnic aspects, with their cultural/intellectual physiognomy, as well as their reflections in the consciousness of the masses[1] – the national question is undoubtedly one of the most difficult and sensitive historical phenomena. In Germany, it has long been and still is one of the most complicated and highly disputed problems. Bound up in this are, above all, a broad range of different – indeed conflicting – social interests and objectives. Some of the reasons behind this are to be found in the historical context.

Historical developments in the German-speaking part of Europe were highly contradictory and anything but linear. They did not – as in other parts of western and, in certain cases, also in eastern Europe – lead to a general congruence of ethnic, linguistic, governmental and national factors. On the contrary, during the transition from medievalism/feudalism to modern bourgeois society, they resulted in deep-rooted governmental and social differences which, in extreme cases such as the Netherlands, Switzerland, Austria and Luxembourg, also led to the foundation of independent nations. Indeed, on the edges of the German-speaking area the German-speaking segments of the population, such as the Alsatians and Lotharingians in France, were even integrated into another national state. Favouring these separatist movements was the fact that, in distinction to western Europe, the German-speaking area was not characterized by the centralized government needed by capitalism and, in the majority of cases, achieved in the form of Absolutism, but, until well into the nineteenth century, the region was dominated by particularism, by the so-called German multi-state particularism (*Mehrstaatlichkeit*). This gave the elimination of national fragmentation and the creation of a centralized national state a special vehemence. Although the beginnings of this process can be seen at the time of the early bourgeois revolution (*frühbürgerliche Revolution*), the nineteenth century was completely dominated by the national question.

The *kleindeutsch* national state created under Prussian hegemony in 1871 gave rise to new problems. Not only had the German-Austrians been excluded from the formation of the German nation-state following the Prussian victory over Austria in the 1866 war for hegemony in Germany, but they had since then adopted their own national course. With Poles, Danes and Sorbs, the German Empire had also embraced other nationalities without offering them equal rights. Above all, however, the future of the now constituted German nation was dominated by a deficiency of civil democracy consequent on the 'revolution from above'. In the first half of the twentieth century, the interest of the ruling classes – big business and the *Junkers* – in a redivision of the world, led to Germany becoming a danger for other peoples. Two world wars instigated by Germany also plunged the German people into national catastrophes. In the wake of the Second World War, the struggle connected with overcoming this fateful policy in the eastern part of Germany gave rise to new social-historical developments with far-reaching changes in social and governmental structures and on the face of it also in national structures.

Research into the history of the German nation is not well represented in GDR historiography. In a recently published work, Helmut Bleiber has endeavoured to show the reasons for this.[2] There is no specialized history of the national question.[3] At best, an overview can be filtered out from the general Marxist interpretations of German history.[4] In addition, there is a fairly small number of articles and special studies on aspects or parts of the genesis and development of the German nation written by historians, as well as some papers by philosophers and intellectual historians,[5] several of them on the national problem and national policy in the post-war period.[6]

Already the question as to how long the German nation has existed and at what time the nation was formed in Germany is contentious. In so far as this problem is not evaded or consciously left in the balance, one is frequently confronted with the notion that the origin of the German nation dates back to the turn of the last millennium,[7] whereby the German people as an ethnic unity, which was indeed constituted at that time, is equated with nation. Others contend that the German nation has existed since the fifteenth or sixteenth century at the latest in connection with the social and cultural movements and efforts surrounding the Reformation and humanism. For this, along with the common ethnic attributes of language and habits they advance the argument of developing cultural bonds and the inception of a national consciousness.

A historical-materialistic perception of the nation takes these aspects into consideration but applies other standards and shifts the emphasis. It regards the genesis of a nation as an objective historical process which is both a component and consequence of the formation and assertion of bourgeois-capitalist society. A German nation as a new, more advanced form of structure and development of social life in the areas of central Europe settled by Germans began to take shape as the development of the capitalist mode of production set in. It was capitalism with its developed commodity production, an enormously increasing exchange of goods and the developing division of labour which first created qualitatively new economic, social, political and intellectual-cultural relationships, which laid the material foundations for a higher stage of endeavour towards political centralization and processes of assimilation and unification of language and culture. All of this together led to the union of larger territories and the groups of peoples populating them, who were mostly of the same, but sometimes also of a different, ethnic origin, creating new, larger, more stable social units, that is, nations.[8]

From a Marxist point of view with regard to the history of Europe, these processes began in the fifteenth century. With the primitive accumulation and the formation of capitalist modes of production, above all manufactories (*Manufakturen*), and with the simultaneous outbreak of social and political struggles to remove feudal barriers, culminating in several waves of bourgeois revolutions and constituting a complete revolutionary cycle, the transition from feudal to bourgeois society was initiated and carried through step by step, at a different pace in different countries. Just as capitalist society matured, so too did the related constitution of nations, bourgeois in their social character, over a long period of time, spanning several centuries. It was only the victory of capitalism achieved either in the wake of successful bourgeois revolutions or by way of social reforms, which economic constraints and the pressure of popular movements had wrested from the ruling nobility, that brought about the conclusion of national formation in a country. The nation was therefore in a double sense revolutionary in origin. It was closely connected with revolutionary changes in the economic and social structures of society in the transition from feudalism to capitalism. And as a rule it was only finally constituted after severe social and political struggles to overthrow backward feudal conditions and establish bourgeois social relationships.

This view of the actual birth of nationhood, however, does not deny those elements in the formation of a nation which were already developed and set free prior to the onset of capitalism in feudal society. Above all, it was the ethnic foundations of the subsequent nation which were laid in Germany, just as in other European countries during the age of feudalism. Ethnic foundations are the language as well as specific characteristics of the culture and everyday life, manners and customs, traditions, mentality and social psyche. They are essential prerequisites for the foundation of nations. Nations are distinguished by ethnic characteristics.

The German people were formed as a qualitatively new ethnic and social unit through the integration and assimilation of ethnically distinguishable and older population groups – above all Germanic tribes, Celts and Slavs – during the early Middle Ages in historical struggles lasting for centuries, during which time slavery and pristine society declined and feudalism was born. From the ninth century onwards, 'German' – in Latin 'theodiscus' – was repeatedly used to mark off the large tribes in the empire of the Eastern Franks from the Romance and Slavonic language groups, and after AD 1000 became generally used.[9] The subsequent formation of the German people was reflected in this. Ethno-genesis and the formation of nations do not run simultaneously in European history but rather constitute historical processes belonging to two completely different historical epochs. The formation of new peoples as ethnic-social units took place here in the early feudal period, in the second half of the first millennium, whereas nations were fully formed only with the rise of bourgeois-capitalist relations.

Frederick Engels called the new ethnic groups which had arisen with feudalism the 'modern nationalities'.[10] The medieval *Nationalitäten*, nationalities (Carlton Hayes), *national'nosti* or *narodnosti* in Soviet ethnography, constitute historically pre-national socio-ethnic forms of integration which make up, on the one hand, as historical pre-forms, 'historical antecedents of the modern nations' (Jenö Szücs, p. 173), on the other hand precisely the natural-historical-ethnic basis of these subsequent nations. The new peoples that emerged around the turn of the millennium formed the basis of the constitution of states; and hereby the elementary tendency 'of the nationalities beginning to develop into nations. Throughout the Middle Ages, of course, language and national borders remained far from identical; yet every nationality with perhaps the exception of the Italians was represented by a specially large state in Europe, and the tendency to create nation-states, which became increasingly and consciously evident, constituted one of the essential levers of progress in the Middle Ages.'[11] This tendency was furthered by economic developments which were connected above all with the growing production of goods and the ensuing trade in the towns. These economic ties, however, still remained unstable. And as regards a lasting political centralization which could create favourable political prerequisites for the later formation of nations, they remained ineffective when, as in Germany, there was no alliance between the Crown and towns.

Around the turn of the fifteenth to the sixteenth century the tendencies of a further development of the medieval-feudal nationality to a bourgeois German nation took on a new quality. The actual formation of the nation was now initiated. Decisive for this were new economic and social developments in Germany, which were accompanied by sharpening socio-political contradictions and revolutionary uprisings. Two things brought about a sudden change: since the close of the fifteenth century capitalist relations of production concentrated in single regions had begun to evolve.[12] Their maturation within the framework of feudalism was possible and in no way required a national state already dominated by the bourgeoisie; indeed a bourgeois class capable of seizing power still did not exist,[13] but needed centralized states, which Engels called 'the great monarchies based essentially on nationality'.[14] This allowed the full development not only of bourgeois society but also of the modern nation. Since a centralized state formed by the union of royal centralized power and the burghers of towns (Städtebürgertum) did not materialize in Germany as opposed to other western European countries, an enormous backlog of social conflict built up at an early stage.[15] From this grew the Reformation and the Peasant War in Germany, the first early bourgeois revolution. This was also an attempt, with the revolutionary attack on the prevailing feudal conditions, to limit particularism and thus to create more advantageous terms for the development of the bourgeois German nation.

This situation of social conflict also unleashed strong impulses for national integration. The attempts to reform the Empire in the fifteenth century had already indicated a need for closer political unity amongst the German-speaking territories. It was during the struggle to throw off the heavy papal yoke that the community of interest by way of language and national and ethnic characteristics was for the first time articulated in literary form. The formation of the nation now under way was also given its first conceptual expression.[16] From the fifteenth century onwards when the term 'German nation' appeared first, it was used repeatedly. The reference to the Empire as the 'Holy Roman Empire of the German Nation', first used in 1486, was generally adopted from the beginning of the sixteenth century. The term 'German nation' was widely employed from the Reformation onwards as an expression of common aims and interests of the Germans. It was used by Luther as well as by Ulrich von Hutten and the humanists. Wendel Hipler's Heilbronn Programme of 1525 was based on a pamphlet dating from the year 1523 entitled 'German nation's need' (*Teutscher Nation notturft*) and aimed at 'The Order and Reformation of all estates in the Roman Empire' (*Die Ordnung und Reformation aller stendt ym Römischen Reich*).[17]

The early bourgeois revolution of 1517–25 suffered a defeat which had wide-reaching negative consequences for the formation of the nation in Germany. It took place under essentially less advantageous conditions than in the great west European countries. A centralized state based on the whole of German nationality failed to materialize. Feudal fragmentation remained and became consolidated for centuries. The progress of the bourgeoisie within the system of particularist states was inhibited, retarded and crippled. This was the reason why the development of the economic basis necessary for national union lagged behind.[18] Finally, centrifugal forces gained significant margins of freedom which enabled their segregation from the powerless authority of the Empire. In the early stage of developing capitalism, in its 'manufactory period' (*Manufakturperiode*) and particularly owing to political fragmentation, the binding force of economic relationships was, on the one hand, not strong enough to prevent the break-up of parts of the Empire which were developing economically at different rates of speed and intensity. On the other hand, the socio-political drive of the early bourgeois revolution was not strong enough to bring about the gradual transformation of the whole of German nationality in the waning Middle Ages into a bourgeois nation embracing all Germans.

Nevertheless, the Reformation and Peasant War did emit impulses of national formation. The passionate quarrel with the Catholic Papacy, the principal ideological force of European feudalism and the secession from the Catholic Church promoted the evolution of a national consciousness.[19] The Peasant War which affected large areas of Germany had a similar effect and increased the feeling of solidarity amongst German peasants and plebeians, even though the peasants had no national aspirations and their efforts aimed rather at strengthening the village communities and participation in the territorial Diets

(*Landstände*).[20] The great achievements in literature and art during the revolutionary period transmitted impulses for national integration.[21] Not least of all came the decisive step towards the standardization of the language which came about in the turmoil of the early bourgeois revolution, namely the emergence, thanks to Luther's work, of the New High German literary vernacular.[22] It spread and won such wide recognition that it became not only the common written language of the later German nation, politically united in the German Empire of 1871, but also of the Austrians and the German-speaking Swiss. The

> struggle of the parties in this revolution which affected all classes, released a great cultural revolution. Books, pamphlets and speeches reached wide circles, places of higher learning became the tool of religious struggle, and lastly the revolution made a great contribution to the development of a standardized German language in the form of Luther's translation of the Bible. The early bourgeois revolution reinforced to a high degree the national consciousness of the *Bürgertum* and other strata of the people.[23]

In the centuries separating the early bourgeois revolution and the Great French Revolution the formation of the nation made only little headway in Germany. The economy stagnated and society suffered a catastrophic decline during the Thirty Years' War. With a weak capitalist manufactory base, which owing to feudal fragmentation only developed moreover within territorial boundaries of separate states, and created only few transcending economic ties, no national market came into existence. The *Bürgertum*[24] as the leading social force in the formation of bourgeois society and its victory over feudal power, and with that, also the leading force in the process of forming the nation, remained economically weak and at first largely confined within the boundaries of the territorial states. 'The manufacturing and commercial bourgeoisie participated in the power struggles of the German princes . . . In this way and as a consequence of economic weaknesses, territorial fragmentation reinforced the already existing tendency to provincialism and parochial narrow-mindedness.'[25] The *Bürgertum* was still not able to establish itself as a class at the national level and advance its own interests as national goals.

Nevertheless, national consciousness, expressed for the first time by various social forces during the epoch of early bourgeois revolution, did not vanish. It experienced a visible revival in the eighteenth century when the economic recession was superseded by an upturn in the development of capitalist manufactories in various German territories.[26] This presaged the rise of a new conflict situation and necessary social changes. Currently developing German national consciousness, asserted and furthered by historians, lawyers, philosophers and, above all, literature, increasingly freed itself from the initial orientation towards the Empire, without, however, wholly propagating a narrow so-called territorial patriotism (*Landespatriotismus*).[27] Above all, however, it was not only the interests of the *Bürgertum* but also of the working popular classes which found expression, together with national thinking bound up with cosmopolitan ideas. For more than a century the principal theme remained the internal fragmentation and Germany's ensuing impotence compared with the politically centralized states of western Europe which was found particularly painful and fateful. Bourgeois progress and national unification were increasingly understood as an entity. Representatives of the Enlightenment and German classical literature, philosophy and music, who drew strength and gained profound insight in large measure from the historical upheavals which were maturing during the eighteenth century and attained their revolutionary solution in 1789, promoted national thinking and education[28] and guided German national culture to its apogee even before the internal social forces in Germany had grown sufficiently to be capable of effective action leading to a revolutionary transformation of society.

The territorial framework within which a German nation emerged from the end of the eighteenth century was in no way clearly defined. The old 'Holy Roman Empire of the German Nation' which collapsed under the blows of the French revolutionary armies in 1806 had long ceased to be the example to follow. The absence of a politically centralized ruling power, which the Empire had never possessed, and German particularism favoured notions that considered as a German anyone with a command of the German language and who had come under the spell of German culture and mentality. Johann Gottfried Herder's notions that it was primarily the ethnical, linguistic and cultural factors which formed the basis of nationhood[29] provided, with the widely acclaimed 'cultural nation' (*Kulturnation*), a concept which attempted to define the complicated historical realities existing within the German-speaking area – as, incidentally, was also the case with numerous east European peoples who still did not possess their own states.[30]

However, before the end of the eighteenth century historical decisions had already been made which positively ruled out the notion of one German nation covering all the area of German-speaking central Europe. *En route* from the feudal Middle Ages to modern bourgeois society, between the fifteenth and the end of the eighteenth centuries, during the 'manufactory period' of capitalism, there had been important cases of breakaways of societies and states from the Holy Roman Empire of the German Nation, which had led to national emancipation. This fact, of course, also bore consequences for the constitution of the German nation. Medieval German nationality, which certainly revealed a marked difference between Bavarians, Swabians, Franconians, Saxons and Thuringians, primarily due to previous tribal developments, nevertheless had the appearance of a relative ethnic unit and was accepted as such by the governing nobility during the Middle Ages, but was not completely incorporated in the German nation which emerged with the rise of bourgeois society.

The independence of the Dutch is relevant only in so far as they lived within the area of the States General belonging to the Empire. They went their own way, however, both ethnically and linguistically with a written vernacular having developed from a lower Franconian dialect. Capitalist development and revolutionary bourgeois emancipation accelerated these tendencies and at an early stage led to the creation of a mature bourgeois nation which Marx termed 'the head capitalist nation of the seventeenth century'.[31] The social and economic prerequisites for the political separation of the Dutch from the Empire and for their national independence had been established with the capitalist relationships which spread more rapidly there than in other parts of the Empire, and which not least of all were encouraged by the geographic situation and the ensuing participation in world trade. Yet it was the bourgeois revolution, the struggle for national independence from Spain, waged between 1566 and 1609, which brought about the breakthrough, created the Dutch state, constituted the Dutch nation and finally led to the secession of the Dutch from the Empire at the Treaty of Westphalia in 1648.

Switzerland also finally left the Empire in 1648. In this case large sections of the German-speaking population developed their own state and ultimately their own nation. The peculiar development of the Swiss, reaching back to the thirteenth century, had emerged from the struggle of mostly free peasants organized in rural communities, and of larger towns against feudal tutelage and for greater autonomy from the Empire. This development had already reached such proportions in the sixteenth century that the Swiss Reformation led by Zwingli and Calvin developed its own forms which differed from those in Germany, and the Swiss peasant revolts were not directly connected with the Peasant War in Germany. The unification of the four different nationalities, German, French, Italian and Raeto-Romansch-speaking groups, in a centralized bourgeois state revealed a self-evident common national identity, a Swiss national consciousness which however only reached completion with the bourgeois reorganization of the Swiss Confederation in the first half of the nineteenth century and with the victory of the liberals in the *Sonderbundkrieg* of 1847 and the acceptance of a new federal constitution in 1848.[32]

In Germany it was also around the turn of the nineteenth century that bourgeois national formation entered its decisive phase. There were two processes largely responsible for this. *First*, the transformation to a bourgeois society began in large parts of Germany. The impulse was provided by the Great French Revolution of 1789 which incidentally also permitted the integration of German-speaking Alsatians and Lotharingians in the French National Union with a minimum of complication.[33] The direct and indirect influence of this revolution and the influence of internal revolutionary movements initiated, largely through reforms, the dismantling of feudal relationships in several German states. Whilst in Austria Joseph II's reforms carried out in the sense of Enlightened despotism were not followed immediately after 1789 by the upsurge of revolutionary moves to change society, and thus bourgeois reorganization did not yet get under way, German territory west of the Rhine which had been annexed by France from 1795 to 1815, comprising several West German states belonging to the *Rheinbund* and above all Prussia following its sensational military defeat near Jena and Auerstedt, was completely caught up in the bourgeois upheaval. The era of reform from 1806 to 1813 released forces and created scope for a rapid development of capitalism. Prussia, next to Saxony (which however only initiated its bourgeois revolution in 1830),[34] became the economically most powerful and in capitalist terms most highly developed German state. Thanks to the progressive course Prussia was taking, she also acted as a magnet for all national forces in the anti-Napoleonic struggle for independence. *Secondly*, from the end of the eighteenth century the Industrial Revolution spread to Germany and completely established itself between the 1830s and 1860s, replacing the manufactory stage by modern industrial capitalism.[35] Only then did bourgeois society gain a secure economic base to fall back on.

The ascendancy of bourgeois society which went hand in hand with this 'dual revolution' strongly impelled the formation of the German nation. Only now was the economic foundation of the nation established and in the absence of a centralized state, yet in opposition to state particularism, there emerged a national market. The founding of the *Zollverein* (Customs Union) in 1834 marked the turning-point.

Contrary to the situation in the western European countries the capitalist economy created an economic alliance before this was consolidated by political centralization. The extension of the German *Zollverein* more or less already anticipated the geographical boundaries of the German nation constituting itself politically.

The classes of bourgeois society emerged out of the rapid development of capitalism during the first half of the nineteenth century and after 1830–40 confidently concerned themselves with national affairs. This applied first and foremost to the bourgeoisie which, according to its social position as the leading representatives of bourgeois society, regarded itself also as hegemonic in the struggle for the solution of the national question, and shaped the character of the emerging nation. Bourgeois intellectuals had by their participation in German Jacobinism,[36] in the classical period of German literature and Romanticism, in the struggle against the system of Napoleonic repression and in the poetry of the German *Vormärz*, further moulded German national consciousness and decisively contributed to its diffusion. After 1840 the German bourgeoisie, in the meantime stronger and having matured into a class of national significance with claims to political power, assumed the leadership of the anti-feudal opposition which coincided with the bourgeois national movement.

This national movement became a mass movement for the first time after 1830. The national question in the sense of a union of Germans in a politically unified national state was a cause which was also taken up by other classes of the German people. The national aims and activities against external repression by Napoleon's France between 1806 and 1813 were not only supported by liberal and patriotic aristocrats and intellectuals, but also to differing degrees by peasants, the petty bourgeoisie and plebeians.[37] It is true that this social base of the national movement, constituted in the face of an external enemy, constricted once more for a short period in the aftermath of the War of Liberation when the emphasis shifted from the desire to throw off the foreign yoke to internal problems, the creation of a united bourgeois nation-state which could only be achieved against the reactionary aristocratic and monarchic forces at home. Yet it preserved an intellectual vanguard in the students' fraternities (*Burschenschaften*) which became politically more and more radical. From 1830 onwards its social base expanded again, increasing in revolutionary determination and political radicalism[38] with the revolutionary resistance against the hegemony of Princes and particularism. From the mid-1830s the nascent workers' movement also began to intervene in the national struggle[39] with a new social impetus which went well beyond the aims of the bourgeoisie, and which combined nationalism with an internationalism fed by the common interests of all workers, independent of their nationality. The revolts of 1830–1 in various German states, the *Press- und Vaterlandsverein* and the Hambach festival of 1832, Büchner's *Hessischer Landbote* of 1834 and the manifesto and statutes of the proletarian *Bund der Gerechten* of 1838 provided just as much proof of the social breadth of the national movement as the Rhineland crisis of 1840, the democratic literature of the period preceding the March Revolution of 1848 (*Vormärz*), the Offenburg manifesto of the democrats of 1847, and the Heppenheim democratic resolutions of the liberals of 1847; as well as the national-unitarian democratic aims of the extreme left party in the anti-feudal German opposition, the League of Communists, which were based on the French resoluteness, the *nation une et indivisible* of 1793–4.

It was a characteristic of the formation of the bourgeois nation in Germany that it lacked a centralized state based primarily on the same nationality. This gave the national movement a particular importance and made the national question the dominant topic in the struggle for the bourgeois reform of the country. The nation could only complete the formation if, together with the enforcement of bourgeois social conditions, the aristocratic and monarchical pillars of German particularism were destroyed or at least sufficiently weakened to allow the creation of an economically and socially united nation-state under the auspices of the bourgeoisie. This dual task influenced the German national movement in the nineteenth century and gave it an outstanding position. As the bourgeois reforms began to unshackle capitalism and the Industrial Revolution strengthened the bourgeoisie, so the question of centralization of the state became the most urgent necessity. Since the liberation from foreign repression in 1815, the demand for completing independence through internal national unification of the nation on a bourgeois basis was a consistent component in the vocabulary of political movements. All the anti-feudal forces followed this aim to varying political degrees, each according to their own social position.

Like the movement for bourgeois reforms, the formation of the nation also reached its climax in the revolution of 1848–9.[40] Its central goal from the liberals to the communists was the political unification of the nation into a common state. The revolution was the most important attempt to constitute the German nation on a democratic and revolutionary basis, and thus make bourgeois democracy the essence of the nation. The revolution sent out the hitherto strongest impulses for national integration. In contrast to previous revolutionary attempts which like the merely episodic Republic of Mainz of 1792–3 or the revolts of 1830–1 remained regional, the 1848 revolution immediately took on a national dimension. It spread through all the German states and above all for the first time it broke the omnipotence of the reactionary forces even in the largest and strongest German states, Prussia and Austria, which up till then had remained untouched by serious revolutionary upheavals. If the movement for national independence in the reformist period from 1806 to 1813 had created a national consciousness aimed at a foreign enemy which went beyond the intellectual bourgeoisie to incorporate also the people, this national consciousness was given a much more solid base thanks to the, at least temporarily successful, common struggle of the various social classes against the internal enemies of national unification. The mutual efforts to reform the internal life of the nation had a lasting effect. For the first time ever, the German nation appeared to be institutionalized, and with institutions of a revolutionary origin wrested from the ruling class. The German National Assembly in Frankfurt was created and functioned as the parliamentary executive of the whole nation,[41] even if it did not do justice to its revolutionary duties. The developing movement of associations also attained national dimensions by gaining bourgeois-democratic rights. Especially, the petty bourgeois democratic and workers' organizations strove hard for national unity precisely because of state particularism. This applied to the central committee of German democrats as well as to the unions of book printers and cigar workers, and above all to the Leipzig-based workers' brotherhood which regarded itself as the representative of all German workers, including those of Austria.[42]

A successful revolution would have ended similarly to that in France from 1789 to 1795 in the founding of either a centralized monarchy, or a federal or indivisible republic. Its defeat postponed the conclusion of this process. As the aristocratic and monarchical counter-revolution managed despite important concessions to the bourgeoisie to keep a firm hold of policy-making, it was able to exert a decisive influence on the final outcome of the formation of the German nation. However, in contrast to the pre-revolutionary era it was no longer able to maintain a strictly anti-national stance. Discerning representatives of the reactionary powers, particularly of Prussia, abandoned their inflexible role as protectors of German particularism and themselves adopted national demands. The revolution as well as economic factors had been responsible for this change of attitude. The Prussian policy of unification of one such as Radowitz in 1849–50 already signalled this change.[43] Frederick Engels' subsequent statement, . . . 'and all that has happened since then in our country has been merely a continuation of 1848, merely the execution of the last will and testament of the revolution',[44] is also and in particular valid for the formation of the German nation.

The question as to its territorial extension from the beginning of the nineteenth century appears to be answered best, of course, *cum grano salis* by reference to the loosely merged German territories in the German *Bund* (Confederation) of 1815. The fact that East Prussia and Schleswig were not affiliated to the German Confederation whilst Bohemia and Moravia, inhabited (largely) by Czechs, were included, sounds a note of caution. The adamant refusal of the Czech liberals to take part in the elections to the German Assembly in the spring of 1848 reveals the enormous difficulties contained in a reference to the German Confederation as a territorial framework for the nation-state to be created.[45] Keeping this in mind, it must also be remembered that contemporary considerations and endeavours of, above all, Greater German-democratic provenance regarding the unification of the Germans in one nation, accepted the German Confederation – despite severe condemnation of its reactionary role – as a provisional starting-point. Helmut Bleiber's recent question deserves further consideration, that is, whether the assessment of the German Confederation as an institution of the German Princes for their mutual assurance of the status quo does not require supplementation in so far as the Confederation was considered by the national forces between 1815 and 1867 as the preordained and accepted theatre of operation, which they wanted to fill with bourgeois substance, and whose very foundation was a concession to national-bourgeois ambitions and desires of the time.[46] After the founding of the *Zollverein*, however, there was a more realistic alternative to which the Prussia-orientated liberal bourgeoisie finally gave preference.

A further territorial contraction of the German nation took place after 1850 owing to economic developments which led not least by way of the *Zollverein* to much closer economic ties between the small and medium-sized German states and the Prussian power-house, and with this to greater political dependence. There had long been historically separatist tendencies in Austria which, as recent research claims, pointed to impulses for an independent nation-state from the beginning of the nineteenth century onwards.[47] But up to the revolution of 1848–9 the question, as to whether the German-Austrians would join the German nation or go their own way, remained undecided. The German-Austrians played an enthusiastic part in the German national movement precisely during the revolution. It was the defeat of the revolution which spoiled the chance of their inclusion in a Greater German democratic republic and with this their integration in the German nation. The tendency to exclude them had already become apparent during the revolution when the liberal and moderate democratic majority in the National Assembly decided in favour of a Prussian-led *kleindeutsches Reich* in the spring of 1849. As a revolutionary national constitution from below did not succeed in 1848–9, the victorious counter-revolutionary forces, namely in Prussia, set about the task of national unification themselves, and coupled the founding of a German nation-state directly with the dynastic conflicts of both of the German hegemonial powers, thus predetermining further segregation.

Prussia's victory over Austria in 1866 meant the exclusion of German Austria from the national state completed under Prussian leadership. After this the German-Austrians embarked on their own historical course which within a century led to the founding of a separate Austrian nation. This tendency prevailed despite powerful annexationist efforts following the demise of the Habsburg Monarchy and the founding of the Austrian Republic in 1918 and the *Anschluss* by Hitler's Germany in 1938.[48] The *Anschluss* of 1938 to 1945 did nothing to encourage integration in the German nation. On the contrary, the bitterly painful experience of National Socialist fascism rather contributed considerably to the cultivation of an Austrian national consciousness and in this way ensured that Austrian national emancipation became irreversible. The decisions following the dissolution of the German Confederation in 1866–7 also constituted a significant turning-point in the path of the people of Luxembourg to a state of their own and to their own national identity. In this case too, segregation based on international law, according to the opinion of Luxembourg historians, led to the founding of a small but stable separate national community.[49]

If owing to the exclusion of Austria the German nation in the process of completion only embraced a part of German-speaking central Europe in the second half of the 1860s, it also witnessed the failure to form the nation by way of a bourgeois revolution 'from below'. The democratic and revolutionary activities of the period from 1789 to 1871 in their entirety certainly supplied the most important socio-political thrust for German national unification. The bourgeois movement for national unity led by liberal democratic and proletarian groups also experienced a further boost after 1859 which forced the ruling circles in Prussia to act. 'Even if *Landtag* decisions, newspapers and shooting-club festivals were not able to bring about German

unity, liberalism did subject the Princes to pressure', Bismarck
admitted, 'which made them more inclined to grant concessions to the
Empire.'[50] The ruling *Junkers* in Prussia kept the upper hand, not least
because they understood the requirements of bourgeois development,
in particular the demand for unity in a national state, which they
adopted as their own, and forced through not merely by reforms but
also partly by revolutionary means. Bismarck with the help of the
Prussian army realized his concept of a 'revolution from above', which
linked the expansion of Prussian power with the fulfilment of immediate economic and political needs of bourgeois society at home, and
with the forceful exclusion of the Habsburg Monarchy as the leading
power in Germany.[51] The wars of 1864, 1866 and 1870–1 and the
accompanying economic, social and territorial changes brought the
bourgeoisie in Germany to economic power, created the German
bourgeois national state and with the constitution of the state more or
less completed the formation of the German nation.

Centuries-old processes of national formation were brought to an end
with the founding of the German Empire and a significant historical
step forward had been achieved. The particularist barriers were
removed and the economic needs of the bourgeoisie were satisfied.
German capitalism enjoyed the very best conditions for development
thanks to the establishment of a centralized national state, economic
unification and protection from foreign interference. Bourgeois society
had gained a wide area of operation for the settlement of internal
contradictions in the politically united nation-state. The counter-pole
to the bourgeoisie, the working class, also benefited. It grew considerably with the rapid upward trend of the capitalist economy, and was
now able above all to form nation-wide, to organize and wage its
struggle against the bourgeoisie on a national scale. Over the following
decades a process of national consolidation in Germany took place on
the existing bourgeois foundations within the framework of the
German Empire by way of complex and contradictory economic,
social and political developments.[52]
    Following the founding of the state, however, the German nation
was saddled with exceptionally heavy burdens, resulting from the
anti-democratic way in which the German Empire was created. The
'revolution from above', despite bourgeois democratic concessions,
had prevented bourgeois democracy from becoming the decisive force
in national life. It was not a politically self-confident bourgeoisie
inspired by democratic and republican ideals of a victorious bourgeois
revolution which became the dominant national force, but a capitalist

Junker class with which the bourgeoisie allied itself in a reactionary class compromise against the democratic elements of bourgeois society. The influence of non-bourgeois classes and democratic forces in national life was reduced to a minimum. The maintenance of political power of the *Junkers*, the reactionary class compromise between the bourgeoisie and *Junkers*, the Prussianization of Germany, the supremacy of militarism, essential limitations on bourgeois democracy and the seizure of the national idea by reactionary elements, all combined to restrict the progress achieved in the course of the founding of the bourgeois national state, and considerably exacerbate the immanent contradictions inherent in every bourgeois nation.

Thus already in the 1880s Frederick Engels saw the achievements of national unity threatened by the reactionary Prussian character of the Empire. 'The German Empire', he wrote in a letter to Bebel, 'is in danger of being destroyed by its Prussian base.'[53] And he considered it in the interests of the nation to preserve the centralized nation-state, created along with the Empire. This was an achievement which, however, 'required completion and improvement by a movement from below'.[54] It was the German working class whose political movement in the form of Social Democracy was playing an increasingly greater role in national life, which Engels regarded as the social vehicle and promoter of such democratic 'completion and improvement' for the German nation-state. With this idea Engels intimated that with the constitution of the nation (which compared with other countries was late, and from the point of view of bourgeois-democratic development was incomplete), in the first place, a starting-point for historical processes of a new quality had been reached; and in the second place, the responsibility for the fortunes of the nation was bound to pass from the bourgeoisie to the working class.

Up to the middle of the twentieth century it had still not been possible to resolve successfully the profound contradiction which had accompanied German national development ever since the founding of the Empire, that is, between the interests of the majority of the nation, in a peaceful coalition of Germany, and the policy of expansion, conquest and annexation espoused by her ruling classes. In the twentieth century the rise of imperialism brought this contradiction to a head. The power-hungry German monopolistic bourgeoisie, which had arrived too late when the world was being carved up, wanted to force its redivision by military means and ultimately even aimed at its domination. Backed by a potentially strong economy, it plunged the world into two disastrous wars. In view of the threat to the nation which was already becoming obvious during the First World War,

Engels' proposed social revival by limitation and destruction of the power-base of the big bourgeoisie and the *Junkers* appeared to be a historical necessity. The representatives of the revolutionary working class, particularly the German left wing grouped around Liebknecht and Luxemburg, articulated these needs most clearly,[55] although democratic elements in the bourgeoisie were also beginning to be conscious of this.[56]

The November Revolution of 1918 was an attempt to embark upon a democratic and socialist renewal of the very foundations of the German nation. It did not really get under way and failed. Even far-reaching democratic changes to the political structures existing in the framework of a bourgeois society, as envisaged by parts of the workers' and soldiers' councils, were prevented by the military might of the counter-revolution. The bourgeois parliamentary Weimar Republic initiated important bourgeois democratic rights and created a more liberal arena which improved the chances of a bourgeois democratic alternative, providing that the potential combined force of the workers and middle classes could attain sufficient political strength. However, as the power of the big bourgeoisie and *Junkers* remained unbroken and the old state and military apparatus retained its dominant influence in social life, the achievements of the November Revolution were under threat from the very beginning and were dismantled one by one after the end of the twenties. The revolutionary workers' movement resisted this fateful development from the start. The German Communist Party's (KPD) 'Programmatic statement regarding the national and social liberation of the German people', submitted in 1930, saw the solution in a socialist reorganization of the nation. The National Socialists' bid for power could not be prevented, because the German workers' movement remained divided and thus could not develop into the political force uniting all the democratic elements of society. The establishment of the fascist dictatorship was the first step on the road to the Second World War and another national catastrophe.

The military defeat of Hitler-fascism by the forces of the anti-Hitler coalition also meant the end of the German Empire. At the same time, this presented another opportunity of socially renewing the terms of the nation's existence and steering Germany on to the path of peaceful development by eliminating the social forces which had driven the country to the edge of ruin. The German nation within the territorial confines laid down by the Potsdam Agreement in August 1945 became the point of reference for such a policy.[57] This treaty gave the German people the possibility of creating anti-fascist democratic conditions to form the basis of a united democratic republic to replace the German Empire which was destroyed in the Second World War.

This aim was pursued most vigorously by the German working class and its revolutionary vanguard, the KPD, which in the Soviet-occupied zone united with the SPD (German Social Democratic Party) to form the German Socialist Unity Party, the SED. In its party manifesto it demanded 'a united German anti-fascist parliamentary republic'.[58] In such an anti-fascist democratic and united Germany the long-term struggle between bourgeoisie and working class for the leadership of the German nation and its social reorganization in favour of socialism was to be decided. In the Soviet-occupied zone, where thanks to the presence of a socialist occupation power and a united workers' movement favourable conditions for such a reorganization existed, these were successfully implemented after 1945 with the creation of anti-fascist democratic structures.

In the Western zones too, which were occupied by the USA, Britain and France, there were initially strong moves in favour of such a development. Several party manifestos demanded curbs on the power and influence of the large corporations. Even the CDU (Christian Democratic Union) in its Ahlen manifesto of February 1947 denounced the capitalist economic system and its striving for profit and power and called for the socialization (*Vergesellschaftung*) of the mining and large-scale iron and steel industries. But restorative tendencies rapidly gained the upper hand. To bourgeois power elites, in the process of re-establishment and backed by the Western occupation powers, the creation of an anti-fascist democratic and united Germany (one of the terms of the Potsdam Agreement) in which the shape of conditions of existence of the whole German nation could be debated openly and politically, appeared as too great a risk. The implementation of the Potsdam Agreement was blocked in the Western zones in order to prevent a change in the balance of power in Europe. The old ownership and power structures of the bourgeoisie were restored and consolidated. Under the motto of 'rather half of Germany wholly than only half of whole Germany' the West opted for the division of the formerly united German nation and the creation of a separate West German state. The points along this road were the inclusion of the Western zones in the Marshall Plan in 1947, the separate monetary reform in 1948 and the founding of the Federal Republic of Germany (FRG) in 1949.[59] This meant the destruction of economic unity and the division of the unified (*einheitliche*) state territory of the German nation. The eventual integration of the Federal Republic in the NATO Alliance, despite initial reservations within its own ranks, and despite the resistance of democratic public opinion, sealed the division of Germany and made the process of disintegration of the formerly unified German nation seem likely. As the economic and political power structures in the Federal Republic remained within the capitalist framework, the German nation continued to evolve there along bourgeois lines.

In the German Democratic Republic, which was founded as the second German state within the territory of the Soviet-occupied zone in response to the creation of the West German state in October 1949, the anti-fascist democratic process of reorganization took a socialist path. The leaders of the new socialist German state, however, pursued the aim of reunification in the belief, and with the provision, that even after the creation of the Federal Republic, the process of restoration was reversible. After an initial belief that all-German elections might lead to an understanding between the two German states, it later seemed that a confederation would still be feasible.[60] They were willing to accept a compromise for the sake of unity. All of the corresponding offers, more than a hundred in all, made by the GDR government to the government of the Federal Republic and the *Bundestag*, as well as the well-known peace treaty draft drawn up by the Soviet Union for a united democratic German state in the spring of 1952, were emphatically rejected by the ruling circles in the Federal Republic. Instead of entering into negotiations, they pursued their policy of claiming the sole right of representation. The GDR was regarded as a transient episode which could be ignored.

The social changes in the GDR certainly also had an influence on the national structures and the character of national relationships within this German territory. During the course of socialist reorganization the conditions of social existence of national life began to change. According to Marxist understanding, there began a transition from a bourgeois to a socialist nation; it was assumed that a new social type of the German nation, a socialist German nation, was beginning to take shape. It was assumed that socialism created its own adequate national structure and form of development by a process of renewing the social base of existence of the nation, and this also applied to socialism in the GDR. Since every society needs its own independent structure and form of development according to its respective type, a united German nation serving as a framework of development for capitalism in the FRG, as well as socialism in the GDR, was not possible.[61]

There were in fact tendencies which became visible in the GDR from the 1960s onwards and which pointed to a separate social development and the growth of a certain GDR identity, which together could be comprehended as the beginnings of a separate national identity. These tendencies were first reflected upon in philosophical discussions from the early 1960s, when a socialist society began to emerge from its own foundations.[62]

When it also became evident in the 1960s that the power structures in the Federal Republic had been consolidated, and that in the foreseeable future emerging anti-imperialist developments could not be counted upon, and at the same time both German states were becoming increasingly accepted and recognized by their neighbours, and had become independent and significant factors in the power system and stable peaceful post-war order in Europe, the SED immediately arrived at the sweeping conclusion that a separate socialist nation was taking shape in the GDR in contrast to and independent of bourgeois national development.[63]

At the SED's eighth party congress the thesis was first formulated that

> the socialist revolution which is leading to the renewal (*Erneuerung*) of all existing forms (*Existenzformen*) of human society, is also completely renewing (*erneuert*) the nation . . . In contrast to the Federal Republic where the bourgeois nation continues to exist and where the national question is determined by the irreconcilable class contradictions between the bourgeoisie and the working masses, here in the German Democratic Republic, in the socialist German state, the socialist nation is in the process of development.[64]

This so-called 'two-nations theory' has rightly been identified as, by and large, a politically expedient theory. In view of the flexible political concept of 'two states and one nation' developed by the socialist-liberal coalition in the Federal Republic in 1969–70, the alternative concept of the SED of two German nations was meant to justify the intended demarcation between the GDR and the Federal Republic, not only politically (*staatlich*) and socially, but also nationally.

It should not, however, be forgotten that since the 1960s, with the GDR's independent social and political development, rudiments of a new, socially conscious GDR identity have in fact become evident, and have also been noted and defined outside the GDR.[65] Following the initial discussions in the early 1960s there was an incontestable need for scholarly debate to concern itself further with these phenomena. The ideas expressed were, however, more differentiated than the terse, all too rigid and misleading declaration of the SED, that a socialist nation was in the process of development in the GDR.

During the debates of the 1970s nobody was under the illusion that the birth of a socialist German nation in the GDR was a short-term venture, to say nothing of an already completed historical process. At all events the predominant opinion was that, as in the case of all national formations, it was a question of processes with wide-reaching historical dimensions which continue over many decades and several generations. It was, however, recognized that these processes were under way and under certain circumstances were given real possibilities also by Western authors.[66]

The interpretation developed in the GDR of a socialist nation in the process of formation in that country was based above all on the fact that new economic, social and political foundations had been laid: an independent, sovereign and socialist state with increasingly worldwide recognition; a separate and effective economic organism based on the public ownership of the most important means of production; a new social order in which the bourgeoisie no longer existed and which was dominated by workers, peasants, intelligentsia and the middle strata; a socialist national culture gaining in its own right with its own reception of that which was valuable from the shared cultural heritage of other German-speaking countries and uniting this with artistic reflections of socialist reality.

In the scholarly debates, however, there was no doubt that the renewal of the social basis of existence of national life only constituted the initial stage of a national transformation. This was defined by the term 'establishment' (*Konstituierung*) of the socialist nation. To reach its final completion and maturity, defined by the term 'consolidation', a longer period of several decades, even spanning several generations, was envisaged. Two things seemed to be decisive for these processes extending over a long time.

First, the connection between socialism and the German *ethnos* was still in its infancy. Marxist comprehension of the nation in the GDR which on this point used conclusions emanating from Soviet ethnography,[67] regarded the fusion of traditional ethnic attributes and characteristics of the German people, of German nationality, that is, the whole complex of historical life-styles and forms of communication, habits, customs, traditions, behaviour, mentality, cultural and sociopsychological peculiarities, with the new social organism as a decisive condition for the regeneration of national life. At the same time attention also had to be paid to the development of new habits and forms of communication specific to socialism.[68] It was only the connection between socialism and German nationality which could impart to the GDR its own unmistakable national flavour.[69]

It goes without saying that this process under the peculiar circumstances of coexistence with the Federal Republic of Germany, a capitalist state which emerged from the same nation and whose citizens possessed the same ethnic characteristics, could only develop along contradictory lines and was bound to be accompanied by strong counter-current tendencies, and would historically span several generations.

Secondly, no less important for national formation is the growth of a separate national identity. A society developing in its own right can, in the end, only reach national maturity to the extent that it discovers its own national self-identity. Employing Marx's terminology regarding the formation of the working class,[70] it is only with the emergence of a separate stable national consciousness that a society progresses from a 'nation-in-itself' (*Nation an sich*) to a 'nation-for-itself' (*Nation für sich selbst*). It remains to be asked whether, and to what extent, in the last decades the citizens of the GDR have developed an identity of their own which is durable, and whether this already constitutes a new national consciousness or is merely imbued with, or superimposed by, an overlapping national self-identity connected with the German nation constituted in the nineteenth century.

In order to characterize the new facets of the national question in the decades of post-Second-World-War Germany, reference has been made to the 'division of the nation' or 'two states of one nation', postulating the continued existence of a united German nation. In contrast, there was the view, held above all in the GDR but also by non-Marxists, of a possible or already occurring national separation which was defined either by the term 'binationalism',[71] or else the development towards two German nations. If such tendencies were really at work, they cannot merely be explained by internal developments in Germany, but can only be understood in terms of their international interdependence and dimension. After 1945 Germany was an important focal point of international confrontation between opposing social systems and political and military blocks. When considering German 'binationalism' in the second half of the twentieth century, it must be remembered that these global conflicts had particularly profound and far-reaching consequences precisely here. After all, the demarcation line between the two systems had run through the middle of Germany. The nation in general possesses a high degree of stability. Within its framework in which social conflicts are fought out, it can as a rule cope with the most intense internal disputes without breaking down or disintegrating. It has been accurately noted: 'It therefore requires extraordinary circumstances which do not only originate within the nation; it requires class conflict of epochal dimensions and a far-reaching internationalization of class conflict to challenge the historical existence of a nation.'[72]

The dramatic events of the autumn of 1989 in the GDR, the revolutionary overthrow of the power structures of Stalinist bureaucracy and the vain attempt at democratic regeneration of the socialist society have clearly revealed the limits of assumed 'binationalism' and have cast doubt on the thesis of the formation of two German nations, one bourgeois and one socialist, to which I myself subscribed.[73] The ethnic and common national consciousness of the Germans in both states which has developed over centuries, has proved stronger and more stable than the embryonic disintegration caused by social antagonism, which also certainly led to the appearance of independent forms of social life and reflected the beginnings of a separate GDR identity.

The 'two-nations theory' which in the scholarly debate intended to articulate above all actual development trends and recently actuated processes rather than completed results, nevertheless fell victim to a 'foreshortened perspective' and precipitately anticipated what in long-term historic dimensions was a possible development. The error of judgement ensued, on the one hand, from the overestimation of the strength of social factors to which was indiscriminately ascribed general primacy in national development, namely from an overevaluation of the effects of new economic, social, political and ideological components on national consciousness. On the other hand, there was an underestimation of the stability and durability of the ethnic-national ties shared by men and women in both states and the resultant feeling of national solidarity.

A significant reason for the exaggerated expectations and premature notions of the birth of a socialist nation in the GDR was the overestimation of the quality and standard of socialist development, whose historical limitations were manifested by the social crisis. The hitherto ill-begotten administrative-bureaucratic form of socialism and its failure to link socialism with democracy inhibited, hindered and even prevented a widespread identification with state and society by the citizens – a prerequisite for the growth of national identity. Since an open democratic atmosphere did not exist and all opposition and criticism were regarded exclusively as hostile rather than as important and constructive impulses for social progress, neither a consensus with the new social order, nor with those dissatisfied with and opposed to the bigotry, structural errors and faulty developments of the society, could be achieved. On the contrary, it led many citizens to an increasing dissociation from this society, from withdrawal into private life to mass exodus from the GDR.

Finally, the fact should not be overlooked that since the mid-1970s (Helsinki Agreement) there has been a change in international relations from open confrontation and segregation to convergence and the practical implementation of the principles of peaceful coexistence. If the respective social and political developments in the GDR and the FRG had been essentially forced by the Cold War and the escalation of the East–West conflict from the 1940s to the beginning of the 1960s, with the possible consequence of 'binationalism', strong counter-effects have emerged from the tendency to dialogue and international co-operation, to the construction of the 'European House', which had led to the strengthening and revitalization of existing national ties between the people of both German states. The masses of visitors to the East from the West and the growing numbers in the other direction have also furthered this development. The policies of both German states have reflected the new tendencies from as early as the first half of the 1980s with the formula of shared responsibility.

The revolutionary process of regeneration which began in the GDR in the autumn of 1989 has created a new and open-ended situation in the German question. The GDR government recommended the elevation of shared responsibility to a contractual relationship. Political forces in both German states have taken up the plan of a confederation and have set their sights on this goal. However, there are increasing calls for direct reunification in the GDR as well as the FRG, whereby such a solution could only result in the annexation of the GDR by the Federal Republic. All of these ideas are based on the fact that the Germans continue to exist as a nation and see themselves as such. At the same time not least of all the popular movements in the GDR – as has been observed in the East as in the West from quite different standpoints – have clearly shown that certain elements of a separate GDR social identity exist, whose future, of course, depends on the existence and stability of the GDR as an independent democratic society. The process of co-operation and establishing closer links between the two states of the German nation or direct unification is considered by the leading political forces in both East and West, particularly with a view to the interests of Germany's neighbours and to the guarantee of peace and security on the European continent, and in its immediate dependence on the attempts to overcome the division of Europe and their results in the construction of a peaceful European House. The German problem can only be understood and resolved to the satisfaction of all peoples and states if it remains embedded in the processes of unification in the whole of Europe, in the construction of a European peace system and in the gradual coalescence of the European nations. The German question, that is, the actual organization of forms of social and political life of the Germans as a nation, proves – as it has for centuries – to be a European and hence an international problem.

NOTES

This contribution was completed in 1988 and revised (in the main its last part) in December 1989 during the events that led to the end of dual German statehood.

1 Cf. P. N. Fedossiev *et al.*, *Der Leninismus und die nationale Frage in der Gegenwart* (Moscow, 1974).

2 H. Bleiber, 'Nationalbewusstsein und bürgerlicher Fortschritt – Zur Herausbildung von deutschem Nationalbewusstsein in der Zeit der bürgerlichen Umwälzung (1789–1871)', in H. Bleiber and W. Schmidt (eds.), *Demokratie, Antifaschismus und Sozialismus in der deutschen Geschichte* (Berlin, 1988), pp. 170ff.

3 Short surveys are contained in: A. Kosing, *Nation in Geschichte und Gegenwart. Studie zur historisch-materialistischen Theorie der Nation* (Berlin, 1976), pp. 78–109, and W. Schmidt, *Nation und deutsche Geschichte in der bürgerlichen Ideologie der BRD* (Berlin, 1980).

4 *Lehrbuch der deutschen Geschichte (Beiträge)*, vols. I–XII (Berlin, 1959–69); *Geschichte der deutschen Arbeiterbewegung in acht Bänden* (Berlin, 1966); *Deutsche Geschichte in drei Bänden* (Berlin, 1965–8); J. Streisand, *Deutsche Geschichte in einem Band* (Berlin, 1974, 5th edn 1980); *Grundriss der deutschen Geschichte* (Berlin, 1979); *Deutsche Geschichte in zwölf Bänden*, vols I–V (Berlin, 1982–8); *Deutsche Geschichte in 10 Kapiteln* (Berlin, 1988).

5 Cf. *Zeitschrift für Geschichtswissenschaft (ZFG)*, 10 (1962), *Sonderheft: Beiträge zum nationalen Geschichtsbild der deutschen Arbeiterklasse* (particularly the articles by Ernst Engelberg, Heinz Wohlgemuth, Karl Obermann, Heinrich Scheel, Günther Vogler and Hans-Joachim Bartmuss); J. Streisand, 'Das Problem des Nationalcharakters', in F. Klein and J. Streisand (eds.), *Beiträge zum neuen Geschichtsbild* (Berlin, 1956), pp. 27ff; H. Strobach, 'Zum Volksbegriff bei Marx und Engels', in W. Küttler (ed.), *Das geschichtswissenschaftliche Erbe von Karl Marx* (Berlin, 1938), pp. 170ff; W. Brandt, 'Zu Fragen der Entstehung und zum Inhalt der von Karl Marx und Freidrich Engels begründeten Theorie der Nation', Ph.D. diss. (Jena, 1973); H. König, *Zur Geschichte der bürgerlichen Nationalerziehung in Deutschland zwischen 1807 und 1815*, part 1 (Berlin, 1972), part 2 (Berlin, 1973); H. Hanke and T. Koch, 'Zum Problem der kulturellen Identität', *Weimarer Beiträge* (1985), no. 8.

6 G. Benser, 'Sozialistische Nation und nationale Politik in der Geschichte der DDR. Bemerkungen zu Forschungs- und Diskussionsfragen', in *Zur Formierung der sozialistischen deutschen Nation. Thematische Information und Dokumentation der Akademie für Gesellschaftswissenschaften beim ZK der SED*, series A, no. 42 (Berlin, 1984); J. Hofmann, 'Nationsentwicklung und nationale Politik der SED.

Thesen zu Etappen und Problemstellungen', in *ibid.*; Hofmann, *Ein neues Deutschland soll es sein. Zur Frage nach der Nation in der Geschichte der DDR und der Politik der SED* (Berlin, 1988); Hofmann, 'Zur Entwicklung der sozialistischen deutschen Nation in der DDR – Erfahrungen und Perspektiven', *Einheit* (1988), no. 8, 734–42; A. Kosing, 'Theoretische Probleme der sozialistischen Nation in der DDR', *Deutsche Zeitschrift für Philosophie* (1975), no. 2; Kosing, 'Die Dialektik von Nationalem und Internationalem', in *Dialektik des Sozialismus* (Berlin, 1981), pp. 294ff; A. Kosing and W. Schmidt, 'Zur Herausbildung der sozialistischen deutschen Nation', in *Erfolgreiche Jahre. Der Beitrag der SED zu Theorie und Politik der entwickelten sozialistischen Gesellschaft* (Berlin, 1982), pp. 209–30; W. Schmidt, 'Deutsche Geschichte als Nationalgeschichte der DDR', *Beiträge zur Geschichte der Arbeiterbewegung (BZG)* (1983), no. 3.

7 W. Conze, *Die deutsche Nation. Ergebnisse der Geschichte* (Göttingen, 1963), pp. 10, 15; in more detail, Conze, '"Deutschland" und "deutsche Nation" als historische Begriffe', in O. Büsch and J. J. Sheehan (eds.), *Die Rolle der Nation in der deutschen Geschichte und Gegenwart* (West Berlin, 1985), pp. 21ff; see also: G. Kotowski, 'Deutschland und Österreich seit 1945', in *ibid.*, p. 222. Regarding the national question in the Middle Ages see primarily H. Beumann and W. Schröder (eds.), *Nationes. Historische und philologische Untersuchungen zur Entstehung der europäischen Nationen im Mittelalter* (1978–87), vols. I–VII, especially vol. I, *Aspekte der Nationenbildung im Mittelalter. Ergebnisse der Marburger Rundgespräche 1972–1975* (Sigmaringen, 1978); and here above all W. Schlesinger, 'Die Entstehung der Nationen. Gedanken zu einem Forschungsprogramm', pp. 11–62. For a relativistic approach to the medieval concept of the nation see H. Beumann, 'Zur Nationenbildung im Mittelalter', in Otto Dann (ed.), *Nationalismus in vorindustrieller Zeit* (Munich, 1986), pp. 21–4. For a Marxist analysis of the three historically most important conceptual variants of the nation see J. Szücs, *Nation und Geschichte. Studien* (Cologne and Vienna, 1981), pp. 163ff. For an almost total rejection of Szücs's treatment see J. Ehlers, 'Nation und Geschichte. Anmerkungen zu einem Versuch', *Zeitschrift für historische Forschung*, 11 (1984), 205ff. As many others, Ehlers maintains that the 'nation' has existed since the Middle Ages and that it differs from the 'modern nation' 'merely' in the way its physical basis was massively enlarged. Also non-Marxists have called such an extended notion of the nation in question; see Dann's Introduction in *Nationalismus in vorindustrieller Zeit*, pp. 7ff. Also J. Kocka, 'Nation und Gesellschaft. Historische Überlegungen zur "deutschen" Frage', *Politik und Kultur*, 1 (1981), 12ff.

8 Kosing, *Nation in Geschichte und Gegenwart*, pp. 58ff. Concerning recent non-Marxist research on the question of the birth of the nation which, in contrast to the earlier predominantly intellectual history approach, clearly asserts the economic and social processes in society and sees them in connection with capitalist developments regarded as modernization processes, and attaches great importance to social communication, cf. K. W. Deutsch, *Nationalism and Social Communication* (Cambridge, 1966); Deutsch, *Nationenbildung, Nationalstaat, Integration* (Düsseldorf, 1972); O. Dann (ed.), *Nationalismus und sozialer Wandel* (Hamburg, 1978); T. Schieder and O. Dann (eds.), *Nationale Bewegung und soziale Organisation* (Munich and Vienna, 1978); Dann, *Nationalismus im vorin-*

dustriellen Zeitalter; Bleiber, 'Nationalbewusstsein und bürgerlicher Fortschritt', pp. 171–2.

9 *Grundriss der deutschen Geschichte*, pp. 79ff; J. Hermann *et al.*, *Deutsche Geschichte*, vol. I: *Von den Anfängen bis zur Ausbildung des Feudalismus Mitte des 11. Jahrhunderts* (Berlin, 1982), pp. 391, 455ff; *Deutsche Geschichte in 10 Kapiteln*, pp. 66ff; J. Hermann, *Die Nordwestslawen und ihr Anteil an der Geschichte des deutschen Volkes* (Berlin, 1973).

10 F. Engels, 'Über den Verfall des Feudalismus und das Aufkommen der Bourgeoisie', in Marx/Engels, *Werke (MEW)* (Berlin, 1956–74), vol. 21, pp. 395ff; regarding the definition of the term 'nationality' used here cf. J. V. Bromlej, *Ethnos und Ethnographie* (Berlin, 1977), particularly pp. 133ff; N. M. and S. T. Kaltachtschjan, *Nation und Nationalität im Sozialismus* (Berlin, 1976), particularly pp. 14ff; Szücs, *Nation and Geschichte*, pp. 166, 173ff; Kosing, *Nation in Geschichte und Gegenwart*, pp. 15ff.

11 F. Engels, 'Über den Verfall', in *MEW*, vol. 21, p. 396.

12 Adolf Laube and Günter Vogler *et al.*, *Deutsche Geschichte*, vol. III: *Die Epoche des Übergangs vom Feudalismus zum Kapitalismus von den siebziger Jahren des 15. Jahrhunderts bis 1789* (Berlin, 1983), pp. 12ff; A. Laube, M. Steinmetz and G. Vogler, *Illustrierte Geschichte der deutschen frühbürgerlichen Revolution* (Berlin, 1974), pp. 8ff.

13 Cf. G. Zschäbitz, 'Über den Charakter und die historischen Aufgaben von Reformation und Bauernkrieg', *ZfG*, 1964, no. 2, 277ff; Zschäbitz, 'Über historischen Standort und Möglichkeiten der frühbürgerlichen Revolution in Deutschland (1517–1525/26)', in M. Kossok (ed.), *Studien über die Revolution* (Berlin, 1969), pp. 35ff, particularly pp. 43ff.

14 F. Engels, 'Dialectics of nature', in Marx/Engels, *Collected Works (MECW)* (Moscow, 1987), vol. 25, p. 318.

15 G. Bendler, in *Deutsche Geschichte*, vol. III, pp. 99ff; Bendler, 'Von der Hussitenbewegung bis zum Abfall der Niederlande. Zu den Vor- und Frühformen der bürgerlichen Revolution', *Jahrbuch für Geschichte*, 10 (Berlin, 1974), 9ff; *Grundriss der deutschen Geschichte*, p. 145.

16 G. Vogler, 'Perspektiven der deutschen Nationalentwicklung beim Übergang vom Feudalismus zum Kapitalismus', *ZfG Sonderheft*, 1962, 347ff; also Conze, '"Deutschland" und "deutsche Nation" als historische Begriffe', pp. 26–8.

17 Laube, Steinmetz and Vogler, *Illustrierte Geschichte der frühbürgerlichen Revolution*, pp. 257–60.

18 Streisand, *Deutsche Geschichte in einem Band*, pp. 77ff.

19 Laube, Steinmetz and Vogler, *Illustrierte Geschichte der frühbürgerlichen Revolution*, pp. 73ff, 93, 126ff, 159ff, 186ff.

20 G. Vogler in *Deutsche Geschichte in 10 Kapiteln*, p. 151, and in *Deutsche Geschichte*, vol. III, p. 186.

21 *Deutsche Geschichte*, vol. III, pp. 129ff, 184ff; E. Ullmann, 'Martin Luther und die Kunst der Reformation', in H. Bartel, G. Brendler, H. Hübner and A. Laube (eds.), *Martin Luther. Leistung und Erbe* (Berlin, 1986), pp. 108–15.

22 R. Grosse, 'Luthers Bedeutung für die deutsche Sprache', in *Sitzungsberichte der Akademie der Wissenschaften der DDR*, 1984/12 G (Berlin, 1984), pp. 24–31; J. Schild, 'Zum deutschen Sprachschaffen Martin Luthers. Schwerpunkte und

Entwicklungstendenzen der Forschung', in Bartel *et al.* (eds.), *Martin Luther. Leistung und Erbe*, pp. 101–7; Schild, 'Zu einigen Entwicklungstendenzen der deutschen Sprache zur Zeit der frühbügerlichen Revolution', in G. Brendler and A. Laube (eds.), *Der deutsche Bauernkrieg 1524/25* (Berlin, 1977), pp. 174–84.

23 E. Engelberg, 'Probleme des nationalen Geschichtsbildes der deutschen Arbeiterklasse', *ZfG Sonderheft*, 1962, 27.

24 H. Hoffmann and I. Mittenzwei, 'Die Stellung des Bürgertums in der deutschen Feudalgesellschaft von der Mitte des 19. Jahrhunderts bis 1789; *ZfG*, 1974, no. 2, 190–207; I. Mittenzwei, 'Zur Klassenentwicklung des Handels- und Manufakturbürgertums in den deutschen Territorialstaaten', *ZfG*, 1975, no. 2, 179–90.

25 Hoffmann and Mittenzwei, 'Die Stellung des Bürgertums', p. 205.

26 I. Mittenzwei, 'Wirtschaftspolitik – Territorialstaat – Nation. Die Haltung des preussischen Bürgertums zu den wirtschaftlichen Auseinandersetzungen zwischen Preussen und Sachsen (1740–1786)', *Jahrbuch für Wirtschaftsgeschichte*, 1970, part III; Mittenzwei, *Preussen nach dem Siebenjährigen Krieg. Auseinandersetzungen zwischen Bürgertum und Staat um die Wirtschaftspolitik* (Berlin, 1979).

27 G. Schilfert, 'Zur Problematik von Staat, Bürgertum und Nation in Deutschland in der Periode des Übergangs vom Feudalismus zum Kapitalismus', *ZfG*, 1963, no. 3, 515–34; also: H. Schulze, 'Die deutsche Nationalbewegung bis zur Reichseinigung', in Büsch and Sheehan (eds.), *Die Rolle der Nation der deutschen Geschichte und Gegenwart*, pp. 84ff; W. Frühwald, 'Die Idee der kulturellen Nationsbildung und die Entstehung der Literatursprache in Deutschland', in D. Dann (ed.), *Nationalismus in vorindustrieller Zeit*, pp. 129ff.

28 J. Streisand, *Geschichtliches Denken von der Frühaufklärung bis zur Klassik* (Berlin, 1964); K. H. Günther, *Geschichte der Erziehung* (Berlin, 1987), pp. 215ff.

29 J. G. Herder, *Briefe zur Beförderung der Humanität* (Berlin and Weimar, 1971), particularly vol. I, pp. 6off, 267ff, 292ff, 319ff, vol. II, pp. 63ff, 16off, 225ff, 262ff; Herder, *Zur Philosophie der Geschichte*, ed. W. Harich (Berlin, 1952), vol. I, pp. 323–35, vol. II, pp. 467ff; E. A. Menze, 'Johann Gottfried Herder – Nationsbegriff und Weltgefühl,' *Politik und Zeitgeschichte*, B 1/86 (4 January 1986).

30 Cf. M. Wawrikowa, 'Johann Gottfried Herder und die polnische Idee zur Philosophie der Geschichte in der ersten Hälfte des 19. Jahrhunderts', *Germanica Wratislaviensis*, 44 (1984), 101ff.

31 K. Marx, *Capital: A Critical Analysis of Capitalist Production*, in Marx/Engels, *Gesamtausgabe (MEGA)* (Berlin, 1990), 2nd section, vol. 9, p. 651; see also B. Töpfer, 'Die frühbürgerliche Revolution in den Niederlanden', *ZfG Sonderheft*, 1962, 51–70; G. Brendler, 'Zur Problematik des bürgerlichen Revolutionszyklus, in M. Kossock (ed.), *Studien zur vergleichenden Revolutionsgeschichte 1500–1917* (Berlin, 1974), pp. 29–52, particularly p. 52: 'The early bourgeois revolutionary cycle contributed to the undermining of the already fragile unity of the Empire and to the continuation of the process of dissolving this universally medieval structure. Where the early bourgeois revolution succeeded, namely in the Netherlands, it led to the secession of the country from the Empire. On the other hand, the early bourgeois revolution's breakdown in Germany

was one of the salient historical reasons for the long-lasting malady of the Empire.'

32 G. Hunziker, *Die Schweiz und das Nationalitätsprinzip im 19. Jahrhundert* (Basle and Stuttgart, 1970), particularly pp. 10ff, 16ff; P. Dürrenmatt, *Schweizer Geschichte* (Zurich, 1963), vol. I, pp. 79ff, vol. II, pp. 597ff; *Geschichte der Schweiz und der Schweizer* (Basle and Frankfurt on Main, 1986), pp. 593ff, particularly pp. 600–7; S. T. Kaltachtschjan, *Leninizm o suščnosti nacii i puti obrazovanija internaciol'noj obščnosti ljudej* (Moscow, 1976), pp. 193ff. During the 1848–9 revolution the liberals interestingly invoked the secession of Switzerland and the Netherlands from the Empire when they argued for the exclusion of Austria from a united Germany under Prussian leadership. Cf. *Deutsche Zeitung*, no. 61 (2 March 1849), 2nd suppl., p. 2.

33 F. Engels, *Die Rolle der Gewalt in der Geschichte* in *MEW*, vol. 21, pp. 444ff. For the following cf. *Deutsche Geschichte*, vol. IV: *Die bürgerliche Umwälzung von 1789–1871* (Berlin, 1984), pp. 48ff, 85ff.

34 K. Czok, *Über Traditionen sächsischer Landesgeschichte Sitzungsberichte der Sächsischen Akademie der Wissenschaften zu Leipzig, Philologisch-historische Klasse*, 123, no. 4 (Berlin, 1983), pp. 18ff.

35 *Deutsche Geschichte*, vol. IV, pp. 215ff.

36 H. Scheel, *Deutscher Jakobinismus und deutsche Nation, ein Beitrag zur nationalen Frage im Zeitalter der Grossen Frazösischen Revolution* (Berlin, 1966).

37 H. Scheel, 'Die nationale Befreiungsbewegung 1813/15', *ZfG Sonderheft*, 1962, 323–36; H. Scheel (ed.), *Das Jahr 1813. Studien zur Geschichte und Wirkung der Befreiungskriege* (Berlin, 1963); H. Heitzer, *Insurrectionen zwischen Weser und Elbe. Volksbewegungen gegen die französische Fremdherrschaft im Königreich Westfalen 1806–1813* (Berlin, 1959); *Der Befreiungskrieg 1813* (Berlin, 1967).

38 H. Bock, 'Bürgerlicher Liberalismus und revolutionäre Demokratie. Zur Dialektik der sozialen und nationalen Frage in den deutschen Klassenkämpfen von 1831 bis 1834', *Jahrbuch für Geschichte*, 13 (Berlin, 1975); H. Bleiber and J. Kosim (eds.), *Dokumente zur Geschichte der deutsch-polnischen Freundschaft 1830–1832* (Berlin, 1982).

39 W. Kowalski, *Vorgeschichte und Entstehung des Bundes der Gerechten* (Berlin, 1962); W. Schmidt, 'Nationales und Internationales im Bund der Kommunisten', *ZfG*, 1986, no. 3, 222–38; from a non-Marxist point of view: W. Conze and D. Groh, *Die Arbeiterbewegung in der nationalen Bewegung* (Stuttgart, 1966).

40 W. Schmidt, G. Becker, H. Bleiber, R. Dlubek, S. Schmidt and R. Weber, *Illustrierte Geschichte der deutschen Revolution von 1848/49* (Berlin, 1988); K. Obermann, 'Demokratie und Nation vor und in der Revolution von 1848/49', *ZfG Sonderheft*, 1962, 305–22.

41 G. Hildebrandt, *Die Paulskirche. Parlament in der Revolution 1848/49* (Berlin, 1986).

42 H. Schlechte (ed.), *Die allgemeine deutsche Arbeiterverbrüderung 1848–1850* (Weimar, 1979).

43 R. Weber, 'Von Frankfurt nach Olmütz. Zur Genesis und Politik des Gothaischen Liberalismus 1849/50', in H. Bleiber, G. Hildebrandt and R. Weber (eds.), *Bourgeoisie und bürgerliche Umwälzung in Deutschland* (Berlin, 1977), pp. 361–94; K. Canis, 'Joseph Maria von Radowitz, Konterrevolution und preussische Unionspolitik', in H. Bleiber, W. Schmidt and R. Weber (eds.),

Männer der Revolution von 1848, vol. II (Berlin, 1987), pp. 449–86; W. Schmidt, 'Bemerkungen zur Rolle der bürgerlichen Revolution im Lernprozess der Junkerklasse', in *Forschungs- und Darstellungsprobleme einer historischen Biographie, Sitzungsberichte der AdW der DDR, 1984, 16 G* (Berlin, 1985), pp. 40–7.

44 F. Engels, *Ludwig Feuerbach and the End of Classical German Philosophy*, in Marx/Engels, *Selected Works in Two Volumes (MESW)* (Moscow, 1962), vol. II, p. 360.

45 G. Wollstein, *Das 'Grossdeutschland' der Paulskirche. Nationale Ziele in der bürgerlichen Revolution 1848/49* (Düsseldorf, 1972).

46 Bleiber, 'Nationalbewusstsein und bürgerlicher Forschritt', pp. 170ff.

47 For the formation of the Austrian nation cf. F. Kreissler, *Der Österreicher und seine Nation. Ein Lernprozess mit Hindernissen* (Vienna, Cologne and Graz, 1984), particularly pp. 446–546; E. Bruckmüller, *Nation Österreich. Sozialhistorische Aspekte ihrer Entwicklung* (Vienna, Cologne and Graz, 1984); 'KPÖ immer für Österreich. Podiumsdiskussion über die österreichische Nation und die Herausbildung des österreichischen Nationalbewusstseins', *Weg und Ziel 37, Sondernummer* (December 1979); W. R. Garscha, 'Alfred Klahr und die Rolle der nationalen Frage im Kampf der KPÖ gegen die Bedrohung Österreichs durch Hitlerdeutschland', in *Geschichte des Marxismus-Leninismus und der marxistisch-leninistischen Geschichtswissenschaft 1917–1945. Wege zu ihrer Erforschung und Darstellung* (Leipzig, 1985), pp. 64ff; Garscha, 'Überlegungen zur österreichischen Nationswerdung. Die Etappe 1932–1938', *Bulletin des Arbeitskreises 'Zweiter Weltkrieg'* (Berlin, 1988), no. 1–4, pp. 47–69; for the standpoint of GDR historiography cf. *Deutsche Geschichte*, vol. IV, pp. 509ff; elucidated by Helmut Bleiber, 'Deutschland und Österreich im 19. Jahrhundert', in *ibid.*, pp. 6–31, particularly pp. 11ff, 18.

48 H. Rumpler, 'Österreich. Vom "Staat wider Willen" zur österreichischen Nation (1919–1945)', in J. Becker and A. Hillgruber (eds.), *Die deutsche Frage im 19. und 20. Jahrhundert* (Munich, 1983), pp. 239–67; G. Botz, 'Das Anschlussproblem (1918–1945) – Aus österreichischer Sicht', in R. A. Kann and F. E. Prinz (eds.), *Deutschland und Österreich. Ein bilaterales Geschichtsbuch* (Vienna and Munich, 1980), pp. 179–98, further reading pp. 532–6.

49 G. Tausch, 'Deutschland und Luxemburg vom Wiener Kongress bis zum heutigen Tage. Die Geschichte einer Entfremdung', in J. Becker and A. Hillgruber (eds.), *Die deutsche Frage im 19. und 20. Jahrhundert*, pp. 185–220. Tausch says in the 'epilogue' of his study: 'The sacrifices of the Second World War finally turned the people of Luxembourg into a nation. They demonstrated with their blood the proof of the "Nation Luxembourgeoise" so ridiculed by Treitschke . . .'

50 O. Fürst von Bismarck, *Gedanken und Erinnerungen*, vol. I (Stuttgart, 1889), p. 293; cf. also Bismarck's telegram to Otto von Manteuffel of 11 August 1866 in O. von Bismarck, *Die Gesammelten Werke. Politische Schriften*, vol. VI (Berlin, 1929), p. 120: 'if it is to be revolution then we should rather instigate it than suffer it'.

51 E. Engelberg, *Bismarck. Vom Urpreussen zum Reichsgründer* (Berlin, 1985), particularly pp. 451ff, 603ff; Engelberg, 'Über die Revolution von oben. Wirklichkeit und Begriff', in E. Engelberg, *Theorie, Empirie und Methode in der Geschichtswissenschaft* (Berlin, 1980), pp. 339–84; Engelberg, 'Die Evolution in

der Geschichte macht früher oder später eine Revolution notwendig', in S. Miller and M. Ristau (eds.), *Erben deutscher Geschichte. DDR–BRD: Protokolle einer historischen Begegnung* (Hamburg, 1988), pp. 100–8.

52 Regarding this complex of problems cf. from a non-Marxist point of view the contributions concerning problems of the political, economic and cultural integration of the Germans, Jürgen Kocka, Helmut Böhme and (only superficially) Peter Gay in Büsch and Sheehan (eds.), *Die Rolle der Nation in der deutschen Geschichte und Gegenwart*, pp. 118ff, 137ff, 181ff; from a Marxist point of view: H. Bartel and E. Engelberg (eds.), *Die grosspreussisch-militaristische Reichsgründung 1871. Voraussetzungen und Folgen*, vol. II (Berlin, 1971), especially the contributions by Horst Bartel and Gustav Seeber; and also G. Seeber, 'Reichsgründung und Nationalbewusstsein. Zum nationalen Selbstverständnis der Klassen im Deutschen Reich', in M. Weissbecker and H. Gottwald (eds.), *Klassen, Parteien, Gesellschaft. Dieter Fricke zum 60. Geburtstag* (Jena, 1987), pp. 5–20.

53 Frederick Engels to August Bebel, 13/14 September 1886, in *MEW*, vol. 36, p. 524.

54 F. Engels, 'Zur Kritik des sozialdemokratischen Programmentwurfs 1891', in *MEW*, vol. 22, p. 236.

55 *Geschichte der deutschen Arbeiterbewegung*, vol. II (Berlin, 1966), particularly pp. 187ff, 245ff; H. Wohlgemuth, *Burgkrieg, nicht Burgfriede! Der Kampf Karl Liebknechts, Rosa Luxemburgs und ihrer Anhänger um die Rettung der deutschen Nation in den Jahren 1914–1916* (Berlin, 1963); A. Laschitza and G. Radczun, *Rosa Luxemburg. Ihr Wirken in der deutschen Arbeiterbewegung* (Berlin, 1980).

56 O. Groehler (ed.), *Alternativen. Schicksale deutscher Bürger* (Berlin, 1987) (biographies of Walther Rathenau, Hugo Junkers, Ludwig Quidde, Paul Freiherr von Schoeneich, Helene Stöcker, Max Josef Metzger and Friedrich Graf von der Schulenburg).

57 For the following cf. literature listed in note 6 above.

58 L. Berthold and E. Diehl (eds.), *Revolutionäre deutsche Parteiprogramme* (Berlin, 1964), p. 205.

59 E. Nickel, *Die BRD. Ein historischer Überblick* (Berlin, 1988), pp. 46ff.

60 J. Hofmann and D. Säuberlich, 'Nationale Frage und Nationsentwicklung in der Politik der SED von der Mitte der 50er Jahre bis 1963', in *Jahrbuch für Geschichte*, 31 (Berlin, 1984), 41–70.

61 Kosing, *Nation in Geschichte und Gegenwart*, pp. 120–8.

62 A. Kosing, 'Illusion und Wirklichkeit in der nationalen Frage', *Einheit*, 1962, no. 5, 13–22; D. Säuberlich, 'Das Problem der Nation in der Strategie und Taktik der SED in der ersten Hälfte der 60er Jahre', Ph.D. diss. A (Akademie für Gesellschaftswissenschaften, Berlin, 1984).

63 K. U. Koch, 'Das Problem der Nation in der Strategie und Taktik der SED in der zweiten Hälfte der 60er Jahre', Ph.D. diss. A (Akademie für Gesellschaftswissenschaften, Berlin, 1985).

64 Minutes of the Eighth Party Conference of the German Socialist Unity Party (Berlin, 1971), vol. I, p. 56.

65 H. Apel, *DDR. 1962-1964-1966* (West Berlin, 1967); cf. also H. Heitzer, *Andere über uns. Das DDR-Bild des westdeutschen Imperialismus und seine Kritiker* (Berlin, 1969), pp. 174ff.

66 K. Jaspers, *Freiheit und Wiedervereinigung. Über Aufgaben deutscher Politik* (Munich, 1960), pp. 46ff; W. Schlesinger, 'Die Königserhebung Heinrichs I. Der Beginn der deutschen Geschichte und die Geschichtswissenschaft', *Historische Zeitschrift*, 221, no. 3 (1975), 5, 530ff; G. Schweigler, *Nationalbewusstsein in der BRD und der DDR* (Düsseldorf, 1973); E. Kitzmüller, H. Kuby and L. Niethammer, 'Der Wandel der nationalen Frage in der Bundesrepublik Deutschland. Nationalstaat und Nationalökonomie', *Das Parlament*, 33 (1973); K. Sontheimer and W. Bleek, *Die DDR. Politik, Gesellschaft, Wirtschaft* (Hamburg, 1979); K. Sontheimer, 'Der Wille zur Einheit', *Die Zeit*, 20 October 1972; H. Mommsen, 'Auf der Suche nach der Nation. Zur Geschichte des deutschen Nationalbewusstseins', *Evangelische Kommentare* (1979), no. 10, 565ff; Mommsen, 'Nationalismus und transnationale Integrationsprozesse in der Gegenwart', *Das Parlament*, 9 (1 March 1980), 9ff.

67 Above all: J. V. Bromlej, *Ethnos und Ethnographie* (Berlin, 1977), pp. 35ff, 116ff.

68 Cf.: Sief-third Congress, 8–12 April 1987, Zürich, Switzerland. Bibliographie The Life Cycle, pp. 48–60; also: U. Mohrmann, 'Sitten und Gebräuche im Lebenszyklus der DDR-Bürger. – Eine volkskundliche Forschungsaufgabe', in *Zur Formierung der sozialistischen deutschen Nation*, pp. 110–18; expanded in *Abhandlungen und Berichte des staatlichen Museums für Völkerkunde Dresden* (Berlin, 1989); Mohrmann, 'Alltag und Festtag in der DDR. Zu unserem Umgang mit "volkskulterellen" Traditionen', *Ethnographisch-archäologische Zeitschrift*, 27, no. 1 (Berlin, 1986), 27–41; bibliography: *Untersuchungen des Bereichs Ethnographie der Humboldt-Universität Berlin zu ethnographischen Gegenwartsproblemen*, compiled by a group of students under the supervision of Walter Rusch (Berlin) in *ibid.*, pp. 152–60; H. Hanke, 'Kulturelle Traditionen des Sozialismus', *ZfG*, 1985, no. 7, 589ff; H. Hanke and T. Koch, 'Identifikation und/oder Emanzipation. Nochmals zur Frage der kulturellen Identität', *Weimarer Beiträge*, 35, no. 10 (1989), 1589–1608.

69 Also from a non-Marxist point of view a connection between German nationality and socialism in the GDR has been noted. Cf. K. Sontheimer and W. Bleek, *Die DDR. Politik – Gesellschaft – Wirtschaft* (Hamburg, 1979), p. 61: 'Today socialism is no longer merely the preserve of political institutions and ideology, it has also become incorporated, in a particularly German variation, in the social thought and behaviour patterns of the East Germans.'

70 K. Marx, *The Poverty of Philosophy. Answer to the Philosophy of Poverty by M. Proudhon*, in *MECW* (Moscow, 1976), vol. 6, p. 211.

71 As in E. Kitzmüller, H. Kuby and L. Niethammer, 'Der Wandel der nationalen Frage in der Bundesrepublik Deutschland', *Aus Politik und Zeitgeschichte. Beiträge zur Wochenschrift 'Das Parlament'*, no. 33/73 (18 August 1973), 14.

72 Benser, 'Sozialistische Nation und nationale Politik in der Geschichte der DDR', p. 32.

73 For a self-critical analysis of the two-nations theory see J. Hofmann, *Wie weiter mit der deutschen Nation?* (Berlin 1990); W. Schmidt, 'DDR und nationale Frage. Selbstkritische Anmerkungen zur These von der sozialistischen Nation', *Wissenschaftliche Mitteilungen der Historiker-Gesellschaft der Deutschen Demokratischen Republik*, 1990/1, 54ff.

SEVEN

NATIONALISM AND NATION-STATE IN GERMANY

HEINRICH AUGUST WINKLER

UNTIL recently, the history of nationalism in Germany has mainly been treated as the history of its thinkers, with the focus on ideas and not on interests. The research methods have been those of the intellectual historian and not of the social historian. They tend to be phenomenalist rather than analytical.

The problems with this approach are evident. In 1972 the American historian Robert Berdahl mentioned some of the questions which still have to be answered satisfactorily:

What was the relationship between the ideas and the political reality? How did the ideas of the intellectual elite become the experience of the nation? Or, if early nationalists merely articulated sentiments that were felt less keenly by a broad spectrum of the population, what new experiences generated the new nationalist thought? Finally, what happened between 1800 and 1848 that increased the appeal of nationalism as a political movement?[1]

Although Berdahl is concerned with the period preceding the March Revolution of 1848 in Germany, his dissatisfaction with the results of the existing body of research can still be expressed in general terms. If we want to explain the *origins* and *changes* which took place in German nationalism, we must first enquire into its social preconditions. What functions did German nationalism have? Which strata of society supported it? Did the functions and proponents change in the course of time – and if so, why?

I will try to show that the new approach permits a better *periodization* of German nationalism than the traditional one. Furthermore, it appears to me that German nationalism is only *comparable* on an international plane when an approach is adopted which combines the perspectives of social and political history. Such an approach may help us to draw a clearer distinction between the more general and the specifically national characteristics of nationalism. Finally, this approach offers an opportunity to incorporate explanatory models of systematic social science, to examine them critically and to make a contribution to a historical *theory* of nationalism.

In this essay, I would like to concentrate on three problems. *First*, I will look at the phase in which German nationalism was an expression of *bürgerlich* emancipation or, to put it another way, an ideology of modernization held by the aspiring *Bürgertum*. *Secondly*, I want to discuss the reasons and consequences of the change in the function of nationalism which turned a 'left-wing' into a 'right-wing' ideology. *Thirdly*, I would like to examine the question of why nationalism diminished in Germany – and not only there – after the Second World War.

I

My first thesis is: *From the period preceding the March Revolution of 1848 to the founding years of the German Empire, the national slogan was primarily an expression of the desire for* bürgerlich *emancipation. The demand for national unity was directed against the land-owning aristocracy as the upholders of territorial state fragmentation. In distinction to this, the* Bürgertum *saw itself as the social embodiment of German unity whereby the educated stratum placed particular emphasis on German national culture, which it created, while industrial and commercial entrepreneurs saw political unification as arising mainly from the need for a national market. The second argument came more and more to the forefront as industrialization progressed: the creation of a German national state would not least enable Germany to reduce its economic backwardness in comparison with industrially advanced England. In this respect, early nationalism was an ideology of modernization. The economic challenge presented by England had a no less enduring impact on German nationalism than the political challenge thrown down by Napoleonic France.*

The degree to which nationalism was the product of the consciousness of being economically inferior to England can be seen from the well-known politico-economic demands of Friedrich List – his programme for an 'educational' tariff system – as well as from the protectionists he influenced. However, even the growing free trade movement considered the German national state to be a *conditio sine qua non* of economic progress.

To the same extent to which free trade forces prevailed after 1848, the *grossdeutsch* nationalists lost ground to the *kleindeutsch* nationalists: the programme of economic liberalism could only be realized with Prussia and against the Habsburg Empire.

Pre-1848 revolutionary nationalism in Germany was no more pacifist than any other type of nationalism. List was not the only one in favour of extensive annexations. The Romantic dream of the 'springtime of nations' – of the International of the Nationalists – was destroyed by the actual course taken by events in the revolutions of 1848–9: national differences were a major reason for their failure. In distinction to the revolutionaries of 1789, only very few liberals thought it still necessary to look for the humanitarian legitimation of their own national demands and, therefore, the compatibility of these demands with the interests of others. In those cases where legitimation of this kind was attempted, as by Marx and Engels, it was above all used to distinguish between 'revolutionary' and 'counter-revolutionary' peoples, in other words, between legitimate and non-legitimate national movements. Belonging to the first category were the Poles; to the second, the Czechs, Slovaks and the South Slavs.

What, then, is the 'German Fatherland' is a question that the liberals of 1848 tended, in the main, to answer tactically. Where Germans assimilated a foreign nationality (as in the case of the Mazurs in East Prussia), the deputies of the *Paulskirche* in Frankfurt invoked the subjective decision of those concerned. However, if the Germans (i.e. those in Alsace and Lorraine) had been assimilated by another nation, the 'objective' principle to be applied was, 'to the extent that the German tongue is to be heard'. In cases of doubt, that which was already in the possession of a German State would have to be defended. Hence, notwithstanding the different language and the contrary will of the population, the greater part of the province of Posen (Poznań) should have become part of Germany according to the resolution of the National Assembly. One thing, however, was self-evident for the liberals of all shades: 'national' and 'progressive' were two sides of the same coin.[2]

Even as late as 1860, the liberal *Bürgertum* were so sure of their position as the true upholders of national unity that, in 1861, the democrat Hermann Schulze-Delitzsch would have preferred to call the newly founded party of 'determined liberals' – the German Progressive Party – the 'National Party', because this notion not only 'encompasses the policy of German unification but also all other tendencies in the party with regard to its fight against dynastic politics'. At the same time, the *National-Zeitung* – the organ of the right wing of the Progressive Party – described the territorial fragmentation of Germany as a consequence of the 'foundations of the feudal state system' whereas 'the division of the nation . . . has been overcome by the German *Bürgertum*'. It continued by saying that 'in this connection, we speak of the *Bürgertum*, and not of the people as such, in order to give greater emphasis to the social aspects of the struggle which the political doctrine has all too often lost sight of'.[3]

The revolution of 1848–9 and the Prussian constitutional conflict of 1862 to 1866 led the liberals – who, in a narrow sense, were the political representatives of the property-owning and educated *Bürgertum* – to the conclusion that they could neither bring about 'freedom', that is, greater *bürgerlich* influence on the state, nor 'unity' in a frontal attack against the old, established forces. For the liberals, it appeared too early for a revolutionary trial of strength because the bulk of the rural population east of the river Elbe *still* followed the *Junkers*. On the other hand, the liberals also considered it too late for a *bürgerlich* revolution because, increasingly, the proletariat *no longer* backed the policies of the liberals.

The Prussian liberals regarded themselves as being handicapped by the territorial fragmentation of Germany because this situation strengthened the feudal and military character of old Prussia at the same time as weakening the *Bürgertum*. According to the liberals, non-Prussian Germany relied on Prussia providing the military back-up in case of emergency, while the small and medium-sized states dispensed with a strong army. Thus in 1859 the liberal politician Max von Forckenbeck said: 'Without a change in the German situation, the existence of a reasonable and free constitution is impossible in Prussia in the long run. If the German situation remains as it is, there will and must be nothing but a further expansion of the military state in Prussia . . .' In 1864 the Berlin *National-Zeitung* wrote that if military service continued to be regarded as the most important and highest-ranking profession, then neither the Prussian people nor their representatives would gain in freedom. 'It has come to the point where anybody who has retained an interest in the civic duties of the state is given the honorary title of "windbag" and only the achievements and the obedience of the soldier are thought to be of benefit to the state.'[4]

The less the chances of having liberal demands carried through in the Prussian state, the more the nationalist idea was seen as the quintessence of general progress. Although it may sound paradoxical: thinking in the categories of national power was an expression of the internal political impotence of the Prussian *Bürgertum*; national pathos a reflection of its social insufficiency. According to the *National-Zeitung* of 3 August 1865, the route taken by the liberals would have to be 'from unity to freedom'.[5] Prompted by this expectation, a year later the right wing of the 'determined liberals' decided definitively in favour of a partial collaboration with Bismarck and, consequently, for a shelving of those demands which, *de facto*, would have meant the introduction of parliamentary government in Prussia. For twelve years German domestic politics were dominated by the pact between the national liberals and the enlightened representatives of the *ancien régime*. During this period – from 1866 to 1878 – the national slogan had *one* function: it served to secure the claim of the liberal *Bürgertum* to be the legitimate majority. It was the ideological means of a *Bürgertum* which had attained one of its two main objectives: national unity. This goal, although it had been reached in principle, was still held by the liberal *Bürgertum* to be endangered from within and it was only by parrying this (real or imagined) danger that it thought it would be able to extend its political influence.

At this time, the domestic direction taken by liberal nationalism had three main aims: on the one hand, it was against the strata of feudal upholders of 'specific Prussianism' and the other 'particularists', on the other hand, it was against Catholic 'ultramontanists' and, finally, against the socialists. In the context of the *Kulturkampf* and under the impact of the Paris Commune, the traditional anti-feudal moment in liberal nationalism had been joined by anti-clerical and anti-socialist components. While the anti-feudal tendencies were still linked with ideas of modernization, the anti-socialist justification for the national slogan – repelling proletarian internationalism – already reflected the *bürgerlich* interest in retaining the status quo.

Anti-clericalism fell between two stools. On the one hand, it was part of the liberal tradition of Enlightenment and progressive thinking and, subjectively, was seen as an aspect of the struggle against medieval backwardness. On the other hand, the means used to fight supra-national political Catholicism – in the words of the *National-Zeitung* of 21 October 1877, the 'black horde of Romans without a fatherland' – compromised the very liberal principles used to justify this struggle. In this sense, the *Kulturkampf* was very much a preliminary round in the suppression of the Social Democratic movement after 1878. Because the anti-clerical element was clearly in the forefront of *bürgerlich* nationalism between 1870 and 1878, it is possible to apply the thesis of the historical ambivalence of liberal anticlericalism as a whole to the liberal nationalism of those years. However, although this nationalism still had the appearance of an ideology of modernization, by this time, fears of being defeated by a majority of votes had taken such a hold that it turned partially into illiberalism.[6]

II

The change in the function of nationalism, which increased in pace and was completed in the late 1870s, was reduced to a brief formula by the liberal Reichstag deputy, Ludwig Bamberger, in 1888:

> The national banner in the hands of the Prussian ultras and the Saxon guildsmen is a caricature of what it once was. This caricature came about very simply when the defeated opponents appropriated the cast-off garb of the victors and after turning, re-dyeing and trimming it to suit their own fashion, were able to strut around as the laughing heirs of the national movement.[7]

Bamberger's sarcastic judgement can be presented in the form of a second thesis: *A slogan of the liberal* Bürgertum *up to the founding period of the German Reich, during the late 1870s, nationalism developed more and more into an instrument of the right for use against left-wingers of all shades, that is, left-wing liberals as well as Social Democrats. Beside protectionist industrialists, the upholders of the new, right-wing nationalism were forces which up to then had tended to keep at a distance from the national movement: Prussian large landowners and small manufacturers tired of competition.*

A fundamental precondition for the political turn-around of the late 1870s – the end of economic liberalism and the domestic predominance of political liberalism; the beginning of an era of protectionist tariffs and the conservative/national liberal collaboration – was the economic crisis of the 1870s, caused by the breakdown of the Vienna Stock Exchange in 1873. It was a period of diminished economic growth, international price deflation and a predominantly pessimistic economic mentality. According to the propaganda of the right, it was the liberals, that is, liberal Jewish finance capital, the 'Golden International', who were responsible for the crisis.[8]

In consequence of the slower rate of economic growth, the distribution struggle intensified. The crisis boosted the Social Democrats and the Marxist teaching of the class struggle. Whoever wanted to distance himself from the proletariat had to profess himself in favour of nationalism: for both the independent 'old middle class' (*Mittelstand*) and the 'new middle class' of officials and white-collar employees, ideological dissociation from Marxist internationalism was of vital significance for their survival as a *Stand*. Above all, the nationalism of the middle strata (*Mittelschichten*) had the function of ensuring that this distance from the 'unpatriotic companions' of the socialist proletariat was maintained. For the middle strata, nationalism was a confirmation of their claim to embody the 'normal moral standards' of society (M. Rainer Lepsius).[9] In the late 1870s, to be a nationalist no longer meant being anti-feudal but instead anti-internationalist and, very frequently, anti-Semitic.

Although the liberal version of nationalism continued in being after the so-called 'internal founding of the Reich' in 1878–9 (*innere Reichsgründung*), it came under a previously unknown degree of pressure from the Right to prove its legitimacy. In 1878, when the protectionists demanded German colonies overseas not least as a 'safety valve for the rumbling volcano of the social question', free trade circles countered with the aim of increased 'German colonization' in Posen. As was to be expected, the protectionists replied that the two forms of colonization were by no means mutually exclusive.[10]

No matter how much the left-wing liberals felt themselves to be a direct part of historical progress, they believed that they were unable to make any headway against the unbroken might of the old ruling classes by purely domestic political means. Just as the later national liberals had welcomed the dispute with Austria during the Prussian constitutional conflict – because it would introduce a new dynamism into the domestic struggle for power – thirty years later, the liberal sociologist Max Weber believed that it would only be possible to weaken the political grip of the *Junkers* and break away from the encrusted structures of the authoritarian state by adopting a prestigious German world policy. Nothing demonstrates the power of self-preservation of the German *ancien régime* better than the desperate means to which its 'determined liberal' critics resorted.[11]

The transition from left- to right-wing nationalism was not peculiar to Germany. In the last quarter of the nineteenth century most countries turned to protective tariffs and the more advanced industrial nations tried harder to divert their domestic conflicts into other channels – namely, by conquering colonies overseas. But differently from western Europe, the traditions of early liberal nationalism in Germany were not strong enough to be able to form an effective corrective to right-wing nationalism in the age of imperialism.

Unlike French nationalism, German nationalism did not experience a phase in which it could assume the banner of human ideals. On the contrary, it came about during the fight against the foreign domination of Napoleon, which claimed this very banner as its own. From a political point of view, Germany did not experience an 'epoch of liberalism' during the nineteenth century. The Weimar Republic rested on a much weaker foundation than the highly industrialized democracies of western Europe and North America. In these countries, the majority of those social strata, which, with the onset of the world economic crisis in 1929, formed the mass basis of a fascist movement – National Socialism – in Germany, remained true to their traditional parties.

What was it, then, that made National Socialism so attractive for the middle strata – from which it recruited large sections of its mass support – as well as significant segments of the agrarian, military and industrial 'ruling elite'? In principle, Hitler's movement promised to retain the traditional social order and destroy democracy which appeared to be endangering this traditional system. Only in a country with a long authoritarian tradition could openly anti-democratic slogans gain a majority. With their extreme nationalism, the National Socialists were able to draw a veil over the incompatibility of the promises which they made to the various social strata. The 'Führer' cult also had the task of giving the movement's heterogeneous social basis a common focal point – and Hitler was the sole charismatic leader of the Right.

Hitler himself was well aware of the social function of nationalism. His slogan of 1924 – 'Marxist internationalism can only be defeated by a fanatical, extreme nationalism with the highest social ethic and moral standards' – can very well be given a 'functional' interpretation.[12] However, a purely functionalistic explanation of National Socialism would be misleading. National Socialist policy which, in the last analysis, was Hitler's policy cannot be deduced from the interests of powerful economic groups. Furthermore, this policy was not simply a sophisticated social technology. If Hitler had only used anti-Semitism to divert the aggression of the petty bourgeoisie from capital to the Jewish scapegoat, he could not have killed the Jews. And if, as some 'new left' authors maintain, anti-Semitism was only a piece of social manipulation, why did the National Socialists try to keep this act of mass murder from the German people? Clearly, Hitler did not expect the 'final solution of the Jewish question' to have a socially integrative function.

Even more deviant than the neo-Marxist 'deduction' of anti-Semitism is another, specifically 'right-wing' explanation of the National Socialist genocide of European Jews. In early 1986, Ernst Nolte proposed the thesis that the holocaust was a copy – if a rather distorted copy – of the Russian original, the Gulag Archipelago. If one is to believe this, Hitler wiped out the Jews in order to prevent himself being exterminated by the Bolsheviks – in other words, he carried out an 'Asian act' in a kind of putative self-defence.

Nolte's relativist intention, which sparked off the so-called 'German historians' dispute' (*Historikerstreit*) with this very thesis, is obvious.

National Socialism is meant to appear as a mainly reactive phenomenon and the murder of the Jews historicized. However, Nolte's violent speculation ignores, along with many other factors, a major difference: unlike Russia or Pol Pot's system in Cambodia, Germany had knowledge of a long tradition of the rule of law. The systematic elimination of Europe's Jews must be seen against the background of Western values, in the creation of which Germany itself had also been involved. Viewed from this perspective, the holocaust was a state of crime of unparalleled magnitude.[13]

Without doubt, National Socialism is the most extreme example known to history of an ideology which came to have an independent existence. It required a high level of militarization of German society through the First World War, the national trauma of defeat in 1918, a 'middle-strata panic', caused by the world economic crisis, as well as the traditional anti-liberalism of the social elites, to make possible the National Socialist 'seizure of power'. And it required a group of 'military desperadoes' (Wolfgang Sauer) – a group socially uprooted in the wake of the First World War – who combined extreme *bürgerlich* fears with a deep contempt of the *Bürgertum*, in order to push nationalism to the utmost conceivable consequence.[14] At the end, the nihilistic negation of all concrete interests was marked by the delusive ideas of nationalism and racism. Nationalism was not only used to manipulate the masses but it also blinded those who considered themselves to be masters of manipulation.

III

My third thesis is: *After the Second World War, in Western Europe in general and West Germany in particular, nationalism no longer played the same role as an ideology of integration as after the First World War. Besides having been compromised by National Socialism, fundamental changes in the international political scene, as well as a new set of economic circumstances, contributed to nationalism losing its functional raison d'être in the Western world.*

At first glance, it would appear that the post-Second World War situation offered a particularly fruitful setting for a new German nationalism: the division of Germany, the flight and the expulsion of millions of Germans from the east of the 'Reich' and from countries which had been the victims of National Socialist aggression provided a suitable background against which nationalist agitation could flourish. Nevertheless, there was a much smaller echo to nationalist slogans in the Federal Republic of Germany than in the Weimar Republic. I see three main reasons for this:

First: National Socialism also compromised nationalism for a large part of those strata which helped Hitler to power. Even during the 'Third Reich', numerous middle-strata followers of National Socialism felt cheated of the hopes they had placed in the 'seizure of power'. It was not until war had broken out that the consumer co-operatives were disbanded; the hated department stores – another favourite target of small traders – remained in being until the collapse of the 'Third Reich'. With regard to nationalism for the German people, much more sobering than National Socialist economic policies were the experience of war and the consequences of war. In distinction to the post-First World War years, after 1945, there was no really representative social force which disputed that Germany's leaders had started the world war Germany had just lost. After the Second World War, only fringe groups tried to disseminate the legend that Germany was innocent of having begun the war. The ruins of the cities, the misery of those expelled from their homelands and the plight of the whole nation spoke an eloquent language: they were evidence of the price to be paid for the national blindness. In the post-war years, there were of course nationalist groups and slogans. In retrospect, however, what appears to me to be most in need of explanation is not the existence of such groups and slogans but much rather the fact that the response to them has been so limited. The explanation why nationalism in the 'old' Federal Republic of Germany was less attractive than in the majority of the other larger west European states is undoubtedly to be found in the experience of the catastrophe which ensued from extreme German nationalism.

Secondly: The National Socialists countered the widespread fear of social decline with the promise of national ascent. In 1945 social decline had gone as far as it could for the majority of Germans. Social fears were not so much caused by the sensing of an inside as an outside threat. Although consciousness of this was not a good basis for a policy of nationalist isolation, it was for a policy of Western integration. And this is a major reason for the success of the Catholic Rhinelander and notorious anti-nationalist, Konrad Adenauer. However, it was also the opportunity for the Social Democrats to portray themselves as a 'national' party, a party of German unity. The fact that the moderate Left favoured a national policy while the moderate Right pursued a supranational policy is, as the Swiss journalist Fritz René Allemann remarked as early as 1956, an important difference between 'Bonn' and 'Weimar'.[15] Nevertheless, the policy of Western integration was only possible because the victorious Western powers accepted West Germany as a political partner within relatively few years after the end of the war – this is another fundamental difference from the Weimar Republic. In contrast to 1918, after the Second World War the victors occupied Germany and, thereby, caused an incomparably deeper breach in political, military and social continuity than was the case after the First World War. To a large extent, the rapid rehabilitation of the West German successor state to the German Reich by the Western allied powers cut away the ground from under any national resentment against these very powers.

Thirdly: Extreme nationalism has always played the role of a compensation ideology. As the American psychologist Daniel Katz has noted, nationalism can act as an enhanced psychic income for broad population strata, that is, compensation in the form of collective prestige for material privations. Nationalism permits the projection of hate and animosity on to 'out groups'; through a collective experience of success, it can reduce personal frustration and help to transfer libidinous desires to group symbols. One of Katz's most important findings is that, under certain circumstances, people have a particularly great need for nationalism while, under other circumstances, nationalism can lose virtually all significance, that is, when people are able to lead a fulfilled and rich life as individuals, they have no need of an extraordinary significance for their group.[16]

In my opinion, this insight is not only important for the analysis of German nationalism. Very clearly, the economic prosperity of the Federal Republic has contributed greatly to the weakening of nationalism: symbolic compensation such as offered by nationalism is less in demand when there are good chances of obtaining material satisfaction. Much speaks for W. W. Rostow's theory that societies which have entered the age of 'mass consumption' are less susceptible to aggressive nationalism than societies which are still in the early stage of 'economic maturity', that is, in Rostow's terminology, the phase immediately following 'take off'. Despite all the misgivings regarding this theory of 'the stages of economic growth', it is nevertheless evident that there is a close link between economic and social development on the one hand and nationalism on the other.[17]

A glance at the countries of the 'third world' today confirms the finding based on the observation of early European nationalism: in the majority of cases, nationalism is aimed at overcoming economic backwardness. However, besides *material* backwardness, one-sided *political* dependence or discrimination is a factor which tends to promote nationalism. Nationalism only suffers a functional loss in those cases where a society does not have the feeling of economic backwardness and one-sided political dependence. If this is true, then sweeping accusations of foreign nationalism coming from the mouth of Western 'beati possidentes' represent the opposite of historical understanding.[18]

The remarks made above about the diminishing attraction of nationalism in Germany after 1945 were essentially based on the experience of the 'old' Federal Republic. It was not a nation-state and it increasingly saw itself as a 'post-national' community. A new 'constitutional patriotism' came to replace traditional German nationalism in the Federal Republic: a loyalty to the state based not on ethnic principles but on the universal values of liberal democracy.[19]

Yet the 'old' Federal Republic no longer exists. Should we therefore reckon with the emergence of a new German nationalism in the wake of the union of the Federal Republic and the German Democratic Republic in 1990? Until the autumn of 1989 the restoration of German unity was an aim to which West German policy paid lip-service but scarcely pursued in any active sense. Since the days of Willy Brandt's social–liberal coalition, the Bonn government had aimed to alleviate human conditions and to assist the gradual democratization of the GDR. Opposition groups in East Germany wanted a German Democratic Republic which lived up to its name; they did not want a new German national state. They believed that the demand for reunification was counter-productive since it provided an alibi for the opponents of reform amongst the leadership of the SED. 'Reunification or us': that was the alternative which Honecker and his colleagues tried to impress not only on Gorbachev but on most of the non-aligned and Western states as well.

The regime of the SED collapsed when it became clear to the whole world, including the Soviet Union, that it could no longer guarantee stability. The mass exodus via the Federal Republic's embassies in Warsaw and Prague and across the Hungarian frontier with Austria was the point of no return: the 'Honecker system' could no longer maintain the walled frontier nor suppress the internal opposition. On the other hand, the Soviet Union could not come to the aid of the SED without arresting Gorbachev's reform movement and thereby prompting a world crisis.

This Soviet non-intervention represented Moscow's most significant intervention in German politics since 1945. The Kremlin realized that the GDR was threatening to become the focal point of a crisis with international dimensions. A destablized GDR could no longer fulfil the geostrategic functions which it had fulfilled since its foundation, namely as a material basis for the Soviet Union's aspiration for parity with the USA in world politics. Almost overnight the unwritten law which for four decades had determined international politics was nullified: the principle that peace in Europe depended on the parity of the superpowers and that this in turn depended on the division of Germany. In releasing the GDR Moscow gave up its hegemonial aspirations and thus inaugurated the definitive end of the post-war era.

Until the hurried opening of the Berlin Wall on 9 November 1989 the demonstrators in Leipzig, Dresden and East Berlin had demanded democracy in the GDR and not German unity. Only in the middle of November was the popular slogan 'We are the people' gradually drowned out by others: 'We are *one* people!' and 'Germany, a united fatherland!' The national slogan was the slogan of the hitherto silent majority, not that of the active and largely intellectual opposition. The slogan became popular because it was capable of expressing everything that the mass of the population of the GDR wanted to articulate: the anger over the presumptions of the SED type of socialism, the rejection of a third way into the no man's land between capitalism and communism, the demand for material parity with the privileged Germans in the Federal Republic. The demand for unity was an expression of impatience, which surprised those who for many years had been irritated by the apparently limitless patience of the East Germans, compared with the Poles, for example. Even now the demand was not premature. The East Germans only then began to demand unity when that demand could no longer endanger their newly won freedom. Rarely have the masses acted so perfectly in accordance with the principles of *realpolitik* as in the autumn of 1989 in the GDR.

There was little evidence of nationalist fervour in Germany during the process of unification. In the 'old' Federal Republic joy over the fact of unity was soon mingled with concern about the economic cost, over sacrifices to be made on behalf of the East Germans, the real losers of 1945. Indeed since the dramatic collapse of the GDR the gulf which had developed between the two German states has become fully visible for the first time. Some West Germans are disturbed rather than pleased by the union with the 'poor relations' in the East. They see it as a threat both to their standard of living and to the 'Western' life-style to which they had become accustomed during the decades of division. There is in the Western part of Germany a strong desire to maintain the existing order of things – a desire which will not readily be undermined by appeals to national solidarity.

In the former GDR the socialist internationalism which had been propagated for decades has scarcely left any traces. Anti-Polish and anti-Semitic prejudices are commonplace, and more survived here of the historical mythology of German nationalism than in the 'old' Federal Republic. The empty doctrine of anti-fascism which the government imposed from above effectively prevented any critical evaluation of recent German history. East German society is also much less 'multicultural', that is, more homogeneous in ethnic terms, than West German society. There is considerable evidence for the emergence of a 'delayed nationalism' in the former GDR: an assertive feeling of identity on the part of Germans who want to prove that they are particularly good Germans, precisely because they have been disadvantaged by history.[20]

The political culture which has developed in West Germany since the Second World War is of course sufficiently dynamic to cope with such regressive tendencies. The fact that the united Germany is tied into the European community and into the Atlantic alliance acts as an obstacle to the pursuit of an independent nationalist course by Germany. Unlike the first German nation-state, which foundered on its own ambitions, the second German nation-state has been formed with the agreement of its neighbours. The aggressive German nationalism of the past is burned out. In accordance with the wishes of the majority of Germans, the newly united Germany does not aspire to be a classical nation-state but part of a European federal state. However, whether this vision will be translated into political reality does not depend on the Germans alone.

NOTES

1 R. M. Berdahl, 'New thoughts on German nationalism', *American Historical Review*, 77 (1977), 65–80.
2 Works on this subject include: H. Rothfels, 'Das erste Scheitern des National-staates in Ost-Mittel-Europa 1848/49', in *Zeitgeschichtliche Betrachtungen* (Göttingen, 1959), pp. 40–53; G. Wollstein, *Das 'Grossdeutschland' der Paulskirche. Nationale Ziele in der bürgerlichen Revolution 1848/49* (Düsseldorf, 1977).
3 H. A. Winkler, *Preussischer Liberalismus und deutscher Nationalstaat. Studien zur Geschichte der Deutschen Fortschrittspartei 1861–1866* (Tübingen, 1964), p. 32.
4 *Ibid.*, pp. 29ff.
5 *Ibid.*, p. 78.
6 H. A. Winkler, 'Vom linken zum rechten Nationalismus. Der deutsche Liberalismus in der Krise von 1878/79', in Winkler, *Liberalismus und Antiliberalismus. Studien zu politischen Sozialgeschichte des 19. und 20. Jahrhunderts* (Göttingen, 1979), pp. 36–51 at p. 41.
7 L. Bamberger, 'National', in *Nation*, 22 September 1888, reprinted in *Bamberger Political Schriften* (Berlin, 1897), vol. V, pp. 203–37 at p. 217.

8 H. Rosenberg, *Grosse Depression und Bismarckzeit. Wirtschaftsablauf, Gesellschaft und Politik in Mitteleuropa* (West Berlin, 1967).

9 R. M. Lepsius, *Extremer Nationalismus, Strukturbedingungen vor der nationalsozialistischen Machtergreifung* (Stuttgart, 1966), pp. 9ff.

10 Winkler, *Vom linken zum rechten Nationalismus*, p. 46.

11 M. Weber, 'Der Nationalstaat und die Volkswirtschaftspolitik', in Weber, *Gesammelte politische Schriften*, 2nd edn (Tübingen, 1958), pp. 1–25 at p. 23.

12 A. Hitler, 'Warum musste ein 8. November kommen?', *Deutschlands Erneuerung*, 4 (1924), 107, quoted by T. W. Mason, *Arbeiterklasse und Volksgemeinschaft. Dokumente und Materialien zu deutschen Arbeiterpolitik 1936–1939* (Opladen, 1975), p. 5.

13 E. Nolte, 'Vergangenheit, die nicht vergehen will', in *Historikerstreit. Die Dokumentation der Kontroverse um die Einzigartigkeit der nationalsozialistischen Judenvernichtung* (Munich, 1987), pp. 39–47.

14 W. Sauer, 'National Socialism: totalitarianism or fascism?', *American Historical Review*, 73 (1967), 404–24.

15 F. R. Allemann, *Bonn ist nicht Weimar* (Cologne, 1956), p. 274.

16 D. Katz, 'Nationalism and strategy of international conflict resolution', in H. C. Kelman (ed.), *International Behaviour: A Social-Psychological Analysis* (New York, 1965), pp. 354–70.

17 W. W. Rostow, *The Stages of Economic Growth: A Non-Communist Manifesto*, 2nd edn (Cambridge, 1971).

18 H. A. Winkler, 'Der Nationalismus und seine Funktionen', in Winkler (ed.), *Nationalismus*, 2nd edn (Königstein, 1985), pp. 5–46.

19 D. Sternberger, *Verfassungspatriotismus* (Hanover, 1982); J. Habermas, 'Eine Art Schadensabwicklung', in *Historikerstreit*, pp. 62–76.

20 For a more detailed account of developments in Germany since autumn 1989, see H. Winkler, 'Das Ende der Nachkriegszeit', in W. von Sternburg (ed.), *Geteilte Ansichten über eine vereinigte Nation. Ein Buch über Deutschland* (Frankfurt, 1990), pp. 268–76.

EIGHT

THE NATIONAL IDENTITY
OF THE AUSTRIANS

ERNST BRUCKMÜLLER

Nationalism – a world intoxicated with collective nomenclature. For example, the fact that I am an Austrian means that I share a common label with an abundance of repellent individuals; because of this, I do not want to accept that I be categorized solely in terms of such a concept.

Heimito von Doderer, *Repertorium. Ein Begreifbuch von höheren und niederen Lebens-Sachen*, ed. D. Weber (Munich, 1969), p. 164

AUSTRIA

To simplify the discussion we will define 'Austria' only as the territory constituting the Republic of Austria since 1919 and since 1945; it follows that the inhabitants of this territory may logically be described as 'Austrians'. This, however, cannot avoid the complications arising from the fact that this Austria was for a long time a part of a much greater power structure, which was also known as 'Austria'. It is preferable to call this greater power structure 'the Habsburg Monarchy' for the period after 1867. In doing so, one should not forget that the name 'Austria' had been identified with the *Land* of the same name which had existed since 1156, and which is today the province of Lower Austria. The *Land* of Upper Austria (Austria above the Enns) is also included in this definition of 'Austria'. Moreover, the western half of the Habsburg Monarchy was unofficially known as 'Austria' after the *Ausgleich* (Austro-Hungarian Compromise) of 1867. Its inhabitants were officially in possession of 'Austrian' citizenship. It should be pointed out that this last version of Austria corresponds to almost all of *present-day* Austria, together with territories of significant proportions which belong to existing Italy, Romania, Poland, and the former Czechoslovakia, USSR and Yugoslavia.

OVERVIEW OF THE QUESTION OF NATIONAL IDENTITY

The national question has been variously conceived of in history. However, in this instance, we will deliberately lay aside certain conventionally adopted attributes of a 'nation', such as language, national tradition, culture, racial origin, and so on. The distinguished Viennese historian Wilhelm Bauer, himself a German nationalist, warned in 1918 against the use of such attributes:

> Neither characteristics of race or racial origin, nor even a common language are decisive factors. Children of the same parents can in certain circumstances belong to different nations! The modern national idea is almost solely based on personal disposition, and in the last resort it is simply which nation an individual *feels* himself to be a part of that is decisive, not which one he physically or linguistically, or otherwise, belongs to. This explains also why contemporary expressions of nationalism from time to time seem to take on a quasi-religious complexion. Religion and national feeling [*Volkstum*] share a similar origin in the irrational and thus they also come together in the way that they and their influence are fought over . . . [1]

If we accept Wilhelm Bauer's description of national consciousness as a matter governed by 'personal dispositions', that is, by levels of emotional consciousness, then it would seem appropriate to seek out the areas of identification which motivated and still motivate the Austrians of the nineteenth and twentieth centuries. In other words, the question is: upon what national or linguistic (or other) unity is Ernest Renan's *plébiscite de tous les jours*[2] based in the case of Austria.

Of course, the majority of people in traditional pre-industrial societies had no opportunity to take part in such a plebiscite. Hugo von Hofmannsthal percipiently described this state of affairs in 1916: 'Only a few years ago – time gradually blurs the outlines and reduces the profile of everything in life – a man would have felt himself to be a subject of the princely Schwarzenbergs, or of the abbey of Melk, not just a Lower Austrian or Austrian.'[3]

The development of 'nations' is therefore inextricably linked to the process of the modernization of society. This process may be briefly characterized by its various components: de-feudalization and the rise of a class society, industrialization and commercialization of the economy, the establishment of supraregional markets, the integration of numerous small regions into larger political units, and the development of the modern state through the setting up of bureaucracies, as well as extensive territorial, tax and power monopolies. These processes, which began slowly in the sixteenth century, showed a marked acceleration in the eighteenth century, and reached their apogee in the nineteenth century; also, it may be said, their certain conclusion with the completion of the state's formation after 1948. The result of them was to liberate people from ancient bonds. Clearly there was now a need for new identification figures, since the old ones were disappearing (compare the quotation from von Hofmannsthal). The new identification symbol for the nineteenth century (and indeed for the twentieth century) was the *nation*. This brings us to the problem that the undeniable and documentable social modernization processes within the territory of the Habsburg Monarchy, precisely as regards the German-speaking inhabitants, produced no unambiguous national identity.

The reasons for this were as follows: when the Republic of Austria was formed after the First World War, it defined itself as 'German Austria, *Deutsch-Österreich*'. It wanted to be the nation-state of the German-speaking Austrians, or, in contemporary terminology, of the 'Germans' within the Austro-Hungarian Monarchy, or at least within its western half. As an expression of the 'national' right of self-determination, this Republic declared itself on 12 November 1918 at the same time to be a part of the newly born Republic of the German Reich. The Austrians themselves, or at least their most important representatives, clearly saw themselves as 'Germans'. Even when this self-attachment did not exclude for many people a consciousness of being Austrian, it undoubtedly became an important precondition for the incorporation of Austria into Nazi Germany in 1938, and the extensive participation of many Austrians in the military and racist havoc wreaked by the National Socialists. This 'German' self-identification by Austrians was also shared by many foreign contemporaries: British and Yugoslav politicians, for example, signalled acceptance in 1938 of the incorporation of Austria into the German Reich, because the Austrians were in reality Germans, and therefore should logically be united with the larger German state.[4] (Of course, as will also be shown later in this essay, between 1918 and 1938 this 'German' self-identification was by no means general and uncontroversial.)

When the Republic of Austria was reconstituted after the Second World War, it defined itself as 'Austria'. The word 'German' was so rigorously avoided that the subject 'German' was no longer taught in the schools, but instead 'the language of instruction' (*Unterrichtssprache*). Certainly this formulation also represented an attempt to dissociate the state from Germany, and thus from co-responsibility for Nazi crimes. The protagonists of this new Austrian self-definition were, as a rule, completely genuine 'Austrians', whose anti-Nazi commitment and 'anti-German' sense of their Austrian identity is not in doubt (for example, the Chancellor, Leopold Figl, or the Education Minister, Felix Hurdes). In exactly the same way as could the advocates of a 'German' identity, they were able to point to a long chain of historical and cultural evidence legitimizing the new ideological stance. This ranged from the emphasizing of non-Germanic elements in the Austrian population (Illyrians, Celts, Romans, Slavs) through the earlier constitutional autonomy of the Austrian duchy within the Holy Roman Empire, to the function of the supranational Habsburg state as the 'bulwark' of the Christian West against any barbarians who came from the East.

From the 1960s on Austrian self-confidence has grown to such an extent that one can now, without inhibition, speak of an Austrian national identity. Table 8.1 shows the percentages of Austrians who agreed to one or other of two propositions at specified times. *This national identity refers unambiguously to the territory comprised by the Austrian Republic.*[5] Within this unambiguous and ascertainable national identity, however, *quite diverse identification models* are frequently to be observed.

Table 8.1. *Perception of national identity among Austrians*

Proposition	Percentage agreeing in:				
	1964	1970	1972	1980	1987
1 Austrians constitute a nation	47	66	62	67	75
2 Austrians are slowly beginning to think of themselves as nation	23	16	12	19	16
Totals of 1 and 2	70	82	74	86	91

For some groups the small-scale but courageous Austrian resistance against the Nazis plays a major role as the symbol of Austrian national identification. Others, again, carry around with them in their Austrian consciousness more or less substantial slabs of the Habsburg past (in the form of notions of 'Mitteleuropa'). It remains unclear for how many people Austria is still a German, if autonomous, nation-state. After the recent resistance to the concessions of greater rights to Austrians whose language is Slovene, Croat, Hungarian or Czech, this group also cannot be totally ignored.

THE METHOD

Nations arrive at an understanding of themselves through myths and symbols. Their national holidays are often dedicated to the myth of revolutionary or military successes. Their flags and anthems glorify the victories of their forefathers with the aim of instilling and anchoring a sense of community in the here and now. Nations achieve their identity by means of demarcation from other national groups.

We will first investigate the different indicators of 'national' consciousness in the present, the national symbols of the Austrians, the myths, flags, anthems and collective experience of success, which serve as the focal points of national consciousness. At the same time, it is important to analyse the demarcation from others which are present in the Austrian psyche, in terms both of negative stereotypes of other nationalities, and of collective sympathies.

From the findings that emerge we will attempt to formulate a historical answer to the questions raised.

SYMBOLS, MYTHS AND NEGATIVE STEREOTYPES

Anthems, Flags, National Holidays

The text of the Austrian national anthem was written by the Austrian poetess Paula (von) Prevadović (whose name, significantly, is Croatian). The melody adopted was that of an eighteenth-century Masonic hymn attributed to Mozart. The necessity for a new anthem was already evident in 1918, since the *Kaiserlied* ('God preserve . . .') had become inappropriate. At that time the Chancellor, Karl Renner, had himself tried his hand at composing lines to the melody of the distinguished composer Wilhelm Kienzl ('German Austria, you marvellous land . . .'). The somewhat bombastic anthem failed to achieve much popularity and furthermore was always regarded by the Right of the political spectrum as a work of the Left; it was eventually replaced by Ottokar Kernstock's composition 'Be blessed eternally . . .', which had the undoubted advantage that it could be sung to the magnificent music of Haydn's *Kaiser* hymn. Of course, this advantage was cancelled out by the ever weightier disadvantage that the melody had long been used to accompany the extremely imperialistic *Deutschland-Lied* of Hoffmann von Fallersleben (both in Germany and by German nationalists and National Socialists in Austria). The consequence was that in 1945 Haydn's beautiful strains appeared hopelessly compromised. In short: a new anthem was a part of the new Austrian identity of the Second Republic; while its rather tedious melody could not compete with Haydn's, it at least had the advantage that it was impossible to confuse it with the *Deutschland-Lied*.[6]

The flag presented fewer problems: at the suggestion of Wilhelm Miklas, later the Federal President, 'red-white-red' was chosen in 1918, a solution which endured even after 1945. This colour combination harked back to the gules, a fesse argent arms of the archdukes of Austria, which had been familiar since the thirteenth century, and with which, from earliest times, all sorts of mythical tales had been associated. In the late Middle Ages it was regarded as the coat of arms of 'New Austria'. In modern times the red-white-red pointed stylized shield in conjunction with the imperial double eagle functioned as a sort of state coat of arms of the emerging Habsburg statehood. A flag with the red-white-red colour combination had existed since 1786 as an official naval flag (featuring a crowned red-white-red shield in the centre). It remained in use as a flag of the imperial and Austro-Hungarian navies (with minor alterations) until 1918. The official state colours until 1918 were of course black and yellow, inherited from the old Holy Roman Empire.

The newly designed federal state coat of arms of 1918 could also be carried over to the Second Republic, with the small, but significant, alteration that the talons of the eagle were adorned, after 1945, with a burst chain. This was a reference to the regaining of independence from Germany. However, it is interesting that not only in the souvenir industry, but also in the minds of many Austrians, the old double eagle of the Monarchy is still in very good standing.[7]

The National Holiday shows less continuity. In the First Republic the 12th of November was designated a National Holiday, that being the date of the official proclamation of the Republic. The political Right, who saw in this a yearly reminder of their very modest role at that time, and of the (albeit shortlived) power of Social Democracy, disliked this National Holiday intensely. By 1933 it was no longer being observed with much enthusiasm, and in 1934 it was discontinued. Under the corporate state dictatorship, the 10th of May became the National Holiday (Day of Youth). After 1945 there was no return to the tradition begun in 1918. Only in 1965 was the 'Day of the Flag', which had been celebrated since 1957, declared a National Holiday. This day is 26 October, the date in 1955 when the *Nationalrat* (the Austrian parliament) passed the resolution concerning the permanent neutrality of Austria. With this resolution, the commitment entered into in Moscow was fulfilled. This stipulated that, after the State Treaty was signed and in force, Austria would adopt a position of permanent neutrality on the Swiss model. It was to take effect on the first day following the expiry of the ninety-day deadline by which, calculated from the coming into force of the State Treaty on

27 July 1955, the allies for their part undertook to withdraw their troops.[8]

In contrast to other holidays of this kind, on this day no great military victory, nor any successful revolution, achievement, or proclamation of independence is celebrated. Certainly the day is closely associated with the attainment of complete autonomy and sovereignty, the culmination, as it were, of that long process which had begun in April of 1945, and which reached its climax in an atmosphere of euphoria on 15 May 1955 with the signing of the State Treaty. Yet the day is hardly laden with emotional connotations (and it is also significant that the official propaganda advised that it be marked by somewhat trivial activities, such as hiking). On the positive side, the Austrian National Holiday offers no opportunity for nationalistic or chauvinistic excesses.

Focal Points of National Symbolism

The opinion poll in 1980, which has already been referred to, included among its questions one which asked which *Bundesland* (Federal Land) embodied to the greatest extent the specific individuality of Austria. Vienna, named by 30 per cent of those polled, came out well ahead of the Tyrol (14 per cent) and Lower Austria (9 per cent). In particular, young people and the educated stratum identified Austria at that time with Vienna.[9] This result cannot be ascribed to an excess of local Viennese pride, since, in Vienna itself, according to the same poll, such feelings are not at all evident.[10]

Vienna, of course, had become a large and important town early in its history. In 1207 it was already regarded as the second town of the Empire after Cologne. In 1361 Rudolph IV called Vienna 'the capital city of all our territories and realms', and this pivotal function of the city was underlined by the founding of the university and the enlarging of St Stephen's (the principal church), as well as by efforts to establish a bishopric. In 1548 Wolfgang Schmeltzl called the Viennese Hofburg (Court Castle) the 'House of Austria', for, in a precise sense, this was the central building of that lineage which called itself 'Haus Österreich' (*casa d'Austria*). The central buildings, turned into highly revered focal points for the dynasty and the people of Austria, were extended in the baroque period. Then the Karlskirche (Charles Church) was erected as the central sanctuary, for which all the Habsburg lands provided financial support. In this period also, the accumulation of treasures and sacred objects in Vienna gathered momentum: the famous art collection from Ambras was transferred here in various stages, likewise, for example, the wonder-working icon of the Virgin from Maria Pötsch (from Hungary). In the nineteenth century central temples of a (secularized) cult of art arose on the Ringstrasse: the Hof- (now Staats-) Oper, the Burgtheater, the Kunsthistorisches Museum and Naturhistorisches Museum (which came into being from the court collections), and the building of the Musikverein. At the same time, the population increased: from around 180,000 in 1750 to 208,000 in 1791, to 430,000 in 1850 and more than 2 million in 1910.

In the nineteenth century the centralizing functions of Vienna were even more numerous and by the same token even more contradictory. Until the rise of Berlin from about 1870, Vienna was the largest German city; now it became suddenly also the largest Czech and Jewish city of central Europe. Vienna became the centre of Austrian liberalism, of German centralism, but also of conservative Catholicism, of anti-Semitism, and of the Marxist-orientated labour movement. Vienna, therefore, besides its magnetic attraction as the distant seat of imperial power, so well described by the writer Manès Sperber, also brought upon itself the accumulated hatred of 'pure' nationalists (Czech as well as German) for the mixed population of the imperial capital; the hatred of the anti-Semites for the large number of Viennese Jews, the hatred of the anti-Marxists for Social Democracy. In Adolf Hitler these feelings of hatred seemed to be, at the same time, paradigmatically combined with a never quite conquered admiration for the grandiose Vienna of the Ringstrasse.

In 1918 Vienna lost its central functions in the area of the Habsburg Monarchy; and in 1938 that also in the area of the Republic. Today, Vienna has become geographically peripheral even inside Austria, as well as in relation to the rising European community. Of the 2 million inhabitants in 1910, scarcely 1.5 million remain. The lingering nostalgia for Vienna's central function that has endured post-1945 is expressed, for example, in the assistance given by the Austrian Federal Lands to the reconstruction of the cathedral of St Stephen's. And, of course, in the results of opinion polls.[11]

Personalities as Figures of National Identification

Certain personalities have always been important totem figures of national identification. The poll in 1980 in respect of deceased political leaders resulted in a pronounced lead for Empress Maria Theresa over the politician Karl Renner, Emperor Francis Joseph and Julius Raab, another politician; but in terms of familiarity and estimation of their importance for Austria (or to what extent they were characteristic for Austria), this quartet was easily put in the shade by two composers: Johann Strauss and Wolfgang Amadeus Mozart.

Amongst living Austrians, Bruno Kreisky was singled out as possessing in even greater measure the attributes that summed up the meaning and characteristics of Austria. He even came out ahead of two such important personalities from the worlds of sport and entertainment as the skier Annemarie Moser-Pröll and the actor Heinz Conrads.[12]

There is no need to go into the possible underlying reasons for the high value placed on music and composers, on Maria Theresa and on Francis Joseph. More interesting (and more surprising) is the overwhelming role of Bruno Kreisky in forming the Austrian identity of the recent past. Albert F. Reiterer in his book *Die unvermeidbare Nation* has dealt with the temporal coincidence of the consolidation of the Austrian national consciousness with the period of Kreisky's tenure of office. As symbol of the 'modernization' of Austria pursued by the Austrian Socialist Party (SPÖ) since 1970, and equally because of his high international profile, Kreisky has become (well beyond the confines of the SPÖ) an identification and integration figure for Austrians. He can therefore be seen to some extent as a 'charismatic leader'.[13] In addition, Kreisky was certainly also the symbol for a new Austrian consciousness, no longer bound up with old associations such as 'Catholic', 'Habsburg', and so on.

National Myths

Indeed, an 'obligatory' national myth of Austria no longer exists today, with the possible exception of the State Treaty. The reasons for this may be found in the history of the last three or four generations of Austrians, who could experience no historical event prior to the State Treaty of 1955 which could be regarded as integrative and formative of identity: 1918 was for the Left 'Revolution', for the Right defeat and disintegration. 1938 was for all German nationalists and those who identified with Germanism a success and a triumph, while for all who identified with Austrianism, for Jews and for political opponents (on the Right and on the Left) of National Socialism, it was a catastrophe. By the same token, 1945 meant catastrophe for the large number of Austrians who considered themselves German and were National Socialists, but joy for the resurrection of Austria on the part of those who were on the losing side in 1938. Not until 1955 could the whole of Austria join in celebrating the withdrawal of the occupying powers. Here lies the 'collective success' which a shared collective consciousness requires every bit as much as the collective experience of jointly secured existence within stable borders.

'Successes', which one generally finds to be interpreted in the sense of events that formed the identity of other nations, are few and far between in the history of Austria. The Austrian army had not succeeded in winning in war for a long time, and no successful revolution can be pointed to which strengthened consciousness of a shared identity. Moreover, the formation of the nation-states that border present-day Austria (Germany, Italy, Czechoslovakia and former Yugoslavia) was achieved always at the expense of the old Austria, whose centre is identical with the centre of contemporary Austria, and whose ruling classes were resident here and experienced those foreign successful integration processes as bitter defeats. One has to go back, therefore, to the contribution to the strengthening of Austrian identity made by Prince Eugene of Savoy, the Turkish wars and, if need be, Archduke Charles or Field Marshal Radetzky, in order to restore to the Austrians some of that heady enthusiasm that arose out of 'their own' military victories. This awakening of the echoes of past glories was a feature of the First World War and of the period between 1933 and 1938.[14]

This phenomenon is surely also one of the historical grounds for the uncertain foundations of collective pride in the nation which the opinion polls reveal.[15]

Demarcations, Negative Stereotypes of Other Nations, Collective Sympathies

Since it would seem inappropriate to enquire into negative stereotypes of other nations, the tireless pollsters have tested the amount of sympathy, and the extent to which there are assumptions of inherent affinity, with Austria's neighbours. It is, of course, precisely from one's neighbours that one is most concerned to establish lines of demarcation in order to demonstrate one's individuality. In answer to the question: 'Which nation seems to you the most sympathetic?' (Austria itself was a permitted answer in this case), Austria was the choice of 33 per cent, followed by Germany (26 per cent), Switzerland (11 per cent), the USA (4 per cent) and France (3 per cent). When one compares this investigation with that into the 'greatest inherent affinity' with neighbour states, the following results emerge: Germany attracts the greatest number of positive replies (70 per cent), followed by Hungary, level pegging with Switzerland (10 per cent), Czechoslovakia (5 per cent) and Yugoslavia, on the same score as Liechtenstein (1 per cent each)[16] These data, collected in 1980, do not differ significantly from those collected in 1987. Germany still leads with 64 per cent, ahead of Hungary with 16 per cent, Switzerland (10 per cent) and Italy (3 per cent). Inherent affinity with Czechoslovakia was now assumed by only 2 per cent of Austrians, while Yugoslavia scored the same as Liechtenstein (1 per cent each).[17]

THE FORMATION OF THE STATE ON AUSTRIAN SOIL[18]

The rise of modern nations is always associated with the territorial expansion of domains and with the integration of splinter territories into larger configurations. These become states as a result of a strengthening of institutional infrastructure, in particular through the monopolization of military and tax administration. A natural consequence usually is that a centre arises which is uniquely representative of the new state entity.

This is the usual pattern in western Europe. If one looks at the history of Austria, which is inextricably bound up with that of the Habsburgs since 1282, one observes numerous stages of precisely this process:

1 After the victorious Carolingian feudalism had dissolved the old tribal system of the Bavarians and Carantanians, the first stage of the concentration of power out of fragmented twelfth-century feudalism began. It resulted in the *Länder* (domains) of Austria, Styria, later Tyrol, Carinthia, Salzburg, Upper Austria and Vorarlberg. The *Länder* developed an extraordinary capacity for resistance against all later attempts to subordinate them to the modern concept of a state. The bearers of land consciousness (*Landesbewusstsein*) were the estates, composed of the nobility, the prelates (mostly the heads of the old monasteries), representatives of the towns and, in some *Länder*, elected legal functionaries of princely rural courts (*ländliche Gerichte des Landesfürsten*). These land estates were the military arm and the advisers of the Prince. In the late Middle Ages, they increasingly absolved themselves from their military obligations by the granting of taxation. At the same time, their most important aristocratic members were feudal landlords, from which resulted a conflict which was not resolved until 1848, for these feudal lords were permanently reluctant to share the surplus produced by peasants with the Princes. Thus, in the struggle for the formation of a modern state, the most important aim of the Princes became the monopolization of taxation of the peasantry.

2 If the process of the concentration of domains advances further, new and larger areas arise, which embrace an increasing number of such *Länder*. In the territories of present-day Austria this process began with the joint rule of Princes of the so-called Babenberg line over the *Länder* of Austria and Styria in 1192. The Habsburgs took over these two *Länder* in 1282, acquired in addition in 1335 Carinthia and Krain (the central part of the present-day Republic of Slovenia), in 1363 Tyrol, and in 1500 Gorizia (parts of which today lie in Italy, former Yugoslavia and Austria). By 1520, the Habsburgs had acquired a large part of present-day Austria (without Salzburg, Burgenland and the Innviertel in Upper Austria); in addition they possessed those parts of South Tyrol that now lie in Italy, small portions of Friuli and Istria (with Trieste), and almost all of Slovenia. Moreover, they had significant estates in Alsace and in the Swabian lands between the Rhine and the Danube.

In an institutional sense, the Prince of all these domains (until 1519 Emperor Maximilian I) and their Diets stood in opposition to each other. Accordingly, the emperor, who was obliged to be absent from his 'hereditary domains' (*Erblande*) much of the time owing to his Burgundian and imperial duties, attempted to set up bureaucratic structures, *soi-disant* 'governments'. From the time of Ferdinand I (1522–64) such arrangements were a permanent feature. Also joint assemblies of most or all Habsburg domains were occasionally held, as, for example, in 1518 in Innsbruck. It is interesting to note that out of such assemblies could grow estates representation for the newly emergent states (Land Assemblies General, Estates General, States General). And from such assemblies could be derived national assemblies of a revolutionary nature, as in the France of 1789. What is important here is that the tradition of the Land Assemblies General was discontinued and was not taken up again. In the same way, the projects for the formal integration of these 'hereditary domains' into an individual *kingdom* were not carried through. Consequently, the future Austrian nation lacked two central symbols – the Austrian crown and an Austrian parliament.[19]

3 From 1526 the Habsburgs were not only the Princes of the Austrian *Länder*, but (usually) also German kings and Holy Roman Emperors, as well as Kings of Bohemia (with Moravia and Silesia), and of Hungary (with Croatia). As a result, they inherited from the Hungarian kings direct confrontation with the Ottoman Empire; and as inheritors of Burgundy, they found themselves in competition with the House of Valois in the West. The diversion of 1522 made the German

branch of the Habsburgs appear relatively insignificant in comparison with the dominant Spanish line. All the same, after the abdication of Charles V, the imperial crown remained with the line of Ferdinand I, which lent it a not inconsiderable aura of 'splendour'.

The competitive tensions throughout Europe, which have already been hinted at, implied a huge need for money, since now it was necessary to pursue an unbroken succession of armed conflicts (with France, with the Ottoman Turks, with the Estates in Germany which turned Protestant). Military and financial administration therefore became the vital concerns of the court-'state'. The 'formation of the state' can therefore be understood as a process in which the authority of the (court-) state of the Princes was extended to an ever greater range of activities and territories. A fundamental necessity was the suppression of the powers of the Estates, which, for reasons that have already been indicated, showed little enthusiasm for approving the ever-increasing tax requirements of the Habsburgs. The conflicts between Princes and Estates came to a head between 1519 and 1620. The suppression of this resistance from 1620 onwards had a further consequence: the Austrians of today are *not* able, like Englishmen or Dutchmen, to draw on a tradition of successful resistance by the Estates to the king as part of their national mythology.

4 Between 1620 and 1740 administrative penetration of the different Habsburg kingdoms and domains, and their integration into a single 'state' proceeded only slowly. In spite of the transformation of Bohemia and Hungary into hereditary domains (1627 and 1687), the violent suppression of Protestantism and the expulsion of many Protestant nobles and burghers, neither a thorough unification of the administration ensued, nor a basic transformation of society. This remained unwaveringly feudal. But its fundamental conservatism also maintained the Estates and *Länder*. The new Habsburg court aristocracy acquired full feudal residential rights in the countries where their possessions lay, and, what is perhaps more important, they became successive supporters of traditional identification with one's own country (*Landesbewusstsein*). The Habsburgs never succeeded in making the aristocracy financially dependent on them (as, for example, was the case with Louis XIV). *This unbroken tradition of regional aristocratic power provided variously an important nucleus for the subsequent formation of modern national consciousness in Bohemia and Hungary.*[20]

All the same, the period between 1680 and 1720 furnished substantial material for the formation of the Austrian state and national mythology. The victories of Prince Eugene and other commanders did not only extend Habsburg hegemony into south-east Europe, they also supplied vital ingredients in terms of national myths which retained their significance even into the twentieth century. The so-called 'Pragmatic Sanction' (1713), to which all the Estates of all the kingdoms and *Länder* were signatories, placed the monarchial union of the Habsburg possessions on a permanent constitutional footing which actually lasted until 1918. New economic policies attempted to bind together more closely the *Monarchia Austriaca* whose components were still rather loose in the economic sphere, and to raise economic productivity.

The reasons why the state formation of the Habsburgs at this time, despite some advances, failed to achieve decisive unification, are usually explained by the following factors:

The Habsburgs were not only the heads of their hereditary kingdoms and domains, but also Emperors of the Holy Roman Empire. Although, after the failure of Charles V and after (at latest) 1629, the Habsburgs had no more chance to incorporate this empire into their state, they still remained heavily involved in its events, even more noticeably between about 1670 and 1710 than before and after these dates. As a result, the relations between 'Emperor and Empire' remained as a rule oppositional, and did *not* lead to the strengthening of the ties between the hereditary domains and the Empire: the Imperial Diet (Reichstag) and District Diets (*Kreistage*), the organs of the 'Empire', had no competence in the hereditary domains, where the 'Emperor' really was the sole overlord. The imperial history of the Holy Roman Empire may therefore be fundamentally interpreted as the successful history of the warding off of Habsburg state formations in the empire, and of own state formation by the great Estates and the Emperor. The politico-social integration processes on German soil in no way favoured any kind of 'German unity' (a fact which is overlooked by all those, who, in arguing for the 'German' character of Austria, stress the centuries-old association with the old 'Empire'). On the other hand, the Empire cost the Viennese court a great deal in terms of paying attention to its problems and resources.

In this period the rulers relied for their legitimization less on the bureaucracy than on religious and monarchial representation. These found expression in the building of numerous castles, monasteries and churches, in sumptuous pilgrimages and processions, in theatrically staged masses and devotional displays. The architectural expression of this 'pietas Austriaca' is not only to be discerned in the building of Klosterneuburg, Melk, St Florian or Göttweig (on whose grandiose stairway fresco Charles VI himself is depicted as Phoebus Apollo riding in the chariot of the sun), but also in the Vienna Karlskirche, the Hofbibliothek, the plague monument on Graben street in Vienna, and so on. By 1700 baroque Catholicism seems to have found a considerably wider measure of acceptance in society at large. This is even demonstrated, for example, in the choice of names amongst the population. An important reason for this acceptance lies in the shrewd exploitation of regional and local saints, and of shrines. These were now enthusiastically promoted, and also incorporated into the official 'state cult'.

The highest authorities of the central administration for the individual territories were the so-called 'chancelleries' (one each for Hungary, Bohemia, Austria, Transylvania, and so on). The high-level bureaucracy of the chancelleries was recruited from the regional aristocracy, who simply ran them in pursuit of their own interests.[21]

In addition, the central administration was made more complex during the period of division (from 1564 on), when individual courts and central administrations arose in Innsbruck and Graz. These maintained their own bureaucratic existence even after the reunification of the Habsburg lands (in 1620 and 1665 respectively) until 1749.

5 The centralization and unification efforts received powerful impetus from the great political crisis following the death of Charles VI in 1740. After this had been overcome, Maria Theresa began immediately in 1749 to carry the process of state formation decisively forward by means of wide-ranging changes. Military and tax reforms reduced the influence of the Estates, the freedom from taxation enjoyed by the aristocratic and ecclesiastical landowners was lifted, and district officers now represented the Prince also before the peasantry (who until then had only dealt with agents of their feudal landlords).

A 'state' actually did now arise, that did not, however, embrace all the Habsburg domains, but essentially only Bohemia, Moravia-Silesia, and the Austrian *Länder*. Hungary was largely untouched by the military and tax reforms of Maria Theresa; together with Milan, Belgium and Tyrol, Hungary remained outside the unified customs area uniting the Bohemian-Austrian domains with Trieste, established in 1775.

This process was accelerated under Joseph II, not to say radicalized. His ecclesiastical, educational, fiscal and administrative reforms aimed at creating a unified state entity (now also inclusive of Hungary), whose official language was German. Priests (*Weltpriester*), officials and officers as the most important servants of the state were to serve the concept of the unified state. No consideration was to be given to traditional prerogatives and attitudes, and especially none to traditional regional and local autonomies. This was to be done away with, both enjoyed by the communes and the Estates.

THE JOSEPHINE STATE AND THE PROBLEM OF THE FORMATION OF THE NATION

With the dissolution or repression of traditional feudal and communal autonomies, as well as of regional and religious identification models, the isolated individual was confronted with the question of his identity. The *bürgerliche* nation of men free of feudal dependency was about to be born.

Maria Theresa and Joseph II understood 'national education' (*Nationalbildung*) as above all a problem of bringing up a people to identify themselves with their state.[22] The Enlightenment must have given these efforts added pathos: the metamorphosis from a subject of the state (*Staatsuntertan*) to a (more or less) 'citizen' (*Staatsbürger*) was imminent. The latter expression was, incidentally, already in use under Joseph II, and was also adopted in the *Allgemeine Bürgerliche Gesetzbuch* (Book of Civil Law) which came into force in 1812.[23]

As a result of these developments the Habsburg state was faced with the following questions:

1   Did the standard-bearers of national consciousness, pertinent to this state, correspond to an already existing bourgeoisie (or one in the process of emerging)?
2   Was this class so widespread that it could function as the standard-bearer of a nation that encompassed the entire monarchy?
3   Were symbols and myths available which could replace the traditional identification models and, at the same time, work in favour of the integration of the Habsburg state?

The *first* question cannot be answered wholly in the negative. It is beyond dispute that from 1770 a new, bourgeois, class was arising. It was drawn from lawyers, publishers, book printers, merchants, notaries and above all, civil servants (*Beamten*). The majority of writers in Josephine Vienna came from the circles of civil servants, who were able to build up for a short while an extremely interesting variant of the critically aware literary public described by Habermas. However, the preponderance of civil servants (or people in some way dependent on the state) in the ranks of the new class indicates very clearly the parameters and limitations of bourgeois existence. Although he was concerned with the state and public affairs, the civil servant remained dependent on the state (which still meant on the Prince), and thus restricted in his capacity for critical initiative. It is difficult to deny that the 'nation of *Hofräte*' (Court Councillors – an upper rank of the Austrian bureaucracy), so poignantly depicted by Hermann Bahr as a society of officials floating in the orbit of imperial authority, showed the beginnings of a bourgeois nation. It was, however, one that lacked the potential or the capacity to grow decisively beyond its own confines.[24]

At the same time, this already provides a partial *second* question. For the most part, this bourgeois society was confined to Vienna, at any rate as a mass phenomenon – even when there were, of course, local examples of it in Lwów/Lemberg, Graz, Kraków/Krakau, Brno/Brünn, Innsbruck, Pest, Ljubljana/Laibach, and so on. And in the regional centres outside Vienna, apart from amongst the protagonists of bureaucratic centralization and an emergent 'German' entrepreneurial bourgeoisie, the need for new national identifications not centred on Vienna and the Habsburgs, but centred on one's own *country and one's own nation*, was being catered for. Thus, for the time being (and in fact for a long time to come), loyalty to the Emperor, land patriotism (*Landespatriotismus*) and loyalty to the *new nation* as experienced by means of a common language coexisted without difficulty. The concept 'nation' could at one and the same time be applied to the monarchy as a whole and to an individual *Land* (such as Styria); or, merely, to a linguistic grouping.

Certainly the representatives of this new (Austrian) consciousness were predominantly German-speakers. As officials they had to carry out the unifying centralization of Joseph II, which was effected through the medium of the German language. At the same time there existed many causes of friction between the (North) German literature of the Enlightenment (Nicolai) and the Viennese literati. It would seem permissible therefore to characterize this emerging national consciousness as 'German-Austrian': its protagonists in Josephine Austria thought of themselves as 'German', but at the same time distanced themselves from 'non-Austrian Germany'. This mental distancing reflected cultural differences which flowed from diverse confessions and state formations (Catholicism versus Protestantism, Austria versus Bavaria and Prussia, and so on).

Such distancings were revealed not only in the literary feud with Nicolai, but also in the efforts to found an Austrian Masonic Lodge independent of Berlin, and also in the tendency of the Austrian *Illuminati* towards an organization completely independent of Bavaria. Since, in the Josephine decade, the (bureaucratic) core of the bourgeois society came together with officers and the high nobility in the lodges, one can identify Austrian Freemasonry with the kernel of the emergent nation.[25]

At the same time Josephinism undoubtedly gave important impetus to the development of modern national consciousness amongst Magyars, Czechs, Slovenes, and so on. Although that is not relevant to our theme, it should be noted that Joseph II's centralization and administrative Germanization called forth, notably in Hungary, a passionate insistence on national independence; the natural consequence of this was that the national languages became increasingly symbols of national identity. Because of the determined opposition to the centralizing and 'German' unification of Joseph II (who undoubtedly was not concerned with 'Germanization' in the nineteenth-century sense), it was of course more or less impossible that the non-German linguistic groupings could feel themselves to be a part of a (German-) Austrian nation as such.[26]

Coming now to the *third* question, it is probable that Josephinism, through its struggle against Church and court ceremonial, against the ostentation of baroque Catholicism and costly pilgrimages, itself limited the effectiveness of the mythology that potentially worked in its favour. Although the myth of 'the good emperor' continued to influence the rural masses, the rationalized apparatus of state under Joseph II, with its armed forces and civil service, proved to be in no way promotive to myth creation. Among others, this was *also* because the aim of these establishments, namely the favourable outcome of foreign policy and, if need be, military successes, was not fulfilled: the policy of expansion both in Bavaria and the Balkans (the Turkish war) failed.

Undoubtedly Joseph II and his reforms were *also* available to the Josephine Austro-consciousness as identity-building myths. That also meant, however, that a shift of policy in a reactionary direction could explode the mythology that gave direction to the previously described bourgeois strata. Extremely interesting evidence of this is provided by the Josephine writer Johann Baptist Alxinger, who wrote as follows to Nicolai in 1796 after the end of the liberal period of Josephinism:

> the banning of books and clericalism [*Pfaffentum*] are the only defences which we erect against the feared revolution, although our fears are groundless. After much heart-searching, I have eventually reconciled myself to no longer being an Austrian, but simply a German. While this officially inspired feud with the sciences persists, how can a scholar identify himself with his country . . .[27]

It is therefore logical that the anti-French patriotism of the Napoleonic wars did *not* revolve around the budding Enlightened German-Austrian consciousness of the Josephine decade. Instead, it was bound up with the traditional feelings of regard for the caring Prince who from 1804 was also, and from 1806 was only, the Austrian Emperor. These attitudes underlay not only the anthem written by Lorenz Leopold Haschka and set to music by Joseph Haydn, which essentially expressed the wish that God should preserve and protect the good Emperor Franz (Francis II), but also the planning and preparation of a general arming of the population in answer to the French *levée en masse*. Voluntary detachments and the militia (*Landwehr*) remained circumscribed by custom and tradition. Besides an 'Austrian' militia, there was a 'Styrian' militia, a 'Bohemian' legion under Archduke Charles, and so on (see page 205). Also the contemporary anti-revolutionary journalism of Hormayr was at pains to align itself with the historical traditions of the *Länder* of the empire.[28]

The failure of Josephinism resulted too in the failure of the first conceptualization of a bourgeois German-Austrian nation, in the viable form in which it was manifest in the Josephine literature of the Enlightenment (and in the Austrian Freemasonry of 1786). Subsequently, monarchial patriotism was obliged to orientate itself almost exclusively towards the person and institution of the Emperor. Of course, for those to whom such an orientation seemed infantile, the period preceding the March Revolution of 1848 (*Vormärz*) could already provide new models with which to identify.

GERMAN NATIONAL CONSCIOUSNESS IN AUSTRIA

This new identification model was supplied by a belief in the grace conferred by the language of Luther and of the Weimar classics. Not the 'impure' German of the Viennese popular theatre, mixed up, as it was, with Austrian dialect and countless echoes of Romance and Slav languages, but the language of the North German Protestants seemed now to be the medium through which the Austrian Germans discovered their new language-oriented identity. The 'necessary union of peoples' (in the words of the Czech historian and politician František Palacký) of the Austrian imperial state became an unnecessary evil in the eyes of those who, in opposition to the drift and irresolution which characterized the intractable problems of old Austria, upheld the clearly defined concept of the nation-state. This was the position of the German Left at Frankfurt in 1848. With this grouping of the Left some Austrians and, notably, some Germans from Bohemia were

closely identified. The German nation-state was already conceived of
as an authoritarian state in which the Slavic populations of Prussia
and Austria were to be handled as subjugated peoples; this, for
example, was the attitude of the poets Friedrich Hebbel and the aging
Ernst Moritz Arndt.[29]

Only a few people, such as Count Friedrich Deym, or Victor Baron
Andrian-Werburg, took to an alternative to the new nationalism based
on linguistic groupings, with a vision of a supranational Austrian
nation which would embrace all the nationalities of Austria. This
position was also similar to that of Alexander Baron Helfert. In the
event, the revolution of 1848 did not bring about a revolutionary
Austrian nation that transcended language groupings, but rather
completed the formation of nationalism based on national tongues.
From now on Germans and Czechs confronted each other in the
Czech Lands (Bohemia, Moravia and Silesia) and no longer, as in
1790, 'German Czechs' (Deutschböhmen) and 'true born Czechs'
(Stockböhmen).[30]

The development of a national consciousness among the non-
German nations was accelerated by the new German national consciousness. Effectively, German had been the language of the army,
the civil service and the bourgeois society within the Habsburg
Monarchy. The new nationalistic presumption that anyone who spoke
German also be considered a German, accelerated the build-up both
of national consciousness and of a new bourgeois language culture
among 'the others'. The Czech and Slovene bourgeoisies now began
consciously to use 'their' languages, in place of the nationalistically
perceived German.

If we say that, in 1848 and afterwards, new language-based
nationalism grew in strength, the following characteristics should be
noted of the deepening and expansion of German national consciousness in Austria:

1 German national consciousness in Austria was propagated by
writers, journalists and students (vide the Schiller celebrations in
1859). It penetrated somewhat wider social layers as a result of its
dissemination by teachers and the professions. From the 1880's on it
could variously enjoy strong institutional support through the network
of societies for the promotion of German education and the protection
of German interests. *German language groupings in the national border and
battle zones were more susceptible than the German-speaking Tyroleans or the
Lower Austrians; and the bourgeois social groups more so than the peasants.*[32]

2 *The especially democratic and emancipatory ethos which certainly was part and parcel of the youthful nationalism until 1848, had evaporated shortly after the revolution; the German bourgeoisie of the Habsburg state made its peace with that state, in whose existence it had a vested interest both as the entrepreneurial and as the bureaucratic class.*

It was guaranteed through the status quo, and even without any legal advantages, enough social advantages to enable it to renounce part of the democratic demands made in 1848. On the whole it was satisfied with the confirmation of fundamental rights for the individual (1867), and an additional sweetener was provided by the favourable electoral law arising out of the part-constitutionalization of the imperial state.[33]

3 Precisely on these grounds the German bourgeoisie was obliged to reject the struggles for emancipation of the non-German nations: the demands of the Czechs, Slovenes, Croats and Italians for greater autonomy, and greater recognition in terms of suffrage, was perceived as a threat to property and privilege (*Besitzstand*) – a key expression in the confrontation of the late nineteenth century. *Both* sets of motives contributed to the fact that German national consciousness in Austria was early on allowed to become defensive, authoritarian and rigid.[34]

4 Regarding the type of state appropriate to German national consciousness, it is clear that the overwhelming majority of the nationally conscious German Austrians wished to preserve the Habsburg Monarchy, together with their relatively privileged position within it. However, from the 1880s on, destructive radical forces associated with the name of Georg von Schönerer began to threaten it, forces which found favour particularly amongst students and academics. In these circles could be heard with increasing stridency the demand only sporadically raised in 1848: namely, that the Monarchy should be broken up and its German-speaking parts (which naturally included the whole of Bohemia!) should be incorporated into Bismarck's German Empire.[35]

5 The relationship of German national consciousness in Germany to that in Austria is interesting. That the traditional dislike of Protestant Germany (especially Prussia) for Catholic Austria continued as before could be seen from the hardly deniable fact that German national consciousness, before and after 1848, paid ever-decreasing attention to Austria; from 1870 it was concentrated wholly on the new German Empire. Needless to say, this did not go down well with the radical

German nationalists of Austria! The German attitude to the Austrians was memorably summed up by the famous historian Theodor Mommsen, when he remarked that the Bavarians were a half-way stage (*Übergang*) between Austrians and human beings.[36]

6 The progress of national consolidation seems to have satisfied, until 1900, also those German Austrians who shared a German national consciousness, and who hitherto had managed to achieve very little in developing it. Now, traditional identification with one's own country (*Landesbewusstsein*) grew ever stronger when it was provided with a 'German' dimension.[37]

THE AMBIVALENCE OF GERMAN AUSTRIAN NATIONAL CONSCIOUSNESS

Without doubt the accelerating process of national identification through language meant that those who, like the historian Anton Gindely, wanted to be neither Czech nor German, but Bohemian (*böhmisch*) and loyal to the Emperor, became an increasingly rare species. None the less we may assume that an old-fashioned patriotism, centred on the person and institution of the Emperor, especially amongst the peasant masses of the Monarchy, was still a factor to be reckoned with even until the First World War. This patriotism fell away amongst all language groupings of the better educated classes. Whether we can describe such loyalty as 'Austrian' must remain an open question. What is true is that those strata of society that had most strongly identified themselves with the Emperor and the Monarchy remained, even under the Republic after 1918, relatively the least receptive to a German orientation. The prominent Austrian Social Democrat Otto Bauer may be regarded as a reliable witness when he speaks of 'the opposition on economic grounds of the capitalist class, and on political grounds of the monarchists' towards the *Anschluss* with Germany, and also of the 'traditionally' Austrian tendency (*Österreichertum*) of the 'old Viennese patriciate and the old Viennese petty bourgeoisie'. These, together with the separatist tendencies of the *Länder*, and together with capitalists, monarchist officers, nobility and clergy, would have rejected the *Anschluss*.[38]

One can, perhaps, hazard the generalization that the German Austrians clung to the Habsburg Monarchy in proportion as they were economically dependent upon its continued existence. This would apply to businessmen whose entire market was the huge closed customs area of the Monarchy, civil servants, officers, and the

Viennese bourgeoisie who profited from the central role of Vienna within the Empire. Over and above these, those sections of society should be taken into account who were (still) unaffected by the new nationalistic mentality, such as the aristocracy and, above all, the Catholic peasantry. To the extent that the new nationalisms assumed a racist complexion (as was always the case with German national-ists), also especially in the eyes of the Jews the Monarchy must have gained in value. The identification of many Jews with the Habsburg Monarchy is evidenced by numerous literary works (and was, on this account, an important factor in intensifying the hostility of anti-Semitic nationalisms towards both the Habsburg Monarchy *and* the Jews).[39]

There is, of course, another side to the coin: namely, that the most intense 'German' consciousness of all may be ascribed to those groups who were able to formulate 'national' demands and Utopias from a basis of youthful radicalism unconstrained by any economic depen-dence – typically students, and a number of radical demagogues (Schönerer) and writers. Equally, Germans in marginal situations in relation to other nationalities were haunted by anxieties about the continuation of their national existence. So also, the political con-sciousness amongst the petty bourgeoisie of towns in 'the provinces' assumed more pronounced German national characteristics. Here one failed to profit from the existence of the great Monarchy; on the contrary, one had long experience of the cumulative vacuuming effect, whereby economic and cultural values were sucked back into the great maw of over-mighty Vienna. The 'provincialization of the provinces' led, therefore, not to increasing identification, but to a critical distancing from the centre. This was especially the case in the areas that lay closest to the new German Empire, and where one could easily compare the dynamism of the economy over the border with stagnation at home. It was therefore in just such sleepy and pictur-esque small and middle-sized towns as Krems or Salzburg that all sections of the bourgeoisie (middle and petty bourgeoisie) became German national.[40]

In theory the same should have held true for the working class, who were indoctrinated not only with internationalism by their leaders, but also with a belief in the superiority of 'German' culture. But at any rate the Czech workers around 1900 saw themselves unambigu-ously as part of the Czech nation, and by the same token led the emancipation from the German Austrian labour movement. It could also have been the case that the large Viennese working class itself was influenced by the Viennese identification with Austria (after all, the highest wages were paid in Vienna). This would explain the distinctly cool reception given to Otto Bauer and other Social Democrat leaders by the Viennese workers in 1918–19, who were seemingly unimpressed by the politicians' enthusiastic advocacy of *Anschluss* with Germany.[41]

Our thesis is therefore this: that the German-speaking Austrians in the nineteenth century developed an ambiguous collective consciousness. On the one hand, it was 'Austrian' in the sense of being orientated towards the existing framework of the Habsburg Monarchy. Probably the best description of this situation was written by the economist Friedrich von Wieser in 1905: 'The German Austrian in the time of our grandfathers and fathers was German, because he was an Austrian, and because for him it was impossible to separate the concept 'German' from the concept 'Austria' . . .'[42]

In the identification with the Monarchy was included as a rule a quite unconscious assumption of the 'German' predominance in the state structure: in other words, a basic identification also of the German Austrians with the bureaucratic and military apparatus, with the authority of government and civil servants.

These possible areas of identification collapsed in 1918. All that remained of the old way of thinking was identification with 'Germanism'. And this, naturally, became all the more intense, as the search for intellectual and morale-boosting compensation for the defeat of 1918 gathered momentum. Otto Bauer once said, with some justification, that it was the Viennese bourgeoisie who lost the war and it was their empire which was smashed to pieces. At last, therefore, the *Anschluss* idea could take root even in the bourgeois circles of Vienna. And, indeed, the desperation of impoverished (petty) bourgeois houseowners and clerks was to work to the advantage of National Socialism from 1932 onwards (for example, in the Viennese local elections of that year). In contrast with the magnetic pull of Germany, the small new Republic of Austria (so called since the Treaty of St-Germain in 1919) could in no way be seen as a meaningful focus of national identification.

Even the smaller groups of those who consciously regarded themselves as Austrian, and whose voices were scarcely audible above the din of *Anschluss* propaganda, were forced to consider how a greater national unity could be achieved, and how the small republic could be formed in such a way as to carry conviction.[43]

The scenario first changed in 1933: with the seizure of power by the Nazis in Germany, not only the automatic identification of the Left with the German Reich was thrown into question. Engelbert Dollfuss's

Christian Social ruling faction also had to come to terms with the new situation. Both groupings, naturally from completely different standpoints, sought to tailor Austria to the 'better' Germany, as opposed to the Hitler-Germany: Austria as the refuge of German democracy, and Austria as preserver of the (Catholic) German imperial idea, a concept which had no home in neo-pagan National Socialism any more. After the rising of 12 February of the *Schutzbund* (Social Democratic semi-military organization) against the dictatorship, the gap between the Left and the government became unbridgeable, and all efforts on the part of the former to effect a reconciliation were discontinued. The Social Democrats remained fixated on an imaginary German unity, and in the end approved the successful *Anschluss* with the German Reich in March 1938, seeing it as the foundation for the long-awaited pan-German revolution. Only in the small Communist Party (and closely following Stalin's writings on the national question) was an attempt made to enshrine the notion of Austrian individuality within the concept of the Austrian nation.[44]

For the government camp the establishment of an ideological basis for the corporatist *Ständestaat* was even more urgent. A theoretical construct of the 'Austrian' was cobbled together. Of course, he was perceived as 'German', or rather as 'better German', by the overwhelming majority of its begetters. Only a few, like Ernst Karl Winter, Hans Karl Zessner-Spitzenberg or Dietrich Hildebrand (himself a refugee from the Nazis), took the idea to its logical conclusion, and projected the Austrians as a completely individual nation. This viewpoint remained permanently a minority one. In particular, Federal Chancellor Kurt Schuschnigg thought of himself so strongly, and with such emotional allegiance, as 'a German', that for him resistance to Hitler's blackmail was enormously difficult (not only because of Austria's weakness). It was not by chance that Schuschnigg's famous valedictory speech on the evening of 11 March contained a refusal to 'shed German blood', nor that it ended 'with a German word and a German salute'.[45]

If the 'German' element in the Austrian's self-definition appeared finally to have got the upper hand as a result of the mass hypnosis of 1938, the actual experience of 'German unity' had a devastatingly sobering effect. True, many Austrians profited from the plundering, expulsion and extermination of the Viennese Jews, in which the natives enthusiastically took part. True, also, the stimulus to the armaments industry created jobs. But the experience of the war, the German defeat, the oppression, the poverty (and not least the quartering of German refugees from the bombing on Austrian territory,

which was considered to be less vulnerable) – all this resulted in the
'Austrian' components of the collective consciousness coming strongly
to the fore again. Even before 1945 the evil 'Piefke' (a traditional
pejorative term for Germans) had become a hostile stereotype. Clearly
such feelings came more easily to those strata of the population whose
'German' consciousness was never more than skin-deep: the Viennese,
the Communists and the Catholic peasantry. By 1943 Adolf Schärf for
the Social Democrats and Lois Weinberger for the Christian Socials,
in talks held independently of each other with the German resistance,
had both established the claim to Austrian independence in the event
of a successful revolt against Hitler. 'The *Anschluss* is dead', Adolf
Schärf is supposed to have said – and this from a man who, in
common with many other Social Democratic intellectuals, had felt
himself far more spiritually at home in 'Weimar' than in *k.u.k.*
(imperial and royal) Vienna.[46]

National Socialism thus permanently weakened the German orientation of the Austrians. To be 'German' was clearly not a very
desirable objective after the experiences of 1938 and 1945. This
challenge should not simply be viewed as collective opportunism: not
a few Austrians also experienced the resurrection of Austria in 1945
emotionally, as the resurrection of a homeland whose value had only
been truly appreciated when it no longer existed.

The already relatively long experience of a secure existence, allied
to a degree of material prosperity, should therefore ensure that the
Austrian sense of national identity enjoys a further untroubled development. On the other hand, the 'German' elements in the Austrian
consciousness are of course still discernible, albeit diminishing: the
controversy surrounding the presidential elections in 1986 has possibly
reawakened memories of old conflicts. But there is little real evidence
that it has led a large part of the Austrian population to seek a way
out of these difficulties by again retreating into a 'German' identity.
Although small groups have indeed reacted in this way, on the whole,
the mental dissociation from Germany, but also from National Socialism, is today significantly more pronounced than in 1980.[47]

In the context of the 'successful' history of the Second Republic it
has become easier for modern Austria to come to terms with a rich,
albeit contradictory, history with extremely diverse identification
figures ranging from Maria Theresa to Bruno Kreisky, from Karl
Renner to Francis Joseph. At the same time the Austrians have come
to accept a sense of their identity which is no longer dependent upon
the greater geopolitical context within which their history unfolded.

NOTES

1 W. Bauer, 'Österreich', *Österreich, Zeitschrift für Geschichte*, 1 (1918–19), 6.

2 E. Renan, *Qu'est-ce qu'une nation?* (Paris, 1882).

3 H. von Hofmannsthal, 'Österreich im Spiegel seiner Dichtung' (1916), in Hofmannsthal, *Ausgewählte Werke. Erzählungen und Aufsätze* (Frankfurt on Main, 1957), 593–604, p. 598.

4 For example, this was the attitude of the British Ambassador in Berlin, Sir Neville Henderson, or of Milan Stojadinović, the Yugoslavian Prime Minister. See H. Haas, 'Die Okkupation Österreichs in den internationalen Beziehungen' and A. Suppan, 'Anschluss und Anschlussfragen in Politik und öffentlicher Meinung Jugoslawiens', both in R. Neck and A. Wandruszka (eds.), *Anschluss 1938 (Wissenschaftl. Kommission zur Erforschung der österreichischen Geschichte der Jahre 1918 bis 1938, Veröffentlichungen Bd. 7)* (Vienna, 1981), pp. 41ff and 69ff.

5 F. Kreissler, *Der Österreicher und seine Nation. Ein Lernprozess mit Hindernissen* (Vienna, 1984); G. Wagner, 'Österreich. Von der Staatsidee zum Nationalbewusstsein (I) – Die Meinungsumfragen über die österreichische Nation 1956–1980 (II)', in Wagner (ed.), *Österreich. Von der Staatsidee zum Nationalbewusstsein* (Vienna, 1982), pp. 109ff; P. A. Ulram, *Österreichbewusstsein 1987* (Vienna, 1988) (Chronology of a project of the Jubilee Fund of the Austrian National Bank carried out by Gerald Stourzh and Peter A. Ulram. See also G. Stourzh, *Vom Reich zur Republik. Studien zum Österreichbewusstsein im 20. Jahrhundert* (Vienna, 1990), especially pp. 102–4.

6 Regarding anthems see E. Früh, 'Gott erhalte? Gott bewahre! Zur Geschichte der österreichischen Hymnen und des Nationalbewusstseins zwischen 1918 und 1938', *Österreich in Geschichte und Literatur*, 32 (1988), 280–315; the texts of the Austrian anthems may be found in F. Grasberger, *Die Hymnen Österreichs* (Tutzing, 1968).

7 On state symbolism see Wagner, *Österreich*, pp. 257–66. On the high value placed on the Double Eagle see the results of opinion polls in 1980 in: *Das österreichische Nationalbewusstsein in der öffentlichen Meinung und im Urteil der Experten* (a study made by the Paul Lazarsfeld Society) (Vienna, 1980), p. 45: 45 per cent of those asked believed that the Double Eagle was a good coat of arms for Austria (in competition, however, with half-baked suggestions such as skiers, ski-jumpers, mountain and forest, a waltzing couple, and so forth).

8 G. Stourzh, *Geschichte des Staatsvertrages 1945–1955. Österreichs Weg zur Neutralität*, 3rd edn (Graz, Vienna and Cologne, 1985).

9 *Das österreichische Nationalbewusstsein*, p. 32.

10 Both the polls of 1980 and 1987 show that the Viennese exhibit less regional patriotism than the inhabitants of other Federal *Länder* (with the exception of Lower Austria). On the other hand, the Viennese see themselves strongly as 'Austrians', in this respect only outdone by the Lower Austrians; also, of course, above averagely 'European' or 'citizens of the world', cf. Ulram, *Österreichbewusstsein 1987*, p. 23; the tables supplied here constitute the first empirical evidence of the interrelation of *Land* and national consciousness.

11 I have explored these relationships further in an essay which appeared under

the title 'Wien und die österreichische Identität', in E. Busek (ed.), *Von den Hauptstädtern und Hintersassen* (Vienna, 1987), pp. 19–36; in this also the further references.

12 *Das österreichische Nationalbewusstsein*, pp. 39 and 40.

13 A. F. Reiterer, *Die unvermeidbare Nation. Ethnizität, Nation und nachnationale Gesellschaft* (Frankfurt on Main and New York, 1988), p. 262. I myself have observed in my book *Nation Österreich. Sozialhistorische Aspekte ihrer Entwicklung* (Vienna, 1984), p. 221: 'In the case of Austria, her history since 1945 – her *national reconstruction*, the achievement of the *State Treaty*, a certain reputation in the world at large of a few *leading politicians* (Kurt *Waldheim*, Bruno *Kreisky*) obviously contributed to this consciousness-raising phase of the joint national effort.' In fact, the presidential election of 1986, which revealed an astonishingly defiant attitude on the part of Waldheim to his service in the German army, radically altered the international perception of Austria. Within the country, Waldheim's stance undoubtedly reflects the feelings of some Austrians, as an expression of the *German* dimension of the Austrian national consciousness. The reactions to Waldheim's statement (and lapses of memory) demonstrate, however, that no comprehensive national solidarity could be built around his attitudes and personality. Whether the whole controversy has had a destructive effect on the Austrian national consensus, it is too early to say. Whatever the truth of that will turn out to be, it need hardly be said that my analysis of 1984 has been refuted by subsequent events.

14 It was no accident that Hugo von Hofmannsthal concerned himself with Prince Eugene and suchlike during the First World War. On the relationship between the evocation of the age of the Turkish wars and the ideological foundations of the so-called *Ständestaat* (the corporatist form of the dictatorship of the Right in Austria between 1934 and 1938), see M. Mitterauer, 'Politischer Katholizismus. Österreichbewusstsein und Türkenfeindbild', *Beiträge zur historischen Sozialkunde*, 12 (Vienna, 1982), 111ff.

15 Ulram, *Österreichbewusstsein 1987*, compares with the results of 1980 and comes to the conclusion that since then pride in sporting and political achievements has largely given way to the exaltation of cultural values (pp. 26ff). What is important is that over twenty years the opinion that Austrian national consciousness only dates from 1945 has not only continued to be held, but has increasingly gained adherents (Ulram, pp. 11–14).

16 *Das österreichische Nationalbewusstsein*, pp. 29ff.

17 Ulram, *Österreichbewusstsein 1987*, pp. 30–3.

18 The following exposition is based on material in E. Zöllner's *Geschichte Österreichs*, 7th edn (Vienna, 1984). The interpretation suggested is also to be found, minus certain modifications which will be indicated here in the text, in Bruckmüller, *Nation Österreich*.

19 The plans for a kingdom are now concisely summarized (with literature) in E. Zöllner, *Der Österreichbegriff. Formen und Wandlungen in der Geschichte* (Vienna, 1988), pp. 31ff.

20 There is a massive literature on Czech and Hungarian national 'reawakening'. An exceptionally good introduction is provided by H. Raupach, *Der tschechische Frühnationalismus* (Darmstadt, 1969, unrevised reprint of 1st edn, 1939).

Comparable is M. Hroch, 'Das Erwachen kleiner Nationen als Problem der komparativen sozialgeschichtlichen Forschung', in T. Schieder and P. Burian (eds.), *Sozialstruktur und Organisation europäischer Nationalbewegungen* (Munich and Vienna, 1971), pp. 121ff; see also M. Hroch, *Die Vorkämpfer der nationalen Bewegungen bei den kleinen Völkern Europas* (Prague, 1968).

21 B. Holl, *Hofkammerpräsident Gundaker Thomas Graf Starhemberg und die österreichische Finanzpolitik der Barockzeit (1703–1715)* (Vienna, 1976), pp. 64 and 215.

22 R. Meister, 'Die Idee einer österreichischen Nationalerziehung unter Maria Theresia', *Anzeiger der philologisch-historischen Klasse der Österreichischen Akademie der Wissenschaften*, 1946, p. 16; E. Wangermann, *Aufklärung und staatsbürgerliche Erziehung. Gottfried van Swieten als Reformator des österreichischen Unterrichtswesens 1781–1791* (Vienna, 1978).

23 An example of an earlier use of the concept of 'citizen' may be found in L. Bodie, *Tauwetter in Wien. Zur Prosa der österreichischen Aufklärung 1781–1795* (Franfurt on Main, 1977), p. 260: the writer Rautenstrauch insults the publisher Wucherer, who comes from the imperial town (*Reichsstadt*) of Reutlingen, by telling him that he does not deserve 'the honourable name of an Austrian citizen'. For 'citizen of the state' as a legal definition in the book of Civil Law for West Galicia (1797) see W. Ogris, 'Zwischen Absolutismus und Rechtsstaat', in R. G. Plaschka and G. Klingenstein (eds.), *Österreich im Europa der Aufklärung* (Vienna, 1985), vol. I, p. 374; also important is H. Strakosch, *Privatrechtskodifikation und Staatsbildung in Österreich* (Vienna, 1976), first published in English as *State Absolutism and the Rule of Law. The Struggle for the Codification of Civil Law in Austria 1753–1811* (Sidney, 1967).

24 In so far as I have revised my view (1984) that in practice no bourgeois nation can be observed in the context of the 'Hofrats'-nation of the Habsburg aristocracy and civil servants, see Bruckmüller, *Nation Österreich*, particularly p. 91. On the rise of middle-class society at this time see Bodie, *Tauwetter*, pp. 72ff; also important is E. Wangermann, *Von Joseph II zu den Jakobinerprozessen* (Vienna, 1966); the English edition: *From Joseph II to the Jacobin Trials*, 2nd edn (London, 1969) (1st edn 1959).

25 E. Rosenstrauch-Königsberg, 'Erste Schritte auf dem Weg zum österreichischen Nationalbewusstsein', in R. G. Plaschka and G. Klingenstein (eds.), *Österreich im Europa der Aufklärung* (Vienna, 1985), vol. II, pp. 895–918. The reference to the contemporary differentiation between 'Austria' and 'non-Austrian Germany' (which corresponds fairly exactly to the fact of a largely achieved statehood on the one hand, and an as yet unshaped version of it, except in the large territories of Prussia, Bavaria, Saxony or Hanover) may be found in Bodie, *Tauwetter*, p. 64. On p. 66 Bodie sums up: 'However that may be, in the Austrian literature of the Enlightenment there is already a national problem, which the identification of Austrian writers with the "German" national feeling of "non-Austrian Germany" (which came to the fore in just this period), very considerably aggravated . . .'

26 This is dealt with in the contributions to this volume which discuss the development of national consciousness amongst the Czechs, Magyars, and Croats.

27 Bodie, *Tauwetter*, p. 427.

28 The events of this period have already attracted considerable attention among scholars as potentially expressive of national solidarity, although not in revolutionary (no more than in bourgeois) terms. See especially the voluminous work of A. Robert, *L'Idée nationale autrichienne et les guerres de Napoléon: l'apostolat du Baron Hormayr et le salon de Caroline Pichler* (Paris, 1933); further, A. K. Mally, 'Der Begriff "Österreichische Nation" seit dem Ende des 18. Jahrhunderts', *Der Donauraum*, 17 (Vienna, 1972), 48ff; P. Berger, 'Graf Stadion über die "österreichische Nation"', *Der Donauraum*, 20 (Vienna, 1975), 193ff; Bruckmüller, *Nation Österreich*, pp. 92ff.

29 F. Heer, *Der Kampf um die österreichische Identität* (Vienna, 1981), pp. 204ff; H. Lengauer, 'Kulturelle und nationale Identität. Die deutsch-österreichische Problematik im Spiegel von Literatur und Publizistik der liberalen Ära (1848–1873)', in H. Lutz and H. Rumpler (eds.), *Österreich und die deutsche Frage im 19. und 20. Jahrhundert* (Vienna, 1982), pp. 189–211.

30 See, for example, C. Stölzl, *Die Ära Bach in Böhmen. Sozialgeschichtliche Studien zum Neoabsolutismus 1849–1859* (Munich and Vienna, 1971). On the conception of Andrian-Werburg and others see R. A. Kann, *Das Nationalitätenproblem der Habsburgermonarchie*, 2nd edn (Graz and Cologne, 1964), vol. I, pp. 8off; vol. II, pp. 29, 97ff (the – first – English edition of Kann's voluminous opus is titled *The multinational Empire*, New York, 1950). Further, F. Fellner, 'Die Tagebücher des Viktor Franz von Andrian-Werburg', *Mitteilungen des österreichischen Staatsarchivs*, 26 (1973), 328ff.

31 For example, the autobiography of the Slovene politician, J. Vosnjak, *Spomini* (Ljubljana, 1982) ('spomini' = reminiscences, memoirs).

32 P. Molisch, *Geschichte der deutschnationalen Bewegung in Österreich von ihren Anfängen bis zum Zerfall der Monarchie* (Jena, 1926).

33 J. Redlich, *Das Österreichische Staats- und Reichsproblem. Geschichtliche Darstellung der inneren Politik der Habsburgischen Monarchie von 1848 bis zum Untergang der Monarchie* (Leipzig, 1920, 1926), vols. I–II. Here in particular vol. I/2, p. 71.

34 *Ibid.*, p. 27.

35 Kann, *Nationalitätenproblem*, vol. I, pp. 99ff; B. Sutter, 'Die politische und rechtliche Stellung der Deutschen in Österreich 1848–1918', in A. Wandruszka and P. Urbanitsch (eds.), *Die Habsburgermonarchie 1848–1918*, vol. III/1 (Vienna, 1980), pp. 154–339, particularly pp. 215ff.

36 Sutter, 'Die Deutschen', p. 205.

37 Bruckmüller, *Nation Österreich*, p. 147; for the 'German' interpretation of traditional *Landesbewusstsein* see many passages in Sutter, 'Die Deutschen', *passim*.

38 O. Bauer, *Die österreichische Revolution* (Vienna, 1923). Reprinted in Bauer, *Werkausgabe*, vol. I (Vienna, 1975), here pp. 682ff. On the general, anonymous patriotism for the Emperor still existing in 1914–18 see Heer, *Kampf*, pp. 321ff.

39 That did not prevent very many highly cultivated and well-to-do Jews from identifying themselves with a *Deutschtum* (Germanness) which went well beyond culture alone. Perhaps the most influential exponent of this type was the editor of *Neue Freie Presse*, Moritz Benedikt. A more gentlemanly, but

perhaps more significant, representative of the same line was the distinguished scholar Theodor Gomperz. See R. A. Kann, *Theodor Gomperz. Ein Gelehrtenleben im Bürgertum der Franz-Josef-Zeit* (Vienna, 1974).

40 The essential youthfulness of the 'pure' nationalist factions, and the various backgrounds to their struggles, which were often only explicable in psychoanalytic terms, are all frequently referred to by Friedrich Heer in his great work *Der Kampf um die österreichische Identität.* For the development of German nationalist attitudes in the Austrian *Länder* see H. Haas, 'Von liberal zu national. Salzburgs Bürgertum im ausgehenden 19. Jahrhundert', in I. Ackerl, W. Hummelberger and H. Mommsen (eds.), *Politik und Gesellschaft (Festschrift Neck)* (Vienna, 1981), pp. 109–132.

41 Bauer, *Revolution*, p. 623.

42 Kann, *Nationalitätenproblem*, vol. I, p. 57.

43 For instance, the group centred on the journal *Vaterland*. On this see J. Papiór, 'Vaterland' (1927–1938). Eine (gross) österreichische Zeitschrift', *Österreich in Geschichte und Literatur*, 32 (Vienna, 1988), 20–30.

44 Cf. *Arbeiterzeitung*, 15 October 1933 (Discussion paper, contributed by Gerald Stourzh, in E. Rauter, ed., *Schriftenreihe des Arbeitskreises 'Dr. Karl Renner'*, vols. III and IV, *Dr. Karl Renner Symposium 1983 and 1984*, p. 82. On the Communist line on the nationality question see Rudolf (pseudonym of Alfred Klahr), 'Zur nationalen Frage in Österreich', *Weg und Ziel*, 1937 vol., March and April, reprint special issue of *Weg und Ziel*, 1979. On the Social Democrats, particularly Otto Bauer, and their line in 1938, see Kreissler, *Der Österreicher*, pp. 112ff, 175ff, 253ff.

45 Heer, *Kampf*, pp. 425ff. See also A. F. Reiterer, 'Vom Scheitern eines politischen Entwurfes. "Der österreichische Mensch" – ein konservatives Nationalprojekt der Zwischenkriegszeit', *Österreich in Geschichte und Literatur*, 30 (Vienna, 1986), 19–36.

46 R. Luža, *Österreich und die grossdeutsche Idee in der NS-Zeit* (Vienna, Cologne and Graz, 1977); L. Weinberger, *Tatsachen, Begegnungen und Gespräche* (Vienna, 1948), p. 135; A. Schärf, *Österreichs Erneuerung 1945–1955* (Vienna, 1956). From such sources it can be confirmed that resistance to National Socialism was disproportionately strong in those that were more markedly 'Austrian' oriented: that is, the Communists and the Catholic Conservatives; see E. Hanisch, 'Widerstand in Österreich 1934–1945', *Aus Politik und Zeitgeschichte, Beilage zur Wochenzeitung Das Parlament*, B 28/88, 8 July 1988.

47 Interestingly the results of opinion polls contradict the subjective impression of the author. Certain reinflamed 'German' emotions which I was bound to notice, for instance, on the occasion of a lecture by the noted German historian Michael Stürmer in Vienna (17 March 1987), or in connection with the rather feeble contribution by K. D. Erdmann, 'Drei Staaten – zwei Nationen – ein Volk?', *Geschichte in Wissenschaft und Unterricht*, 35 (1985), 671–83, still seem to be the preserve of minorities, albeit of minorities not without influence. *These* emotions are again being displayed more openly. On the other hand, a parting from the 'German' past is now (not before time!) more clearly articulated by the majority; while in 1980, 34 per cent of those asked said that the *Anschluss*

of 1938 had 'finally brought about the natural union [of Austria] with the German people', in 1987 the figure had sunk to 20 per cent (which is none the less still a remarkably high figure). See also A. Pelinka, *Zur österreichischen Identität. Zwischen deutscher Vereinigung und Mitteleuropa* (Vienna, 1990); E. Bruckmüller, 'Das Österreichbewusstsein', in W. Mantl (ed.), *Politik in Österreich. Die zweite Republik: Bestand und Wandel* (Vienna, 1992), pp. 261–78.

NINE

THE CZECHS

ARNOŠT KLÍMA

THE national question belongs undoubtedly among the most complicated historical problems. In this respect each individual nation has
had a different experience. Manifold historical conditions which varied
in each individual case have played a decisive role. While studying
the national question one has to bear in mind the many changes since
the Middle Ages which were connected with economic and political
conditions. Whereas modern nationalism and the process of solving
the national question was very closely linked with the beginnings of
capitalism one should be aware of the fact that the foundations of the
development of nations had already been laid during the Middle Ages.
Therefore it will be necessary, at least in the case of the Czech nation,
to devote our attention to this problem.

THE MEDIEVAL NATION

Regarding the Czech Lands it was significant that medieval Bohemia,
as well as Moravia, was inhabited not only by Czechs but also by
Germans who lived in compact entities, especially in towns where
they soon formed a German-speaking patriciate exercising decisive
influence on the towns' administration. Already very early we can
observe that the clergy, such as the chronicler Cosmas (1045–1125),
were consciously expressing a common Czech national feeling. The
explanation for this can be found in the immigration of the German
clergy that filled the native Czech clergy with fear of competition for
senior posts. This was why the first recorded evidence of a growing
national consciousness came precisely from the Czech clergy. Cosmas,
for instance, agreed with the magnate Kojata's opposition to the
election of the German Lanz to the office of Bishop of Prague.[1] In his
chronicle he also recorded that Prince Spytihněv 'earned everyone's

admiration because he ordered the expulsion within three days of all Germans from Bohemia wherever they are found, whether rich or poor or pilgrim . . .'[2] It is important to realize that Cosmas and his contemporaries saw the Germans primarily as foreigners.[3] Above all, the policy of inviting foreigners to Bohemia was resented, especially their presence on the Royal Council, which some Czechs regarded as the greatest of misfortunes, particularly when German 'guests' were appointed.[4]

The influx of German colonists to Bohemia in the twelfth century created a rosary of town settlements which became the centres of handicraft and mining. Without this inflow of skilled labourers, without their experience and wealth, the rapid growth of mining towns, which meant so much for the expansion of political power of the Czech kings, could not have taken place. This happened especially under Václav (Wenceslas) II (1287–1305) who was offered the Polish and the Hungarian crowns. Under such circumstances, when immigrants occupied such influential positions in towns, it was the *language* which became the most important mark of distinction between the two ethnic groups in the country. Indeed, the Czechs associated their language with defending their nationality and demanded that all dignitaries should know Czech.[5]

At the beginning of the fourteenth century the German patriciate in Prague and Kutná Hora even mounted a conspiracy. On 15 February 1309 the German burghers arrested the two leading Czech noblemen, Jindřich (Henry) of Lipé and Jan (John) of Vartemberk, the former being the most powerful feudal lord and the High Marshal of King Jindřich (Henry) of Carinthia. Jindřich of Lipé had under his command a considerable armed force of mercenaries which he put at the king's service, and under contemporary conditions he could be considered as a minor condottiere, a precursor of Wallenstein.[6]

It would of course be a mistake to regard this conspiracy as a kind of class struggle between the burghers and the feudal lords. The German patriciate of Prague and Kutná Hora simply wanted to share power with the nobility. For this reason they demanded the right to marry their children with those of the nobility. According to the chronicler Otokar of Styria the patricians tried twice to convince the king that they acted in his interest. If the king joined them and rejected the feudal parasites, so they argued, he would become a genuine sovereign for the benefit of the kingdom. The chronicler recorded that the king had declined to accept this offer and remained a 'mere spectator' during the struggle between the patriciate and the nobility.[7] Eventually, the conspiring German patricians had to flee from Prague and Kutná Hora when Jindřich of Lipé captured the capital.

The uprising of the German patriciate against the Czech nobles left a strong echo in the versified chronicle attributed to Dalimil. The chronicle reads: 'if the lords had remained in their right senses the foreigners would not have sprawled all over Bohemia . . . O lords, you now can see for yourselves whether you follow wise counsel when you give castles to foreigners. Had they not had somewhere to imprison you they would not have dared to rise against you . . .'[8] This sentiment then led the author of the Dalimil chronicle to oppose all foreigners, especially Germans, and inspired him to recommend his king 'to have in his Council Czech nobles only, to prevent foreign guests from settling, to use one's own language and to abandon the alien tongue'.[9] Dalimil also referred to the episode, taken over from Cosmas' chronicle, that Prince Spytihněv 'drove out of the country all Germans within three days . . . and all other foreigners as well'.[10]

With regard to the situation in the fourteenth century one must agree with František Graus 'that already during the Middle Ages one discerns a shaping of a kind of national consciousness' mainly because Bohemia had for centuries been a classical country of national tension. It was this phenomenon which contributed to the emergence of national consciousness.[11] Another Czech medievalist, František Šmahel, convincingly points out the highly significant fact that the Czechs had a relatively strong state in which their unifying bond was, above all, their language.[12] He argues that for more than a century Czech public opinion was influenced by everyday contact with indigenous Germans as well as with other aliens and that, therefore, Czechs readily accepted patriotic and national challenges. During the Hussite period, however, especially at the time of the crusades against the Czechs, 'Czech nationalism was . . . predominantly defensive'.[13] Šmahel quotes in this context Jan (John) Hus's words after the invasion of Bohemia by the Meissener and Bavarian armies in 1401: 'When the Bavarians and Meisseners invaded Bohemia and burned down villages, tortured and murdered poor souls, I grieved about these atrocities and said that in this respect the Czechs are more miserable than dogs and snakes because they do not defend their kingdom, although they have just reason for doing so.'[14]

During the Hussite era the main features of the Czech nation, according to Šmahel, were language (*lingua*), origin (*sanguis*) and faith (*fides*). It was no accident that the Czech followers of Hus's teaching built the Bethlehem Chapel in which preaching was to be done only in the Czech language. During the same period grants and gifts for the *Natio Bohemorum* increased to such an extent that within twenty years the University of Prague had three colleges for poor students. It was in this context that in October 1419 representatives of the Hussite nobility presented Emperor Sigismund the following demands:

1 Foreigners should not be entrusted with office.
2 Germans should not be appointed town councillors, especially not in those towns where Czechs could and should rule.
3 Legal disputes in Bohemia should be conducted in the Czech language.
4 Czechs should have the 'first voice' in the kingdom, and also in the towns.
5 Bible reading and singing in Czech in the churches should not be hindered.[15]

This Hussite patriotism or national consciousness emanated from priests, noblemen and burghers. Josef Macek believes that 'the defence of one's native country against international reaction . . . helped to mobilize the feeling of national unity and to overcome divisions in the Hussite camp'.[16] Because not only Hussites belonged to the Czech language community but also their Catholic adversaries, Šmahel is convinced that during Hussitism the principle of faith was more important than that of native country and nation.[17]

Long before the Hussite movement the Czech-versus-German relationship had begun to shape conditions in Bohemia and it continued to do so during and after the Hussite period. Thus also during the reign of Jiří (George) of Poděbrady in the Message to the inhabitants of Hradec, Orel and Pardubice in 1469 the Germans are again labelled as enemies of God and the call was: 'Out of Bohemia, evil German soul.'

Šmahel is asking whether Hussite nationalism 'was anomalous because of its early maturity and its almost total social impact' and to what extent it anticipated the Czech nationalism of the nineteenth century. František Graus also points out that during the fourteenth century the Czechs created a very vivid national consciousness but he refuses to consider Czech nationalism of the Middle Ages as a precursor of modern nationalism of the nineteenth century. He maintains, however, that in the Middle Ages the Czechs were fast developing into a unified society capable of forming a modern nation.[18]

It is obvious from what has been said so far about the medieval Czech nation, about its language, about its relations with foreigners, especially Germans, about the defence of the Czech nobility's interests against alien newcomers, be it in the Royal Council or in the towns' administration, about the attitude of the clergy to aliens, that the relationship to foreigners, specifically to Germans, played a crucial role in the rise of Czech national consciousness. We encounter this national consciousness within the Czech medieval nation in the clergy as well as in the nobility. In the urban population it appears only during the Hussite era and it is surely this connection with the Hussite movement which created the anomaly referred to by Šmahel. The medieval nation differs substantially from the modern nation in that it does not include the non-privileged groups in towns and in the countryside. To all intents and purposes the Czechs qualify as a medieval nation of the feudal era.

The frequent encounters of clergy and nobility with foreigners, especially with Germans, and during the crusades as well with the Papal Curia in Rome, led the noted nineteenth-century Czech historian František Palacký to conclude that 'the main content and principal feature of the entire Czechomoravian history is . . . the perennial intercourse and strife of the Slavonic world with Romanism and Germanism'.[19]

NATIONAL REVIVAL – BIRTH OF THE MODERN NATION

The modern nation is inseparably connected with the rise of capitalism and differs substantially from the medieval nation which consisted of privileged strata of society. In the Czech Lands this process followed a specific path. In contrast to the Middle Ages the Czechs did not have their own state in the eighteenth and nineteenth centuries. Their country became part of the Habsburg Monarchy with German as the administrative language and the Czechs as a subjugated nation. The uprising of the Czech Estates in 1618 which led to the formation of a government of thirty directors ended in defeat at the battle of the White Mountain on 8 November 1620. Henceforth the nobility spoke German, Spanish or French, the patricians in the towns German. Thus the significant mark of the medieval Czech nation, the Czech language, was confined to the peasantry and the urban poor. Under these unfavourable circumstances deep economic changes were taking place within feudal society. Next to agricultural activity on the large feudal estates and on small peasant holdings handicrafts increasingly developed. Wool, flax, cotton and silk were used for the production of textiles. In addition to textile production which was partly conducted by rural industry and partly in manufactories, the production of iron and glass increased. All these products found a market in towns and abroad. Although agriculture was to remain the major productive activity, handicrafts and manufactories rapidly developed during the second half of the eighteenth century. When in 1781 serfdom was abolished in the Czech Lands a free labour market emerged. The surplus landless rural population moved to nearby towns in search of a livelihood in the newly founded workshops and manufactories. These country people spoke Czech and as their numbers increased the Czech-speaking population in the towns and particularly in the suburbs grew significantly. They swelled the ranks of the emerging proletariat working in new workshops, living mainly in common dormitories, and eating very sparingly because wages were low.

At the same time some members of the intelligentsia, often sons of handicraftsmen, clerks and servants who studied at the university, turned their attention to the study of the Czech language and literature which had once flourished in their homeland. Giving proof of their interest in drama and theatre they began to translate foreign plays into Czech and to write Czech plays themselves which were staged by amateur groups. In this respect Prague, the capital city, began to play a major role. In the suburbs, as for instance in Smíchov and Karlín but also in the inner New Town, manufactories came into existence where many Czech workers were employed. It is not surprising therefore, that in 1786 a theatre built of wood – the *Bouda* (Shack) – was set up in the Horse Market (today's Wenceslas Square) right in the centre of Prague. It also was frequented by craftsmen and workers enjoying plays performed in the Czech language which had been written by young authors of Czech origin, mainly by Václav Thám and Prokop Šedivý. Czech plays began to be shown also outside Prague as for instance, from 1786, in the town of Vysoká nad Jizerou in northern Bohemia. Prague also saw the publication of newspapers in the Czech language. It is against this background that we have to see the awakened concerns of several educated Czechs (who earned their living as tutors in aristocratic families) with Czech history, language and literature. Among them, above all, F. M. Pelcl (Pelcel, Pelzel) and Josef Dobrovský studied the subjects in depth. The former worked first as a tutor in the family of the Counts of Sternberg (Šternberk), later as librarian and archivist for the Counts Nostitz (Nostic). In 1774 Pelcl published a Czech history in German which appeared in the Czech language in 1791–6. Josef Dobrovský who was also employed as a tutor in the Nostic family became an authority on the Czech language and literature, and founder of Slavonic philological studies.

Although the first Czech scholars wrote their works in German they are nevertheless regarded together with the playwrights, actors and journalists as the 'awakeners' of the Czech nation. Their activities regarding the revival of the Czech past and propagation of all that was Czech were designed to awaken Czech national consciousness. A movement arose known as the Czech National Revival. Since the end of the eighteenth century the modern Czech nation seemed to have acquired most of the features characterizing a modern nation in the period of capitalism. The Czech nation lived closely together in Bohemia and Moravia, and thus inhabited a common territory; it spoke the same language, it shared a common economic life and common culture and possessed a national consciousness. In contrast to the medieval nation, all who spoke Czech and felt themselves to be Czech were considered to be part of the nation whatever social class they belonged to, be they noblemen or burghers, proletarians or peasants. This formation of the modern Czech nation took place between the end of the eighteenth century and the middle of the nineteenth century.

As indicated above, the modern Czech nation did not have its own state – it did not possess sovereign rights. It was subjected to the ruling nation who were Germans. They held the majority in the Bohemian Diet and in the town councils and they occupied the positions in the bureaucracy of the provincial and district administration. Under these conditions the representatives of the ascendant Czech intelligentsia set out to accomplish a not altogether easy task: to acquire *equal rights* for the modern Czech nation with that of the German nation in the Czech Lands. This called for exhausting plodding work lasting half a century. It fell upon the members of the Czech intelligentsia who by and large came from families of craftsmen living in smaller towns. Through the media of the theatre and newspapers the Czech intelligentsia endeavoured to introduce Czech as the language of instruction in schools. It tried hard for the establishment of a Czech 'industrial school' intended to train future industrial employees in the mother tongue. Furthermore, Czech social life began to be organized through public entertainments and balls; through the printing of books and journals, including the establishment of the publishing house *Matice česká* (Czech Mother); through the publication of the large dictionary of the Czech language (Josef Jungmann) and the reconstruction of the historical past of the Czech nation (František Palacký) and, last but not least, through the foundation of the social centre *Měšťanská beseda* (Civic Club).

Occasions to meet socially were provided by Czech lawyers and doctors who received students, clerks, young poets, playwrights and other guests in their salons where home and international affairs were debated. Here friendly links developed with representatives of other Slav nations finding themselves in a similar, if not worse, situation. The Slav question began to play a significant role. This was aided by the passage of Russian troops under Marshal Suvorov through the country during the Napoleonic wars at the end of the eighteenth century. Also Russian armies fought on Moravian territory in the battle of Slavkov (Austerlitz) in 1805. Friendly contacts were also fostered with Poles, Slovaks, Serbs and Croats. Slav solidarity strengthened the national consciousness of the Czech intelligentsia.

The country's economy was growing. Apart from textile mills, especially cotton printing factories, the first engineering works and factories for the production of a variety of commodities were established. By 1827 the authorities had decided to organize industrial exhibitions: in 1828, 1,498 home-produced commodities and in the following year 2,200 products were put on show. It was evident that the country was experiencing rapid economic and industrial growth. This encouraged entrepreneurs in 1833 to found their own *Jednota ku povzbuzení průmyslu v Čechách* (Association for the Encouragement of Industry in Bohemia) in Prague on the pattern of the French *Société d'encouragement pour l'industrie nationale*. It dealt with industrial and economic problems and a Czech section of the Association began to function in 1843. Thus step by step the Czech middle class won the struggle for participation in the country's economic life.

The unprecedented upsurge of Czech cultural life provoked fears and doubts in the ranks of the bureaucracy whether this had not gone too far and whether the Czechs as an underprivileged nation within the monarchy were not demanding more than was admissible. In 1842 the Prague police director Muth pointed out that within several scientific societies, such as the Royal Bohemian Society of Sciences and the Society of the Patriotic Museum in Bohemia, the Czech language was supplanting German. Moreover, *Matice česká* officially requested that Czech instruction should be extended from elementary to higher schools. There was a whole crop of Czech associations which advocated the exclusive use of the Czech language. This was very dangerous, the police director complained, and should be stopped. It is important to realize that the Czechs in Bohemia and Moravia at the time numbered about 6.5 million (70 per cent) whereas the Germans numbered about 2 million (30 per cent). But the German minority enjoyed full political rights while the Czechs had almost none.

Several enlightened personalities among the nobility occupying high positions of influence in the Czech Lands felt that it was unjust to suppress the Czech nationality which formed the majority in the country. Count Leo Thun wrote in his memorandum of 1842 that the existence of the Czech nationality was a fact of life. He pointed out that strong national movements were present in various parts of Europe and one had to accept this also in the Czech Lands. The suppression of the Czech language, he argued, did not make sense because it would harm the intelligentsia and promote instead craftsmen, workers and peasants into positions of national leadership who in turn could integrate the national cause with their class demands.

An important form of activity was reading and discussion circles which met in public houses to argue about such controversial topics as Absolutism, aristocratic privileges, feudal subjection of peasants, and social problems of the working people. Naturally, the political situation in the neighbouring countries was also discussed using information from foreign newspapers, especially the *Augsburger Allgemeine Zeitung*, to which some of the Prague coffee houses subscribed. Interesting articles were read aloud and translated for the public. When the Czech journalist Karel Havlíček returned from Russia, his article 'The Slav and the Czech' became widely known because of his analysis of conditions in Russia and his discussion of the relations of Czechs to Russia. Information about the internal conditions in Germany and Russia stimulated representatives of the Czech intelligentsia to debate the political future of the Czech nation. They definitely wished the Czechs to achieve full equality with the Germans in the Czech Lands within the Austrian framework, for they feared that a political union with either Germany or Russia could be more dangerous for them than their further development in Austria. As part of Germany they realized that they would eventually succumb to Germanization as did the Elbe Slavs many centuries before. But in Austria they would live alongside other Slav nations – Poles, Serbs, Croats, Slovenes and Slovaks – which would give them a certain protection and thus they could continue the struggle for national equality. After Havlíček's report about the situation in Russia they feared that an attachment to Russia would take the Czechs into the much worse social and political conditions of Tsarist autocracy. On the basis of such thinking the Austroslavic political concept arose during the 1840s which aimed at the transformation of Absolutist Austria, in which the Habsburg dynasty shared power with the German aristocracy, into a federal state of nations enjoying equal rights.

We can therefore summarize that between approximately 1780 and 1848 a national revival took place in the Czech Lands which led to the making of the modern Czech nation. This process began with the early efforts of the Czech intelligentsia to strengthen national consciousness; it then continued with efforts to achieve equal national rights, and led to the formulation of the particular political concept of Austroslavism. Now there could be no doubt that the 6.5 million Czechs in Bohemia and Moravia were a nation albeit without a state. They had their schools, newspapers, theatres and publishing houses. They published Czech books and plays as well as scientific works which gained recognition. The works of their scholars such as the philologist Josef Dobrovský, the historian František Palacký, the ethnographer Pavel Josef Šafařík and the philologist Josef Jungmann received attention abroad.

THE REVOLUTION OF 1848: THE CZECH POLITICAL PROGRAMME BETWEEN GREATER GERMANY AND AUSTRIA

The bourgeois revolutions of 1848 spread throughout central Europe, including Austria and the Czech Lands. Revolutionaries demanded the abolition of the remnants of feudalism and the establishment of capitalist conditions. The course of the revolution varied from country to country: there were situational differences in the German states, in Austria, in Hungary and in the Czech Lands. As far as the Czech Lands were concerned, it is important to bear in mind that apart from the Czech-speaking majority there was a substantial German-speaking minority which, in addition to bourgeois demands, also voiced national demands connected with the revolution in neighbouring Germany.

From the very beginning of the Austrian revolution and in the wake of the fall of Absolutism and its representative Chancellor Metternich, the Czech bourgeois intelligentsia had counted not only on the introduction of fundamental civil rights but also on achieving equality between the Czech and German languages. The Czech bourgeois intelligentsia was not striving for an independent state for, in the spirit of Austroslavism, it wanted the Czech Lands to remain part of Austria which was to be transformed into a federal state of equal nations. Germans as well as Czechs, Poles, Magyars, Southern Slavs and Italians were to possess self-governing units with their own administrations and schools in which official business and teaching were to be conducted in the national language. Already in March 1848 representatives of the Czech intelligentsia and bourgeoisie had addressed a petition to the Emperor in Vienna in which they demanded, apart from the abolition of remnants of feudalism such as villeinage and

corvée, freedom of the press, religious freedom, personal safety, local
self-government, equal status for the Czech and German languages,
and the establishment of a Bohemian *de jure* state entity in the
framework of the Austrian Monarchy.

The Viennese court and government, after delaying negotiations,
accepted the demands by issuing a Cabinet decree on 8 April 1848.[20]
Henceforth the Czech language was to receive equal status with
German in all branches of state administration and public education;
every stratum of the population was to be represented in the Bohemian
Diet on the basis of the broadest suffrage. Furthermore, the Kingdom
of Bohemia was to have its highest offices restored in Prague. It
seemed that the Cabinet decree of 8 April 1848 had satisfied the
demands of Czech politicians. However, the very next day representatives of the Germans from Bohemia (*Deutschböhmen*)[21] handed their
protest against the decree to the Minister of the Interior, Pillersdorf,
in Vienna. In view of the further course of the revolution none of the
concessions made in the decree came into force.

The relationship between Czechs and Germans in Bohemia deteriorated gravely because of the revolution inside Germany itself. At the
end of March 1848 political representatives from the German states
met in the city of Frankfurt and decided to set a date for all-German
elections leading to a Constituent National Assembly of a future
united Germany. It was understood that a unified Germany was to
encompass the German Confederation established between 1815 and
1820 of which the Czech Lands – Bohemia, Moravia and Silesia –
were also part. Therefore they were also to be integrated into the
proposed united Germany. A *Vorparlament* (Preliminary Parliament)
of fifty members under the presidency of Alexander von Soiron was
entrusted with the preparation and realization of the election until the
convocation of the all-German National Assembly. Because at the
time only two Austrian politicians were present in Frankfurt the
Vorparlament decided to invite six more representatives from Austria,
including two from Bohemia. For the Germans from Bohemia the
publicist Franz Schuselka was elected, for the Czechs the historian
František Palacký who received the letter informing him of his election
and inviting him to come to Frankfurt on 10 April 1848.

Palacký did not accept the invitation and refused to go to Frankfurt.
He explained the reasons for his refusal in a long letter to Alexander
von Soiron. Palacký's letter, which he discussed with several Czech
politicians in the *Měšťanská beseda*, is an important document dealing
with Czech policy regarding Germany, Austria and Russia. Palacký
argued that the major task of the German National Assembly would

be the unification of Germany and the creation of a unified German nation and that he understood this endeavour. He, however, did not think of himself as being German and although the Czech nation was a small one, Palacký continued, it never considered itself nor was it considered by others as part of the German nation. Therefore Palacký expressed his conviction that Frankfurt was not the place for him. If the negotiations in Frankfurt were to succeed in establishing a united Germany, Palacký went on, this would inevitably result in the collapse of Austria as an independent empire. Palacký considered this detrimental because the existence of an independent Austria remained the best security guarantee for the small nations of central and south-eastern Europe. Furthermore, he pointed out, Tsarist Russia would just expand its influence into central and south-east Europe. Consequently, the small nations living in that area – Slavs, Romanians, Magyars, Greeks, Turks and Albanians – would not be able to resist this pressure unless they were joined in a large Danubian federative state. Palacký felt that Austria was predestined to play the role of a barrier against Russian expansionism. He wrote: 'Certainly, had the Austrian state not existed since long ago we ourselves would have to endeavour to create it as soon as possible in the interest of Europe, indeed of humanity itself.' This then was for Palacký a further reason why the Czech nation should link its future with Austria and not with Germany.

Palacký's third reason against Czech participation in the Frankfurt National Assembly was his fear that the success of the German revolution would inevitably lead to the establishment of a republic. With regard to Austria, Palacký rejected such a form of government, for the break-up of Austria would lead to the creation of several small republics unable to withstand the power of a 'universal Russian monarchy'. Although the Czech leader did not spell it out in his letter he knew well that the establishment of an Austrian republic would strengthen the influence of the German-speaking bourgeoisie which, in the main, supported the joining of Austria with Germany. The far weaker Czech bourgeoisie and its intelligentsia needed political allies in its effort to carry through its policy which relied on the preservation of Austria and its transformation into a federative state of equal nations. Such allies could not be found among the German-speaking bourgeoisie but only among those strata of society which desired to preserve Austria as a sovereign independent state: the court, the aristocracy and bureaucracy. Thus a strange alliance came about between the Czech bourgeois intelligentsia, on the one hand, and the Austrian court and aristocracy, on the other. For this the Czech bourgeoisie was repeatedly strongly criticized. However, this policy was dictated by political tactics arising from the contemporary situation.

Consequently, the Czech political programme found itself between a Greater Germany and Austria in the course of the 1848 revolution. The Czechs opted for an Austria that was to be completely unlike the one before the revolution. Prince Metternich's absolutist-feudal regime was to be replaced by a federation of equal and autonomous national units in which fundamental civil rights were to be guaranteed. Criticism of the Czechs, then or later, for having joined the counter-revolution and for having helped to preserve Austria emanated from a misunderstanding. Although it was true that the Czech political programme of 1848 was for the preservation of Austria as a state, it was to be a state based on bourgeois freedoms in which the national question was to be solved along the road of a federation of equal nations. This would be entirely different from the pre-revolutionary state since, as a result of the revolution, it would be a state of citizens not of feudal subjects.

The 1848–9 revolution in Austria was defeated in the end. The Czechs, like other nations of the Monarchy, remained a subjugated nation. After 1849 their efforts to attain equality as a nation continued albeit under even more restrictive conditions because the neo-Absolutism of Alexander Bach, in order to prevent nationalist unrest, harshly suppressed any national movement. It was obvious that under these new conditions the Czech bourgeoisie and intelligentsia had to resume the fight for national equality in Bohemia and Moravia where Czechs represented the majority of the population but remained an oppressed nation without equal rights.

DUALISM

After the defeat of the revolution in 1849 neo-Absolutism ruled over Austria for ten years but was powerless to deal with the complexities of conflicts at home and abroad. Especially unresolved remained the national question which continued to be the probing stone of any political settlement in Austria. This time the insurrection started in Austria's north Italian provinces which counted on French assistance. In 1859 the Austrian army was defeated on the battlefields of Magenta and Solferino and the situation in the Monarchy seemed conducive to reforms both in the imperial and provincial administration. On 20 October 1860 an Imperial Diploma was issued 'for the organization of internal legal conditions in the Monarchy' which stipulated that in future laws could be promulgated, amended and abrogated only by the provincial Diets or the Imperial Parliament (*Reichsrat*). Also the constitutional institutions of the Hungarian kingdom were revived. However, the Magyars rejected the October Diploma because the concessions in the direction of dualism seemed insufficient to them. Prime Minister Count Goluchowski had to resign and on 13 December 1860 Anton von Schmerling was appointed his successor. Against Goluchowski's conception of 'historical-legal individuality' Schmerling enforced dualist centralism. His draft constitution was made public in February 1861. According to this draft, known as the February Constitution, Austria was to have a 'full' and a 'restricted' *Reichsrat*. The 'restricted' sessions were to be devoted to matters concerning all non-Hungarian parts of the Monarchy, while the 'full' sessions concerned the Empire as a whole. In practical terms this reform meant the introduction of dualism, although this was not openly stated, because Hungarian affairs were to be dealt with separately.

The Czech politicians began to realize the danger of Austria transforming itself into a dual state of Austria-Hungary. They decisively opposed such a political solution which would leave nationalities in the Austrian half under German rule, and those in the Hungarian half under Magyar rule. This meant that their federalist conception would in practice have no chance of succeeding. In the period which followed Czech politicians fought against the impending dualism and their leader František Palacký, opposed the dualist solution in the Upper House (*Herrenhaus*) in Vienna. When during 1861 Palacký realized that he alone could achieve nothing against the forthcoming dualist settlement, he announced 'passive opposition' and the Czech deputies in the Bohemian Diet followed suit in 1863. On 9 November 1864 the Czech politician František Ladislav Rieger published his programmatic article against the threat of dualism in the journal *Národ* (Nation) for which Palacký wrote a series of eight articles between April and May 1865, later published as a pamphlet entitled *The Idea of the Austrian State*. According to Palacký the guiding principle in the nineteenth century had become *the idea of equality among nations* which in Austria could assume the form of federalism. He came to the following conclusion:

> If, however, the idea of a modern Austrian state is to be reversed and this empire which is so diverse and unique in the world is not going to grant equal justice to all, but supremacy and power of one over the others, and if the Slavs will in reality be declared a subordinate race

... internal peace will change into unrest ... and finally awaken strife and struggle ... the day on which dualism is proclaimed will also become inevitably the day on which Panslavism of the least desirable form will be born ... We Slavs will contemplate these developments with genuine anguish though without fear. Before Austria was, we were, and when Austria no longer is, we still shall be.

Events followed in rapid succession. Austria's dispute with Prussia over Schleswig-Holstein led to the outbreak of war in 1866. On 3 July 1866 Austria was defeated at the battle of Sadova and, after the capture of Brno, was forced to sign the armistice of Mikulov. Prussia achieved her aim of ousting Austria from Germany and brought about the dissolution of the German Confederacy. But the Prussians also interfered in Austria's internal affairs by enabling the Magyars to organize the Hungarian Legion. In this situation the radical faction in Hungary led by Kálman Tisza gained decisive power and demanded the unconditional independence of Hungary. What the Austrian aristocratic politicians had proved incapable of doing was performed by the newly appointed Foreign Minister, Baron Ferdinand Beust, who was a Saxon. On 20 December 1866 he left for Pest where he negotiated the dualist agreement with Count Gyula Andrássy to which the Emperor gave his assent on 8 June 1867. The Austrian Monarchy was thus transformed into Austria-Hungary. The fears of the Czech politicians were confirmed and all their protests and passive opposition in the Bohemian Diet had been of no avail.

A further stage in the protracted evolution of the political conception of the Czech nation began which was to last until the First World War. During this period the Czech national movement had again to fight as a movement of a subordinate nation for equality with the Germans in the Czech Lands. This period of Czech national politics is characterized as the 'piecemeal period' because Czech politicians had to be satisfied with small and partial concessions from the government. There was no ambition to come forward with a grand political scheme. One of the reasons for this passivity was the relatively rapid economic growth in the country in spite of the crisis of 1873–9. Capitalism matured in the Czech Lands leading to the establishment of new factories and to the increased employment of workers and this helped to generate a fuller social and cultural life. The Czech bourgeoisie participated in this development and, because it had no faith in a great political movement, it seemed to be content with small successes in everyday life. In fact it was the Czech workers who took up the demand for national equality in Austria. In 1873 the Social Democratic newspaper *Dělnické listy* (Workers' Letters) wrote:

We declare that we shall always and everywhere demand the broadest political freedoms and social equality. We declare that now and always we regard our Czech nationality as sacred and untouchable, and we regard it as our foremost duty to make the greatest sacrifices for it to succeed and to prosper ... We demand that a workers' assembly of all nationalities in Austria be convened to agree on a common programme, and to express itself especially on the nationality question which is so important in Austria, to lead them to a just recognition of all and thus to contribute to the development and perfection of the different nations.[22]

However, only a momentous event such as the First World War was able to produce a fundamental change.

THE FIRST WORLD WAR, THE INDEPENDENT STATE AND THE CZECHOSLOVAK NATION

When the First World War broke out the Czech bourgeois politicians did not have a common political concept. The majority of Czech political parties, including the Social Democrats, believed that Austria would survive and that the Czech Lands would remain part of it. The only exception was the tiny radical State Rights Party (*státopravní strana*) with little influence which demanded the break-up of Austria-Hungary and the establishment of an independent Czech state. Meanwhile the Czechs, obeying the mobilization orders, were leaving for the battlefronts.

The first economic difficulties became evident as early as 1915. Austria was not prepared to endure a prolonged war; soon bread and flour rationing was introduced; food was scarce and prices rose rapidly. In front of shops long queues formed and women waited for hours to obtain the essential staple food for their families. Often they had to leave the towns to get hold of something to eat in the countryside. While unrest spread at home, desertions were taking place at the battlefront. On the Russian front groups of Czech soldiers walked over to the enemy and in April 1915 the bulk of the Infantry Regiment No. 28 from Prague conspicuously joined the Russians on the other side. Out of 2,000 soldiers only 150 remained on the Austrian side. In May of the same year about 1,600 soldiers and officers of the Infantry Regiment No. 36 from Mladá Boleslav allowed themselves to be captured by the enemy. It was obvious to the authorities that the Czechs did not want to fight for the preservation of Austria-Hungary and they initiated a wave of arrests. Among the arrested were well-known public figures such as Karel Kramář and Alois Rašín who were prominent in the Young Czech Party, Václav Klofáč who led the National Social Party, Josef Scheiner who headed the mass gymnastic organization *Sokol* (Falcon), and others who were sentenced to death. However, the death sentences were not carried out.

Apart from this another trend in Czech politics began to assert itself, represented by the Deputy for the Realist Party in the *Reichsrat* (Imperial Parliament) and Professor of Philosophy at the Czech University in Prague, Tomáš Garrigue Masaryk. In autumn 1914 Masaryk decided to transfer his political activity abroad in order to bring about a change in the thinking about the Czech question. When he became Professor at the new School of Slavonic Studies at London University he gave the Inaugural Lecture 'The Problem of Small Nations in the European Crisis' on 19 October 1915. In it he pleaded the case for the political independence of small nations such as Poles, Serbo-Croats and Czechs. Shortly afterwards Masaryk took practical steps. On 14 November 1915 Masaryk, in conjunction with the like-minded young Czech sociologist Edvard Beneš and the Slovak astronomer Milan Rastislav Štefánik (who served as airforce officer in the French army), published in the name of the Czech External Committee a momentous document in favour of an 'independent Czechoslovak state'. This was, after several centuries, a new conception of Czech national policy which broke all ties with Austria in its endeavour to establish an independent state. Such a radical policy could be pursued only abroad. Exiled Czech politicians could count on the support of Czech organizations in the United States, Russia, Britain and France. In February 1916 the Czechoslovak National Council (originally *Conseil National des Pays Tchèques*) was established in Paris with Masaryk as its Chairman, the Deputy of the Agrarian Party Josef Dürich as Vice-chairman, Beneš as General Secretary and Štefánik as Member of the Council.

By the middle of November 1916 Czech politicians representing practically all shades of political opinion constituted a National Council in Prague and the Czech Union at the *Reichsrat* in Vienna. After the death of the Emperor Francis Joseph I, the new Emperor Charles I announced a general amnesty on 1 January 1917 as a result of which the death sentences on Karel Kramář and the other Czech politicians previously found guilty of treason were commuted into life imprisonment. On 27 February 1917 the revolution broke out in Russia which became a republic. This was of great import for the further conduct of the war as well as for Czech politics. It should be explained that already in Russia Czechoslovak Legions had been formed consisting of prisoners of war and of Czechs and Slovaks settled in the Tsarist Empire. The fact that Czechs and Slovaks had their own armed formations fighting on the side of the Entente against Austria-Hungary was of great political importance.

At the same time a wave of resistance swept the Czech Lands which prompted 222 Czech writers and representatives of Czech cultural life in May 1917 to publish a manifesto exhorting the Czech deputies vigorously to defend the nation's interest with a view to a future democratic Europe of free nations. On 30 May 1917 the spokesman for the Czech Union in the *Reichsrat* indeed declared that it would 'strive for the unification of all branches of the Czechoslovak nation in a democratic Czech state, including the Slovak branch of the nation that inhabits an area continuous with the historical Czech home-land'.[23] The activities of the Czechoslovak Legions in Russia, France and Italy and of the politicians of the Czechoslovak National Council led to the declaration of the French government on 29 June 1918 recognizing the claims of the Czechoslovak government on 9 August, and the US government's recognition followed on 3 September. E. Beneš informed the governments of the Entente that the Czechoslovak National Council in Paris had constituted itself as the Czechoslovak government. Two days later T. G. Masaryk presented the so-called Washington Declaration in the USA which proclaimed the independence of the Czechoslovak nation whose future state would be a republic.[24] The Washington Declaration was officially conveyed to the US government on 17 October 1918. Ten days later the Austro-Hungarian Foreign Minister Gyula Andrássy declared that his government accepted the American President's terms for an armistice. On the following day, on 28 October 1918, representatives of the National Committee in Prague took over power; it declared itself the Constituent Assembly of the independent Czechoslovak state and, in line with this act, promulgated its first law proclaiming the foundation of the Czechoslovak state, based on the joining up of the Czech Lands with Slovakia.

Thus after centuries of endeavour it was the First World War and the struggle of the Czech and Slovak people and their representatives at home and abroad which brought about the establishment of the independent Czechoslovak state. Its historic importance is undisputed and, significantly, after a thousand years the Czech Lands were again united with Slovakia which led to the concept of the *Czechoslovak nation*. Consequences of this notion were ambiguous because a section of Slovaks was convinced that the Slovaks constituted a separate nation deserving autonomy, and this they pursued. On 28 October 1918 the independent Czechoslovak Republic was born but it lasted only twenty years.

THE SECOND WORLD WAR AND THE ESTABLISHMENT OF THE STATE OF CZECHS AND SLOVAKS

When the Second World War broke out in September 1939 the Czechoslovak Republic had already been destroyed. Its German-speaking frontier districts had been annexed to Nazi Germany by the Munich Agreement of 30 September 1938, and Slovakia with the support of Germany declared itself an independent state on 14 March 1939. On the next day, 15 March 1939, the truncated Czech Lands were invaded by the German army and incorporated into the Third Reich as the 'Protectorate of Bohemia and Moravia'. During the war that followed Czechs and Slovaks fought against Germany. Resistance was organized at home and abroad. Czechoslovak units fought alongside the Red Army and with the British forces in Africa and Europe. The Slovak uprising in August 1944 is seen as the starting-point of the liberation of Czechoslovakia.

From the beginning of the war it was accepted in the West and in the Soviet Union that after victory the independent Czechoslovak state would be restored, and so it was. During its rapid advance the Red Army with the Czechoslovak Army Corps in its ranks crossed the eastern border of Czechoslovakia in the winter of 1944 and by stages occupied Slovakia, Moravia and Bohemia. On 5 April 1945 the Czechoslovak government, which had been formed in exile, met in Košice and issued its first programme. In it the government pledged that the new state would be based on *complete equality of Czechs and Slovaks*. This was to remove former antagonisms. It took, however, until 1968, when the law about the federative state of Czechs and Slovaks was promulgated giving each nation its government, parliament and all offices of the internal administration of the country.

The establishment of the state of two equal nations, Czechs and Slovaks, is one of the important results of the Second World War and, for the moment, the end point of the national status of the Czechs in historical context. This took shape first in the Middle Ages from a state and national existence; through the rise of the modern nation in the epoch of the National Revival, to the formulation of a political programme in the revolution of 1848, followed by the political struggles of the nineteenth century which ended with the birth of the

Czechoslovak state in 1918, until the present federative state of Czechs and Slovaks.[25]

NOTES

1 F. Graus, 'Die Bildung eines Nationalbewusstseins im mittelalterlichen Böhmen', *Historica*, 13 (1966), 22.
2 *Kosmova kronika česká* (Cosmas's Czech Chronicle) (Prague, 1947), vol. II, p. 14.
3 Graus, 'Bildung', p. 24.
4 J. Šusta, *Král cizinec, České dějiny* (King the Foreigner, Czech History), vol. II/1 (Prague, 1939), p. 48.
5 Graus, 'Bildung', p. 40.
6 Šusta, *Král cizinec*, pp. 14–18.
7 *Ibid.*, pp. 38–9.
8 *Dalimilova kronika* (Dalimil's Chronicle), CII (Prague, 1948), p. 88.
9 *Ibid.*, CVI, p. 219.
10 *Ibid.*, XLV, XLVI, pp. 46–7.
11 Graus, 'Bildung', p. 5.
12 F. Šmahel, *Idea národa v husitských Čechách* (The Nation-Idea in Hussite Bohemia) (České Budějovice, 1971), pp. 184–5.
13 *Ibid.*, p. 178.
14 *Ibid.*
15 *Ibid.*, pp. 20–1.
16 J. Macek, 'Národnostní otázka v husitském revolučním hnutí' (The national question in the Hussite revolutionary movement), *Československý časopis historický*, 3 (1955), 17.
17 Šmahel, *Idea národa*, pp. 101, 105.
18 Graus, 'Bildung', p. 48.
19 F. Palacký, *Dějiny národu českého v Čechách a na Moravě* (History of the Czech Nation in Bohemia and Moravia), vol. I, 3rd edn (Prague, 1976), p. 12.
20 A. Klíma, *Revoluce 1848 v českých zemích* (Revolution 1848 in the Czech Lands) (Prague, 1974), p. 19.
21 It appears that in 1793–4 the difference between *Deutschböhmen* (German Czechs) and *Stockböhmen* (true-born Czechs) was statistically registered for the first time. Cf. M. Teich, 'Bohemia: from darkness into light', in R. Porter and M. Teich (eds.), *The Enlightenment in National Context* (Cambridge, 1981), p. 163 n. 70.
22 A. Klíma, *Počátky českého dělnického hnutí* (Beginnings of the Czech Working-Class Movement) (Prague, 1949), pp. 25–7, 75.
23 O. Urban, *Česká společnost 1848–1918* (Czech Society 1848–1918) (Prague, 1982), p. 612.
24 V. Olivová, *Dokumenty ke vzniku Československa roku 1918* (Documents on the Origin of Czechoslovakia in 1918) (Prague, 1968), pp. 119–121.
25 It ceased to exist on 1 January 1993 when two seperate republics came into being: the Czech Republic and Slovakia. (Editorial note before going to press.)

TEN

THE NATIONAL QUESTION IN HUNGARY

EMIL NIEDERHAUSER

'IT is true that most Slavic peoples and indeed Germanic and Romance peoples had conflicts with some of their neighbours some of the time; the Magyars had trouble with all of them most of the time.'[1] Robert A. Kann is right in making this statement. But he did not take into consideration the fact that Slovaks and Croatians or the Romanians and Croatians lived rather far from each other and for this reason had not many points of conflict. The Hungarians lived in the centre of the country, and thus indeed had contact and therefore conflict with all of them.

MEDIEVAL HUNGARY

From its beginnings medieval Hungary was a multiethnic state. The conquering Hungarian tribes, themselves of various ethnic origins, found Slavonic tribes here. During the course of the Middle Ages different Western settlers, mostly Germans, arrived; peasants and townspeople, and from the East, Turkish ethnic elements, reached these parts. They were given territorial privileges. Vlachs, the present-day Romanians, appeared in the eastern part of the country in Transylvania. At the turn of the eleventh and twelfth centuries, King Ladislas I and King Coloman conquered Croatia, which became a 'Regnum Socium' endowed with a wide-ranging autonomy.[2]

From the late Middle Ages onwards large numbers of Southern Slavs appeared seeking refuge from the Ottoman conquest. As the central part of Hungary was under Ottoman occupation from 1541 until the end of the seventeenth century, more changes occurred in the ethnic composition of the country.[3] When the Ottomans departed from Hungary, large areas of the country were sparsely populated, and the Habsburg government moved German settlers in, mainly to the southern areas. By the end of the eighteenth century, the Hungarians were in an ethnic minority in comparison to the other nationalities, though individually these were of a smaller number, allowing the Hungarians to retain their relative majority.[4]

Traditional society is always more sensitive to social and political differences than it is to ethnic and linguistic differences. Therefore this multinational combination did not create conflicts.

The nobility (*nemesek*) and the clergy both equally belonged to the feudal elite the 'Natio Hungarica', the usual privileges of which order they were able to enjoy. Thus, this feudal elite was Hungarian as was the Croatian in Croatia. It could happen that the nobility and the serfs were of different ethnic backgrounds, while the town-dwellers were of yet a third ethnic group, but they were only made aware of these differences in a social context.

Historiography was inclined to see the national question in the relationship, or rather in the constant disputes, between the Habsburg king and the feudal estates. But a real national question in the modern sense of the word arose only in the late eighteenth century, under the influence of the French Revolution. The situation changed radically. The movement towards national rebirth, or awakening, took place simultaneously amongst Hungarian and other ethnic groups.[5] This movement, a general phenomenon of eastern Europe, can be traced back to the following model: an ethnic community linked usually by a common language becomes conscious of its unity, or rather an intellectual elite begins to advertise this unity.

The generally held view was that the nation as a community had existed since time immemorial, but was at present dormant and needed to be awakened; this is how the movement got its name. The movement consists of two phases, the cultural and the political. The cultural phase shapes the national identity, which consists of two important components: the national language, which in countless cases has to be created out of numerous dialects, and a historical consciousness. It is during the political phase that the demand for local autonomy will appear with the free use of the national language in the administration and finally the emergence of the nation-state.

This theoretical model does not approximate to the historical events in all their complexity, but serves as a tool in their interpretation. Before going into more detail, we have to mention the fact that the nations in Hungary may be divided into two types according to their social composition:[6] one in which some kind of feudal elite had existed, the other in which it had not. In Hungary only the Magyars and the Croats belonged to the first type. They were in a fortunate position, because their elite had been governing their respective countries for

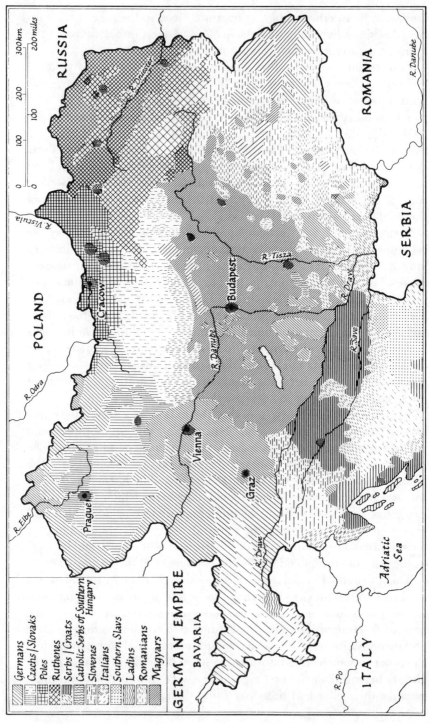

1 Ethnic divisions of the Habsburg Empire, *c.* 1910 (based on a map in C. A. Macartney, *The Habsburg Empire 1790–1918,* 1968)

centuries, and thus their historical consciousness was closer to the actual development, while the other nations had recourse only to myths. The possibility of a legal political life in the Diets was another of their advantages.

In this respect historical Hungary under the crown of St Stephen was divided up into the following parts: Hungary proper (roughly speaking present-day Hungary, Slovakia and Vojvodina), Croatia and Transylvania. Croatia had its own feudal Diet, the *Sabor*, but was obliged to send deputies to the Hungarian Diet, which consisted of two houses. In the Upper House sat the high church dignitaries and those born into the aristocracy (*született arisztokraták*), while in the Lower House sat the elected representatives of the nobility, of the free royal towns and chapters. Transylvania had its own Diet, where the so-called three nations, the Magyars, the Szeklers and the Saxons, were represented. (The Szeklers are an ethnic group of debatable origin, but by this time had a distinctly Hungarian national identity, and spoke Hungarian.) The Saxons were German settlers from the twelfth century, who had received territorial autonomy from King Andreas II in 1224.[7]

The nobility, comprising nearly 5 per cent of the entire population, was conscious of belonging to the 'Natio Hungarica', that is, to the privileged elite.[8] This resulted in a particular kind of consciousness: to be 'Hungarus', which meant more or less that they were inhabitants of the Kingdom of Hungary (which to contemporary thinking also included Transylvania).[9] It was precisely due to the impact of the movement of national awakening that 'Natio Hungarica' was beginning to become the Hungarian nation. Up until 1844, Latin was the official language, the laws being formulated in Latin, but after 1790 Hungarian translations were added to them. In the Hungarian Diet Hungarian gradually replaced Latin in the debates. As a result of this the various members of the nobility, who were of different ethnic origins, slowly became Magyarized and made a great effort to learn Hungarian. Only the Croatian noblemen and aristocrats did not take part in these developments. They kept the Latin language and their Croatian ethnic identity, which in a similar way led to the emergence of the modern Croatian national consciousness.

It is clear from what has been said so far that the majority of the rest of the nationalities in Hungary did not take part in political life, because they did not belong to the elite classes. The Germans were in the most favourable position, slowly becoming Hungarian town-dwellers, but taking comfort from the fact that Hungary was part of the Habsburg Empire where German was the major state language.

The German peasants were not affected by the national movement. The Serbians, partly town-dwellers, partly free soldier peasants on the Military Border in the southern part of Hungary, were also in a better position.[10]

A few of the Romanians were also border-guards, but the majority were peasants, that is, serfs, and they had a very small intelligentsia which comprised mainly Orthodox and Uniate clergymen. The Slovaks were in a similar situation, being denominationally also divided, 80 per cent Catholic, the rest Lutherans. Only the Serbs were united in their Orthodox Church, which possessed a wide-ranging autonomy providing the possibility of some political life. The Ruthenes (Carpatho-Ukrainians), living in the north-east corner of historical Hungary (present-day Carpatho-Ukraine in the former USSR), were also peasants with a small number of Uniate clergy. A minority of these clergy wavered between Russian or Ukrainian national identity, while the peasant masses remained untouched by national problems.

There was a small number of other ethnically different inhabitants, Slovenes in the western counties, Greeks, Armenians and Jews. The Jews, during the course of the nineteenth century, became Magyarized. So these ethnic minorities did not cause national problems.

One other factor has to be taken into consideration. The nations mentioned lived on the whole in the geographically definable Hungary. The Croatians lived in Croatia and Slavonia, which was separated by a geographically recognizable border from Hungary proper. The Slovaks lived in the north and north-west, the Romanians in the east, Serbians in the south and the Magyars in central and eastern areas.

However, it is not quite as simple as that. Mainly as a result of the changes which occurred during the Ottoman period, a significant part of the ethnic groups intermingled as they settled, for instance in the Vojvodina and in Transylvania. Germans lived practically in every town, but the German peasants lived scattered throughout the whole country, as did the Slovaks in the southern areas (even in present-day Hungary). Croatian settlements could be found around Budapest. The Hungarian noblemen and officials of the administration lived all over Hungary, with the exception of Slavonia and Croatia, though Hungarian landowners of large estates lived in the latter, too. These mixed settlements, which did not have obvious boundaries, became an important element of later events. Quite clearly it was impossible to draw clear-cut ethnic borders between the various nations without turning some of them into minorities.

The next event, the movement of national rebirth (revival, awakening), was simply a superficial phenomenon under the guise of which the beginning of modernization was taking place, the development of capitalism, shaping a modern state and society along Western lines. In the so-called 'reform era' (1830–48), the Hungarian nobility made spectacular efforts to further the advancement of this development towards a modern statehood. The Diets voted many laws to this effect and as they had to confront a hostile Vienna, the struggle took on the form of a national movement.[11] (In fact the various movements of national rebirth in eastern Europe did not usually pay much attention to economic and social questions; the Hungarian nobility and many of the aristocrats were unique in this respect.)

At the same time, this race towards a modern statehood and a modern society was connected with the acceptance of the French model of a nation-state, though the leaders of the Hungarian reform movement were aware of the fact that the Magyars were in a minority in comparison to the other nations put together, even if we leave out the Croats because of their feudal autonomy. This is why the Hungarian political elite was afraid of Panslavism, the collaboration of the Slav nations inside Hungary with Russia. This fear was not entirely without foundation, but may have been exaggerated.[12] It was precisely those groups of the reform-minded nobility who were radicals on social issues (especially the emancipation of serfs as a fundamental question) who were also radicals on the national question, that is, intolerant of non-Magyars. The more conservative-thinking members of the political elite emphasized the multinational composition of the country and the insurmountable difficulty of assimilating all the non-Magyars. The most prominent of these was Count István Széchenyi, a leading figure of the reform movement.[13]

It was the generally held opinion of the political elite that liberal individual rights granted to everyone, irrespective of nationality, would satisfy the intelligentsia of the non-Magyar nations, not to mention their peasantry, if the full emancipation of the serfs took place. It was also expected that this intelligentsia would follow the example of the nobility and become Magyarized. After the relative calm at the turn of the nineteenth century in the relationship between the Magyars and other nations, certain effects of the efforts at Magyarization taking place in the schools and other cultural institutions, though ineffectual, upset the intelligentsia. Hungarian public opinion demanded the rights of the Magyar language in place of the official Latin and the semi-official German, but also in place of the other languages. The intellectuals of the other nations protested. Articles were published in the newspapers on the controversial issue, political leaflets appeared. 'Sollen wir Magyaren werden?' said the pamphlet distributed by the Slovak Samuel Hoitsy, one of many in German, so that it could be understood by everyone, including people abroad. (German was a sort of 'lingua franca' in the entire Habsburg Monarchy). Both sides published articles debating the issues, first in the *Frankfurter Allgemeine Zeitung*.[14]

Public opinion reacted nervously on both sides. However, the national dispute affected only public opinion, a negligible part of society. Coexistence, as in countless years gone by, continued to be practised. Hungarian families, nobles and burghers, habitually sent their children to German, Slovak or Serbian families, usually for a year, 'to be exposed to German' as they said in Hungary, in order to learn the respective language, German or Slovak, etc. They in turn received German or Slovak children into their homes to learn Hungarian. With the growing dominance of the Hungarian language, this kind of 'peaceful coexistence' began to disappear. Among the large peasant masses national conflict was, as yet, virtually non-existent.

THE REVOLUTION OF 1848–9 AND THE ROAD TO THE AUSTRO-HUNGARIAN COMPROMISE (1867)

The situation suddenly changed during the course of the 1848–9 revolution. The real purpose of the revolution was the abolition of the feudal system, the establishment of modern democratic institutions, the liberation of the serfs, the declaration of civil rights and freedom of the press – the beginnings of modernization. In Hungary this change took place without bloodshed.[15]

Contemporaries were more interested in the national aspects of the change. Hungary got a government responsible to the elected Parliament (the election took place during the summer of 1848), a government responsible to all the provinces of the Crown of St Stephen including Transylvania and Croatia.

The last feudal Diet had already voted for the union of Transylvania with Hungary, the old claim of the national movement, and this was passed by the Diet of Transylvania too. The relationship between the governments of Vienna and Hungary remained unclear and this caused the armed confrontation later. It could not be described as more than a kind of personal union between Hungary and the western territories of the Monarchy. However, the newly elected Parliament did have the right to pass laws, which had to be sanctioned by the king. It looked as though the Hungarian national question was solved in this way. Hungary received its independence from the government of Vienna. A new Hungary came into being, a Hungarian nation-state, at least such was the opinion of the political elite, which believed that its claims and plans of social and political change had been realized.

The union with Hungary was voted for by the feudal Diet of Transylvania, which apart from the Saxons included only members of the 'Natio Hungarica' in both the new and the old sense of the word. The Transylvanian Diet voted this union in the absence of the Romanians, though the latter undoubtedly by this time formed the majority of the inhabitants. Only the bishops of the two Romanian National Churches were present, an insignificant minority. Thus the non-Magyar nations of Hungary were excluded from political life. The Croatian Diet refused to recognize the competence of the Hungarian government or Parliament. The Hungarian government, composed of the most brilliant representatives of the reform movement, men of exceptional talent devoted to the national cause, and all the other political leaders continued to hold their earlier opinions: civil rights and equality before the law and the belief that all the liberal achievements of the revolution would surely satisfy the members of the non-Magyar nations. In the first few bright days of the revolution it really seemed that (with the exception of Croatia) the other national movements greeted with joy the bloodless victory of the revolution: the liberty, equality and fraternity realized for all.

There was just one more thing they wanted added to these glorious achievements: the acceptance of their separate nationhood, the acknowledgement of the fact that they constituted nations. But this was the one thing that the leaders of the revolution were not willing to recognize. The old concept of 'Natio Hungarica', mixed with the new national thinking based on the French model, made it impossible for them to make room for these claims.[16] The slogan for a unified Hungarian political nation was not yet declared, but it was clear that in Hungary this was the only possibility.

The leaders of the other nations organized mass meetings, demanding their national rights, the Serbs their church assembly. It was the Serbs who first began an armed uprising against the Hungarian government, the Croats and Romanians followed and guerrilla fighters were organized even among the Slovaks. The civil war between the Magyars and the other nations coincided with Hungary's war of independence against the Austrian army. As each consecutive Austrian constitution recognized the existence of the various nations and their equal rights, the leaders of the non-Magyar nations turned to the Austrians for help against the Hungarians. The Hungarian government considered this treason. Even during the last few days of the revolution, in face of the Russian intervention on the side of Austria, the Hungarian Parliament voted an act acknowledging the rights of non-Magyars to use their own language only on local and minor administrative levels and for the right of maintaining their own schools. True, this was the first nationality act in Europe, but two weeks before the capitulation of the Hungarian army, it did not seem too convincing.

The collapse of the armed resistance was a serious blow to the Hungarian national movement. The neo-Absolutist system in existence since August 1849, but only established formally at the end of 1850, reduced Hungary simply to a province of the Austrian Empire. Transylvania, Croatia and the newly established Vojvodina were detached from Hungary proper. Local government, which had been formerly in the hands of the nobles, was suppressed and Austrian civil administration was introduced. At a local level they could not dispense with the help of the Hungarian civil servants who were mostly Magyars.[17]

According to a contemporary saying, the non-Magyar nations received from Austria as a reward what the Magyars received as a punishment. Only the Serbs received territorial autonomy; the Croatians retained theirs. But neither the Slovaks nor the Romanians received territorial autonomy, which they had formerly claimed, though it had been promised to them when Vienna needed their support.

Vienna continued to need this support against the Hungarian national movement. The émigrés, under the leadership of Lajos Kossuth, tried to regain full independence with the aid of foreign powers. Kossuth introduced a plan for a Danubian confederation including Hungary, Romania, Serbia and Croatia, a federation of independent states. Public opinion in Hungary rejected this plan and the possibility of a break with the Habsburg Monarchy.[18] Although Kossuth's plan retained the territorial integrity of Hungary (again with the exception of Croatia), the political elite within Hungary was searching for some form of compromise with the Austrian government.[19] The general opinion was that territorial integrity (this time including Croatia) could not be maintained unless Hungary remained part of the Habsburg Monarchy, a large European power. Constitutionalism was re-established in the Monarchy in 1861, but the Hungarians were not willing to take part in an imperial parliament representing all the territories of the Empire. In 1863–4 the Viennese government organized a Diet in Transylvania, but as the Hungarians boycotted the sessions, the Romanian and Saxon deputies constituted a majority and agreed to being separated from Hungary.[20] In this way the government tried to play off Magyars against non-Magyars. But even measures such as these could not break the Hungarian political elite. In 1865 Francis Joseph began informal talks with the leading figures of this group. The military catastrophe of 1866, the impact of the exclusion of Austria from Germany, led to the Austro-Hungarian Compromise of 1867, the political agreement between the Emperor and the Hungarian elite.[21]

The Compromise restored constitutional life in both Austria and Hungary with governments responsible to their respective Parliaments, with a high property qualification for suffrage. The system was not a personal but a real union of the two countries with a common foreign policy, a common army and common finances. These were administered by common ministers, who were not responsible to the two Parliaments. A similar Hungarian–Croatian Compromise[22] followed in 1868 which re-established the autonomy of Croatia with its own Parliament called the *Sabor*, with councillors presiding in various departments, in fact ministries which on the other hand were not responsible to the *Sabor*. Common legislation affecting the two countries went on in the Hungarian Parliament with Croatian deputies also present at these sessions. Croatia was represented in the government by a Croatian minister. With this arrangement the Croatian problem was eliminated to some extent, though it continued to be part of the national question.[23] The Croatian resistance against Hungarian dominance did not disappear. However, the royal governors in Zagreb, called Bans, appointed by the king on the recommendation of the Hungarian government, managed to maintain this arrangement, very often by suspending constitutional life. In any case the national question was reduced to the situation within Hungary (including Transylvania, which had been united with Hungary once more in 1867) and the relationship between Austria and Hungary.

THE NON-MAGYAR NATIONS FROM THE COMPROMISE TO THE BREAK-UP OF THE DUAL MONARCHY

So far a lot has been said about the ethnic composition of Hungary from the Middle Ages onwards, but without any kind of data as to the ratio of the nations to each other. So far we have refrained from using such data for lack of exact figures. The first census took place in 1851 and then regularly every ten years from 1869. It was the mother-tongue, not the nationality, that was taken into account during the census. Apart from the first census held by Austrian officials, the

Table 10.1. *Ethnic composition of Hungary, 1850–1910*

	1850 %	1880 %	1890 %	1900 %	1910 %
Hungarians	44.5	46.7	48.6	51.4	54.5
Germans	11.6	13.6	13.1	11.9	10.4
Slovaks	15.0	13.5	12.5	11.9	10.7
Romanians	17.3	17.5	17.1	16.6	16.1
Croatians ⎱	2.9	2.9	2.5	2.5	2.5
Serbians ⎰				1.2	1.1
Slovenes	5.1	4.6	4.5	3.1	3.0
Jews	0.4	0.5	0.5	—	—
Others	2.1	—	—	—	—
	1.1	1.1	1.1	1.4	1.7
Actual number in millions	11.6	13.7	15.1	16.8	18.26

results of the following ones are deemed to be questionable by foreign scholars, sometimes by Hungarians too. It is possible that certain amendments were made in favour of the Hungarians, but it is our opinion that no doctoring of the results took place on a large scale in the twentieth-century manner. Had that been so, the number and proportion of Hungarians would have been far greater. Because of a lack of other sources, even if the calculations are not completely reliable, the breakdown of the percentages offers us some indication of the numbers, which is probably not too far from reality. As Croatia was inhabited mostly by Croatians, with a significant minority of Serbians in the eastern parts and an insignificant number of Hungarians, the data given in Table 10.1 include Hungary proper (including Transylvania) but without Croatia. Only percentages are indicated, with approximate total populations given at the end of the table.[24] From 1900 the Slovenes were counted among 'Others'. The Jews also after their emancipation were classified according to mother-tongue.

As can be seen, the Hungarians constituted an absolute majority (and a slight one at that) only from 1900. In 1910, counting even Croatia, they composed only 51.5 per cent of the whole population. If the data were falsified, it was a modest effort and that is the least one can say.

On the other hand, it must be added that the percentage of non-Magyars did not correspond with their participation in political life. These proportions formed the basis of the political events and debates up to 1918.

Contemporaries regarded the national question politically as merely the relationship of Hungary to Austria and its place within the Dual

Monarchy. The meaning and evaluation of this dualistic system continues to be discussed in Hungarian historiography up to the present day, and to expand this subject would take another essay.

The point is that one section of the political elite was on the whole satisfied with dualism, because it guaranteed, or seemed to guarantee, territorial integrity. In 1875 they formed the Liberal Party, which managed, apart from 1906–10, to retain an absolute majority and therefore power in Parliament. They tried to increase Hungarian influence in affairs of 'common interest', but remained loyal to dualism. Another section of the elite, however, backed by a large mass of Hungarian voters, vehemently criticized the dualistic system. Their aim was personal union with Austria solely, based on the unity of the dynasty, but without common expenditure and with an independent customs system. The Independent Party, together with the other opposition parties, won the elections in 1904. The king tried to govern with a ministry of officials, who were planning to introduce universal suffrage. This was precisely the reason for the opposition leaders accepting the king's conditions and forming a government which continued the dualist system.[25]

Universal suffrage would have led to an increase in the numbers of non-Magyar representatives in Parliament. That is to say that the real national question was the problem of the non-Magyar nations. The Nationality Act of 1868,[26] the second after the abortive act of 1849, assured the cultural rights of the non-Magyar nations, their rights to schools in their mother-tongue, to form economic associations, banks, and so on. The government and the law tacitly recognized the existence of non-Magyar nations. A simple manifestation of this was that the banknotes in circulation bore their value not only in Hungarian, but in all the other languages spoken in Hungary. But this relative equality of rights was secondary to the principle that in a political sense only one nation existed in Hungary, the Hungarian nation, the members of which were all inhabitants of the country without difference as to race, language or denomination. This principle, already in existence in the Reform Era, as mentioned above, became one of the guiding principles of the whole political movement after 1867. The idea of the nation-state led inevitably to this result.

The Nationality Act did not satisfy the non-Magyar nations, but it could have made possible some sort of coexistence, had it been realized as to the letter and especially as to its spirit. In the first years after the Compromise the political leaders endeavoured to this end. The leading figure of the Compromise, Ferenc Deák, made an important speech in Parliament in favour of the establishment of a secondary school for Serbian speakers, supporting his argument at Novi Sad with the fact that the Serbians were equal citizens of Hungary.[27] In the course of time, however, reality became further and further removed from the letter of the law. Cultural associations such as the *Matica srpska* (founded in 1826 in Pest) existed and published periodicals, annuaries, and so on.[28] But the Slovak institution of a similar nature, the *Matica slovenská*, was banned for Panslavistic agitation in 1875.[29] Only on the economic front could the government not enforce its opinions on the various nationalities and neither could it prevent, for instance, Romanian-owned savings banks from beginning to flourish.

The various churches advanced the cause of the non-Magyar nations, the Orthodox Church for the Serbs and the majority of the Romanians, and the Uniate for the Ruthenes and the rest of the Romanians. These Churches were considered by contemporaries to be 'national' Churches. As may be seen, the Slovaks and the Germans did not have their own national Churches as they were divided in their adherence to the Catholic and Lutheran faith. But even in the latter cases the Church was not merely a place for worship in the respective languages, as their role in education was even more important. The Churches, with the exception of the Slovaks', all supported secondary schools, where the pupils were instructed in their mother-tongue. The prelates of the Church sat in the Upper House and could thus represent their nationality. State education was only just emerging and that, too, had to be held in the language of the local inhabitants. In 1883 the government decreed a law making the teaching of Hungarian compulsory in secondary schools. For elementary schools it was not compulsory until 1907. The avowed aim of the act was that every citizen in Hungary should be able to express himself in the state language, not an unusual requirement by twentieth-century standards.[30]

Contemporaries nevertheless considered the act to be a shaming instrument of Magyarization. This phenomenon has to be mentioned here and the question of natural assimilation. The idea of a nation-state was, without doubt, the ever-increasing guiding principle of the Hungarian statesmen. Consequently attempts were made to assimilate the non-Magyars. Hungarian cultural groups were established with the express aim of spreading the Hungarian language and an attachment to Hungary. Amongst these were the Hungarian cultural society for Upper Hungary (i.e. Slovakia), another one for Transylvania and a third for southern Hungary (roughly contemporary Vojvodina).[31]

The suppression of the three secondary schools teaching Slovak in 1874 (again on account of alleged Panslavistic activities) was a further sign of enforced assimilation.[32] These efforts were widely supported by Hungarian public opinion. It must be added that in fact these steps involved resistance on the part of the nations concerned.

On the other hand, it is undeniable that a natural assimilation was taking place, especially in the fast-developing towns and industrial centres. Budapest, for instance (united in 1873), which in the mid-nineteenth century was still a German city with a not insignificant non-Magyar population (Serbs, Greeks, Slovaks, etc.), after the turn of the century had become exclusively a Hungarian-speaking capital city.[33] The natural assimilation went on understandably as a result of modernization and industrialization. Therefore this affected those nations with a more modern social structure, whereas those with a more archaic structure resisted more effectively. According to the estimations of Peter Hanák, between 1890 and 1914, when modernization permeated the whole of Hungary (with the exception of Croatia), the different nations must have lost by assimilation to the Magyars more than a million people. Of these, 400,000 were Germans (in the cities), 300,000 Slovaks, 200,000 Jews, 100,000 Southern Slavs and 50,000 Romanians and Ruthenes.[34] The role of social structure can be clearly seen in these figures. Perhaps an explanation is needed merely for the number of the Slovaks. They had arrived in Budapest in large numbers to work in the building industry and in factories. Ján Bobula, a leader of a Slovak political party which after 1867 had tried to collaborate with the government, later became János Bobula, the owner of a large factory in Budapest and an esteemed citizen of the capital.[35] To be Magyarized was undoubtedly a prerequisite of an economic, political or cultural career.

Another element of the national question was the high rate of emigration to America, the United States in particular.[36] It is difficult to give precise numbers as many of the emigrants subsequently returned. It is roughly estimated that the number of emigrants who left indefinitely may have been 3 million. Between the two wars the ruling elite were actually blamed for having let the government encourage emigration and thus lose a large number of people. In fact the majority of them were non-Magyars, mainly Slovaks and Serbs, although with a significant Magyar minority. The government had in fact helped to advance emigration in the hope of getting rid of non-Magyars and unruly elements of the Magyars.

The members of the Lower House were almost exclusively Hungarian. This was the result of the high electoral census and government pressure, so convincingly exposed at the turn of the century by R. W. Seton-Watson (Scotus Viator).[37]

In fact it was aimed partly against the non-Magyars (let us remember the fear of general suffrage), but mostly against the opposing Magyar parties. Of course it is obvious that under these conditions non-Magyar politicians had little opportunity of entering the political scene or Parliament. So they preferred to boycott it. Several political parties emerged among the non-Magyar nations (with the exception of the Germans), but the Slovak and Romanian national parties distanced themselves from political life.

The situation changed at the turn of the century. Corresponding to the progress made on the economic and social front, a new political elite emerged among the Romanians and Slovaks, which rejected the political passivity, and in small numbers got into Parliament. Prime Minister István Tisza tried to reach a compromise with the Romanian National Party, which in effect represented the largest minority, with regard to political representation, schools and other cultural institutions. On a local level talks went on up to the First World War.[38]

Around 1900 there emerged within Hungarian Society a small left-wing group, centred around the periodical *Huszadik Század* (Twentieth Century)[39] which criticized the semi-feudal social structure and demanded democratic reforms, these being the most urgent national questions. Oszkár Jászi, one of their prominent leaders, dealt with the national question as well as other matters.[40] He demanded that the Nationality Act should be applied and that Hungary should be reorganized on national lines – in effect, the establishment of an eastern European Switzerland. But even this very progressive politician could not abandon the idea of territorial integrity. During the last months of the First World War he published a book expounding this solution. The Social Democrats were not able to visualize anything else either. They insisted on the principle of the Second International – one country, one labour party. For this reason they acknowledged the existence of a Croatian Social Democratic Party. But within Hungary it was only in the last few years that they were willing to establish committees within the party in order to spread propaganda amongst the workers of the non-Magyar nations.[41]

FROM TRIANON TO OCTOBER 1956

The break-up of the Dual Monarchy at the end of 1918 and the Peace Treaty of Trianon in 1920 brought about a completely new situation.[42]

The area of Hungary was reduced (excluding Croatia) from 282,000 sq. km to 93,000 sq. km and the number of inhabitants was reduced from 18 to 7.6 million. Two years later Hungary lost yet more of its western areas to Austria. The territory acquired by the partly newly formed states, Czechoslovakia, Romania and Yugoslavia, was inhabited on the whole by non-Magyar nations. As precise ethnic frontiers could not be drawn anywhere, about 3 million Magyars found themselves among the former nationalities under the sovereignty of foreign states. This was the great reversal of roles, the dominating Magyars becoming subservient to the neighbouring states. The majority of the Magyars lived in a wide belt on the other side of the frontier.

This was a serious blow to the Hungarian national consciousness. Dreams of territorial integrity vanished. The national question in a formal sense, that is, full independence from Austria, was resolved, the 'common' affairs disappeared. It now became clear that the real national question was not that of sovereignty and national customs area. Hungary had become independent (as far as a small state can preserve its independence), but one in three Magyars lived outside the country.

The new Hungary was no longer a multinational state. The number of non-Magyars dwindled significantly. The German peasants (who had not become Magyarized) represented the largest non-Magyar minority, but they were dispersed over the whole country, like the other minorities, without any territorial unity.

After the two revolutions – the democratic October Revolution of 1918, and the revolution of 1919 establishing the Soviet Republic, the system, symbolized by the name of Governor Miklós Horthy, became far more conservative than before 1918. The ruling elite, in order to legitimize its rule, began to make passionate propaganda to get the Peace Treaty of Trianon revised.[43]

Marxist historical writing of a later date speaks much about the fact that only the economic and social interests of the ruling classes were behind this revisionism: the loss of big estates, banks and factories and the desire to slow down social discontent by blaming every problem on Trianon. It is true that part of this argument is correct. But Marxist historiography refused to recognize for a long time that Trianon was a national catastrophe felt by everyone who had relatives in the neighbouring countries, or those who had fled from there.

The illegal Communist Party recognized this fact, and denounced Trianon as an imperialist peace treaty and demanded national self-determination. The solution, it claimed, would follow in the period after the victory of socialist revolution, which would automatically solve all problems.[44]

The legal political parties in Hungary were technically in favour of territorial revision. This, however, raised several problems. Given the economic situation of the country (military restrictions, etc.), nobody could expect a revision realized by military force, although this idea was not foreign to certain right-wing circles. The majority was for peaceful revision with the approval of the big powers. But this brought about question number two: revision of the frontiers on the basis of ethnic groups, or the reconstitution of all of pre-war Hungary, with the exclusion of Croatia? No one seriously hoped for its return. Left-wing parties, including the Social Democrats, opted for a peaceful revision on the basis of ethnic lines. This solution was in fact accepted in government circles, though official or semi-official propaganda emphasized complete revision. The manipulation of public opinion in favour of revision and against Trianon, which became widespread in the newspaper, schools and from the late twenties on the radio, naturally made an impression on the population. The necessity of the revision of the treaties on an ethnic basis was accepted by left-wing parties and circles. As the former entente powers had refused to take into account the revision of Trianon, Hungarian governments began to seek the help of first Italy, then the Germany of Hitler, enemies of the Versailles system. With their consent and aid Hungary regained a significant part of its previously lost territories, from Czechoslovakia in 1938 and 1939, from Romania in 1940 and from Yugoslavia in 1941.[45] With the exception of the last, it was all achieved without military intervention. In the case of Czechoslovakia it was with the tacit consent of Great Britain and France. As these territorial changes were only transitory, we shall dispense with precise data. But it must be added that it was only in the first case, that of the southern part of Slovakia, that the changes were justifiable ethnically, 80 per cent of the population being Magyar.

In the case of northern Transylvania, Magyars were only in a relative majority; Subcarpathian Ruthenia (Carpatho-Ukraine in the former Soviet Union) was inhabited by Ruthenes (Ukrainians) and in the southern areas the population was so mixed that none of the ethnic groups had a significant relative majority.

Nevertheless, national enthusiasm rose high in the years of reoccupation. Less notice was taken of the fact that Hungary had once again become a multinational country, albeit with a massive Magyar majority of about 80 per cent. These achievements happened simultaneously with Hungary's growing involvement with preparations for war on the side of Germany. The co-operation with Germany was undoubtedly built on a mutual economic need on both sides, Hungary gaining an open market for its agricultural goods and Germany getting food, badly needed in the last years of the war.[46] In order to recover the territories and to conserve them, the Hungarian government and Hungary committed themselves on the side of the Axis powers and had to share their fate in the victory over fascism.

After the defeat of Hungary the frontiers of 1937 were re-established according to the stipulation of the armistice. The change was sanctioned by the Peace Treaty of Paris 1947, with one addition. Three more villages went to Czechoslovakia on the right bank of the Danube near Bratislava. The Košice government, supported by all the political parties of the Czechoslovak government, including the Communists, was to deprive the Hungarians of their rights of citizenship (apart from the active supporters of the resistance movement), and condemned them to resettlement in Hungary. Hungary itself was in a desperate situation, having lost almost half of its national wealth.[47]

The victorious powers were not willing to allow a one-sided expulsion of Hungarians and made an agreement at the beginning of 1946 concerning an exchange of inhabitants. To this end 90,000–100,000 Hungarians were transferred to Hungary in exchange for 70,000 Slovaks who were returned to Czechoslovakia. At the same time, in accordance with the Potsdam decisions, all Germans had to leave Hungary. This measure was suspended in 1948, by which time 200,000 Germans had left (or had escaped before the end of the war), the remaining slight majority regaining its civic rights gradually in the 1950s.[48]

After the events of February 1948 in Czechoslovakia, Hungarians gradually regained civic rights, whilst in the neighbouring countries Leninist-Stalinist policy towards national minorities, as it was called, was able to guarantee certain civic rights to Hungarians. It seemed that the national problem had been resolved on the basis of Marxism-Leninism as the construction of socialism proceeded.

The events of October 1956 in Hungary alarmed Hungary's neighbours, who feared a new wave of nationalist recriminations and revisionism. This did not take place; some 200,000 Hungarians left the country for the West.

The number of non-Magyar nations decreased with the partial expulsion of the Germans and continues to decrease due to natural assimilation, although the government, especially since 1968, has made serious efforts to preserve the minorities, promoting their cultural activities in various ways, helping them to keep their national identity. But as was the case after 1918 the question of the Hungarian nations is no longer a national question. Demographic stagnation, indeed the decrease in the population growth in Hungary, seems more of a threat. The existing situation, namely that every one in three Hungarians lives outside Hungary in neighbouring countries and all over the world, with problems peculiar to those countries, remains a national problem.[49] But this is an issue not covered by this essay.

NOTES

1 R. A. Kann and Zdeněk V. David, *The Peoples of the Eastern Habsburg Lands, 1926–1918* (Seattle, Wash. and London, 1984), p. 4.

2 *Magyarország története*, vol. I: *Elözmények és magyar történet 1242–ig.* (History of Hungary: Prehistory and Hungarian History up to 1242), ed. G. Székely (Budapest, 1984); Gy. Szekfü, *Etat et nation* (Paris, 1945); E. Flachbarth, *A History of Hungary's Nationalities* (Budapest, 1944); Z. Ács, *Nemezetiségek a történelmi Magyarországon* (Nationalities in Historical Hungary) (Budapest, 1984).

3 *Magyarország története*, vol. III: *1526–1686*, ed. Zs. P. Pach (Budapest, 1985).

4 E. Arató, *A nemzetiségi kérdés története Magyarországon* (History of the Nationality Question in Hungary), vol. I: *1790–1840*; vol. II: *1840–1848* (Budapest, 1960).

5 E. Niederhauser, *The Rise of Nationality in Eastern Europe* (Budapest, 1981).

6 Z. I. Tóth, 'Quelques problèmes de l'état multinational dans la Hongrie d'avant 1848', *Acta Historica Academiae Scientiarum Hungaricae 1955*, fasc. 1–3.

7 *Magyarország története*, vol. V: *1790–1848*, ed. G. Mérei (Budapest, 1980).

8 Ibid., vol. V/1, p. 486.

9 M. Csáky, *Von der Aufklärung zum Liberalismus. Studien zum Frühliberalismus in Ungarn* (Vienna, 1981).

10 G. E. Rothenberg, *The Austrian Military Border in Croatia, 1522–1747* (Urbana, Ill., 1960); Rothenberg, *The Military Border in Croatia 1740–1881* (Chicago, 1966); V. Dedijer, I. Božić, S. Cirković and M. Ekmečić, *History of Yugoslavia* (New York, 1974).

11 *Magyarország története 1790–1848*.

12 M. Wesselényi, *Szózat a magyar és szláv nemzetiség ügyében* (A Voice in the Case of the Hungarian and Slavic Nationality) (Bukarest [Leipzig], 1843); E. Kovács, *Szemben a történelemmel. A nemzetiségi kérdés a régi Magyarországon* (In Face of History: The Nationality Question in Ancient Hungary) (Budapest, 1977); *Magyarország története 1790–1848*.

13 G. Barany, *Stephen Széchenyi and the Awakening of Hungarian Nationalism 1791–1841* (Princeton, N. J., 1968).

14 E. Arató, *A magyarországi nemzetiségek nemzeti ideológiája* (The National Ideology of the Nationalities of Hungary) (Budapest, 1983); *A magyar nacionalizmus kialakulása és története* (Formation and History of Hungarian Nationalism) (Budapest, 1964); W. Felczak, *Węgierska polityka narodowościowa przed wybuchem powstania 1848 roku* (The Hungarian Policy with Regard to the Nationalities

before the Beginning of the 1848 Rising) (Wrocław, Warsaw and Kraków, 1964).

15 G. Spira, *A magyar forradalom 1848–49-ben* (The Hungarian Revolution in 1848–49) (Budapest, 1959); I. Deak, *The Lawful Revolution: Louis Kossuth and the Hungarians 1848–1849* (New York, 1979); E. W. Stroup, *Hungary in Early 1848: The Constitutional Struggle against Absolutism in Contemporary Eyes* (Buffalo and Atlanta, Ga, 1977).

16 G. Spira, *A nemzetiségi kérdés a negyvennyolcas forradalom Magyarországán* (The Nationality Question in Hungary at the time of the Revolution of 1848) (Budapest, 1980); Z. I. Tóth, 'The nationality problem in Hungary in 1848–1849', *Acta Historica Academiae Scientiarum Hungaricae 1955*, fasc. 1–3.

17 *Magyarország története 1848–1890*, ed. E. Kovács (Budapest, 1979).

18 R. Gragger, *Die Donau-Konföderation. Ludwig Kossuths Plan einer Lösung des Donaustaatenproblems* (Berlin, 1919); L. Lajtor, *Kossuth dunai konföderációs terve és elözményei* (Kossuth's Plan of a Danubian Confederation and Its Antecedents) (Budapest, 1944).

19 G. Szabad, *Forradalom és kiegyezés válaszutján* (On the Crossing of Roads between Revolution and Compromise) (Budapest, 1967).

20 M. Mester, *Az autonóm Erdély és a román nemzeti követelések az 1863–64. évi nagyszebeni országgyülésen* (Autonomous Transylvania and the Romanian National Claims in the Parliament of 1863–64 in Sibiu) (Budapest, 1936); *Erdély története 1830-tól napjainkig* (History of Transylvania from 1830 to Our Days), ed. Z. Szász (Budapest, 1986).

21 *Magyarország története 1848–1890*; T. Mayer (ed.), *Der österreichisch-ungarische Ausgleich von 1867: seine Grundlagen und Auswirkungen* (Munich, 1968).

22 V. Krestić, *Hrvatsko-Ugarska nagodba 1868 godine* (The Croatian–Hungarian Compromise of 1848) (Beograd, 1969); W. Felczak, *Ugoda węgiersko-chorwacka 1868 roku* (The Hungarian–Croatian Compromise of 1868) (Wroclaw, Warsaw and Kraków, 1969).

23 J. Šidak, M. Gross, I. Karaman and D. Šepić, *Provijest hrvatskog naroda g. 1860–1914* (History of the Croatian Nation) (Zagreb, 1968); V. Jászi, *Tanulmányok a magyar-horvát közjogi viszony köréböl* (Studies concerning the Hungarian–Croatian Constitutional Relation) (Budapest, 1897).

24 *Magyarország története 1848–1890*, vol. VI/1, p. 477; *Magyarország története 1890–1918*, ed. P. Hanák (Budapest, 1978), vol. VII/1, p. 414.

25 *Magyarország története 1890–1918*; F. Pölöskei, *A koalició felbomlása és a nemzeti munkapárt megalakulása 1909–1910* (The Dissolution of the Coalition and the Formation of the National Party of Work) (Budapest, 1963).

26 1868: XLIV. *Törvénycikk a nemzetiségi egyenjoguság tárgyában* (Act Concerning the Equality in Rights of the Nationalities), *Corpus Juris Hungarici. 1836–1868. évi törvénycikkek* (Budapest, 1896), pp. 409–94; P. Body, *Joseph Eötvös and the Modernization of Hungary, 1840–1870* (Philadelphia, 1972).

27 G. G. Kemény (ed.), *Iratok a nemzetiségi kérdés történetéhez Magyarországon a dualizmus korában* (Documents Concerning the History of the Nationality Question in Hungary in the Period of Dualism), vol. 1 (Budapest, 1952), pp. 292–4; B. K. Király, *Ferenc Deák* (Boston, Mass., 1975).

28 *Matica srpska 1826–1926* (The Serbian Matica [Mother]) (Novi Sad, 1927).

29 B. Kostický, 'Zrušenie Matice slovenskej a ďalšia maďarizácia' (The abolition of the Slovak Matica [Mother] and the Continued Magyarization), in Kostický, *Matica slovenská v našich dejinách* (The Slovak Matica in Our [Slovak] History) (Bratislava, 1963).

30 I. Dolmányos, *A 'Lex Apponyi'. Az 1907. évi iskolatörvények* (The School Acts of 1907)(Századok, 1968), no. 3–4; S. Köte, *Közoktatás és pedagógia az abszolutizmus és dualizmus korában* (Public Education and Pedagogy in the Age of Absolutism and Dualism) (Budapest, 1975).

31 X.Y. [Lajos Mocsáry], *A közmüvelödési egyletek és a nemzetiségi kérdés* (The Cultural Societies and the Nationality Question) (Budapest, 1886); Kovács, *Szemben a történelemmel.*

32 L. Ruttkay, *A felvidéki szlovák középiskolák megszüntetése 1874-ben* (The Dissolution of Secondary Schools Teaching in Slovak Language in 1874 in Slovakia) (Budapest, 1939).

33 *Budapest története* (History of Budapest), vol. VI, ed. K. Vörös (Budapest, 1978).

34 *Magyarország története 1890–1918*, vol. VII/1, p. 416; P. Hanák, 'Polgárosodás es asszimiláció Magyarországon a XIX. században' (Bourgeois development and assimilation in Hungary in the XIXth century), *Történelmi Szemle*, 1974, no. 1–2; F. Glatz, *Nemzeti kultúra – kulturált nemzet 1867–1987* (National Culture – Civilized Nation) (Budapest, 1988); G. Barany, 'From aristocratic to proletarian nationalism', in P. F. Sugar and Ivo J. Lederer (eds.), *Nationalism in Eastern Europe* (Seattle, Wash. and London, 1969); F. Gottas, *Ungarn im Zeitalter des Hochliberalismus. Studien zur Tisza-Ära, 1875–1890* (Vienna, 1976); P. Hanák, *Magyarország a Monarchiában. Tanulmányok* (Hungary in the Monarchy: Studies) (Budapest, 1975); Hanák, 'A magyar nacionalizmus néhány problémája a századforduló idején' (Some problems of Hungarian nationalism at the turn of the century), *Történelmi Szemle*, 1960, no. 2–3; K. Gulya, *A horvát kérdés a dualista Magyarországon az elsö világháború elötti években 1908–1914* (The Croatian Question in Dualist Hungary in the Years before World War I) (Szeged, 1972); I. Diószegi, *A magyar külpolitika utjai. Tanulmányok* (The Ways of Hungarian Foreign Policy: Studies) (Budapest, 1984); for broader perspective, E. Gellner, *Nations and Nationalism* (Oxford, 1983); R. Pearson, *National Minorities in Eastern Europe 1848–1945* (London, 1983).

35 B. Kostický, *Nová škola slovenská* (The New Slovak School)(Bratislava, 1959); H. Kálnoki, *Bobula János szereplése közéletünkben* (The Role of János Bobula in Our Public Life) (Budapest, 1879).

36 J. Puskás, *From Hungary to the United States, 1880–1914* (Budapest, 1982).

37 R. W. Seton Watson, *The Southern Slav Question and the Habsburg Monarchy* (London, 1911); Watson, *Corruption and Reform in Hungary: A Study in Electoral Practice* (London, 1911); H. Seton Watson and C. Seton Watson, *The Making of New Europe: R. W. Seton Watson and the Last Years of Austria-Hungary* (Seattle, Wash., 1981).

38 *Erdély története 1830-tól napjainkig*; Z. Szász, 'A Tisza-féle magyar-román "paktumtárgyalások" feltételrendszere, 1910–1914' (The system of preconditions of the Romanian–Hungarian 'pact-talks' conducted by Tisza), *Történelmi Szemle*, 1984, no. 1–2; F. Pölöskei, *Tisza István* (Budapest, 1988); F. Albrecht,

Forrástanulmányok gróf Tisza István nemzetiségi politikájához (Studies in the Sources of the Nationality Policy of Count István Tisza) (Lugos, 1933).

39 G. Litván and L. Szücs (eds.), *A szociológia elsö magyar mühelye. A Huszadik Század köre* (The First Hungarian Workshop of Sociology: The Circle of the Review Twentieth Century, 2 vols. (Budapest, 1973); A. Pók (ed.), *A Huszadik Század körének történetfelfogása* (The Historical Conception of the Circle of the Review Twentieth Century) (Budapest, 1982); Z. Horváth, *Die Jahrhundertwende in Ungarn* (Neuwied on Rhine, 1966).

40 P. Hanák, *Jászi Oszkár dunai patriotizmus* (The Danubian Patriotism of Oszkár Jászi) (Budapest, 1985).

41 *Studies on the History of the Hungarian Working-Class Movement, 1867–1966*, ed. H. Vass (Budapest, 1977).

42 Zsuzsa L. Nagy, *A párizsi békekonferencia és Magyarország 1918–1919* (The Paris Peace Conference and Hungary)(Budapest, 1965); M. Ormos, *Padovától Trianonig* (From Padua to Trianon) (Budapest, 1983).

43 *Magyarország története 1918–1919. 1919–1945*, ed. G. Ránki (Budapest, 1976); G. Juhász, *Hungarian Foreign Policy, 1919–1945* (Budapest, 1979); S. Balogh, 'A bethleni konszolidáció és a magyar 'neonacionalizmus' (The consolidation under the premiership of Bethlen and Hungarian 'neonationalism'), *Történelmi Szemle*, 1972, no. 1–2; Glatz, *Nemzeti kultúra*.

44 See note 41.

45 *Magyarország története 1918–1919. 1919–1945*.

46 G. Ránki, *Economy and Foreign Policy: The Struggle of the Great Powers for Hegemony in the Danube Valley 1919–1939* (Boston, Mass. and New York, 1983).

47 S. Balogh, *A népi demokratikus Magyarország külpolitikája 1945–1947* (The Foreign Policy of the Hungarian People's Democracy) (Budapest, 1982).

48 L. Kővágó, *Nemzetiségek a mai Magyarországon* (Nationalities in Present-Day Hungary), 2nd edn (Budapest, 1981).

49 A general view of present-day situation: J. F. Brown, *Eastern Europe and Communist Rule* (Durham, N.C. and London, 1988).

ELEVEN

THE UNION OF DALMATIA WITH NORTHERN CROATIA: A CRUCIAL QUESTION OF THE CROATIAN NATIONAL INTEGRATION IN THE NINETEENTH CENTURY

MIRJANA GROSS

THE TERRITORIES INVOLVED IN THE INTEGRATION OF THE CROATIAN NATION

When the republics of Venice and Dubrovnik ceased to exist and the Napoleonic era came to an end, most of the territory where the unification of the Croatian nation was to take place belonged to the Habsburg Monarchy. Northern civilian Croatia and Slavonia had traditionally enjoyed autonomy within the crown of Hungary, but this virtually came to an end with the Magyar constitutional laws of 1848. These changes therefore provoked opposition to Magyar domination from the Croatian national movement, and resulted in a revolt led by the *Ban* (traditional governor) Jelačić with soldiers from the Military Frontier.

The nobility, who comprised the *populus politicus* of Croatia and Slavonia, had based their arguments for autonomy on historical claims deriving from the medieval kingdom of Croatia centred on Dalmatia. Their theorists believed that their predecessors had recognized the Hungarian king in the twelfth century by a treaty, and thus preserved the continuity of the Triune Kingdom, that is, the kingdoms of Dalmatia, Croatia and Slavonia. The Magyar interpretation, on the other hand, considered Croatian territory as acquired by conquest, *partes subiugatae or adnexae*, and thus entitled to no modern autonomy based on historic rights.

These noble claims for the re-establishment of a Croatian state with boundaries predating the Turkish conquest, were adapted by the elite now leading the national movement. The territory they claimed comprised first of all civilian Croatia and Slavonia; the Military Frontier, which was under military administration from Vienna; and

Dalmatia. Since the Habsburg Monarchy consisted of two kinds of territory, nations which had a 'historical' reality and which were now within Habsburg borders, and 'unhistorical' nations which had not had a prior state structure, and since the Croats were such a historical nation, it made sense for the leaders of the national movement to use the nobles' historical ideology, weeding out its feudal features to adapt it for modern development. Alongside natural rights, the argument from historic right provided important grounds for claiming an extensive autonomy, which would enable the Croatian elite to direct the process of modernization in its own interest, without interference from Austro-German or Magyar ruling elites; but this claim to autonomy was only credible if the historic territories could be reconstituted. The roots of the Croatian national revival are thus to be found in the 'Illyrian' movement of the years before 1848, and in 1848–9 itself when there was a brief independent government.

The Illyrian movement in northern Croatia as the first stage of the Croatian national revival used the name Illyrian because of its centuries-old continuity from Roman times, and especially since the Renaissance. It was needed to overcome the deeply rooted regionalism of the Croatian lands, and the ideology which was developed originated from the Croatian cultural heritage, Croatian state-right and the idea of the community of Slavs. The leaders of this movement created the most important national and cultural institutions, a standardized language and the framework for future political struggles. The main idea of Illyrianism – to create a common culture for all South Slavs on the basis of a unique literary language – was not adopted into the constitutional programme of the nations on South Slav territory. Therefore from 1848 onwards the terms Croatian and Yugoslav replaced Illyrian to designate the national movement. The Yugoslav ideology of the National Party in northern Croatia, especially from the 1860s onwards, included ideas that were central to Croatian national integration, and the main mobilizing factor for the union of northern Croatia and Dalmatia.

'NATIONALISTS' VERSUS DALMATIAN 'AUTONOMISTS'

The question of a union between northern Croatia and Dalmatia was of great importance in the politics and ideology of state-right, but conditions for the national movement in the two provinces were completely different. After the fall of the republic of Venice, which included Dalmatia, in 1797, nearly every session of the Croatian Estates in Zagreb had insisted upon the union of the kingdom of

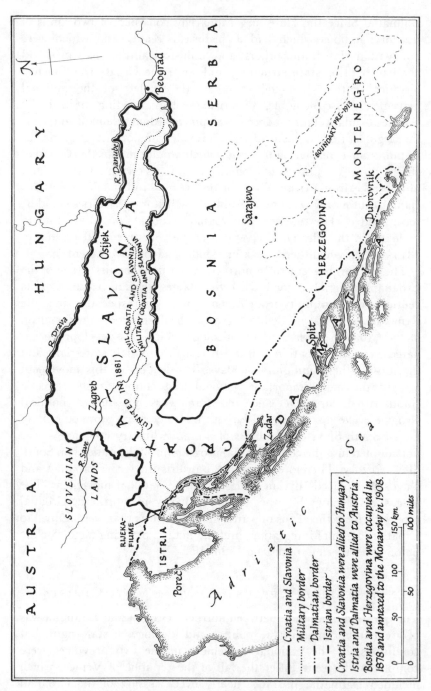

2 The Croatian lands in Austria-Hungary (1867–1918)

Dalmatia with those of Croatia and Slavonia. These gravamina were intensified in 1848 when the principle of the integrity of the Triune Kingdom was adopted implicitly by the Viennese court, with the appointment of Ban Jelačić as governor of Dalmatia. In 1850 the King and Emperor, Francis Joseph, held out hopes that the deputies of Dalmatia and the Diet of Croatia and Slavonia might negotiate on this issue, but in reality there was of course no political activity at all under the neo-Absolutist regime.

Under the Habsburg Monarchy public awareness of the problem of uniting northern Croatia and Dalmatia began when the institution of the *Reichsrat* (Imperial Parliament) was reinforced in 1860. The two deputies from Croatia and Slavonia, Bishop Joseph George Strossmayer and a businessman, Ambrose Vraniczany, stressed the historical political identity of Croatia, derived from the 'very ancient liberal' institutions of the medieval kingdom, insisted that Dalmatia was an integral part of Croatia, and that a union was necessary since Francis Joseph had promised it in 1850. The Dalmatian deputy, Francesco Borelli, argued on the other hand for the historical autonomy of the kingdom of Dalmatia, stressing that it had no connection whatsoever with Croatia. Though he admitted that the majority of the population was Slav in language, mentality and outlook, he pointed out that its higher culture was Italian. While Borelli saw in the high qualities of the Dalmatian intelligentsia the capacity for leading modern Dalmatia, Strossmayer denounced this very intelligentsia for having separated itself from the common people and its language.[1] The *Reichsrat* sessions therefore saw formulated for the first time the contrasting ideologies of the Slav-Dalmatian 'Autonomists', vehement opponents of union with Croatia, and the 'Annexationists' or 'Nationalists' who pressed for this union.

In 1860 the Vienna government issued the October Diploma, which ignored the constitutional claims of the Croatian leaders advanced since 1848. A conference meeting in Zagreb under the presidency of the Ban to prepare constitutional proposals to present to the Croatian Diet therefore appealed to the king to allow union with 'sister Dalmatia', which it claimed had been torn away from Croatia and Slavonia and should now, by historical and national right, come under the same 'constitutional roof'. In reply the king granted permission for representatives from Dalmatia to take part in the conference to discuss the issue. Since the Dalmatians boycotted the conference, the Croatian delegates claimed the union from the king on the basis of his sovereign authority and his invitation to the Dalmatian deputies to the Croatian Diet, thus guaranteeing the kingdom its state-right and legal integrity.[2] The king then ordered the new Dalmatian Diet to debate the union with Croatia, but this was impossible because the majority opposed it. The Croatian Diet therefore voted an address to the king asking for the union of the Triune Kingdom and protesting that the Dalmatian Diet had sent its deputies direct to the *Reichsrat*, regardless of Croatia. It denounced the interference of an 'alien' government in Dalmatian afairs – that is, the cabinet headed by Anton von Schmerling, who supported the Autonomists – and demanded the release of persons arrested as 'political defendants' for speaking out in favour of the union, together with the halting of any further proceedings for the same offence.[3]

Presenting itself as *nos reliquiae Regnorum Dalmatiae, Croatiae et Slavoniae*, the Diet insisted on the integrity of the Triune Kingdom, consisting of civilian Croatia and Slavonia, the Military Frontier (united to civilian Croatia and Slavonia only in 1881), Dalmatia with Dubrovnik and Kotor, the islands of Quarnero, a large portion of Istria, portions of Styria, and Bosnia and Herzegovina.[4] The majority of the Diet rejected the October Diploma as a flagrant transgression of Croatian state-right, and refused to send its deputies to the *Reichsrat*. The Diet argued that the old ties with Hungary had been broken in 1848, but that the Triune Kingdom would be willing to ally itself with Hungary on the basis of equal rights between the two states. This conception of the statehood of the Triune Kingdom was as unacceptable to the king as to the Magyar elite. Francis Joseph therefore dissolved the Croatian Diet. In his decree, he made it clear that the union of Croatia and Slavonia with Dalmatia, as arranged by the two Diets, would depend on the Croatian Diet in future making decisions in conformity with the organization of the Monarchy following the February Patent of 1861.[5]

THE DALMATIAN BACKGROUND

By the resolution of the Congress of Vienna in 1815, Dalmatia had become a part of the Habsburg Monarchy. Austrian Dalmatia consisted of a group of territories: Venetian Dalmatia, so-called Venetian Albania (the region of Boka Kotorska – Bocche di Cattaro), and the republic of Dubrovnik (Ragusa), abolished by Napoleon as an independent state in 1808. Venetian Dalmatia in its turn was composed of different regions. First there were the parts of the ancient kingdom of Croatia, which from 1409 onwards was gradually occupied by Venice but then partly conquered by the Turks in the sixteenth century, leaving Venice in possession of cities on the Adriatic coast, and the islands. In the middle of the seventeenth century Venice's territory was somewhat enlarged, 'the old acquisition', followed by the 'new' at the end of the seventeenth century, and the 'newest' at the beginning of the eighteenth century.

The differences between the old and new territories were potentially significant because the type of society characteristic of the old parts was not extended to the new. In order to organize defence against the Turks in the new territories there had to be a military border with a military-administrative system. It was a society of free peasant-soldiers on state land, only the higher strata of which were gradually integrated into the urban society of the 'old acquisition'. Under French occupation the land became the property of the owners of larger estates, and the peasants. So Venetian Dalmatia had two social systems: the city communes of the coast and the islands, and the peasant society of the hinterland. These two social structures had a deep influence on the Croatian 'national revival' in Dalmatia.[6]

A specifically Croatian ethnic consciousness in this peasant society which preceded a sense of national feeling was not able to guarantee a dynamic process of Croatian national integration. Only the bourgeoisie of the coastal cities created new economic and social relations and could be the predominant influence in this development; but the circumstances were extremely unpropitious for this to take place. During the Venetian, French and Austrian administrations the language of culture and public life was Italian. Dalmatia was grouped with the provinces of Lombardy until 1859, and Venice until 1866, and the latter supplied Dalmatia with officials for its bureaucracy. The schools were Italian and the intellectuals studied at Italian universities, mainly Padua. The majority of the Italian-speaking bourgeoisie in Dalmatia was familiar with the Croatian or Serbian idiom and used it in contact with the peasants, but they had never learned the literary language standardized by the leaders of the Illyrian movement in northern Croatia.

Nevertheless, cultural and commercial contact with the northern Italian provinces, particularly Trieste, and the Italian literary culture of Dalmatia, did not create an Italian national consciousness among the educated strata (with the exception of settlers from Italy). The urban bourgeoisie of the coast was aware of its Slav origin, but felt different from the Slav-speaking common people. The urban elites thought of themselves as belonging to the 'Slav-Dalmatian' nation, existing only in Dalmatia. These Autonomists, opponents of the union with northern Croatia, still maintained the ethos of traditional municipalism. They saw in the city-commune the supreme expression of culture, and for them the framework of their life could not extend beyond the province of Dalmatia. It must be stressed that the cities were very small. Only two of them had more than 10,000 inhabitants. Split (Spalato), the largest, grew from 12,093 in 1857 to 14,513 in 1880. The administrative centre Zadar (Zara) only reached approximately 10,000 inhabitants in 1880. The urban population was formed from what remained of the municipal patriciate, and the new bourgeoisie: merchants, shipowners, the bureaucracy and intelligentsia, craftsmen. There were also many peasants. The privileged elite invested its capital in land cultivated by peasant-tenants. A 'Slav-Dalmatian' ideology was useful only to the richer urban circles in their privileged social position, but they were too narrow and socially too exclusive to impose their interests on the other social strata. After the unification of Italy this oligarchy developed a completely Italian national consciousness and was a small, though economically strong, Italian minority with irredentist tendencies.

SLAV NATIONALISM IN DALMATIA c. 1830–1861

In the 1830s and 1840s, the precursors of 'national revival' emerged in Dalmatia. The revue *Zora Dalmatinska* (Dalmatian Dawn) was a symptom of this development. But the influence of Illyrianism from Zagreb as a Croatian national centre was feeble and had no impact on the shaping of an organized national movement. Although the movement for union was strong in northern Croatia the events of 1848 resulted in no change in Dalmatia. Appeals from the district councils and communes of Croatia to the communes of Dalmatia were generally useless. The future Autonomists in the commune councils were legitimists or favoured the annexation of Dalmatia to Venice. It must be stressed that the Austrian constitution of April 1848 included Dalmatia as part of the Austrian lands.[7]

Conditions changed with some slight economic progress in the fifties based on viticulture and shipping, which fostered the emergence of a liberal middle class and an intelligentsia. The deep gulf between the Italian-speaking oligarchy and the Croatian- or Serbian-speaking common people, that is, a society shaped by its highest and lowest strata, was not in their interest.

In 1860–1, after the collapse of the neo-Absolutist regime in Vienna, groups from the ranks of the urban liberal bourgeoisie and intelligentsia, and the lay priests and Franciscans of rural peasant society, came forward as Nationalists or Annexationists in contrast to the Slav-Dalmatian ideology, which presupposed the existence of a Dalmatian nation. In their eyes this ideology was isolationist and would lead to the Italianization of Dalmatia. Instead they emphasized the Slav, South Slav, Croat and Serb nationality of the overwhelming majority of the Dalmatian population; that is, they identified nationally with the population of Croatia and Slavonia, and with the Slav south in general.

While the Autonomists believed that the progress of Dalmatia depended on the Italian-speaking bourgeoisie with their high economic and cultural level, and not on the uneducated and poor Slav majority, the Nationalists believed in the right of this majority to direct their own destiny. They argued that the Italian-speaking elite were only a small minority in an essentially Slav peasant province.

The majority of the Dalmatian peasants were 'colons' who owned no property and were tenants on the 'master's' land, giving him a fixed portion of their produce, mainly grapes. Some of the colonate were small proprietors. The relationship between landowners – the urban bourgeoisie and the Church – and the colons varied in different parts of Dalmatia. The whole structure inhibited systematic production for the market and entailed hunger and malnutrition for most of the peasant population. Some Nationalists who spoke in the name of the common people were also landowners with colons, and they did not intend to liquidate the colonate, which was in fact preserved until the end of the Monarchy. Although only a small proportion of the peasants had voting rights, they were useful in election campaigns because they were totally dependent on their masters.[8]

It needs to be remembered that Dalmatia was the most backward country of the Habsburg Monarchy, with the highest proportion of the population engaged in agriculture – 86.1 per cent in 1890. The next most backward land was Croatia and Slavonia, with 84.6 per cent in agriculture in 1890.[9]

The Autonomists were the first group to organize themselves politically, with the help of the bureaucracy and the Schmerling regime. In 1860–1 the Nationalists too became active. A number of the intelligentsia entered public life and helped to formulate variants of the Nationalist ideology. In these years of preparation for the national revival, contacts and consultation between the Nationalists in different regions and localities created, step by step, the National Party of Dalmatia, the partner of the National Party of Croatia.

In their early polemics, the Nationalists denounced the Autonomist idea that the Dalmatians were Slavs by nationality and Italian by culture, stressing that the great majority of the population did not know Italian at all, and that the ordinary people could only reach a higher level of education in their own language. The real political conflict began in December 1860, when the conference in Zagreb demanded the union of Dalmatia with Croatia and Slavonia, and Francis Joseph answered with his invitation to the Dalmatians to come and discuss this issue with the conference. But the Autonomist bureaucracy and the city communes objected to this political union, and proposed instead that the Dalmatian Diet should decide on this issue, because it was sure that the Autonomists would have the majority. In agreement with the Minister of State Anton von Schmerling, the governor of Dalmatia, General Mamula, nominated Autonomists as representatives of Dalmatia for the Zagreb conference – and they of course refused to go. Mamula declared himself against union, because of its adverse political consequences for the whole state and because only a minority wanted this union; Schmerling agreed with him; and thus the scene was set for the persecution of the Nationalists. In the meantime thirty-nine communes, led by Zadar and Split, joined the protest action against the union, and a delegation was allowed to come before the king. Much later the Nationalists organized a similar action in favour of the union, consisting of communes only from the Dubrovnik and Kotor districts, but they succeeded in getting support for their cause in other communes too before the Dalmatian Diet opened.[10]

The February Patent of 1861 had instituted the Dalmatian Diet, similar to other Diets in the Austrian part of the Monarchy. It had forty-three deputies and two virilists (the Catholic and Orthodox high dignitaries), and was composed of four houses (curias): one each for the largest taxpayers, the cities, and the chambers of commerce and industry, and the 'exterior' curia consisting of the rural communes. In all but the latter there were direct elections with a tax-paying franchise. For the exterior curia elections were indirect, with every 500 male taxpayers voting for an electoral college which then chose the deputy. The election was valuable even with a low turn-out at the first round; with the authorities' help in 1861 the Autonomists were able to hinder the political activity of the Nationalists and win the elections. Furthermore, the Executive Committee of the Diet was entirely under the Autonomists' control.[11]

After the defeat of the Nationalists, the authorities tried to stop their activity by intimidating them with accusations of high treason against some of the proponents of union, and by removing minor officials and teachers to other positions. In the meantime the majority of the Diet decided against sending their representatives to the Croatian Diet in its discussion of union, thus committing itself to the autonomy of Dalmatia. A delegation of Nationalist deputies therefore went to Vienna to protest against the decision of the Autonomist majority, and a delegation of Autonomists followed them. The delegation from the Croatian Diet, claiming amongst other things union with Dalmatia, was already there and all of them met on the order of the King-Emperor, but naturally this had no result.

SLAV NATIONALISM AND YUGOSLAVISM IN 1861

Several groups of writers and pamphleteers were formulating a Nationalist ideology and political programme around 1860–1, with a view to stirring up a national consciousness among the Italianized Dalmatian bourgeoisie.[12] However, the national, integrationist ideology preached by the Nationalists was not homogeneous: rather, it reflected the historical development of different Dalmatian regions and social structures. Therefore, the South Slav ideology of urban Dalmatia, a Croatian ideology reflecting peasant society, a special Slav ideology espoused by Dubrovnik as continuing the tradition of the independent republic, some particularist tendencies in the districts of Dubrovnik and Boka Kotorska, and a Serbian national integrationist ideology, can all be discerned.[13]

The crucial question for the success of the Nationalist movement was the conflict between the Autonomist oligarchy, wishing to preserve its social privileges, and the weak middle classes wanting to eliminate this predominance by liberalizing social relations. To the Nationalists, the main reason for the deep gulf between the Italianized cities and the Slav peasants was the language barrier which prevented communication between the higher and lower strata. They accused the educated elites of ignoring the need to educate the common people and condemning them to poverty and illiteracy. Therefore the Nationalists wanted to educate the common people in their own language.

The levels of illiteracy were appalling and persistent. In 1880 there was 89.3 per cent illiteracy in Dalmatia, which fell to 78 per cent in 1900. Even in urban Dalmatia literacy was at a low level: the population of Split in 1880 was over 90 per cent illiterate, while the coastal city communes averaged 85 per cent. In the peasant hinterland there was 95 per cent illiteracy. The revivalist movement accordingly made a great effort to open and organize primary schools. In 1867–8 there were 217 schools, with 126 using the Croatian or Serbian language for instruction, 26 Italian, and 65 a mixture.[14] Although there was a growing number of schools they were not successful in combating illiteracy. Until the beginning of the national revival few schools could provide instruction in Croatian or Serbian, so only a negligible proportion of peasant boys learned to read and write, chiefly from priests. During the first years of the revival it was difficult to recruit teachers for schools using Croatian or Serbian as the language of instruction because they were trained in Italian schools. The education of the peasant population also had to surmount the usual difficulties associated with poverty: no school buildings or proper rooms, bad roads, parents needing the children as shepherds, and the reluctance to educate girls.

The urban Nationalists, who also had to learn the Slav idiom themselves because they were educated exclusively in Italian, thought this 'nationalization' should proceed only gradually. The intelligentsia of urban Dalmatia saw in the common people suitable material for a common liberal culture centred on the cities, whereas the conservative intelligentsia with peasant ties, mostly priests, wanted the new society to be based on the continuity of patriarchal values, national conscious-ness and the Christianity of the common people. As the intellectual leaders of the areas where Venetian rule had been of only short duration and where the Croatian idiom was intact, they were the only fluent speakers of Croatian or Serbian. However, at the start these differences were unimportant because the common aim of nationali-zation was to prevent the Italianization of Dalmatia.

The urban nationalists were also strongly influenced by the Yugo-slavism of northern Croatia, but this ideology was considerably altered in Dalmatia because of differing conditions and the slower process of integrating the Croatian nation.[15] Yugoslavism, promoted by Bishop Strossmayer and formulated as an ideological system by another Catholic priest, Rački, was, in a broader sense, the contribution of the Croatian middle-class intelligentsia to the development of a Croatian bourgeois society and culture. Yugoslavism was the integrationist ideology of the Croatian nation, as well as a supranational concept: there was therefore an unstable relationship between the two compo-nents of this ideology.[16]

The Yugoslavism of the Dalmatian urban intelligentsia, which considered the South Slavs as a national entity, was a response to the need to overcome Dalmatian particularism. In Italian the term 'Croatia' had bad connotations because it was used to refer to the Croats and Serbs of the Military Frontier who had fought for the Habsburgs against the liberation of the north Italian provinces in 1848–9, 1859 and 1866. The urban nationalists used the term Croatian to refer to the medieval state, and to the language and ethnic identity of the Dalmatian population, but they still felt that this term was a lower, 'tribal' sort of designation and not a name for a nation.

The trend of the Yugoslavism espoused by the rural intelligentsia on the contrary was to continue to stress the development of a separate Croatian national consciousness within the framework of the broader ethnic, cultural and linguistic community of the South Slavs.

The Nationalist programme of a union with northern Croatia was very important because it connected the Dalmatian bourgeoisie, with their demands for a liberalization of social conditions, with the liberal bourgeoisie of northern Croatia who led the political and cultural initiatives. But some urban Nationalists wanted to preserve the special institutions of Dalmatia in a united Triune Kingdom. Nevertheless, they gradually subscribed to the necessity for union on both ethnic and historical grounds, that is, the ethnic identity of the population, and the fact of Dalmatian territory having belonged to the medieval Croatian state. The Nationalists in both Dalmatia and Croatia thought the success of their claims depended on the reorganization of the Monarchy on federal principles;[17] therefore they were denounced by the authorities of the centralist Schmerling regime, as well as by the Autonomists, as 'Panslavists'.

The movement for national revival included the Serbian minority alongside the Croatian majority. Under the influence of uprisings against the Turks in Serbia, the tradition of the medieval Serbian state and the activities of the Serbian nationalism centred in southern Hungary, the integration of the Serbian nation was also progressing in Dalmatia. The Serbian intelligentsia there was small but included a dynamic group of merchants. Among orthodox Serbs there were only a few Autonomists, whose position was solely the result of the need to co-operate with the regime. The Serbs nurtured a special animosity towards the Autonomist urban oligarchy, because during the Venetian administration and at the beginning of the Austrian it had promoted the so-called Union, that is, the Catholicization of the Orthodox population, but the Greek forms of worship were still allowed.

Yugoslavism, however, was not a Serbian nationalist integrationist ideology. It was based on the idea of the kinship of the South Slavs and the necessity for cultural co-operation, because the Serbs too felt threatened by the Autonomists and by Italianization. Therefore the Serbian elite promoted the nationalist programme of introducing the national idiom as the official language, and the union of Dalmatia with northern Croatia, and showed themselves to be thoroughly supportive of Nationalist activities.

POLITICAL DEVELOPMENTS FROM 1860 TO THE AUSTRO-HUNGARIAN COMPROMISE OF 1867

As we have seen, in the years 1860–1 the Nationalists were as yet unable to resist the powerful Autonomists with their effective organization. However, they were able to lead a systematic political and cultural offensive aimed first of all at winning over the urban middle classes. In 1860–1 the political battles had turned around the question of the union of Dalmatia with Croatia. The Schmerling regime had been resolutely against this union, first because it was not realizable within the centralist system, and because the political claims of the National Party in Croatia were unacceptable to Vienna. Therefore the Schmerling regime had made it clear to the powers that be in Croatia that union with Dalmatia was conditional on their acceptance of the centralist system of the Monarchy and renunciation of claims for Croatian autonomy and statehood. This resulted in some temporary friction within the National Party, with the centre of gravity within the Dalmatian National Party shifting towards a policy of claiming the parity of Croatian or Serbian with Italian as a first step in the national movement.

The turning-point of the national movement was the appearance of the newspaper *Il Nazionale* in 1862 with its Croatian supplement *Narodni list*. It had an immense influence in spreading nationalist ideology among the Italian-educated bourgeoisie. Reading-rooms which acted as centres for Nationalist meetings and a publishing institution, the *Matica dalmatinska*, were also established.

The repressive Schmerling system was at first able to rely on the Autonomist bureaucracy, but there were groups of liberal Autonomists who opposed this regime and therefore had some common interests with the Nationalists. As the National Party was no longer insisting on an immediate union with Croatia, agreement was possible in 1864. The 'Liberal Union' was effected when the Nationalists declared they would no longer oppose the decision of the Dalmatian Diet as to the union with Croatia, while the liberal Autonomists declared they would no longer oppose the gradual introduction of the 'Slav' language into public life on an equal footing with Italian. This agreement did not help the Nationalists to get better results in the 1864 election, but because of this co-operation the Diet was dissolved. The Liberal Union was not, however, a lasting episode.

The most important conditions for 'nationalization' were provided at the level of the communes. The Austrian laws of 1862 and 1869, pertaining to the administration of the communes and Dalmatia respectively, made local self-government possible. Only taxpayers of a certain level were enfranchised; therefore the Nationalists could take over the communes only if they could win over the well-off strata of the towns and the countryside. Though the Viennese central authorities controlled the administration of the communes through the district heads, this self-government was extremely significant for all the non-German national movements. In particular, the Slavs under the Monarchy could gain through the struggles for self-government a more advantageous position for their economic and national interests than they could gain in the Diets, the *Reichsrat*, or in negotiations with the Viennese authorities.[18] Therefore the political movement for 'national revival' in Dalmatia was first of all an embittered fight for the communes. Their councils had the option of introducing the national language into schools and the administration or of obstructing this possibility.

The most eminent leaders of the National Party were Miho Klaić, a liberal and pragmatic politician, adroit in negotiations and an expert in important questions such as finance, education and administration, and the parish priest Mihovil Pavlinović, a conservative in social matters and a representative of the peasant intelligentsia. Before the Hungarian–Croatian Compromise he co-operated well with the liberal intelligentsia and accepted the South Slav ideology professed by Bishop Strossmayer's National Party in northern Croatia.[19]

In 1865 the King-Emperor abandoned Schmerling's German centralism. The new government, headed by Richard von Belcredi, had the task of preparing the reception of the compromise with the Magyar elite worked out by the Minister for Foreign Affairs, Ferdinand von Beust. Francis Joseph wanted to preserve the historical autonomy of Croatia and Slavonia only in a narrow sense, that is to say, as dictated by the interests of the Monarchy as a whole and the Magyar ruling elite; therefore he always resolutely refused Croat claims for statehood based on Croatian state-right. But he did not allow the Magyar elite to wipe out the provincial autonomy of Croatia and Slavonia (as was condoned by the 1848 constitution). However, after his compromise with the Magyar nobility in 1867, it was possible to limit this autonomy as it suited the Magyars. Prime Minister Count Gyula Andrássy was therefore able to carry out the Hungarian–Croatian Compromise of 1868 by force, and without the consent of the National Party.[20]

Under the terms of the Austro-Hungarian Compromise, northern Croatia was left in the Hungarian part and Dalmatia in the Austrian part of the Monarchy. But the new terms did not stop the claims for the union of these lands. The Hungarian government put Croatian autonomy into practice in the narrowest sense possible, as the autonomy of a province and as a concession, not a historically derived right. Against this, Croatian political groups found abundant arguments to support their claim that the Compromise was actually a treaty between two states. In connection with the union of northern Croatia and Dalmatia, it is crucial to note that the Compromise in the Magyar and Croatian texts (which differ in some significant nuances) was declared to be between the Kingdom of Hungary and the 'Kingdoms of Dalmatia, Croatia and Slavonia'. The Triune Kingdom is declared to be a 'political nation', a term understood by the Croatians in the sense of 'nation-state'. This declaration of state-right in the Compromise was by no means carried out in practice, but its ideological impact was immense.

The Croatian version of the Compromise uses the expression 'Kingdoms of Dalmatia, Croatia and Slavonia' whereas the Magyar text avoids the term 'Kingdoms' and puts Croatia in the first place. The term Triune Kingdom, listing Dalmatia first, was consistent with the official term used by the Croatian Diet before and after 1848, as well as with other documents concerning Croatian autonomy and the Habsburg titles. After the Compromise, the Croatian autonomous laws and other official documents were obliged to name Dalmatia last. It is important to note that paragraph 65 of the Compromise states, besides the necessity of the union of the Military Frontier with civilian Croatia and Slavonia, that Dalmatia should be reincorporated and united with Croatia and Slavonia on the basis of 'the Holy Hungarian crown', but that the opinion of Dalmatia must first be obtained. This declaration was in opposition to the Austrian 'December Constitution' of 1867 which included Dalmatia as one of the lands represented in the *Reichsrat*. At the beginning, the statement of a possible union was of no importance. Later, when the National Party in Dalmatia reached a majority in the Diet, this issue affected the very essence of the Dualist system. The Austrian and the Hungarian ministers even combined forces to prevent demands for union in the Croatian and Dalmatian Diets, and there were also objections raised in the *Reichsrat*.[21]

CROATIAN NATIONALISM IN DALMATIA AFTER THE AUSTRO-HUNGARIAN COMPROMISE

The Austro-Hungarian Compromise provoked significant changes in Dalmatia. After the fall of the Schmerling regime in 1865, the new governor, General Joseph Filipović, stopped discriminating against the National Party, and the Viennese authorities decided against hindering a limited 'nationalization'. The heads of the Autonomist bureaucracy were removed and the government made some statements concerning the equal right of Croatian and Italian to be used as official languages. The Autonomists could no longer rely on the unlimited support of the regime.

During the Austro-Italian war in 1866 the attempt by the Italian fleet to occupy Dalmatia was prevented by the Austrian victory on the island of Vis. To the Nationalists, this battle was a defence of their national territory by the Dalmatians themselves, because for the most part the sailors in the Austrian fleet were Dalmatians. The war lost the province of Venice to the Italians, which accelerated the growth of irredentism among the Autonomists, a growing proportion of whom now considered themselves as Italians, not Slav-Dalmatians.

The improved position of the National Party in 1866 deteriorated in 1867–9. As the Austro-Hungarian Compromise was based on Austro-German and Magyar hegemonies, Minister Beust was not inclined to tolerate the progress of 'nationalization' and the possibility that a majority in the Dalmatian Diet might declare themselves in favour of union with northern Croatia. Therefore the Autonomist bureaucracy could hinder the victory of the Nationalists in the elections for the Diet in 1867, and prevent the implementation of decrees helping the introduction of the national language into the administration, judiciary and middle schools. The new governor, Wagner, was instructed to rely on the Autonomists, and allowed the sort of excesses and manipulation by the Autonomists in the elections in 1869 that had also been tolerated in 1865. The Nationalists were even accused of inciting the uprising in Boka Kotorska which was due to the problems aroused by military service in the area.

In 1867 the Autonomist majority in the Diet voted an address of gratitude to the Emperor for having included Dalmatia in the Austrian part of the Monarchy and for thus definitively rejecting the possibility of union with Croatia and Slavonia. After the Hungarian–Croatian Compromise the National Party had none the less some hope that union would occur because of the wording of the Compromise indicating union of Dalmatia with Croatia and Slavonia. They soon found out that the declaration had no practical meaning and that union was definitely precluded. Hence when the Nationalists participated in the election of deputies for the *Reichsrat*, they always stressed their reservations regarding state-right, by declaring that their membership of the *Reichsrat* in no way implied renunciation of the declaration of the rights of Dalmatia, Croatia and Slavonia as a united state. As the majority party the Nationalists were obliged to co-operate with the regime and to accept Dualism.

This situation had changed during the short-lived federalist experiment of the Count Alfred Potocky and Count Edouard Taaffe governments, who tried to co-operate with the Federalists and Slav representatives of the Monarchy. They no longer allowed the Autonomists to put pressure on the Nationalists, so the first 'free' elections for the Dalmatian Diet in 1870 saw the victory of the National Party. Though these federalist tactics were not a lasting episode, they introduced a new epoch for the National Party, which could now be sure of preserving its majority.

However, the electoral victory of the National Party in 1870 did not mean that the aims of 'national revival' were fulfilled. Urban Dalmatia was not yet won over and the Croatian or Serbian language was not yet the official language, though it had made great headway.

The electoral system for the Diet as well as for the communal councils ensured that the bourgeoisie had the majority and were the predominant influence in peasant areas and in southern Dalmatia. The Nationalists had already been able to win a majority of deputies from peasant Dalmatia for the Diet since 1861. In the first communal elections (1865–7) they were able to succeed because of their temporary agreement with the liberal Autonomists. Later the number of Nationalist communes grew steadily. However, at the time of the first communal elections the National Party was only secure in the rural hinterland and in southern Dalmatia. Their adherents in urban areas belonged only to the rather narrow circles of the liberal bourgeoisie and the intelligentsia. The predominance of Nationalists in the 1870 Diet did not mean that urban Dalmatia was 'conquered' for the national movement. Only in the 1876 elections were the Nationalists able to gain a small majority in urban society and to begin eroding Autonomist or Italian sympathies.

Though the security of the National Party rested on its standing in peasant Dalmatia, in general the revivalist movement depended on urban society and had to adapt to its interests. The Nationalists fought bitterly in the strongholds of urban society – the territories of Split, Zadar and the islands. They gradually suceeded in winning the majority in communal elections and by 1882 even took over the most important bastion of Autonomism – the city of Split – and by the end of the eighties the other communes in its territory. Except for a few unimportant small communes, only Zadar, the administrative centre of Dalmatia, kept its Italian majority.

The Nationalist electoral victory in Split in 1882 was a turning-point for the national movement. Split was the centre of the strongest territory economically and socially in Dalmatia and therefore the success of Croatian national integration was connected with defeating Autonomist and Italian interests there and in urban Dalmatia. The victory at Split is seen as marking the end of the revivalist movement because after that the National Party enjoyed the support of the great majority of the Dalmatian bourgeoisie. A broader national movement with new features could now begin.[22]

LINGUISTIC ISSUES AND SERBO-CROAT DIVISIONS

In the twenty years from 1861 to 1882, Croatian or Serbian had become the public language of the educated classes, but the struggle to have it confirmed as the official language had to continue, although the Austrian government stopped favouring Italian after the unification of Italy. The Diet in 1861 had already agreed that deputies could use the 'Illyrian' language, but this opportunity was scarcely used at first because the majority of the deputies had only a slight acquaintance with the language. The situation changed with the progress of the 'national revival', and the 'national Croatian or Serbian language' became the official language of the Diet only in 1883, while the Italian deputies were still allowed to use Italian. So the positions of the two languages had been reversed.

From 1872 the national language had equal status with Italian, in the administration's external affairs and in the judiciary, that is, in public contacts. By 1900 Croatian or Serbian had become the language of instruction in primary and middle schools (with the exception of Zadar) and, with two exceptions, the official language in all communes. The Viennese government opposed the introduction of Croatian or Serbian into the administration of internal affairs, in accordance with their language policy in the non-German provinces in general. After the failure of attempts to introduce German instead of Italian, the national language became the official interior administrative language in 1912.

The revivalist movement in Dalmatia included Croats and Serbs alike, and the national integrational ideology of the urban Nationlists thought of the South Slavs as a single nation. On the eve of the Compromise conditions were ripe for the development of two distinct movements, ideologies and national consciousnesses: the Croatian and the Serbian. The Croatian public in northern Croatia hoped that the Triune Kingdom would be a Croatian national state, but the existence of a Serbian nation within Croatia was acknowledged (although a small group argued that all South Slav were Croats). On the Serbian side, the idea was that all those who spoke the *štokavian* dialect, whether Orthodox, Catholic or Muslim, were Serbs. (The majority of Croats speak this dialect.) Therefore Serbia's mission was to unite all Serbs under Habsburg and Turkish rule in a single Serbian state, and the idea of the Triune Kingdom as a Croatian state was rejected. But in 1867, when the Austro-Hungarian Compromise happened, through the temporary contacts of the Strossmayer group with the Prince of Serbia, the Croatian Diet declared that the Serbian nation within the Triune Kingdom, numerically in the minority, would have equal status with the Croatian nation, the numerical majority.[23]

In Dalmatia before the Compromise there was not as yet any dissent between the Croatian and Serbian elite, as we have seen. Whereas in northern Croatia the Serbs were not members of the federally oriented National Party, being adherents of centralism or dualism, the Serbs in Dalmatia were still strong and active supporters of the National Party. However, there appeared signs of sympathy for Serbian separation from the Croats in the revivalist movement, and for an accentuated Serbian nationalism. After the Austro-Hungarian Compromise this tendency became stronger among the Serbian bourgeoisie in Dalmatia, through the influence of the United Serbian Youth based in southern Hungary, and its propaganda for the unification of all Serbs in a Greater Serbia. Up to this point all the nationalist institutions and public activities in Dalmatia had been integrated: now the Serbs began to organize themselves separately.

On the Croatian side there were also considerable ideological changes. The vague South Slav ideology originating in urban Dalmatia no longer matched the degree of integration between Croats, Serbs and Italians. Yugoslavism in liberal circles persisted but increasingly emphasized the name of Croatia for the nation and the state-right of Croatia in its argument for the union of Dalmatia and Croatia. The name 'Croatia' persisted in rural Dalmatia among the peasants, but an explicit Croatian national ideology had not yet been formulated because the rural intelligentsia had to adapt itself to the need to include the urban elite in the Croatian national movement.

After the Hungarian-Croatian Compromise such an ideology was formulated by Pavlinović. He emphasized the union with northern Croatia on the grounds of the state-right of the Triune Kingdom, which should become the Croatian national state. This state-right, which identified the Croatian state with the Croatian 'political nation', could be construed as including the Serbian population within the area as a 'genetic' nation, with the same rights as the 'Croatian political nation'. But the ideology of state-right could also lead to the argument for eliminating the Serbian nation within the Croatian state.[24] The Serbian intelligentsia in Dalmatia had campaigned for union with northern Croatia when these aims were based on the South Slav ideology of the urban elite, that is, for as long as the name 'Croatia' and a Croatian identity for the future state had not been emphasized, and the idea that Serbia should include all Serbs wherever they lived had not yet gained strength. But after the Compromise there was a clear confrontation between the Croatian and Serbian state-idea, aggravated by the fact that both the Serbian and Croatian factions claimed Bosnia and Herzegovina as part of their national states.

With his Croatian national consciousness and his Catholicism, Pavlinović no longer considered the Croats and Serbs as separate 'tribes' within a South Slav nation, but as separate nations with their own state traditions, religion and culture. Serbs in Croatia should consider they were Croatian citizens, that is, 'Croatians by the land and the Croatian state'. He therefore denied the Serbian right to reject the sovereignty of Croatia within the framework of the Monarchy and denounced Serbia's tendencies to appropriate Croatian territory, emphasizing Croatia's right to Bosnia and Herzegovina.

Among the Croatian leaders of the Dalmatian National Party there was much dissent over liberal and conservative interpretations and support for nationalism. The leaders of the National Party explicitly emphasized the 'total equality' of Croats and Serbs regarding religion, nationality, politics and literature in its 1873 programme. In 1877 they stated that the Croats and Serbs, 'being a nation', have equal rights under the protection of Croatia's state-right. Nevertheless, divergences were growing between the Croatian and Serbian elites, which resulted in the formation of a separate Serbian National Party in 1879, which abandoned the programme of union of Dalmatia with Croatia and Slavonia.

The propaganda of the National Party for union with northern Croatia was no longer allowed, and because of the Diet's address in 1877 claiming this union it was dismissed. No more similar demands were possible. In 1889 the National Party renamed itself the National Croatian Party, repeating its 1877 statement on the Serbs and declaring that it would ask the Emperor to consent to the union at an appropriate time. However, in other statements the party was silent on this issue: the declaration was only a reminder that the union was not forgotten. It must be stressed that after 1889, Governors of

Dalmatia were under permanent orders to dismiss any Diet debating the union.

Because of the opposition of Croatian and Serbian political groups, and the impossibility of action in favour of union, both Vienna and Budapest could keep the two national movements within limits which did not endanger the Dualist system. When a major crisis within Dualism broke out at the beginning of the twentieth century, co-operation between Croatian and Serbian forces could take place on a higher level than before, and political action was co-ordinated in northern Croatia and Dalmatia.[25]

NOTES

1 M. Gross, *Počeci moderne Hrvatske* (The Beginnings of Modern Croatia) (Zagreb, 1985), pp. 450–3.

2 *Spisi saborski sabora kraljevinah Dalmacije, Hrvatske i Slavonije 1861* (The Documents of the Diet of the Kingdoms of Dalmatia, Croatia and Slavonia from 1861) (Zagreb, 1862), parts VI–XLIV.

3 *Dnevnik sabora trojedne kraljevine Dalmacije, Hrvatske i slavonije god. 1861* (The Journal of the Diet of the Triune Kingdom of Dalmatia, Croatia and Slavonia) (Zagreb, 1862), pp. 62–3, 67–71.

4 Rijeka (Fiume) is not mentioned because the city was in 1848 incorporated into Croatia. After the Hungarian–Croatian Compromise it was *de facto* but not *de jure* incorporated within Hungary. M. Gross, 'Dvadeset godina bijesa i očaja ili borba za Rijeku od 1861 do 1881' (Twenty years of wrath and despair or the fight for Rijeka from 1861 to 1881), *Dometi*, 4 (1987), 183–225.

5 The Documents, part III, pp. 287–94.

6 On the national revival there has been much recent literature. See D. Kečkemet, 'Bibliografija narodnog preporoda u Dalmaciji' (Bibliography of the national revival in Dalmatia), in D. Kečkemet *et al.* (eds.), *Hrvatski narodni preporod u Splitu* (The Croatian National Revival in Split) (Split, 1984), pp. 415–43. The best interpretation of the social conditions of the revival is in N. Stančić, *Hrvatska nacionalna ideologija preporodnog pokreta u Dalmaciji* (The Croatian National Ideology of the Revivalist Movement in Dalmatia – M. Pavlinović and His Circle) (Zagreb, 1980). See also: R. Petrović, *Narodno pitanje u Dalmaciji u XIX stoljeću* (The National Question in Dalmatia in the Nineteenth Century) (Sarajevo, 1968).

7 S. Obad, *Dalmaciji revolucionarne 1848/49. godine* (Dalmatia during the Revolutionary Years 1848/49: Selected Sources) (Rijeka, 1987).

8 D. Foretić, 'Društvene prilike u Dalmaciji od polovice XIX stoljeća do prvoga svjetskog rata' (Social conditions in Dalmatia from the second half of the nineteenth century to the First World War), in J. Ravlić (ed.), *Hrvatski narodni preporod u Dalmaciji i u Istri* (The Croatian National Revival in Dalmatia and Istria) (Zagreb, 1969), pp. 48–51.

9 J. Šidak, M. Gross, I. Karaman and D. Šepić, *Povijest hrvatskoga naroda g.*

1860–1914 (The History of the Croatian Nation 1860–1914) (Zagreb, 1968), p. 319.

10 Haus-Hof und Staatsarchiv, Kabinettskanzlei, Vorträge (Schmerling's memorials to the Emperor on Dalmatia, particularly in January and February 1861.)

11 I. Perić, *Dalmatinski sabor 1861–1912. (1918.) god.* (The Dalmatian Diet 1861–1912) (1918)) (Zadar, 1978).

12 There were 56 persons writing 17 booklets and 102 articles or letters to newspapers. N. Stančić, 'Nacionalna integraciona ideologija dalmatinskih narodnjaka 1860/61. godine' (The national integrational ideology of the Dalmatian nationalists in 1860/61), in *Radovi Instituta za hrvatsku povijest XI*, 1978, 183–279.

13 These ideologies are systematically elaborated in Stančić, 'Nacionalna integraciona ideologija'.

14 I. Perić, *Borba za ponarodjenje dalmatinskog školstva 1860–1918* (The Fight for the Nationalization of the Dalmatian Schools 1860–1918) (Zagreb, 1974), p. 80.

15 On the different rhythms and social conditions for the integration of the Croatian nation in particular regions of Croatia see M. Gross, 'On the integration of the Croatian nation: a case study in nation building', *East European Quarterly*, 2 (1981), 209–25.

16 On the national ideologies see my articles: 'Zur Frage der jugoslawischen Ideologie bei den Kroaten', in A. Wandruszka *et al.* (eds.), *Die Donaumonarchie und die südslawische Frage von 1848 bis 1918* (Vienna 1978), pp. 19–39; 'Croatian national-integrational ideologies from the end of Illyrism to the creation of Yugoslavia', *Austrian History Yearbook*, 15–16 (1979–80), 3–33; 'Les traits fondamentaux des idéologies croates d'intégration nationale avant la Première Guerre Mondiale', *Revue des Etudes Slaves*, 56 (Paris, 1984), 373–86; 'O ideološkom sustavu Franje Račkoga' (On the ideological system of F. Rački), *Zbornik zavoda za povijesne znanosti Jugoslavenske akademije*, vol. 9, 5–33. See also P. Korunić, *Jugoslavenska ideologija u hrvatskoj i slovenskoj politici* (The Yugoslav Ideology in Croatian and Slovenian Politics) (Zagreb, 1986).

17 M. Gross, 'Föderationspläne bei den Kroaten: Habsburger Monarchie oder Jugoslawien?', in M. Bernath and K. Nehring (eds.), *Friedenssicherung in Südosteuropa* (Munich, 1985), pp. 99–116.

18 J. Klabouch, 'Die Lokalverwaltung in Cisleithanien', in A. Wandruszka and P. Urbanitsch (eds.), *Die Habsburgermonarchie 1848–1918*, vol. II (Vienna, 1975), pp. 270–305.

19 T. Macan, *Miho Klaić* (Zagreb, 1980). Besides the above-mentioned book of Stančić dealing with Pavlinović's ideology, there are many articles and studies about him. Of special importance is his edited correspondence: A. Palavršić and B. Zelić, *Korespondencija Mihovila Pavlinovića* (Split, 1962).

20 After the revision of the Compromise in 1873 the National Party, having previously rejected the Compromise in principle, came to power under the Ban I. Mažuranić. Only then was Croatian autonomy realized.

21 For example, the royal decree opening the Croatian Diet in 1875 did not mention the Dalmatian issue, thus satisfying the claim of the Hungarian Ministerial Council. The decree of 1878 explicitly prohibited discussion about

Dalmatia. See M. Gross, 'The character of Croatian autonomy in the first decade after the Hungarian–Croatian Compromise, in S. Wank *et al.* (eds.), *The Mirror of History: Essays in Honor of Fritz Fellner* (Santa Barbara and Oxford, 1988), pp. 275–94.

22 N. Stančić, 'Pobjeda Narodne stranke na općinskim izborima u Splitu 1882. god. i problem periodizacije narodnog preporoda u Dalmaciji' (The victory of the National Party in the communal elections in Split in 1882 and the problem of periodization of the national revival in Dalmatia), in Kečkemet *et al.* (eds.), *Hrvatski narodni preporod u Splitu.*

23 An agreement between Prince Michael of Serbia and the leaders of the National Party was possible in 1867. It concerned provoking an uprising in Bosnia and Herzegovina in order to promote the inclusion of these provinces into Serbia. But the prince changed his mind hoping that he could better realize his goal through his contacts with the Hungarian Minister–President Andrássy.

24 This was in particular the idea of the Party of Rights. See M. Gross, *Povijest pravaške ideologije* (The History of the Ideology of the Party of Rights) (Zagreb, 1973). See also from the same author 'Croatian national-integrational ideologies'.

25 R. Lovrenčić, *Geneza politike 'novoga kursa'* (The Genesis of the Policy of 'New Course') (Zagreb, 1972). See also M. Gross in Šidak, Gross, Karaman and Šepić, *Povijest hrvatskaga naroda g. 1860–1914.*

TWELVE

THE NATIONAL QUESTION IN POLAND IN THE TWENTIETH CENTURY

JERZY TOMASZEWSKI

I T would be difficult to say exactly when Polish national consciousness emerged. Traces of it can already be detected in the Middle Ages, in the attitudes of inhabitants of the Polish lands to neighbouring communities speaking other languages and subject to other rulers. Conflicts with Western neighbours – with the vassals of the Holy Roman Empire of the German nation – made a particular contribution to the development of a feeling of national difference, influenced by an awareness of external threat. The literature of the Renaissance clearly testifies to the existence of such an awareness; one has only to recall the frequently cited words of Mikołaj Rej (1505–69), regarded as the father of Polish literature: 'Let all the neighbouring nations know that Poles are not geese, but have their own language.' Perhaps the fact that Polish kings were elected was among the reasons that a sense of loyalty to the dynasty did not develop among the politically and economically ruling nobility (*szlachta*); for no new dynasty arose after the Jagiellonian line died out. However, a consciousness of the unity of the nobility did appear – of a 'nation of nobles' – strengthened by the (not altogether justified) conviction that only in Poland was the 'nobleman on his little plot of land the equal of the Palatine', and that only in Poland did the nobility enjoy a 'golden liberty', unknown in other countries of Europe. From this derived the view that it was an honour for foreigners – even if they were of noble birth and bore a coat of arms – to be raised to the ranks of the Polish nobility; it was not granted to everyone.

Among the nobility living in the united state, previously in two parts (the Crown Lands and the Grand Duchy of Lithuania), the Polish language gradually prevailed, but this did not at first reflect consciousness of belonging to a single nation. When the Lithuanian magnate Prince Jerzy Radziwiłł took over the bishop's capital of Kraków in 1577 he received a letter from his brother (written in

3 Poland, *c.* 1937

Polish), in which we read: 'Mark, my lord, that you are a Lithuanian and not a Pole. And may you be pleased, my lord, to act for the good of your nation, for the Poles treat us with disdain and others as nothing.'[1] The Ruthenian nobility referred to themselves as *gente Ruthenus natione Polonus*. The word *natio* in this case indicated the state to which one belonged, and *gens*, one's national tradition. As the years went by, however, the nobility gradually yielded to the process of Polonization, and by the eighteenth century not only the Polish language, but also the sense of belonging to Polish culture and tradition, and to the Polish nation, prevailed.

One should note that at that time only the nobility considered themselves to be representatives of the nation and only they possessed political rights and the power to influence the fate of the state. According to current estimates, they constituted not less than 8 per cent of the country's inhabitants. The peasant majority of the people – subordinated legally and economically to the nobility – remained outside the nation understood in this sense. Nor were burghers (*mieszczanie*) included. Society in other European countries was similarly structured, with feudal forms of subjection of the peasants. This rather high percentage of noblemen distinguished Poland on the European map. One should not assume, however, that a member of this class was necessarily the owner of significant landed property. A particular characteristic of the historical development of certain Polish lands and of Lithuania was the existence of large numbers of nobles who owned only smallholdings, with a few serfs (*szlachta zagonowa, szlachta szaraczkowa*). The economic position of this group can be compared with that of free peasants in western European states, with the difference that they possessed certain political rights. A significant proportion of the nobility had no land at all (*gołota szlachecka*) and found itself in the employ of the magnates (formally sharing equal rights with them), for whom they performed a variety of services.

The peasant majority spoke a variety of languages, depending on their location within the state. In the western provinces Polish dialects predominated, in the east, Ruthenian dialects (forerunners of the contemporary Belorussian and Ukrainian tongues), in the north-east, Lithuanian. In a few areas inhabitants who had come from the west, and been settled in the countryside by landowners, spoke in German dialects. The Polish language dominated the towns, although some of the inhabitants spoke German or Jewish (Yiddish). But language was no indicator of national consciousness. The ordinary masses were not political subjects, nor did they constitute a nation in the contemporary sense of the word. They can be treated solely as ethnic groups, from which nations were to form only in the future. Religious differences did play a significant role, however. On the whole, peasant groups speaking in Polish dialects professed Catholicism of the Latin rite (although Protestantism dominated in Silesia and in Mazuria), whereas those speaking in Ruthenian dialects were usually Orthodox (although in the north-east there were also Roman Catholics) or members of the Uniate Church, which had been imposed from above; a *sui generis* historical paradox meant that in the nineteenth century this rite became firmly fixed in the peasant consciousness whereas the Russian authorities no less firmly – and perhaps even more so – brutally attempted to enforce Orthodoxy, which the Uniates obstinately opposed. In places where the Uniate Church survived (under Austrian rule) it became a support for the Ukrainian national movement.

It is not easy to explain the process of formation of national consciousness among the peasants. There are records dating from the end of the eighteenth century marking their participation in the battle for Polish independence, particularly during the uprising led by Tadeusz Kościuszko (1746–1817; its leader came from the Polonized Belorussian nobility). This was linked with hopes for improved living conditions and liberation from servitude.

The Jews cherished similar hopes and provided a cavalry regiment under the leadership of the famous Berek Joselewicz (born in 1764, he died on 5 May 1809, leading a Jewish detachment in the Duchy of Warsaw's army created by Napoleon).

One should not, however, draw too far-reaching conclusions from this. Born in 1842 in a village not far from Kraków, Jan Słomka recalls his childhood years thus:

> As for national consciousness in previous times, as I remember the peasants called themselves only Mazovians, and their speech Mazovian; they lived only for themselves, constituting a completely separate mass, quite indifferent to national affairs. I, for example, only began to feel myself a Pole when I began to read books and papers, and I think that other country-folk came to recognize their nationality in more or less the same way ... until recently [the memoir was written at the beginning of the twentieth century. J. T.] there were still many who, if reminded of Poland, would grow angry and curse, saying that only the nobles could want a Poland, so that people would work for them as they had done in feudal times ...[2]

Villeinage and serfdom were abolished by the three partitioning powers, a fact long remembered in the countryside.

Such views gradually faded as Polish Enlightenment developed. And yet in memoirs of the Second World War and occupation one can still find accounts such as the following: 'Yet one should say, for the sake of truth, that the other side of the coin is not so rosy. Two peasant farmers and four workers showed more or less open satisfaction at the occupier's invasion.'[3] These must surely be the last vestiges of a lack of national consciousness during the years of occupation, but they deserve to be noted since they indicate how complicated and drawn-out was the process of its development.

With some simplification, one can say that the liquidation of the social structure of society remaining after the feudal period represents a breakthrough in the process of national awareness pervading the consciousness of the masses. For the peasants this consisted of abolishing serfdom, followed by enfranchisement (which meant the liquidation of villeinage). It should be noted, however, that enfranchisement was instituted (in the nineteenth century) differently in different Polish lands, which were divided at the time between Austria, Prussia and Russia. Great estates were not dismantled and in many regions of the Polish lands conflicts between village and manor continued as before. The question of agricultural reform – that is, the division of great estates among the peasants – remained a central point of the programme of the Peasant parties until 1944 when it was carried out by Poland's post-war government. For the burghers, the breakthrough came with the granting of civil and citizens' rights, also granted, after a considerable delay, to the Jews. In sum, the process of development of national consciousness among those classes who were not part of the nobility only really began in the second half of the eighteenth century, and it was only in the second half of the nineteenth century – when the process of eliminating legal inequalities between the classes was finally completed – that it encompassed the majority of the inhabitants of the former Republic.

This in turn brought many complications. According to the traditions of Polish political thought, all the lands within the former pre-partition borders were considered to be Polish territory, for the noble Polish nation had, after all, dominated them. Hence the stipulation that the state should be rebuilt according to its pre-war borders, a condition supported by many democratic thinkers in Europe in the mid-nineteenth century (including Karl Marx). It was taken as obvious, and therefore beyond discussion, that after the liberation of the peasants, Polish national consciousness must develop throughout this territory, as it had in the country's western and central regions. The Belorussian and Ukrainian languages were regarded as peasant dialects, of local significance, which would defer to an all-Polish language. Reality proved to be rather more complicated.

During the second half of the nineteenth century in the eastern territories of the former Republic a different national consciousness was developing among the local people who spoke languages other than Polish (and often observed religions other than Catholicism of the Latin rite). They were influenced, to a certain extent, by Polish democratic circles. The birth of Belorussian literature at that time is linked with the work of writers coming from historic Lithuania, from the circle of the most outstanding Polish poet, Adam Mickiewicz (1798–1855), who often used Belorussian folk motifs in his poetry. During the January uprising (1863–4) the leader of the insurrectionary detachments in Belorussia, Konstanty Kalinowski (Kastuś Kalinoŭski, 1838–64) published a journal in Belorussian, calling for battle against Russia. Likewise, other Polish writers coming from the Belorussian lands left works in the language of the local populace, thus beginning a national literary tradition. In the second half of the nineteenth century authors appeared whose works were written exclusively in Belorussian. At first they could be printed only beyond the Russian borders, Belorussian works not being permitted until after the 1905 revolution. At first, otherwise conservative Polish landowners supported these changes. They feared the Russification policies of the authorities and they saw in the development of Belorussian aspirations a chance to make the local people independent of Russian influences. Much later the legend arose that the Belorussian movement was the creation of the Tsarist authorities who wished to obliterate Polish influences; it gained wider credence after Belorussian politicians freed themselves from Polish domination.

The Polish contribution to the development of Ukrainian national consciousness was on a smaller scale, although there were some Polish writers who also wrote in Ukrainian. Antagonism, however, was much more acute. Both in the case of Belorussia and the Ukraine, national differences were linked with social differences. Ideas of Polish culture and statehood were represented above all by the nobility and by the intelligentsia who had their roots in the noble tradition (though not necessarily with a noble birthright), whereas the Belorussian or Ukrainian consciousness in the process of formation was linked to the plebeian tradition which had often found itself in opposition to the Polish state (the Cossack wars in the seventeenth century provide a particular example of this). This was illustrated by the linguistic relations which had originally existed in these lands. During the second half of the nineteenth century, and sometimes much later, the

Polish language was acknowledged as the language of the nobility, used by the upper classes in order to communicate, whereas Belorussian, Lithuanian or Ukrainian were used to address the common people. These were 'peasant' languages, as they were sometimes described in daily life in the countryside.

Language conveyed social relations; the adoption of Polish was linked with social advancement. It is no surprise, therefore, to find that for Polish right-wing circles the emergence of Belorussian, Lithuanian or Ukrainian national consciousness constituted a challenge. In traditional understanding, the local peasant – liberating himself from dependence and striving for a higher level of culture – obviously had to become a Pole, just as in Mazovia, Wielkopolska (Greater Poland) or in Małopolska (Little Poland, known as Western Poland). If this failed to occur, it could only be the result of foreign intrigue. Under Russian rule Tsarist machinations were suspected, in the Austrian partition the Habsburgs were held to blame; after 1917 a Bolshevik conspiracy was perceived behind the Belorussian and Ukrainian movements. The dismissal of the process of the development of national consciousness as a 'foreign intrigue' ruled out all possibility of dialogue with neighbouring nations, as their representatives were considered to be traitors of Poland, or at best, people misled by 'foreign agents'. The consequence of such reasoning was a programme formulated by an outstanding politician from the ranks of the national democracy, Stanisław Grabski (1871–1949): 'today, the transformation of the state territory of the Republic into a Polish national territory is a necessary condition of maintaining our frontiers'.[4]

Polish democrats held a different position. An appeal to the people and the recognition of their political rights led to the view expressed radically by Jarosław Dąmbrowski (1836–1871) in 1867: 'each nation has the right to pass decrees only for itself. The need for freedom felt by the nation gives it the unquestionable right to rid itself of patronage; any enforcement of a foreign influence or authority is an act of force. This force becomes even more execrable if it is committed by a nation struggling for its own liberty.'[5]

However, few Polish politicians drew such far-reaching conclusions from the principle of equality. The dominant view was of the necessity of finding some form of federation of nations which had once formed part of the Polish state, that is, the Belorussians, Lithuanians and Ukrainians. Before 1917 it was argued that in this way the more highly civilized Polish nation, which alone was able to create a strong state, would guarantee Belorussian, Lithuanian and Ukrainian independence from Russian influence. Doubtless some Polish activists cherished the secret hope that the Poles would dominate such a federation and would dictate the political and national aspect of the whole. But it was precisely because of this that Belorussian, Lithuanian and Ukrainian partners were found lacking for a union of nations thus conceived. Furthermore, they could reasonably fear that nationalist politicians would gain the upper hand on the Polish side and that any equality of nations and guarantees for the free development of their cultures would be out of the question.

It should be noted that Belorussian, Lithuanian and Ukrainian national consciousness developed relatively late. There were almost no noble classes linked with the traditions of these nations, and it was only the social liberation and political awakening of the peasant masses that made this process possible. It is difficult to trace its course precisely, a course which differed in a number of ways in the case of each of the three nations. The development of Belorussian national consciousness faced great obstacles and delays. Nevertheless, the works of Francišak Bahuševič (1840–1900) can already be seen to include a programme for the development of Belorussian culture and a passionate defence of the national tongue, warning his countrymen against the fate 'of those peoples who first lost their languages – as a dying man loses his power of speech – and then died completely'.[6]

It is worth noting that, although the majority of Belorussian society was Orthodox, many Catholics, including priests, assisted at the birth of the country's cultural renaissance and in the development of its political life. This state of affairs was presumably influenced by the extensive dependence of the Orthodox clergy on the Russian administration, whereas Catholicism was a faith suffering discrimination and therefore found itself to some extent in opposition to social structures existing at the time.

At all events, groups continued to exist – right into the interwar period – of indeterminate consciousness: people aware that they were neither Russians nor Poles, but defining themselves only generally as 'locals', or according to regions (*Poleszucy, Huculi, Łemkowie*, etc.) They spoke Belorussian, Ukrainian or, more rarely, Lithuanian dialects which they called 'peasant' or 'local' speech. Their national consciousness grew only gradually. This was influenced by social conflicts, religious differences, state political influences, or by the clergy (which is why the appointment of parish priests was of great interest to the Polish administrative authorities), political and national organizations, schools, the press, and so on. In some areas ancestry was decisive: the descendants of the *szlachta zagonowa* considered themselves superior to the peasants, though they spoke the same language, often professed the same faith and owned only slightly larger holdings. They referred to themselves as 'Polish nobility' in opposition to the peasants, who could only be 'local', 'Ruthenian', and so on. An important element in the development of national consciousness was overcoming illiteracy which was still widespread in the twentieth century in the Republic's eastern provinces.

In Lithuania's historic lands there was one more, not very numerous group, the so-called natives (*Krajowcy*). As far as language and culture are concerned they should be recognized as Poles, which in any case they declared themselves to be on more than one occasion. However, they were bound to the tradition of the Grand Duchy of Lithuania as the fatherland of the Lithuanians, Belorussians and Poles born there. They rejected federal projects in which Poland was to be the dominant partner, declaring themselves in favour of an independent Lithuania – the common fatherland of people of a variety of cultures. In conditions of acute Polish–Lithuanian conflict this political trend had no chance of success; it did not lead to the creation of a separate nation speaking Polish, but linked with Lithuania.

If the process of the development of national consciousness among the peasants to the east of the Polish ethnic territory was marked by the weakening of Polish cultural influences, in the west – especially under Prussian domination – there were changes of a different character. In Wielkopolska, Pomorze (Pomerania), Upper Silesia and, to a lesser extent, in Warmia and Mazuria, Polish dialects dominated among the rural population. In Wielkopolska and Pomorze a significant section of the population that lived in towns also spoke Polish and the Polish nobility was the politically dominant force. During the nineteenth century, the Prussian authorities undertook a colonization programme in an attempt to bring over German peasant farmers and to support the German element in the towns. They also tried to enforce German language and culture on to the local population via schools. This policy aroused resistance to the German authorities on the part of the Polish populace and also provoked sharp conflicts between the population and the influential, and privileged, Germans. Contrary to the intentions of the administration, this contributed to a strengthening of Polish national consciousness, and prompted co-operation between various strata of Polish society in opposition to pressure from the administration, the threat of Germanization and the acquisition of land by German settlers. The process of urbanization, linked with rural changes, brought about a population flow from the countryside to the towns and, as a result, the weakening of the German position in the latter. In Wielkopolska and Pomorze strong Polish resistance against the Germans developed, which sometimes took on typically nationalistic characteristics.

The question of terminology, linked with the particular traits of the development of national consciousness in central Europe, requires some emphasis here. Thus it has been acceptable to describe the process of the development of this consciousness, the defence of national traditions and cultures, and the social attitudes connected with them, as patriotism. It is only when patriotism led to disdain or hostility towards other nations, and when political programmes expressed the intention of subordinating the interests of minorities to those of one nation, that we speak of nationalism. The difference is crucial in the case of societies who were defending themselves against national oppression. If patriotic attitudes did not exclude – and sometimes even led to – co-operation between discriminated nations against a common threat, then nationalism usually ruled out such alliances. A characteristic slogan adopted by Polish activists in the Prussian partition – each to his own for his own – expressed a programme of supporting only Poles (i.e. Polish production and trade), as opposed to Germans who were favoured by the partitioning authorities. In such circumstances it had the character of self-defence against the oppression of German nationalism. Only in independent Poland, after 1918, did it take on the character of a nationalistic offensive against national minorities.

Relations in the other Polish lands under German occupation developed differently in more than one respect. In the Silesia of past centuries the local nobility had accepted German culture while clinging to local habits and customs; Polish traditions and language were preserved by the ordinary people. In the second half of the nineteenth century a process analogous to the changes in the Ukrainian lands took place: the awakening of Polish consciousness among the plebeian strata, opposing the policies of the administration, and hostile to the German owners and administrators of estates, mines and steelworks. These changes occurred at least partly under the influence of the somewhat distant ancient centre of Polish culture in Kraków; the German–Austrian border did not constitute an impenetrable obstacle.

In Silesia, however, the situation was more complicated than on the eastern borders. The acceptance of German culture brought with it the chance of social advancement, open to Germans and all but closed to youth who declared their Polishness. German society was not exclusively composed of administrators, landowners and capitalists, but also of workers, linked by a common fate and interests with Polish workers. The German language was enforced by schools, the administration and often (though not always) by the Church. A number of elements combined to produce an environment of indifference to national issues; in a situation where Germans were privileged before 1921 and Poles supported after 1921 (when the eastern part of Silesia became part of the Polish state) there arose 'a category of people deriving their source of income from their ideological vagueness'.[7] The difficult economic situation also played a part in this, together with the lack of political stability. In a territory where an acute struggle for the soul of its inhabitants – begun by the Prussian Germanization policies – was taking place, these undecided people were described, as a rule, in pejorative terms. From a historical perspective we perceive above all the drama of societies suffering attempts to deprive them of their native speech and culture, expressed in the often tragic fate of individuals. Today this group cannot be quantified; it probably constituted a small percentage of the inhabitants of Silesia. In Cieszyn, a part of Silesia which came under Austrian rule, this category of people found themselves on the border between Polish, Czech and German culture; a separate party was even set up – the Silesian People's Party – whose supporters were called 'Ślązakowcy'.

Markedly less favourable conditions for the development of Polish consciousness existed in Warmia and Mazuria. These lands, far from the centres of Polish culture, found themselves under the dominant pressure of German politics. As a result, the spread of Polish folk dialects quickly decreased during the nineteenth century and those speaking them were not even aware what they were. A strong sense of separate regional consciousness developed among them, particularly in Mazuria. They defended the local tongue and the predominantly Protestant faith, they did not consider themselves Germans, but often harboured a distrust of Polishness which appeared alien to them. Of course, even in this milieu there were Polish activists who – despite all the difficulties – published Polish newspapers and books, but did not succeed in tipping the scales in favour of Poland during the plebiscite, carried out in the summer of 1920, in circumstances particularly unfavourable for the Polish state. The following years, especially the Nazi period, caused a further weakening in the impact of Polish consciousness, ruthlessly fought by the authorities. Speaking in Polish, even in the seclusion of one's own home, met with threats of severe repression.[8]

*

To simplify somewhat, we can say that at the beginning of the twentieth century Polish national consciousness embraced all strata of society speaking Polish (whether literary, or folk dialects), with the exception of a few small groups in Silesia (within both the German and Austro-Hungarian borders) or the notably more numerous groups in Warmia and Mazuria. In Lithuania there was also a circle, again quite small, of natives (*Krajowcy*) who declared themselves Polish in nationality, but who were faithful to the traditions of Lithuania. In other regions of lands inhabited by Poles the phenomenon of indeterminate national consciousness was the exception rather than the rule. Admittedly, in some areas a strong feeling of a regional bond developed, but it did not clash with the consciousness of a national bond. Such a regional society with a strong sense of its own identity and pride in its traditional peasant culture is characteristic today of the mountain people of the High Tatra. However, when an attempt was made during the Nazi occupation to set up a separate 'Mountain nation' (*Goralenvolk*) on this basis, granting material privileges to people who declared such a national allegiance, the occupier's experiment ended in complete failure. Many of the highlanders joined the Polish resistance movement. On the other hand, a large group (the numbers are difficult to estimate) of the Ruthenian population speaking in Belorussian or Ukrainian dialects (the demarcation between them is a disputable issue) continued to find themselves in the prenational state, possessing only an awareness that they owned an identity distinct from that of the Poles and Russians. Under Austrian rule Ukrainian consciousness had fully developed, and was severely opposed by Polish right-wing groups. Groups maintaining a sense of regional consciousness also existed there (*Huculi, Łemkowie, Bojkowie*), though they were somewhat weaker, and there was also a Ukrainian political trend under Habsburg rule which declared national unity with the Russians. They described themselves traditionally as Ruthenians, quickly rejecting the term 'Ukrainians', then becoming common. This trend could also be found in Subcarpathian Ruthenia, which was part of Czechoslovakia. In the interwar years this group was quickly eroded, acquiring Ukrainian allegiance.

The process of development of national consciousness under Russian rule was quickened by the influence of both revolutions, in 1905 and 1917. In the less oppressive atmosphere following 1905, publishing houses producing works in national languages appeared, accompanied by a growth of intellectual groupings. Towards the end of the First World War the German occupying powers wanted to take advantage of the national aspirations of peoples subjugated by Russia and promoted national systems of education (Belorussian, Lithuanian, Polish, Ukrainian and Jewish), and they promoted or at least tolerated the emergence of independent state organs (Belorussian, Lithuanian, Polish and Ukrainian). The Russian Revolution provided an opportunity to build independent states on the ruins of the tsardom. People's organs of the Soviet authorities appeared wherever Tsarist influence had extended. Created by Belorussian and Ukrainian peasants, they functioned using their own languages. Tongues previously treated as peasant dialects, and hence inferior to the noble (Polish) or administrative (Russian) languages, acquired official status in the new state apparatus.

It is not my intention to offer an analysis of the processes which gave birth to nations in the complicated – and above all volatile – conditions prevailing in the Soviet republics. I will restrict myself to the statement that the policy of supporting national cultures, realized at least during the first half of the 1920s, helped to strengthen national awareness not only in the western regions of the USSR, but also in Poland. The peace treaty signed in Riga in March 1921 left a significant number of people speaking non-Polish languages and usually of non-Polish national consciousness on the Polish side of the borders. The revolutionary events spurred them not only to formulate social programmes, but also to present their own national aspirations. The link between the revolution and the development of Belorussian and Ukrainian national consciousness was sufficiently evident for Polish right-wing circles to treat this phenomenon as the result of a 'Bolshevik conspiracy' and to see the national politics of the first years of Soviet rule almost exclusively as an instrument to destroy the Polish Republic.

The Polish state came into being as a result of the disaster that befell the great powers of central Europe and as a result of the revolution that overtook the whole of central and eastern Europe towards the end of the First World War. The Polish national movement, aiming at the creation of an independent state, was part of that revolution, as were the national movements of other societies of that part of Europe: the Belorussian, Czech, Lithuanian, Slovak, Ukrainian, and others. The Polish Republic was a fruit of that movement; it came into being as a state created by the Polish nation, but extended over an area inhabited also by other national groups. This gave rise to fundamental conflicts. Almost all Polish political parties greeted the creation of the Republic as the realization of Polish national aspirations. The Polish nation regained its lost sovereignty; it freed itself from foreign domi-

Table 12.1. *The national structure of the Polish
population in 1931 (estimate)*

Nationality	'ooos	%
Poles	20,650	64
Ukrainians	5,145	16
Jews	3,133	10
Belorussians	1,966	6
Germans	784	2
Lithuanians	200	1
Russians	140	1
Other	89	0
Total	32,107	100

Sources: J. Tomaszewski, *Ojczyzna nie tylko Polaków* (A
Fatherland not only of Poles) (Warsaw, 1985) p. 50; B.
Makowski, *Litwini w Polsce* (Lithuanians in Poland) (Warsaw,
1986), pp. 26–8.

nation and could decide its own fate, in its own democratic state. In
1931, however, national minorities constituted over a third of the
inhabitants of this state (see Table 12.1). Furthermore, in some
regions these minorities were in the majority; this applied particularly
to the Belorussians and the Ukrainians in the eastern provinces; and
in some northern areas to the Lithuanians also. Of course, the Jews
were not in a majority in any one area (with the exception of a few
small towns in the east), but they made up around 10 per cent of the
population, and so an extremely high proportion. The percentage of
Germans was very small and quickly decreased at the beginning of
the 1920s due to emigration to Germany. In sum, the young state's
national minorities appeared to be sufficiently large for them to aspire
to participation in the formation of policies – if the democratic
programmes of the majority of Polish political parties are to be taken
seriously.

Estimates of the national make-up of the Polish population have
one essential defect: they assume clear and unambiguous divisions
between nationalities. However – as I have indicated above – reality
was rather more complicated. To date, we do not have the means to
calculate how many people belonged to groups of intermediate or
incipient national consciousness. One should also take into consideration that this consciousness proceeded to develop during the interwar
period alongside processes of assimilation. Statistics based on the
census of 1931 show only a specific point in the process of change and
have only an approximate character.

Aspirations to create a Polish nation-state prompted disparate attitudes among Polish society. Right-wing groups – headed by the National Democracy – rejected the notion that in a *Polish* state representatives of *non-Polish* minorities could participate in decisions over the most important questions of state. In Parliament clear political alliances arose naturally on more than one occasion between politicians representing national minorities and Polish left-wing groups, who acknowledged the principle of civic equality more or less consistently. Thanks to this, Parliament chose Gabriel Narutowicz (1865–1922) as President towards the end of 1922. He was supported by the Polish Left and by the national minorities, as opposed to the National Democratic candidate, Maurycy Count Zamoyski (1871–1939), a descendant of the ancient aristocratic family. The new President was spattered with mud – metaphorically speaking – in the right-wing press, and literally, by the nationalistic crowds on the streets of Warsaw. He was soon the victim of a political murder, killed by a mentally unbalanced supporter of the National Democrats.

The national question in interwar Poland had a political aspect – linked with the conflict between a variety of aspirations and programmes – as well as a social, economic and philosophical side. These problems differed slightly in almost every national group.

The greatest similarities can be found in the situation and aspirations of the Belorussians and Ukrainians, and to a certain extent in that of the Lithuanians, although their much smaller numbers and concentration in a relatively small territory meant that the Lithuanian question was of relatively minor importance in Poland. A clear majority of these three societies was made up of peasants, whereas the propertied classes were small in number. There were also relatively few workers; they worked mainly as agricultural labourers or in enterprises connected with the countryside (e.g. in the wood industry, in quarries). The peasants were mainly the owners of smallholdings; one should note, however, that on average the holdings belonging to Ukrainians in the south-eastern provinces were wealthier than Belorussian holdings. This was largely due to unfavourable climatic conditions in the north and less fertile soil.

For the peasant national minorities the land question was of the utmost importance. Large-scale properties were to be found mainly in Polish hands, as were political positions. The landed gentry were the mainstay of Polish influence in the eastern borderlands of the state. The peasants demanded agricultural reform, and thus the parcelling and liquidation of estates. In the central provinces this issue was social and economic in character, in the eastern borderlands it also became a key national question. The conflict between the poor village and the wealthy manor most often corresponded to the conflict between the Polish nobleman (often a magnate; there were estates of over 100,000 hectares) and the Belorussian, Ukrainian and Lithuanian peasant; the tradition of antagonism stretched far into the past. Even if some Polish politicians took up the question of agricultural reform, they still proposed to resettle Polish peasants from other provinces in the eastern borderlands, so that only a part of the reapportioned estates would pass into Belorussian or Ukrainian hands. Such resettlement was actually realized aside from any agricultural reform, particularly in the first half of the 1920s. This exacerbated the Polish–Ukrainian and Polish–Belorussian conflicts, since the newcomers were treated as thieves, stealing land which rightly belonged to the local peasants.

The Polish–Ukrainian conflict was the more acute since in the years 1918–19 the West Ukrainian People's Republic existed for a short time in Eastern Galicia (afterwards part of the Polish state) before its defeat in battle with the Polish army. Ukrainian society treated the Polish administrative authorities as an occupying power. Admittedly some Polish politicians perceived the need to find some kind of compromise with moderate Ukrainian circles, but the extremely nationalistic attitudes of Polish circles in Eastern Galicia proved an obstacle to this. A Ukrainian university was never successfully established (with the sole exception of the illegal university in Lwów), the number of schools with Ukrainian as the language of instruction gradually decreased, and the local authorities employed all manner of oppressive measures against people stubbornly using the Ukrainian language (in some circumstances, Polish law permitted the use of Belorussian, Lithuanian or Ukrainian in court or in addressing the authorities).

In 1922–4 armed detachments existed in the provinces inhabited by Belorussians and Ukrainians. They fought the Polish administration and attacked manors and properties belonging to Poles. They often received help from abroad – from Lithuania and the USSR – and enjoyed the hidden sympathy of the village populace. This movement was successfully crushed, as much by an improvement in the Polish economy after 1925 as by force, although the basic ethnic (national) problems were not solved. After 1929 radical moods grew in conjunction with the great crisis. Nationalist activity increased, particularly among the Ukrainians – the illegal Ukrainian Military

Organization whose members perpetrated terrorist acts against the Poles. In response, a number of arrests (from which Ukrainian deputies were not exempt) followed from mid-September to the end of November 1930 on the recommendation of Józef Piłsudski (1867–1935), and repressive measures directed against many villages; during searches and the hunt for hidden arms the police and army destroyed property, and people were often beaten, particularly those who protested. This so-called pacification strained Polish–Ukrainian relations immeasurably and contributed to a growing hatred of Polish government. Despite the obvious facts, despite the growing conflict which reflected the developed awareness of its own national identity on the part of Ukrainian society, the nationalistic Polish right wing treated the Ukrainians (whom they stubbornly referred to as Ruthenians) as an 'ethnographic mass' which was bound to submit to either Polish or Russian influences. In the 1930s, the administrative authorities made efforts to encourage separate awareness of the regional groups of people speaking Ukrainian dialects; a policy analogous to that carried out by the Germans towards the inhabitants of Mazuria, Warmia and Silesia. In statistical data, the Ukrainians were listed separately from the so-called Ruthenians and support was given to those organizations that cut themselves off from the Ukrainian national movement and declared their links with the Russian nation. Despite all this, Ukrainian self-awareness grew stronger with the passing of time.

Similar tendencies dominated among people speaking Belorussian. Schools with Belorussian as the language of instruction were practically non-existent, numerous obstacles were put in the way of Belorussian institutions and organizations, the use of the Belorussian tongue was eliminated in Catholic churches (Russian was the traditionally dominant language in Orthodox churches), attempts were made to influence Belorussian children by taking them on trips designed to introduce them to the greatness and power of the Republic – despite all this Belorussian intellectuals, social and political activists slowly increased in number. Very often Polish schools, whose task was to strengthen the influence of Polish culture, actually helped the development of Belorussian national consciousness. In the memoirs of an outstanding writer a Polish schoolmistress is mentioned who 'knew our literature and folk poetry and during the few hours devoted to Belorussian language revealed to us our very own native glory'.[9] The very teaching of Polish literature and history provided the pupils with models of love of fatherland and work for its liberation and development, awakening national consciousness.

As a result of pressure exercised by the administrative powers, discrimination against those maintaining Belorussian, Lithuanian or Ukrainian traditions, and finally the activities of Polish schools and organizations, the assimilationist processes among the national minorities (which always occur to some degree) began to gain force, but could not threaten the existence of distinct nations. In this sense nationalist politics failed, but led instead to a sharpening of national conflicts and contributed to the strengthening of nationalistic stances – decidedly hostile towards the Poles – among national minorities in the eastern regions of the state whose population reaped the tragic fruits of this process during the Second World War.

The situation in the western provinces developed rather differently in more than one respect. The creation of a Polish state led, above all, to a fundamental change in the position of the German populace. Previously a privileged social group, they had enjoyed various forms of state support, and, moreover, lived in the conviction of their own cultural superiority. After these lands were incorporated in the Republic they suddenly became a minority, and one viewed with hostility at that, as much by the authorities (though the latter tried to maintain a certain objectivity) as by their Polish neighbours. Many Germans emigrated, in justified fear of vehement hostile reactions on the part of the hitherto discriminated against Polish populace. Such instances were recorded; though I believe that if one takes into account the conditions existing under Prussian rule, there were surprisingly few. Of greater significance was the fact that the Germans ceased to be a privileged group, and a certain section of them saw no prospects for employment in Poland. These were the functionaries of the apparatus of oppression understood in its widest sense – policemen, judges, bureaucrats, and also teachers of whom there appear to have been too many given the needs of what was not after all a very numerous German minority in Poland. Their positions were taken over by Poles. Professional German military personnel also left Poland, and even some landowners sold their estates in order to avoid living in a predominantly Polish (numerically speaking) environment, with authority being exercised by a Polish administration. After 1923 the German Foreign Office (*Auswärtiges Amt*) in Berlin realized that the mass German exodus from Poland was undermining arguments in favour of revising the borders established at Versailles. German consulates in Poland took steps aimed at making emigration more difficult, and before long German organizations began to receive financial help, with the aim of maintaining their strength and influence. In some instances the unemployed parents of children attending German schools received benefits, and thus found themselves in a better position than their neighbours who sent their children to Polish schools. In independent Poland the battle for the soul – so familiar under the partitions – continued.

Such a state of affairs had far-reaching consequences. In Silesia it favoured the continuance – mentioned above – of ideologically neutral groups, and contributed to demoralization, sometimes to personal dramas. Throughout the area of the former Prussian partition it strengthened Polish–German national conflicts, and contributed to nationalistic stances on both sides. Financial help from the Third Reich, in conjunction with political activity, made the quick dissemination of National Socialist influences possible. The situation of Germans who rejected nationalism, above all the Social Democrats, turned out to be particularly difficult. They incurred the hostility of the Polish authorities on two counts: as Germans, and as the organizers of a political movement linked with the Polish Left, questioning the social and political status quo. On the German side – particularly after 1933 – they were treated as a group threatening national unity. The German Social Democrats weakened as a force, but they maintained certain influences among German workers in Poland throughout the interwar period. They later took part in the anti-Nazi underground during the occupation.

There were also a certain number of Germans living beyond the terrain of the former Prussian partition. In the Łódź region they were above all workers and craftsmen, and there were also some businessmen. In other areas they lived mainly in the countryside and worked on the land. During the 1920s they remained on the sidelines of nationalist conflict; later they often succumbed to the poison of Hitlerism.

All the national minorities mentioned so far had one common characteristic: they were members of nations which lived in neighbouring states where they could seek support against the politics of the Polish authorities. Because of this background, conflicts often become particularly acute, especially with Lithuania and Germany. These two states contained Polish minorities within their borders – minorities suffering discrimination in a variety of forms. The Polish government could also justifiably fear that the minorities would become the political instruments of neighbouring states, facilitating the eventual separation from the Republic of its bordering lands. Finding himself in opposition to the government of Piłsudski, General Władysław Sikorski (1881–1943) wrote: 'If we were to . . . shift the eastern borders of Poland to the so-called Curzon line, that is to the Niemen and Bug, and were thus confined to a country with the Vistula as its pivot, conditions would not have permitted us to organize a flexible defence of the state.'[10] It is highly probable that fears of an anti-Polish – spontaneous or inspired – movement of Slav minorities lay behind the Polish government's refusal in 1939 to allow the Red Army to cross the territory of the state in the event of German aggression; this became the direct cause of the failure of the Franco–British–Soviet talks concerning collaboration against the Third Reich.

The situation of the Jews was completely different. First, they were scattered throughout almost the whole state (with the exception of the western provinces, where they constituted an insignificant percentage of the population). Secondly, Poland had no neighbouring Jewish state, which did not in any case exist at that time anywhere in the world, so the Jews could not become a force potentially threatening any part of Polish territory. Thirdly, Jewish organizations had no ambitions to create a separate political organism, and at the most they aimed (though not all of them) to establish autonomous organs of national-cultural self-government. Some Jewish groups declared their absolute loyalty to the Republic, others even took part in its fight for independence. The existence of a Jewish minority within the Polish borders did not therefore create a political threat to the state's interests. It is true that some Jewish organizations declared a pro-gramme of social revolution, and even sympathized with Soviet Russia. This was a result of internal political differences within Jewish society. Analogous political movements also existed in Polish society.

On the other hand, the Jewish question did have real social and religious aspects. In some regions of the country tradesmen and craftsmen were almost all Jewish, and economic conflicts between small farmers and merchants began to acquire nationalist and religious elements. The conviction that trade was basically dishonest was often to be found in the villages, and the merchant who profits because he cheats turned into the stereotype of the Jewish trickster, exploiting the Christian peasant. At the same time the belief that Jews bore the responsibility for the death of Christ persisted in Christian tradition. In Catholic papers for 'the people' there were even – though very rarely – statements to the effect that Jews require the blood of Christian children for the Passover (Pesakh). In the years 1918–21 when the Polish administration and army were still in the process of formation, when local authorities were often in a state of disorganization and with the added upheaval of the Polish–Soviet war, pogroms were known to occur (the bloodiest in Lwów in November 1918) and a variety of excesses took place.

The years of revolution and creation of the Polish state also brought with them an accelerated development of Jewish national consciousness. In traditional orthodox circles, of course, a distance continued to be maintained from secular affairs, and the conviction persisted that the Jews constitute only a religious community linked by history, divine laws and the hope for the coming of the Messiah, but in the new Poland secular groups began to come to the fore of Jewish life who declared their conviction that Jews were a nation like any other. They proposed that Jews should be granted the rights common to national minorities. These differences of opinion even had orthographic consequences. Traditionally in Polish orthography the word 'żyd' [Jew] (in the sense of a representative of a religious community) was written with a small initial letter, whereas in the sense of a member of a nation one had to write 'Żyd' (with a capital initial).

The idea of establishing national-cultural autonomy for Polish Jews had no chance of realization. From the Polish state's political perspective, this would constitute a precedent which if applied to other national minorities would have consequences conflicting with interests of state. It was also rejected by the statesmen of the states of the victorious Entente; during talks between the heads of these states held in 1919, David Lloyd George (1863–1945) stressed that equal rights for Jews in Poland ought to lead to assimilation.[11] Reality proved to be different, however. The assimilatory process embraced only some Jewish circles and was opposed by the majority of Jewish political parties and by Polish nationalists, and Jewish national culture in Poland flourished instead.

The 1930s brought a sharpening of national conflicts in the Polish state. The perceptive observer will see behind them the growth of social conflicts linked with the great economic crisis. The sudden drop in living standards of the rural population strengthened oppositional stances. The land question – with overpopulation becoming more acute in the villages – became decisive for the future. In the eastern provinces this meant an intensification of antagonism between the mainly Polish manor and settlers and the local people who were of a different nationality. At the same time there was a growth of hostility, and even hatred among these people for the administration, which defended the property of landowners and settlers. Of course, there were other causes of dispute, such as the limitation of education in languages other than Polish and the discrimination against non-Polish organizations and societies. The Ukrainians did not forget the traditions of their own statehood. Without a solution to the land problem one could not speak, however, of any compromise solution in the relations between Poland and these minorities.

The Jewish question also had a social basis. In the villages conflicts intensified between the peasant farmer, who constantly received less for his products, and the merchant who struggled for every penny of his earnings to maintain his family. In the towns there was growing competition between various groups of tradesmen and craftsmen. Furthermore, the number of small entrepreneurs began to grow, as the unemployed – despairing of ever finding work – began to trade on a small scale and to carry out various crafts. The number of people wanting to earn a living in this way grew, and the number of potential clients correspondingly decreased. The nationalistic argument reared its head anew in this competitive battle – aimed against Jewish traders and craftsmen. Even if one accepts that the gradual transformation of the structure of Polish trade and crafts was a natural phenomenon, especially its modernization, for which the majority of people carrying out these trades at that time did not have the means, then the basic question must be raised: what was to be done with the people ousted from these traditional professions, in conditions of acute unemployment, when possibilities of emigration were limited by the policies of every state in the world? One should not underestimate the political and philosophical motives behind a number of nationalistic undertakings. Radical groups (though they were not very influential in Poland) drew inspiration from the racist policies of the Third Reich. But quite apart from this, there was no chance of solving the problem of the Jewish minority in Poland without fundamental economic progress and without elimination of, or at the very least a real decrease in, the huge unemployment in the towns.

The German question also had economic aspects, since the strengthening of German nationalistic organizations was made easier due to financial means received from Germany. In this way they had the advantage over those forces in German society in Poland which opposed nationalism, as the latter received no help from Berlin, nor could they count on the help of the Polish authorities. The victory of Adolf Hitler in Germany contributed to the consolidation of nationalistic stances among Germans in Poland. Attempts made by the Polish authorities to counteract Nazi tendencies had no greater chance of success in a situation where a significant part of the German minority felt the Versailles Treaty to be unjust, delivering them into the hands of the disdained Poles.

The national minority question in Poland was not solved during the interwar years. There were too many substantive causes in the way. Attempts at appeasement or at removing conflicts would have had to be based on real economic progress and the solving of social questions – and there was no hope of that. This would not in any case have sufficed. After all, conflict and hostility against the background of ethnic (national) differences had persisted for many decades in the consciousness of antagonistic national groups. Some prejudices had religious authority and several centuries of tradition behind them. The elimination of these elements demanded considerably more time than the twenty-one years of existence vouchsafed to independent Poland.

Such a statement does not preclude critical evaluation of the national policies of the Polish state, or the stances of politicians who too rarely perceived and understood the problems of national minorities. Nor does it entail suspending criticism of nationalistic trends appearing among minorities which approached the whole of Polish society as the enemy, regardless of the fact that there existed Polish groups and oustanding political writers who condemned Polish nationalism.

NOTES

1 J. Bardach, *O dawnej i niedawnej Litwie* (On New and Recent Lithuania) (Poznań, 1988), p. 201.

2 J. Słomka, *Pamiętniki włościanina od pańszczyzny do dni dzisiejszych* (The Memoirs of a Peasant from Corvée to Present Times) (Warsaw, 1983), pp. 163, 165.

3 *Wieś polska 1939–1948. Materiały konkursowe* (Polish Village 1939–1945. Results of a Competition), vol. I, ed. K. Kersten and T. Szarota (Warsaw, 1967), p. 52.

4 S. Grabski, *Z codziennych walk i rozważań* (From Daily Struggles and Considerations) (Poznań, 1923), p. 42.

5 *Radykalni demokraci polscy. Wybór pism i dokumentów 1863–1980* (The Polish Radical Democrats. Selected Writings and Documents 1863–1980) (Warsaw, 1960), p. 13.

6 A. B. McMillin, *Die Literatur der Weissrussen. A History of Byelorussian Literature from Its Origins to the Present Day* (Giessen, 1977), p. 100.

7 Cf. E. Kopeć, *'My i oni' na polskim Śląsku (1918–1939)* ('Us' and 'Them' in Polish Silesia 1918–1939) (Katowice, 1986), p. 107.

8 I was told of this by a fellow student who came from a part of western Silesia

that remained within German borders after 1921. As a result he had practically no knowledge of the Polish language as a child and learned it only after the fall of the Third Reich.

9 Janka Bryl, *Patrzeć na trawę* (Looking on the Grass) (Łódź, 1971), p. 6.

10 W. Sikorski, *Polska i Francja w przeszłości i dobie współczesnej* (Poland and France in the Past and in the Present Time) (Lwów, 1931), p. 114.

11 Cf. *Foreign Relations of the United States. The Paris Peace Conference 1919. Vol. VI* (Washington, D.C., 1944), pp. 624–8.

THIRTEEN

FINLAND: FROM NAPOLEONIC LEGACY TO NORDIC CO-OPERATION

MATTI KLINGE

THE NAPOLEONIC LEGACY

Important elements of modern national feeling were created by the period of the Napoleonic wars: the growth of Romanticism in cultural terms coincided with the mass mobilization of armies, and of all population groups facing the problems of frontier, power, imperium and nation. Politico-national feelings were divided between feelings of victory and pride on the one hand, and apprehensions of disaster and danger on the other. These sentiments had a military and political matrix, but they were interpreted and enlarged into ideologies during the period itself and even more afterwards, in the rapid historical description and assessment of that change.

France was victorious even though defeated; the victories of Arcole, Austerlitz, Jena and Wagram became elements of her national identity, and from about 1840 and especially under the Second Empire a great revival of interest in interpreting the Napoleonic era began. England's victory was also commemorated, with Nelson and Wellington becoming national heroes. In contrast Austria and especially Prussia, even if saved, had to build up their identities on the fact that they had lost important battles and had been occupied by the enemy.

The Russian case is especially interesting. Napoleon's invasion of 1812 was extremely threatening, but the invader was finally forced to an almost complete defeat. This was the result of a *national* uprising against the French, a common battle of all the classes and groups of Russians. In Russia, there was no Romantic national sentiment of any importance, either in the French sense where *nation* was identified with the political idea of *liberté*, or in the German mode, where nation meant *Volk*, a historico-linguistic unity. In Russia, where the old national identification was strictly Christian, a new kind of identification arose with the war and especially with the invasion of Napoleon.

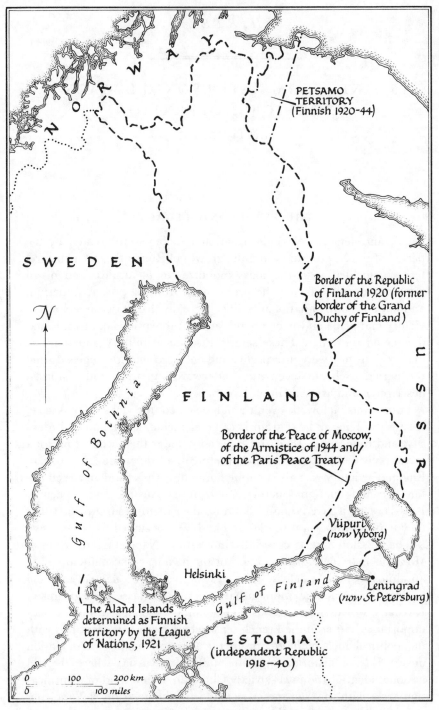

4 Finland's borders in the twentieth century

A striking example of a new feeling of national community is the monument in Red Square in Moscow completed in 1818 by the famous Martos, which represents the village elder Minin and Prince Pozharsky uniting themselves in a national struggle against the Poles in the early seventeenth century – an allegory pointing in reality to the unity of the recent war period. Minin is described in the inscription as *grazhdanin*, which means *citoyen*, *civis*. National feeling means unity of the classes when the *patria* is at war.

In Germany, and, more significantly for Finland, in Denmark and Sweden, the period around 1810 was associated with feelings of defeat and humiliation. Prussia had been defeated in war against France in 1805–7, Sweden in war against Russia in 1808–9. Denmark lost Norway, which was formally conceded in 1814. In this part of Europe, the German Romantic tradition of ethnic and historical enquiry flourished apace, offering a way of positive identification in a difficult situation.

Finland has been a part of Sweden from the earliest consolidation of the realm in the thirteenth century. At Tilsit in 1807, Alexander I and Napoleon divided the world into zones of influence. The coasts and hinterlands of the Gulf of Finland were of great military interest to Russia, especially after 1712, when St Petersburg was made capital of the Empire. In the war of 1808–9, Russia forced Sweden to cede the eastern part of the realm of Finland. From the Russian point of view the aim was to gain hegemony in the Baltic Sea. Russia now had total control of the Gulf of Finland, and with the possession of the western Finnish Turku and Åland archipelago, control of the access route from the Gulf of Bothnia as well. From Kurland and Lithuania up to the northernmost part of the Baltic, the water frontier was now solely owned by the Russian Empire.

The leading Finnish classes understood this politico–military process as representative of current trends: ever since the partition of Poland there had been much defeatism in Sweden. Russia had advanced westwards all through the eighteenth century in Poland, and from the era of Peter the Great, in the Baltic. Sweden had ceded the Baltic provinces, Ingria and Karelia in the Peace of Nystad (1721), and a further part of Finland in 1743. In 1809 it ceded Finland (including Åland), and there were fears over even larger parts of northern Sweden on the western side of the Gulf of Bothnia, at that time occupied by the Russians after a successful campaign over the frozen sea. During the nineteenth century, the Swedes often came back to the fear of Russia – the 'Norrland question'. Sweden's thoughts of defence were built up by a provocative question formulated by a pamphlet in a counterfactual way: How did we lose Norrland? – first the Baltic provinces went, then Finland; when would it be Norrland's turn?

FINLAND AS A GRAND DUCHY

Whereas the educated classes of Finland and the whole of Sweden saw little possibility of winning the 1808–9 war against Russia, the Finnish peasantry fought all over the country with frenzy in a sort of guerrilla war against the Russians. The common people did not wish to become Russians; they wanted to remain Swedish. There was a common fear of the Russian religion and a fear of the Russian social system. The Finns identified themselves deeply with Lutheranism and the old Swedish legal and social order, and respect for and trust in the monarchy.

The new regent, Emperor Alexander I, responded to the feelings of the Finns in a most generous way: Finland was attached to Russia solely for military purposes. Otherwise it became a state in itself, the Grand Duchy of Finland, where the new monarch, an autocrat in Russia, ruled in 1809 as a constitutional monarch with the Diet of the country, composed and working in the same manner as the Swedish Diet. The Swedish legal and official system was maintained, as well as the position of the Church. Continuity became the key word in the everyday life of Finland. For example, 'The Law of the Swedish Realm', the great codification of 1734, was printed several times in Finland under that title during the period of the Grand Duchy until 1917, when Finland became a sovereign country.

But even if Finland, in terms of culture and structures, continued as part of old Sweden, the new 'little Sweden' after 1809, now minus Finland, changed rapidly. A new dynasty of revolutionary origin (the Bernadottes), a new constitution, the rapid flowering of Romanticism and then, later on, an earlier experience of industrialization than in agrarian Finland, all produced a difference between the new Sweden on the one hand, and Finland, still identifying itself with the old Sweden, on the other. A large part of Finnish cultural identity was to consist in a conservative continuation of the way of life and a culture characteristic of the former periphery and now disappearing in the centre.

However, Finnish identity did not emerge solely out of its relation to the past and the tradition of the former capital, Stockholm. The essential feature was its relationship to Russia. In the Diet of 1809, the Emperor-Grand Duke pronounced the famous words constituting the Finnish nation: it was *placée desormais au rang des nations*. He described this national existence by appealing to the maintenance of the old laws and social order. The Finns would not have to think of the old order with any nostalgia – because it was conserved – but only to look forward to peaceful collaboration with the former Swedish co-patriots. The emphasis on the Finnish legal and even constitutional tradition meant an organizational separation from Russia, and in fact Finnish bureaucracy was to have very little to do with the Russian administration during the whole period of the Grand Duchy, the Emperor-Grand Duke himself guaranteeing the union.

The organization of Finland as a part of the Russian Empire has been compared with the position of other Russian territorial acquisitions towards Russia itself. In fact, maintaining local legal and administrative systems was not unusual. What *was* most unusual in the Finnish case was maintaining and strengthening these characteristics during the whole period until the Russian Revolution of 1917, when centralizing tendencies elsewhere tended to diminish and destroy local and national differences – and not only in the Russian Empire. But no other new acquisition had the character of creating a new nation.

Within the realm of Sweden, Finland had been a well-known part of the kingdom, and it was said that it had in olden times been a kingdom itself. Very little evidence can be shown for such theories. The main parts of the Swedish kingdom were the old kingdoms of Svecia and Gothia, but Finland was a duchy, and from 1581 a Grand Duchy. Previously it was called the Eastland as there was also a northern land, Norrland. Finland was sometimes mentioned as a separate unity in formulas like 'Sweden and Finland', but more often included in the formula 'Sweden and Gothia'. In 1650, a leading political theoretician said that Sweden, Gothia and Finland form a *plenissima foederatio*. Some phenomena can be stressed as Finnish peculiarities, such as the more eastern political orientation of the Finnish nobility in earlier times, but mostly the absence of any special Finnishness is striking, if normal local patriotism is not overinterpreted.

The main differentiating characteristic of Finland was its dominant language – Finnish. But the language of the peasantry was not an important issue since the religious and legal systems were in existence. The Bible was in Finnish and the General Law also, pastors preached in Finnish, and in the Parliament in Stockholm there was a Finnish interpreter for the Finnish representatives in the Estate of peasants. Other non-Swedish languages existed also in Sweden, especially German, Danish and Lappish, and previously, Estonian and Lettish.

Laws and decrees were printed in Swedish, but more important still, in Finnish also. Written language in non-religious matters did not really become important in the people's lives until the middle of the nineteenth century with general schooling and the advent of less expensive books, newspapers, indoor lighting, and a need for and interest in learning and communication. Thus the special Finnish identity stressed in the creation of the Finnish nation in 1809 was not based on linguistic definition. For a long time Finnishness meant special administration, law and bureaucracy, both civil and ecclesiastical.

ENLIGHTENED BUREAUCRACY AND EMPIRE CLASSICISM

The role of the bureaucracy can hardly be overstressed in Finnish history. It was due to ideological, structural and also political factors. Indeed to a large extent there were no other structural and political factors: for a long period there was no other political and economic power in the country which could have acted as a pressure group. No great cities existed; it took a long time before Helsinki, declared to be the capital of the Grand Duchy, became in addition a city of economic importance. Rather, it was purely an administrative, military and educational centre, as its architecture indicates. Those three functions dominate the inner city built in St Petersburg Empire Classicism: administration buildings – the Imperial Senate of Finland, now the State Council; the Imperial Palace, now the Palace of the President of the Republic, and so on; educational buildings – the Imperial Alexander University, now Helsinki University, with its great library, its observatory, university gardens and clinics; and military buildings, such as the great barracks of the Imperial Finnish Guards, today the army headquarters, and the buildings of the Finnish Sea Equipage, now the Foreign Ministry. The absence of a wealthy bourgeoisie also meant the absence of a strong liberal pressure group, and that of artists and journalists in any quantity, comparable to that supported by bourgeois patronage elsewhere in Europe.

Also absent was a wealthy landed aristocracy, the Finnish nobility being small and rather poor. Promotion to noble rank continued until 1906, and was still important in the period after 1863, when Parliament began meeting regularly. But those new noblemen were mostly civil and military bureaucrats, very close to the state.

Absent also of course was the court, the Emperor-Grand Duke residing in St Petersburg or its surroundings (Tsarskoje-Selo, Peterhof, etc.) and visiting Finland rather seldom. And, after the 1809 Diet which drew up the constitution, the parliamentary Estates were also absent until 1863, after which they met regularly, but only every third or fifth year. From 1907 there was the unicameral Parliament, elected by universal suffrage including women, but the government (the Imperial Senate for Finland) was not dependent on Parliament's trust, and in fact was without it between 1909 and 1917.

One reflection of the bureaucracy's importance was the fact that a sense of national feeling was not founded on opposition to the fatherland or its institutions: the leading idea was a respect for, even worship of, the regent, and loyalty towards him. The dominant ideology of the Russian Emperors was that of Enlightened autocracy, and much was done to make the bureaucracy really *enlightened*. In this sense, Finland had many advantages. Its Lutheran-ascetic traditions, and the sort of military order of the old Swedish society which resembled nearby Prussian ideals, set the tone for Russian state ideology. The Emperor's fight against corruption drew upon his new subjects' traditions. In general, the Russian state and military organization benefited much from the skill and loyalty of officials recruited in the Western and Lutheran parts of the Empire – Finland, Estonia and Livonia.

Enlightened bureaucracy corresponded with Classicism in style and thinking, and was in opposition to the Romantic trend of the nineteenth century. Taste, harmony, self-command and civic virtue were central ideals – not Romantic individualism, the cult of genius, *la vie bohème* or extravagant fantasy. Of course, many of these phenomena reached the 'Prussian' part of Europe, but were not transformed into or understood as a social ideology.

The University's role in forming an Enlightened bureaucracy for Finland was almost unique: the University, which had been founded in 1640 by Queen Christina, was in 1811 transformed by the Emperor Alexander into a much more modern and enlarged institution, which was then transferred to the new capital, Helsinki, from Turku – the ecclesiastical capital, of Finland – and given the name of Imperial Alexander University in Finland. It was granted a monopoly in the education required for all kinds of learned professions: the ministry, civil service, schoolteaching, medicine and pharmacy, and later on, the training of personnel in agriculture and forestry. Only military training was separate, with Finland possessing its own Cadet School in Hamina (Fredrikshamn), which trained officers for posts throughout the Russian Empire.

It is important to underline that the University was not only a school of bureaucracy, but a free University, whose task was to create a national ideology. The University became, as planned by the Emperor and his counsellors (Archbishop Tengström, Count Speransky, Count Armfelt and others) the centre of almost all the intellectual life of the country, and thereby of all kinds of activity: the arts, journalism, even economic entrepreneurship. The professors and the students played a central role in developing a civic life.

The central line of early Finnish nationalism is that of neo-classical conservatism, identifying Finland and the Finns as something like northern Greeks, a nation in harsh climatic conditions, but sublime in its trust in God and Fate, its sense of duty in the Roman mould. To this was added, in the 1830s, a strong feeling of archaic-artistic legitimation by the *Kalevala*, a collection of folklore made into an almost Homeric epic by Elias Lönnrot, later Professor of Finnish language and literature at Alexander University. At the same time, J. L. Runeberg, lecturer in Greek at the University, depicted the Finns in an idealized, classical manner.

THE FINNISH RESPONSE TO REVOLUTIONARY NATIONALISM

Lönnrot and Runeberg worked in a tradition corresponding to 'official' nationalism, and in opposition to Western, revolutionary ideas trying to find their way into Finland as well. This happened first at the beginning of the 1820s, then at the time of the Polish rebellion in 1831, and again during 1848–9, and also during the Baltic theatre of the Crimean war 1854–6. All these events produced a specific Finnish reaction to a situation whereby the Western liberal and leftist ideologies extended their influence, especially among students, a situation which was of great concern to Russia, as a guarantor of the Congress of Vienna state system in Europe.

The reaction to all these events produced a strengthening of the especially Finnish component of the national ideology. This almost satisfied both parties in the question: for the liberals this could be seen as something national and non-governmental, and from the Imperial point of view, it did not go so far as to encourage revolutionary tendencies.

This is seen especially in 1848, when the students organized a great spring celebration on a green field outside Helsinki: the first Finnish national flag was used, a Finnish national anthem was composed and sung several times, speeches were made and generally a great spirit of solidarity was created. But all this happened in a loyal way with toasts to the Emperor and the heir apparent, who was Chancellor of the University, to the Senate, to Bureaucracy and Fatherland. The national anthem *Vårt Land*, written by Runeberg and composed by the University's music master F. Pacius, is anything but revolutionary: it emphasizes the moral values of nature and the countryside, national destiny, and the Finns' consciousness of all that the future could win through faith, hope and work. In those same days and months, most of the other European students and intellectuals trusted not to fate, hope and work, but to revolution, arms and action.

For the main Finnish architect of the University-based Enlightened bureaucratic patriotism, Archbishop Tengström, the essential goal in 1808–9 had been to protect the Finnish peasant's Lutheran faith and free possession of his lands – not to expose him to Russification on either of these central points. It was of lesser importance if the comparatively small educated classes lost something of their political prerogatives in the parliamentary tradition. Instead the University became a new sort of Parliament, a centre for intellectual activity. This was apparent by mid-century. Finland preserved its special autonomous status in the Russian Empire during the period between the 1848 revolutions and the decline of political liberalism in the 1870s. Much of Finnish development can be seen in contrast to·that of Poland, or to the noble-dominated rule of the Baltic provinces. Finnish rural-based loyal conservatism yielded political dividends every time the Poles, relying on their traditional national pride, rebelled against Russia. So especially around 1863, when the Polish rebellion was crushed and the reforms in Russia stopped, Finland reaped the gains of a new parliamentary life, its own currency (the mark), the declaration of Finnish as the official language of administration and jurisdiction, and a series of modernizing reforms, such as communal autonomy, joint-stock company law, and separation of schools from the Church. Later still came a Finnish army, and something known as proto-parliamentarianism, whereby the leaders of the political parties were nominated senators (ministers) by the new Emperor Alexander III in 1881.

Certainly a very strong role was played by the Finnish rural, peasant, class. It was always the largest though not necessarily the most dominant group in Finnish society, even if the timber industry and other areas of employment began to develop, especially during and after the 1860s, with foreign trade, the expansion of railways and canals, and a money-based economy. Agriculture also developed, especially in the direction of animal husbandry.

During the non-parliamentary period after 1809 peasants did not play any active role in civic society, but their importance was great. The patriotism of Runeberg's and Lönnrot's work was based on an idealization of the Finnish peasantry; being Finnish entailed accepting the peasants as an integral part of the nation. The peasants' language, at least of the majority, Finnish, was understood to be the 'national language', the 'mother tongue', in principle, in spite of the fact that all higher cultural life was carried out, for practical purposes, in Swedish. Thus respect for the language was in line with the government's aims in promoting Finnish: it meant first of all being distinct from Sweden, and secondly, better administration, more *enlightened* government. Finnishness was thus not in any way in opposition to the Emperor's viewpoint; it could make for career difficulties for those of the bureaucratic elite (especially in western Finland) who did not speak any Finnish at all, or whose command of it was weak. From the 1840s the government began to demand training in Finnish from future civil servants, from 1863 Finnish was accepted as an administrative language, and from 1882 it became obligatory when the subject demanded it, so that in the first years of the twentieth century Finnish became the dominant language of the administration.

THE SOCIAL BACKGROUND OF THE FENNOMANIAN MOVEMENT

Although the importance of the peasant role was acknowledged, this meant no participation in the liberal sense. In the 1840s, the young philosopher J. V. Snellman tried to import German and Swedish-influenced political debate into the country. In many respects, he was ahead of his time; conditions in Finland did not yet correspond to the more industrialized, bourgeois areas of western Europe. But Snellman's ideas of 'education of the nation and nationalization of the educated' expressed the important idea of participation. This idea was carried out by a growing press in Finnish. In the revolutionary period 1848–50, the government for some years prohibited publication in Finnish political literature, except on economic and religious issues. But from the 1850s, newspapers and books in Finnish became more common, and due to the economic growth of the peasant class, Finnish-language publication became important. The rise of timber prices brought a great deal of money to the peasants, and important consequences included Finnish publications and Finnish secondary schools.

The estate of the peasantry was one of the four estates of the Diet, and it worked mainly in Finnish. The estate of the clergy, who worked closely with the peasantry, shared much of its outlook. They were

Fennomen, working for culture and education in Finnish, moral conservatism and agrarian values. This meant political conservatism and pro-Russian attitudes, but social progressivism, promotion of social mobility through education, and a demand for better administration, especially for Finnish to be used for a variety of services.

In the other two Estates, the nobility and burgesses, liberal ideas, pro-industrial sympathies and Western orientation were predominant, but did not override a general patriotism, including loyalty to the monarchy. Industrial and other kinds of progressivism were counterbalanced by a certain social conservatism which took a legalistic form in the desire to maintain the special Finnish system of administration and legislation. This meant differentiation from Russia, but also maintenance of social privileges as part of the frequently old-fashioned legal system. This Finnish legalism was often seen as nationalistic and chauvinistic by the Russians. Swedish was valued highly not because it was the language of a Swedish-speaking minority of peasants and fishermen, but because it was the carrier of the cultural and legal tradition of the country, from Swedish times and the formative period of the nineteenth century: Runeberg, Snellman and most of the other founders of Finnish patriotism had written in Swedish.

A very important aspect of Finnish nationalism and national development consists of the transformation of these elites. During the last decades of the nineteenth century and the beginning of the twentieth, the dominant language of Finnish cultural and political life changed from Swedish to Finnish, over a long period of active bilingualism. Bilingualism had old traditions, especially among the numerically largest portion of the educated classes, the clergy. In earlier times, Finnish was the language of practical everyday life, more spoken than written, notwithstanding religious literature dating from the Reformation, whereas Swedish was the language of education, administration and written culture in general. Now Finnish, from the 1840s and the 1860s onwards, rapidly developed into a language of written and philosophical culture. The social background here is telling: Finnish literature was almost always developed by individuals with Swedish – and therefore German and Latin – as a background, as the language in which they had learned to think and write, and had received their higher education. So Finnish was, and became, a language expressing the common Finnish culture, but extended also to its highest forms, maintaining the meaning even while modifying the language to enable it to express ideas of social European cultural tradition. This process had already begun in the sixteenth century, with biblical and legal texts, and was now rapidly extended to the whole field of culture: novels, poetry, science, journalism and administration.

Socially this change was carried out by the Fennomen, that is, people who believed in the future of Finnish-spoken culture and were convinced that this special Finnish culture, with its Swedish and Lutheran roots, could only be maintained in Finland if translated into Finnish. Finland could have been Swedenized – the process was already in a highly developed phase in some social and regional sectors in Finland when the political change occurred. Social factors assured that in spite of change and the promotion of Finnish, Swedenization made headway during the nineteenth century, for upward social mobility was impossible without a good command of Swedish. But in contrast to Ireland, what happened in this process was counterbalanced by the promotion of Finnish.

The state was responsible for promoting Finnish: measures to confirm the grammatical structure and regulate orthography date from the 1810s; a lectureship in Finnish at Alexander University dated from 1828, followed by a Chair; language instruction for priests and civil servants was obligatory from the 1840s, and the administration was bilingual after 1863. But the economic advancement of the Finnish-speaking rural classes had even greater impact as it entailed greater general cultural and political participation. This had the result that elements of the educated classes began not only to declare themselves Finnish-speakers in principle, but also to adopt Finnish increasingly as their language in practice – an aim already canvassed by Snellman and the young Fennomen of the radical 1840s. Much of this was due to the press and to publications in Finnish, but the decisive factor was the establishment of secondary schools where teaching took place in Finnish, starting in the 1850s, but accelerating in the 1880s and 1890s. These schools resulted in the emergence of a new educated class consisting of the offspring of traditionally educated groups such as the clergy, and of upwardly mobile rural groups such as peasants, merchants, and so on. Common schooling created common ideals, marriages and generally speaking a gradual transformation of the dominant culture linguistically and socially. This became a true Finnish model, still exerting influence in the 1950s and 1960s.

Other groups of the educated classes continued to maintain the Swedish-speaking tradition of Finnish culture. Their aim was to stress cultural continuity, and links with Sweden and western Europe in general, coupled with a fear that over-rapid social and cultural development would produce an intervening layer of culturally weak groups, who would be vulnerable to Russification measures were they to be introduced in Finland. Both the Fennomen and the liberals were aware of developments in the Baltic provinces but were confident that Finland's changes would take a different form.

Despite conflicts between Finnish agrarian interest groups, and the Swedish legalist industrial lobby, both shared the main constituent of Finnish patriotism: their attitude to Russia. Even though sympathy to Russia varied, all wanted to preserve an ethnically, legally and religiously non-Russian Finland, and to maintain and develop the special Finnish administration and Parliament. On the other hand, few hoped for a renewal of the union with Sweden, which had now altered its orientation in a union with Norway.

At the start of the nineteenth century, the peasantry was rather homogeneous, consisting mainly of freeholders. But as a result of the high birth rate social conditions changed. Those landowning peasant farmers who were in a position to profit from the continent-wide rise in timber prices, innovations in agriculture and the switch to animal production, with butter in demand in London and St Petersburg, became wealthier and wealthier. But on the other hand, peasants with little or no land were transformed into a rural proletariat, only a portion of whom found a livelihood in the growing but still small cities with their small-scale, albeit increasing, industry, or through emigration to St Petersburg and, later, to America, or by cultivating new land in northern Finland.

THE TWENTIETH CENTURY: POPULIST NATIONALISM, SOCIALISM AND BILINGUALISM

The proletariat became a force in Finnish social and political life very late but to great effect, during the Russian-wide ferment of 1905–7, which was a landmark for Finland too. At this point, after the first elections based on universal suffrage in 1907, the old Fennomanian party developed a strong nationalistic, Finnish-language platform, with the aim of gaining support from the proletariat with a populist programme of nationalism and social reforms. This programme also served to defend themselves from the accusations of the bilingual, legalist front, who thought the 'old' Fennomen had gone too far in their monarchism, and in recent political negotiations, especially the Finno-Russian administrative conflict of 1899–1905.

'Old' Fennomanian populistic nationalism succeeded in shaping a new middle-class nationalism, and some 200,000–300,000 people out of a population of 2.5 million changed their Swedish family names into Finnish in 1906 as a demonstration of political-social identification. But this was mainly a middle-class phenomenon, in which neither the Fennoman 'aristocracy' nor the workers were interested. Workers in the countryside and the towns preferred voting socialist, and their party gained 40 per cent of the mandates in a new unicameral Parliament. This rapidly undermined Fennoman linguistic and social populism. But the latter had already left a lasting legacy in precipitating the creation of a Swedish party, which began to move from the legalist tradition into a Swedish-speaking agrarian and populist direction, and to cultivate links with Sweden. There Swedish nationalism had gained much ground in public opinion, especially after the rupture of the union with Norway. Swedish irredentism, eyeing the Swedish-speaking coastal population of Finland, was on the increase.

If Fennoman populist propaganda and socialist social propaganda created uncertainty in both the Swedish-speaking upper classes and the Swedish-speaking peasantry, who now found themselves together in the Swedish party in 1906, their new *Suecomania* created opposition among many Finnish-speakers. A stronger identification with different cultures and social groups began to gain ground at the expense of the former bilingualism of upper-class society. Many families divided along linguistic lines and had greater difficulty in maintaining links when children went to schools or, as students at university, joined clubs ('nations') affected by linguistic propaganda. These problems were apparent by the 1920s.

The constitution of the Finnish Republic dating from 1919 (still in force), the 1922 language act and the Helsinki University statutes of 1923 all provided for a bilingual state, administration and general cultural outlook. Finnish and Swedish are the national languages, and command of both is required from all officials, civil servants and the educated populace in general. Being educated meant, and still means, bilingualism to some extent. But during the 1920s and 1930s social mobility, propagandistic echoes from 1906–14, fascistic influences common with Europe, and the absence of the Russian factor, put a new language struggle into effect. However, it is important to note that in spite of much agitation practically no legislation was changed: the country remained bilingual. As in the Liberation and Civil War of 1918, the new war against Soviet Russia in 1939–40 and 1941–4 demonstrated the national, patriotic unity of the Finns, true as much in the former war, where the dividing line between Whites and Reds was not one of language.

Since the Second World War Finnish national feelings are mostly anchored in a patriotism concerned with defending the national heritage at a crossroads of different social and historical systems. Finland remains a Nordic country as to its traditions, religion, social system and life style. But it has a special flavour because of its closeness to Russia, as experienced from the period of the Grand Duchy 1809–1917; from the wars in 1918 and 1939–44, fought on both sides with heroism and without the experience of occupation; and from the successful cohabitation (especially in the economic sphere) and mutual respect of the post-war period. Very close co-operation with Sweden and other Nordic countries perpetuates the importance of the Swedish language, but more as a matter of practical utility than as an aspect of national agitation. Popular feeling expressed from time to time has not altered the general consensus.

The Finnish nation and its national character needs to be explained in international context, especially that of rival powers in the Baltic. Economic and social development is a part of this greater context, and ideologies influence both political and social conditions, which are in turn interpreted in both aesthetic and social terms.

NOTE

This essay is based on the author's works on Finnish history:

A Brief History of Finland (6th edn 1990); *Let Us Be Finns! Essays on History* (1990); *Kungliga Akademien i Åbo 1640–1808* (1988); *Kejserliga Alexanders Universitet 1808–1917* (1989); *Helsingfors Universitet 1917–1990* (1991); *Runebergs två fosterland* (1984); *Mellan lojalism och rysshat* (1988); *Studenter och idéer I–IV* (1969–79); *Finlands blåvita färger* (1988).

INDEX

Absolutism, 45, 49, 92, 148, 236
Adenauer, K., 190
agriculture, 89, 232, 277, 325, 329
Alexander I (Russia), 319–20
Alexander III (Russia), 325
Alfieri, V., 63, 72–3, 75
Alfonso II (Asturias), 115
Alfonso III 'the Great' (Asturias-León), 115, 117
Alfonso V (Portugal), 119
Alfonso VI (León-Castile), 119
Alfonso VII (Asturias-León), 117–18
Alfonso X (Castile), 117
Alxinger, J. B., 213
American Revolution, 9, 131
Amsterdam, 129
Anarchism(-ts), 11
ancien régime, 45–6, 48, 132, 185, 187
Andrássy, G., 242, 245, 283
Andreas II (Hungary), 251
Andrian-Werburg, V., 215
Anne of Austria, 45
anti-Semitism, 187–8, 194, 204
Archduke Charles (Habsburg-Lorraine), 205, 214
aristocracy, see nobles(-ility)
Armfelt, G. M., 324
Arndt, E. M., 215
Ausgleich, see Austro-Hungarian Compromise
Austria, xix, 148, 160, 196–221 passim, 317
    Anschluss, 162, 217, 219, 221
    bourgeois society, 212–13
    First World War, 187, 198, 205, 217
    Länder (domains), 206–14 passim
    Länder (Federal Lands), 217
    language(s), 213–15
    'Mitteleuropa', 199
    national symbols, 200–5
    republic, 196, 198–200, 217, 219, 221
    revolution (1848–9), 214–15, 237
    Second World War, 182, 189, 198

Slavic populations, 215
State Treaty (1955), 201–2, 204
Treaty of St-Germain, 219
Vormärz, 158–9, 214
    see also Austria-Hungary; Habsburg Monarchy
Austria, political parties
    Christian Socials, 220–1
    Communists, 220
    National Socialists, 198–200, 204, 219–21
    Social Democrats, 201, 203, 217, 219–21
    Socialist Party (SPÖ), 204
Austria, towns
    Graz, 210
    Innsbruck, 207, 210
    Krems, 218
    Melk, 197
    Salzburg, 218
    Vienna, see separate entry
Austria and
    Bavaria, 212–13
    Czechoslovakia, 196, 205–6
    Germany, 149, 161, 187, 198, 205–6, 212, 216, 218–19
    Hungary, 205–6, 248–66 passim
    Italy, 63, 66, 77, 79, 82, 86–8, 90–1, 93, 196, 205–6
    Liechtenstein, 206
    Netherlands, 130–1
    Poland, 196, 205, 297
    Prussia, 149, 162, 182, 187, 212, 242
    Romania, 196
    Soviet Union, 196, 205
    Yugoslavia, 196, 205–6
Austria-Hungary, 198, 241–3, 245, 258–9, 262
Austrian Monarchy, see Habsburg Monarchy
Austro-Hungarian Compromise, 196, 254, 257–8, 282–5, 287

Austro-Hungarian Monarchy, *see* Austria-
  Hungary
Austroslavism, 236–7
Aytoun, W. E., 26
Azaña, M., 110
d'Azeglio, M., 87, 89–91, 99

Babenbergs (dynasty), 207
Babeuf, F., 66
Bach, A. von, 240
Bahuševič, F., 300
Balbo, C., 73, 85–7
Bamberger, L., 186
Basques, xix, 2, 113, 117
battles
  Agincourt, 40
  Arcole, 317
  Auerstedt, 157
  Austerlitz (Slavkov), 235, 317
  Boyne, 9
  Crécy, 37
  Jena, 317
  Sadova, 242
  Verdun, 55
  Wagram, 317
  White Mountain, 232
Bauer, O., 217, 219
Bauer, W., 197
Bavaria, 212–13
Beauharnais, E. de, 70, 74
Bebel, A., 164
Belcredi, R. von, 283
Belgium, xv, xix, 128–43 *passim*
  Catholicism, 131, 134, 137, 139–41
  Christian Democracy, 136, 138, 141–2
  ethnicity, 130, 136, 143
  Flemings(-ish), 128, 133–6, 139–43
  Industrial Revolution, 135, 141
  liberalism, 135–6, 139, 142
  Meeting Party, 135
  socialism, 136, 139, 142
  Southern Netherlands, 129–30, 132
  Walloon(-s), 128, 133, 137, 140–3
Belgium, languages
  Dutch, 128, 134–6, 138, 142
  French, 128, 133–5, 137–8, 142
Belgium, towns
  Antwerp, 135, 141
  Bruges, 144
  Brussels, 137, 140, 142
  Ghent, 136–7, 141, 144
  Leuven, 130, 142
  Liège, 129, 131, 144
Belgium and Germany
  First World War, 137–8, 144
  Second World War, 139–40
belle époque, 135
Bellegarde, J. J. J. von, 76

Beneš, E., 244–5
Bentinck, W., 75–6
Béranger, P. J. de, 51
Berlin Wall, 20, 193
Beust, F. von, 242, 283, 285
Bianco, C. di St Jorioz, 84
Bismarck, O. von, 153, 184, 216
Blanque, L. A., 81
Blum, L., 55
Bobula, J., 261
Bohemia, xviii, 161, 207–8, 210, 214–16;
  see also Czech Lands; Czechoslovakia
Bonaparte, *see* Napoleon I
Borelli, F., 273
Bosnia and Herzegovina, 274, 289
Boudewijn (Baudouin) of Belgium, 140
bourgeoisie, 39, 51, 55, 88, 96, 158–9,
  164–5, 169, 216, 218–19, 237,
  239–40, 287
  big, 165
  commercial, 154
  liberal, 276, 286
  manufacturing, 154
  petty, 158, 217–18
  urban, 277
  see also Bürgertum; middle class(es)
Brandt, W., 192
Britain, *see* British Isles
British Isles, xv, 1–31 *passim*
  Plantagenets, 31
  reformation, 6
  Stuarts, 7–8
  Tudors, 7
  see also Cornwall; England; Ireland;
    Scotland; Ulster; Wales
British Isles, towns
  Belfast, 9, 12–13, 18
  Cambridge, 15
  Carlisle, 4
  Derry, 16
  Dublin, 3, 5–6, 8–10, 13, 19–20
  Edinburgh, 8, 18, 27
  Glasgow, 13, 27
  Limerick, 10
  London, *see* separate entry
  Manchester, 13
  Southampton, 39
Brittany, xvi, 3, 6, 21, 31, 37, 43, 46, 51
Brno, 212, 242
Bruce, R., 5, 25
Brünn, *see* Brno
Budapest, 212, 242, 261, 290
Buonarroti, F. M., 66, 77, 79–82
burghers, 36, 41, 154, 208, 234, 295, 297,
  327
Bürgertum, 154–5, 182–5, 189
  bürgerlich, 211
Burns, R., 25, 30

Calvin, J., 156
Capet, H., 36
capitalism, 13, 148, 150, 153, 156–7, 159, 163, 167, 228, 234, 237, 242
Carlo Felice (Piedmont), 86
Carlos V (Spain), 107, 129, 208–9
Carpatho-Ukraine, 252, 264, 304
Carson, E., 14
Castil(l)e(-ians), 38–9, 107, 109, 116, 118–21
Castlereagh, R. Stewart, 76
Castro, A., 110–11, 114
Catalonia(-ns), xvi, 31, 107, 109, 117–18, 120
Catholicism(-cs), 6, 8–9, 17–20, 23, 25, 44, 46–8, 54, 56–7, 59, 84–5, 95, 113, 131, 185, 203, 210, 212–13, 260, 281, 288–9, 296, 300
Cattaneo, C., 91–2, 97, 100
Cavour, C., 88–9, 91, 96–9
Charlemagne, 35
Charles I (England), 7–9
Charles I (Habsburg-Lorraine), 244
Charles V (France), 37
Charles V (Habsburg), see Carlos V (Spain)
Charles VI (Habsburg), 209–10
Charles VII (France), 40
Charles VIII (France), 43
Charles IX (France), 43
Charles X (France), 48–51
Charles Albert (Piedmont), 79–80, 86–7, 90–2
Charles the Bald, 35
Charles of Blois, 37
Chartism, 22–3, 25
Churchill, W., 16
class struggle, 81
Classicism, 72, 82
Clemenceau, G., 53
clergy, xviii, 41, 69, 84, 129–30, 217, 228, 232, 249, 276, 328
Clovis, 35
Cobbett, W., 1, 10, 89
Coloman (Hungary), 248
Communism (-ts), 55–6, 58, 77, 81, 91, 159, 165, 193, 220–1, 263
Congress of Vienna, 132
Connolly, J., 13, 18
Conrads, H., 204
Cornwall, 3, 6, 21
Cosmas, 228–9
Costa, J., 109
Counter-Reformation, 85, 130
Cousin, V., 82
Croatia, 270–90 passim
    Habsburg Monarchy, 270–90 passim

Hungary, 207, 248–9, 251–2, 254–6, 261, 270
    see also Dalmatia and northern Croatia
Croatia, towns
    Dubrovnik, 270, 278–9
    Kotor, 274
    Split (Spalato), 276, 278–9, 286–7
    Zadar (Zara), 276, 278, 286–7
    Zagreb, 257, 271, 273, 278
Croatia and Slavonia, 252, 283–4; see also Croatia
Cromwell, O., 8
Crusades, 39
Cuoco, V., 68–9, 74
Czech Lands, xviii, 215, 228–47 passim
    Absolutism, 236
    Austroslavism, 236–7
    economy, 232–5, 242–3
    Frankfurt National Assembly, 238–9
    German question, 228–43 passim
    Germany, 237–45
    Habsburg Monarchy, 232–46 passim
    Hussite movement, 231–2
    language(s), 229–38
    National Revival, 232–7, 246
    Protectorate of Bohemia and Moravia, 246
    revolution (1848–9), 237, 246
    Russia, 235–6, 238–9, 244
    Slav question, 235–6, 241–2
    White Mountain, battle, 232
Czech Lands, political parties
    Agrarian Party, 244
    National Social Party, 244
    Realist Party, 243
    Social Democrats, 243
    State Rights Party, 243
    Young Czech Party, 244
Czechoslovakia, 245–7, 307
    Austria, 196, 205–6
    Czechoslovak National Council, 244–5
    Czechoslovak Republic, 246
    federative state, 246–7
    Hungary, 263
    Munich Agreement, 246
    Washington Declaration, 245
Czechoslovakia, towns
    Bratislava, 265
    Brno, 212, 242
    Hradec, 231
    Košice, 265
    Kutná Hora, 229–30
    Mikulov, 242
    Mladá Boleslav, 243
    Pardubice, 231
    Prague, 229–30, 233, 236, 245

Dalimil's chronicle, 230
Dalmatia, Croatia and Slavonia, *see*
    Triune Kingdom
Dalmatia and northern Croatia, 270–90
    passim
    Autonomists, 273–9, 282, 285–7
    Illyrianism, 271, 276
    language(s), 273–90
    Nationalists, 273, 276–83, 285–7
    peasants(-ry), 275–7, 286
    Slav ideology, 276–9 *passim*
    Yugoslavism, 271, 280–1, 288–9
Dalmatia and northern Croatia, political
    parties
    National Party (Croatian), 271, 277,
        283, 289
    National Party (Dalmatian), 277, 282,
        284–7, 289
    National Party (Serbian), 289
Dąmbrowski, J., 299
Dante, A., 72
David, J.–L., 50
David I (Scotland), 5
Deák, F., 259
Defoe, D., 21
democrats(-cy), 80, 83, 91–9 *passim*
    bourgeois, 159–60, 163
Denmark, 329
Deym, F., 215
Díaz de Vivar, R. ('el Cid'), 119
Dobrovský, J., 233, 237
Doderer, H. von, 196
Dollfuss, E., 219
Doyle, C., 30
Dreyfus, A., 54
Dual Monarchy, *see* Austria-Hungary
Dürich, J., 244
Duroc, M., 70

early bourgeois revolution, 149, 152–4
East Germany, *see* German Democratic
    Republic (GDR)
economy(-ics), xvii, 141, 164, 232–5,
    242–3, 253, 325
    agriculture, 89, 232, 277, 325, 329
    feudal, xix
    Industrial Revolution, 141, 157, 159
    liberalism, 182, 186
    market, 88, 90
    Zollverein (Customs Union), 157–8, 161
education, 52, 56, 211, 215, 260, 279, 305,
    326–7
Edward I (England), 5
Edward III (England), 36
Eleanor of Aquitaine, 40
Elizabeth I (England), 6
Elizabeth II (England), 28
Encyclopédie, 48

Engels, F., 17, 151, 160, 164–5, 183
England, xv, xviii, 7, 10, 14, 16–31 *passim*,
    317
    and Germany, 182
Enlightenment, 65, 71–2, 131, 155, 185,
    211, 214, 297
Enrique IV (Castile), 119
d'Estaing, G., 58
ethnicity, 130, 136, 143, 148, 249, 252

Fabbroni, G., 89
Fallersleben, H. von, 200
fascism(-ts), 55–6, 73, 101 *see also*
    National Socialism(-ts)
Federal Republic of Germany (FRG),
    xviii–xix, 166–8, 172, 189–94
Felipe II (Spain), 107, 120
Felipe IV (Spain), 121
Felipe V (Spain), 107, 121
Ferdinand I (Habsburg), 207–8
Fernando (Aragón), 107, 119
Ferrari, G., 91, 100
Ferry, J., 52
feudalism, 109, 148, 150–4, 206, 237, 254
Figl, L., 199
Filipović, J., 285
Finland, xix, 317–31 *passim*
    Fennomen, 327–30
    Grand Duchy, 320–3, 331
    language(s), 321–2, 326–30
    peasants(-ry), 321, 325–6, 328–9
    Republic, 330
    Russia, 317–29, 331
    Soviet Union, 330
    Sweden, 319–20, 328, 330
Finland, towns
    Hamina (Fredrikshamn), 323
    Helsinki, 322, 324
    Turku, 319, 323
First World War, 24, 137–8, 164, 189,
    198, 205, 217, 242–3, 245, 262, 304
Forckenbeck, M. von, 184
Foscolo, U., 74–5
France, xviii, 6, 9, 35–60 *passim*, 317
    Absolutism, 45, 49
    ancien régime, 45–6, 48
    bourgeoisie, 39, 51, 55
    centralized state, 41
    cocarde, 49
    Commune, 51, 185
    Communist Party, 55
    Crécy, battle, 37
    Encyclopédie, 48
    Estates General, 43–4
    Fifth Republic, 56, 58
    Frondes, 45
    Front National, 59
    la Grande Nation, 50

Jacobins, 54, 58, 66–7
'la Jacquerie', 37
Marseillaise, 52–3
massacre of St Bartholomew, 43
la patrie, 35, 50
Third Republic, 51–3
France (*cont.*)
　Verdun, battle, 55
　Verdun, treaty, 35
　Versailles, treaty, 315
　Vienna, treaty, 50
　see also French Revolution; Paris
France, languages
　Basque, 41
　Breton, 41–2
　Flemish, 41–2
　lanque d'oc, 41
　langue d'oeil, 41
　Latin, 41–2
　Occitan, 41
　patois, 52
　Provençal, 52
France, towns
　Bordeaux, 41
　Brest, 47
　Calais, 39–40
　Dunkirk, 38, 47
　Grenoble, 52
　Lyons, 69
　Marseilles, 44, 47, 52
　Meaux, 42
　Nancy, 52
　Orleans, 36
　Paris, *see* separate entry
　Rochefort, 47
　Saint-Denis, 38
　Saint-Malo, 52
　Sète, 47
　Strasbourg,
France and
　Germany, 158, 185
　Italy, 63–75 *passim*, 81, 91–2
　Prussia, 319
Francis I (France), 40–1
Francis I (Habsburg-Lorraine), 76
Francis II (France), 43
Francis II (Habsburg-Lorraine), 214
Francis Joseph I (Habsburg-Lorraine),
　203–4, 244, 257, 273, 278, 283
Franco, F., 110, 139
Frankfurt National Assembly, 160–2, 183,
　214, 238
　Czech Lands, 238–9
Freemasons(-ry), 54, 56, 77, 200, 212–14
French Revolution, xix, 9, 25, 47–57
　passim, 60, 131–2, 141–2, 249
　Germany, 154–6
　Italy, 63–5, 67

Galdi, M., 64–5, 67–8
Ganivet, A., 108
Garibaldi, G., 78, 94, 96–100
Gaulle, C. de, 35, 56–8
German Democrat Republic (GDR),
　xviii–xix, 149, 167–72, 192–4
　Berlin Wall, 20, 194
　Soviet Union, 192
German Empire (Reich), 51, 154, 163–5,
　186–7, 189, 191, 218–19
Germany, 148–73 *passim*, 181–94 *passim*
　Absolutism, 148
　bourgeois society, 148, 150, 154, 156–8,
　　163
　Bürgertum, 154–5
　capitalism, 148. 150–1, 153, 156–7, 163,
　　167, 193
　colonies, 187
　ethnicity, 148–52, 156, 169
　feudalism, 150-n4
　First World War, 164, 189–91
　Frankfurt National Assembly, 160–2,
　　183
　French Revolution, 154, 157
　Industrial Revolution, 157, 159
　Jacobinism, 158
　Junkers, 149, 163–5, 184, 187
　language, 150–1, 154
　March Revolution (1848), 181
　November Revolution (1918), 165
　particularism, xviii, 148, 152, 158–60,
　　182–3
　Peasant War, xviii, 152–3, 156
　Reformation, xviii, 150, 152–3
　revolution(s) (1848–9), 159–61, 183–4
　Second World War, 149, 165–6, 182,
　　189–91, 194
　socialism, 167, 169, 171, 193
　Vormärz, 158–9
　Zollverein (Customs Union), 88, 157–8,
　　161
　see also Federal Republic of Germany
　　(FRG); German Democratic Republic
　　(GDR); German Empire; Holy
　　Roman Empire of the German
　　Nation; Weimar Republic
Germany, political parties
　Christian Democratic Union (CDU),
　　166
　Communist Party (KPD), 165–6
　Progressive Party, 183
　Social Democrats, 164, 185–6, 190
　Socialist Unity Party (SED), 166, 168,
　　192
　see also National Socialism(-ts)
Germany, society, 181, 194
　bourgeois, 148, 150, 154, 156–8
　capitalist, 150

feudal, 150–1
Germany, towns
  Ahlen, 166
  Berlin, 193, 203
  Bonn, 190, 192
  Cologne, 202
  Dresden, 193
  Frankfurt on Main, 160, 183
  Heppenheim, 159
  Jena, 157
  Leipzig, 193
  Mainz, 160
  Munich, xviii, 246
  Offenburg, 159
  Potsdam, 165
  Weimar, 190
Germany and
  Austria, 149, 161–2, 187, 198, 205–6,
    212, 216, 218–19
  Belgium, 137–40
  Britain, 166, 182
  Czech Lands, 237–45 passim
  France, 158, 166, 182
  Netherlands, 156
  Prussia, 149, 184
  Soviet Union, 167
  Switzerland, 156
  USA, 166
Gindely, A., 217
Gioberti, V., 85–7, 93
Gioia, M., 65, 67
Gladstone, W., 12, 23, 27
Goluchowski, A., 241
Gorbachev, M., 192
Grabski, S., 299
'Great Britain', 4
Great War, see First World War
Guesclin, B. du, 37
Guizot, G., 36–7, 82

Habermas, J., 211
Habsburg Empire, see Habsburg
  Monarchy
Habsburg Monarchy, 162, 182, 196, 198,
  203, 215–19, 238, 241–6
  Croatia, 270–90 passim
  Czech Lands, 232–46 passim
  Hungary, 248–66 passim
  see also Austria-Hungary
Habsburgs (dynasty), 121, 206–9
  Austrian, 129
  Spanish, 129
Hardie, K., 27
Haschka, L. L., 214
Havlíček, K., 236
Haydn, J., 200–1, 214
Heath, E., 20
Hebbel, F., 215

Helfert, A., 215
Henry II (England), 5, 40
Henry II (France), 40
Henry III (France), 44
Henry IV (France), 44
Henry V (England) 40
Henry VII (England), 6, 8
Henry VIII (England), 6
Herder, J. G., 155
Hildebrand, D., 220
Hipler, W., 153
Historikerstreit, xix, 188
Hitler, A., 140, 162, 165, 188, 190, 203,
  220–1, 314
Hofmannsthal, H. von, 197–8
Hoitsy, S., 254
Holy Roman Empire of the German
  Nation, 153, 155–6, 199, 202, 209
  Netherlands, 156
  Poland, 293
  Switzerland, 156
Honecker, E., 192
Hormayr, J. von, 214
Horthy, M., 263
Hugo, V., 51
Hungarian–Croatian Compromise, 257,
  283–5, 287–9
Hungary, xviii, 208, 210, 248–66 passim
  ethnicity, 249, 252, 254, 257–8
  language(s), 251–62 passim
  nobility, 249–57 passim
  October Revolution (1918), 263
  revolution (1848–9), 254–6
  revolution (1919), 263
  territorial revisionism, 263–8
  see also Austria-Hungary
Hungary, political parties
  Communist Party, 263
  Independent Party, 262
  Liberal Party, 262
  Romanian National Party, 262
  Social Democrats, 262, 264
Hungary and
  Axis powers, 265
  Croatia, 207, 248–9, 251–2, 254–8, 261,
    270–90 passim
  Czechoslovakia, 263–5
  Habsburg Monarchy, 205–6, 251, 254,
    256–8
  Romania, 263
  Yugoslavia, 263–4
Hurdes, F., 199
Hus, J., 230
Hutten, U. von, 153

Industrial Revolution, 22, 135, 141, 157,
  159

intelligentsia, 169, 234–7, 239–40, 253, 276, 280, 283, 286, 289
Ireland, xv–xvi, 3, 5–6, 9–20 *passim*, 30–1, 328
  Easter Rising, 13
  Eire, 15, 17–21
  Free State, *see* Eire
  Home Rule, 11–13, 27
  Irish Republican Army, 11, 14–20
Ireland (*cont.*)
  Land League, 11
  Sinn Fein, 12–14, 18–19
  Social Democratic Labour Party (SDLP), 18
  Socialist Republican Party, 13
  Young Ireland, 10
  see also Ulster
Isabel of Castile, 107, 119
Isidor of Seville, 113–14
Islam, *see* Muslims
Italy, 63–101 *passim*, 196
  Absolutism, 93
  Austria, 63, 66, 76, 79, 82, 86–8, 90–1, 93, 196, 205
  bourgeoisie, 88, 96
  Campoformio, treaty, 66, 69, 74
  Carbonari, 77–8
  Democrats, 80, 83, 91–9 *passim*
  economy, 87–91
  England, 67, 75–6, 79, 84
  federalism 64–5 *passim*, 81, 91–2
  French Revolution, 63–5, 72, 83
  Jacobins, 63, 65–6, 74, 77, 79, 81⅛n3, 96, 99
  language, 72–3, 89, 99
  law of copyright, 89
  liberals, 80–2, 86–9, 92, 95
  Napoleon I, 63–4, 66, 69–75, 99
  neo-Guelphs(-ism), 77, 84–6, 92–3
  Papacy, 67, 77, 83, 85–6, 92¼n3
  Party of Action, 99
  patria, 63, 70
  republicans(-ism), 75–80 *passim*, 98, 100
  Restoration, 71, 76, 78, 85
  Risorgimento, 74, 78, 83, 100–1
  Spain, 78
  unification, 95–9 *passim*
Italy, towns
  Bergamo, 94
  Bologna, 77, 89
  Brescia, 64, 74
  Como, 94
  Florence, 71, 73
  Genoa, 88–9
  Leghorn, 89
  Milan, 67, 69, 70, 76, 87, 91–2, 210
  Modena, 64, 79–89, 98
  Naples, 67–9, 87, 97, 99–100

Padua, 275
Palermo, 75, 87
Parma, 98
Pavia, 40
Reggio Emilia, 64
Rome, 64, 74, 83, 85, 92–4, 99, 112
Trieste, 88, 100, 207, 210, 275
Turin, 71
Venice, *see* separate entry

Jagiellons (dynasty), 293
James I (England), 7
James VI (Scotland), *see* James I (England)
Jászi, O., 262
Jelačić, J., 270, 273
Jew(s), 54–6, 59–60, 204, 218, 220, 252, 258, 296–7, 312
  anti-Semitism, 187–8, 194, 203, 218, 261
  finance capital, 186
Jiménez de Rada, R., 113
Joan of Arc, 40, 44
Joselewicz, B., 296
Joseph II (Habsburg-Lorraine), 76, 130, 157, 210–13
Juana 'la Beltraneja', 119–20
Jungmann, J., 234, 237

Kalinowski (Kalinoŭski), K., 298
Kernow, M., 21
Kernstock, O., 200
Kienzl, W., 200
King, T., 20
King Arthur, 3
King John of England, 4
Klaić, M., 283
Klofáč, V., 244
Kościuszko, T., 296
Kossuth, L., 94–5, 256
Krakau, *see* Kraków
Kraków, 212, 293, 296, 302
Kramář, K., 243–4
Kreisky, B., 204, 221

Labour Party, 19, 27, 29
La Farina, 97
Ladislas I (Hungary), 248
Lafayette, G., 49, 79
Laibach, *see* Ljubljana
language(s), xvii, xix, 52, 72–3, 89, 128, 136, 141, 148, 223–5, 229, 251–62 *passim*, 273–90 *passim*, 293–305 *passim*, 308–9, 314, 321–2, 326–30
  Indo-European (origin), 2
  standardization, 154, 275
Lemberg, *see* Lwów
Leopold II (Tuscany), 90

Leopold III (Belgium), 140
Lewis, J. S., 24
Liberal Party, 12, 27, 29
liberalism(-als), 80, 86–9, 92, 135–6, 139, 159, 184, 203, 323
Liebknecht, K., 165
Liechtenstein, 206
Lipé, J. of, 229–30
List, F., 182–3
Lithuania, 293, 295, 298, 300, 304, 308, 311, 319; see also Poland
Ljubljana, 212
Lloyd George, D., 14, 23, 313
Llywelyn the Great, 4
Lognon, A., 35
London, 7, 10, 16, 20, 26, 29, 79–80, 140, 329
Louis XI (France), 43
Louis XII (France), 40
Louis XIII (France), 45
Louis XIV (France), 7, 45–7
Louis XVI (France), 48
Louis XVIII (France), 48, 51
Louis Napoleon, see Napoleon III
Louis-Philippe (France), 48, 51, 79
Low Countries, 129, 143; see also Netherlands
Lönnrot, E., 324–5
Lucas of Tuy, 113
Luther, M., 153–4
Luxembourg, 148, 162
Luxemburg, R., 165
Lwów, 212, 308, 313

Maclean, J., 27
Majorca, 120
Manin, D., 92, 94, 97
manufactories, 150, 232–3
    period, 153, 156
Manx, 31
Manzoni, A., 73, 85
Marcel, E., 39
Maria Theresa (Habsburg), 203, 210–11, 221
Marseilles, 44, 52
Marx, K., 156, 170, 183, 297
Marxism, xvii, 13, 27
Masaryk, T. G., 244–5
Maximilian I (Habsburg), 207
Mazarin, J., 45
Mazzini, G., 67, 75, 80–6, 90–100 passim
Melzi d'Eril, F., 69–70
Menéndez y Pelayo, M., 110
Menotti, C., 80
Metternich, K., 76–7, 90, 237, 240
Michelet, J., 37, 51
Mickiewicz, A., 298
Middle Ages, xviii–xix, 4, 37, 74, 85, 111,

116, 129, 135, 151–3, 155, 201, 206, 228, 230–2, 246, 248, 257, 293
middle class(es), 84, 100, 169, 186, 188, 235; see also bourgeoisie
Miklas, W., 201
Minghetti, M., 89
Mommsen, T., 217
Montfort, J. de, 37
Montanelli, G., 93
Monti, V., 74
Moors, see Muslims
Moravia, xviii, 161, 207, 215; see also Czech Lands
Morganwg, Iolo, (Edward Williams), 23
Morris, H., 6
Moser-Pröll, Annemarie, 204
Mozart, W. A., 200, 204
Murat, J., 71
Muslims, 110–11, 114–19 passim
    al-Andalus, 118
Mussolini, B., 55

Napoleon I, 48, 50–1, 132, 187, 274, 317, 319
    Germany, 157–8
    Italy, 63–4, 66, 69–75
    Poland, 296
    Spain, 75
Napoleon III, 48, 51–2, 95–6
Narutowicz, G., 307
National Socialism(-ts), 162, 165, 188–9
    Austria, 198–200, 204, 219
    New Order, 139
    Poland, 311–12, 214
    'Third Reich', 190
Nazis(m), see National Socialism(-ts)
Nelson, H., 317
Netherlands, 129, 148
    Austrian, 130–2
    Holy Roman Empire of the German Nation, 156
    Northern, 132
    Republic of the United Provinces, 129–30
    Southern, 129–30, 132
    Spain, 107, 156
    States General, 156
    United Kingdom, 132
Nicolai, F., 212–13
nobles(-ility), xviii, 2, 5, 36, 41, 48, 51–2, 69, 73, 79, 84, 129–30, 156, 206, 208, 217, 228–33, 249–57 passim, 283, 293, 295–6, 300–2, 307–8, 321–2, 327
Norway, 319, 329
Nostitzs (Nostic), 233

O'Connell, D., 9–10
Olivares, G. G. de, 121

O'Neills of Ulster, 5
Tyrone, Earl of, 8
Ordoño I (Asturias), 115
Orosius, 106
Ortega y Gasset, J., 109, 114
Otokar of Styria, 229
Ottoman Empire, 87, 207

Pacius, F., 325
Paisley, I., 16
Palacký, F., 214, 232, 234, 236, 238–9, 241
Pallavicino-Trivulzio, G. G., 97
Panslavism, 242, 253, 261, 281
Papacy, 67, 77, 83, 85–6, 92–3, 153, 232
Papal State(s), see Vatican
Paris, 35, 39–40, 45, 49–52, 56, 70–1, 79–80, 91⅛n2, 185
Parnell, L. S., 11
Pavlinović, M., 283, 288
peasants(-ry), xix, 9, 11, 36, 47, 54–5, 84, 96, 136, 153, 156, 169, 206, 210, 217, 221, 234, 236, 252, 275–7, 286, 295–7, 301, 305, 307–8, 321, 325–6, 328–9
Pelcl (Pelcel, Pelzel), F. M., 233
Pest, see Budapest
Peter the Great, 319
Philip of Valois, 36–7
Picavea, R. M., 109
Pidal, R. M., 107, 110, 111
Pillersdorf, F. von, 238
Piłsudski, J., 309, 311
Pisacane, C., 96
Pitt, W., Jr, 9
Pius IX, 86, 92–3
plebeians, 153, 158
Poděbrady, J. of, 231
Poland, xviii–xix, 293–315 passim, 319
Austria, 196, 205, 297
language(s), 293–30-5 passim, 308–9, 314
Lithuania, 293, 295, 298, 300, 304, 308, 311
National Democrats, 307
National Socialism(-ts), 311–12, 314
national structure (1931), 307
peasants(-ry), 295–7, 301, 307–8
Prussia, 297
Republic, 305–15 passim
Russia, 297
Social Democrats, 311
Soviet Union, 305, 308, 312
Poland, towns
Cieszyn, 303
Kraków, 212, 293, 296, 302
Łódź, 311
Poznań, 183, 187

Warsaw, 296, 307
Pompidou, G., 58
Posen, see Poznań
Potocky, A., 286
Poznań, 183, 187
Prevadović, Paula von, 200
proletariat, see workers
Protestantism(-ts), 9, 12, 15, 17, 19, 43–4, 54, 129, 2087, 212, 214, 296, 303
Lutheranism, 260, 320, 325
Prussia, 73, 157, 160, 162, 317
Austria, 162, 182, 187, 212, 216, 242
France, 319
Germany, 149, 164, 184
Poland, 297
Slavic populations, 215

Queen Christina (Sweden), 323

Raab, J., 203
race, xvii, 73, 197, 241
Radetzky, J. W., 91, 94, 205
Radziwiłł, J., 293
Ranza, G., 64
Rašín, A., 243
Rattazzi, U., 99
Reformation, xviii, 6, 129, 150, 152–3, 156, 327
regionalism
France, 58–9
Netherlands, 129
Spain, 109, 112, 116–17, 121
Rej, M., 293
religion, 8–9, 42, 48, 51, 55, 85, 112, 129, 197
Anglican Church, 23
Arian heresy, 113
Calvinism, 7, 43
Christianity, 85, 110
Jansenism, 46, 130
Jewish, 54–6, 59, 110–11
Methodism, 22
Muslim, 59, 110–11, 114–19 passim, 288
Orthodoxy, 252, 255, 260, 281, 188, 296, 300, 309
Presbyterianism, 7, 9
Uniates, 252, 255, 260, 281, 296
see also Catholicism; Clergy; Protestantism
Renaissance, 85, 271, 293
Renan, E., xvi–xvii, 197
Renner, K., 200, 203, 221
revolution(s) (1848–9)
Austria, 214–15, 237, 240
Czech Lands, 237, 246
Germany, 159, 161
Hungary, 237, 254–6
Ricasoli, 3, 89

Richelieu, A.–J. du Plessis, 45
Rieger, F. L., 241
Roederer, P. L., 241
Romania, 196, 256
  Hungary, 263
Romanticism, 72, 82, 84, 132, 158, 317, 319–20
Rousseau, J. J., 82
Rudolph IV (Habsburg), 202
Runeberg, J. L., 324–5, 327
Russell, G., 12
Russell, P., 108
Russia, 317–29 passim
  Czech Lands, 235–6, 238–9, 244
  Finland (Grand Duchy), 320–3
  Moscow, 319
  Poland, 297, 325
  St Petersburg, 319, 322, 329
  Sweden, 319

Saint-Simon, C. H. de, 82
Sánchez-Albornoz, C., 106, 110–11, 121
Santarosa, S. di, 75, 79
Sardinia, 38, 120
Saxony, 157
Schärf, A., 221
Scheiner, J., 244
Schiller, F., 215
Schmeltzl, W., 202
Schmerling, A. von, 241, 274, 278, 282, 284
Schönerer, G. von, 216
Schulze-Delitzsch, H., 173
Schuschnigg, K., 220
Schuselka, F., 238
Schwarzenberg, F., 95
Scorsese, M., 59
Scotland, xv–xvi, 2–4, 7–8, 24–31 passim
  Carlisle, 4
  devolution, 28
  Edinburgh, 8., 18, 27
  Enlightenment, 25
  Glasgow, 13, 27
  Home Rule bills, 27
  Independent Labour Party (ILP), 27
  Jacobite risings, 7, 25
  Kirk, 7, 26
  Scottish Convention, 28
  Scottish National Party (SNP), 27–9
  Union, 7–9, 9, 25, 27
Scott, W., 29
Scotus Viator, see Seton-Watson, R. W.
Second World War, 15–16, 28, 139, 149, 165, 182, 189, 198, 246, 297, 310, 321
Serbia, 256, 288
Seton-Watson, R. W., 262
Shakespeare, W., 30
Shaw, G. B., 23

Sienkiewicz, H., 23
Sigismund (Luxemburg), 231
Sikorski, W., 311
Silesia, xviii, 207, 215, 304
  German, 304, 309
  Polish, 296, 303, 311
  see also Czech Lands
Sismondi, J. C. L. S. de, 74
Slavonia, 252
Slovakia, 245–6, 251, 260, 264; see also Czechoslovakia; Hungary
Slovenia, 207
Snellman, J. V., 326–8
Soiron, A. von, 238
Social Democrats(-cy), 164, 185–6, 190, 201, 203, 243, 263
socialism(-ts), 54–6, 58, 81, 136, 139, 167, 169, 171, 193, 329
Soviet Union, xv, 192
  Austria, 196, 205
  Finland, 330
  Poland (Republic), 305, 308, 312
Spain, xix, 106–21 passim
  Arabs, 114, 116, 118
  autonomiás, 106
  Cazola, treaty, 119
  Jewish, 110–11
  Pyrenees, Peace of the, 107
  Reconquista, 111, 116–19
  Roman, 110, 112–14
  Tudillén, treaty, 119
  Visigoths, 110, 112–17 passim; see also Muslims
Spain, regions
  Aragón, 117–21
  Asturias, 112, 114–17
  Basque, 106, 109, 112, 116
  Cantabria, 112
  Castile, 38–9, 107, 109, 116, 118–21
  Catalonia, 107, 109, 117–118, 120
  Galicia, 112, 116
  Granada, 118–19
  León, 116–17
  Navarre, 117–19
  Valencia, 119–20
  see also Majorca; Muslims, al-Andalus; Sardinia
Spain, towns
  Almería, 118
  Gijón, 115
  Madrid, 109, 121
  Medina Sidonia, 114
  Oviedo, 114, 116
  Seville, 113
  Toledo, 113–14, 119
  Valencia, 119
  Valladolid, 120
Spain and

England, 107
Netherlands, 107, 156
Portugal, 107, 118–20
USA, 108
Speransky, M., 324
Spytihněv, 228, 230
Staël, Mme de, 82
Stalin, J., xvi–xvii, 220
Stendhal, (H. Beyle), 52
Sternbergs (Sternberk), 233
Strafford, T. Wentworth, Earl of, 8
Strauss, J., 204
Strossmayer, J. G., 273, 280, 283, 288
Subcarpathian Ruthenia, see Carpatho-
    Ukraine
Suvorov, A. V., 235
Sweden, 319–20, 328–9
    Stockholm, 321
Switzerland, 148
    Austria, 205–6
    Holy Roman Empire of the German
        Nation, 156
    Netherlands, 156
    Reformation, 156
Széchenyi, I., 253
Šedivý, P., 233
Štefánik, M. R., 244

Taaffee, E., 286
Tengström, Archbishop, 324–5
Thám, V., 233
Thun, L., 236
Tisza, I., 262
Tisza, K., 242
Tommaseo, N., 85
Tory Party, 9, 26, 29
Transylvania, 210, 251–2, 254–6, 260,
    264; see also Hungary
treaties
    Austrian State (1955), 201–2, 204
    Campoformio, 66, 69, 74
    Cazola, 119
    Helsinki Agreement, 172
    Munich Agreement, xviii, 246
    Paris (1947), 265
    Potsdam Agreement, 165–6, 265
    Riga, 305
    St-Germain, 219
    Tilsit, 319
    Trianon, 262–3
    Tudillén, 119
    Verdun, 35
    Versailles, 315
    Vienna, 50
    Westphalia, 156
Triune Kingdom, 270, 273–4, 281, 284–9
Trollope, A., 11

Ukraine, 228
Ulster, 8–9, 13, 15–21, 24
Unamuno, M. di, 109
United States of America (USA), 192
universities
    Aberystwyth, 23
    Ghent, 136–7
    Helsinki, 322–4, 328, 330
    Leuven, 130, 142
    London, 244
    Prague, 231
    Sorbonne, xvi
Upper Hungary, see Slovakia
USSR, see Soviet Union

Václav (Wenceslas) II (Bohemia), 229
Vartemberk, J. of, 229
Vatican, 99–100
Vaurus, bastard of, 42
Venice, 66, 66–7, 91–2, 270–1, 274–6, 285
Verri, P., 65
Victor Emmanuel I (Piedmont), 79
Victor Emmanuel II (Piedmont and
    Italy), 92, 97, 100
Vienna, xvi, 91, 202–3, 211–2, 218–21,
    passim, 237, 241, 253–4, 256, 270,
    279, 282, 290
    Congress of, 90, 274, 324
    Stock Exchange, 186
Visigothic kings, 113–16
Vojvodina, 251–2, 256, 260
Vormärz, 158–9, 214
Vraniczany, A., 273

Wales, xv–xvi, 3, 5–6, 8, 21–4 passim,
    30–1
    devolution, 28
    eisteddfod, 23
    home-rule-all-round, 23, 30
    Plaid Cymru, 23
Wallace, W., 5, 25
Wallenstein, A. von, 229
war(s)
    Anglo-French, xviii
    Anglo-Scottish border, xviii
    Boer, 26
    civil, 6–7, 14, 45, 56
    colonial, 56, 60
    Cossack, 298
    Crimean, 324
    Eighty Years', 129
    Hundred Years', 2, 37, 53
    Independence (Scotland), 5
    Liberation (Germany), 158
    Liberation and Civil (Finland), 330
    Napoleonic, xix, 157–8, 214, 235, 317
    of 1848–9, 96
    Peasant (Germany), xviii, 152–3, 156

Soviet-Finnish, 330
Spanish, 84
Spanish Civil, 139
see also First World War; Second World
  War
Washington, 17
Weber, M., 187
Weimar Republic, 165, 187, 189, 191, 221
Wellington, Duke of, A. Wallesley, 317
West Germany, *see* Federal Republic
  Germany (FRG)
Wieser, F. van, 219
William I (United Kingdom of the
  Netherlands), 132
William II (Germany), 53
William III (England), *see* William of
  Orange

William the Conqueror, 4
William of Orange, 9, 129
Winter, E. A., 226
Wolfe Tone, T., 10
workers, 55, 163–4, 169–70, 218, 233, 236,
  242, 329
working class, *see* workers

Yeats, W. B., 12
Yugoslavia, xv
  Austria, 196, 205–6
  Hungary, 263

Zessner-Spitzenberg, H. K., 220
Zwingli, U., 156